MEMORY FUNCTIONING IN DEMENTIA

ADVANCES
IN
PSYCHOLOGY

89

Editors:

G. E. STELMACH

P. A. VROON

NORTH-HOLLAND
AMSTERDAM • LONDON • NEW YORK • TOKYO

MEMORY FUNCTIONING
IN DEMENTIA

Edited by

Lars BÄCKMAN

Section of Psychology
Stockholm Gerontology Research Center

and

Department of Geriatic Medicine
Karolinska Institute
Stockholm, Sweden

1992

NORTH-HOLLAND
AMSTERDAM • LONDON • NEW YORK • TOKYO

NORTH-HOLLAND
ELSEVIER SCIENCE PUBLISHERS B.V.
Sara Burgerhartstraat 25
P.O. Box 211, 1000 AE Amsterdam, The Netherlands

Library of Congress Cataloging-in-Publication Data

Memory functioning in dementia / edited by Lars Bäckman.
      p.   cm. -- (Advances in psychology ; 89)
   Includes bibliographical references and index.
   ISBN 0-444-88920-5
   1. Alzheimer's disease. 2. Memory disorders. 3. Memory disorders
in old age.   I. Bäckman, Lars. II. Series: Advances in psychology
(Amsterdam, Netherlands) ; 89.
RC523.M45   1992
616.8'31--dc20   92-11600
                                                           CIP

ISBN: 0 444 88920 5

pp. 119 - 134 : Copyright not transferred

This book is printed on acid-free paper

Printed in The Netherlands

v

Contents

Contributors

Lars Bäckman (Chapter 4)
Section of Psychology
Stockholm Gerontology Research Center
Department of Geriatric Medicine, Karolinska Institute
Stockholm, Sweden

William W. Beatty (Chapter 8)
Department of Psychiatry and Behavioral Sciences
University of Oklahoma
Oklahoma City, OK, U.S.A.

James T. Becker (Chapter 2)
Alzheimer's Disease Research Center,
University of Pittsburgh,
Pittsburgh, PA, U.S.A.

Leonard Berg (Chapter 10)
Department of Neurology and Neurological Surgery
Washington University in St. Louis
St. Louis, MO, U.S.A.

Nelson Butters (Chapter 5)
Department of Psychiatry
University of California School
San Diego School of Medicine
Psychology Service
San Diego VA Center
San Diego. CA, U.S.A.

Lawrence A. Coben (Chapter 10)
Department of Neurology and Neurological Surgery
Washington University in St. Louis
St. Louis, MO, U.S.A.

Malcolm B. Dick (Chapter 7)
Center for the Neurobiology of Learning and Memory
University of California, Irvine
Irvine, CA, U.S.A.

Han F. A. Diesfeldt (Chapter 11)
Stichting Verpleeghuizen Nederland
Psychogeriatrische Dienst
Laren, The Netherlands

Olga B. Emery (Chapter 9)
Department of Psychiatry
Dartmouth Medical School
Hanover, NH, U.S.A.

William C. Heindel
Department of Psychiatry
University of California School
San Diego School of Medicine
San Diego, CA, U.S.A.

Agneta Herlitz (Chapter 4)
Section of Psychology
Stockholm Gerontology Research Center
Department of Geriatric Medicine, Karolinska Institute
Stockholm, Sweden

Anthony F. Jorm (Chapter 12)
National Health & Medical Research Council
The Australian National University
Canberra, Australia

Michael D. Kopelman (Chapter 3)
Academic Unit of Psychiatry
St. Thomas's Hospital
London, England

Beata Lipinska (Chapter 4)
Section of Psychology
Stockholm Gerontology Research Center
Department of Geriatric Medicine, Karolinska Institute
Stockholm, Sweden

Oscar L. Lopez (Chapter 2)
Alzheimer's Disease Research Center
University of Pittsburgh
Pittsburgh, PA, U.S.A.

Alex Martin (Chapter 6)
Cognitive Studies Unit
Laboratory of Clinical Sciences
National Institute of Mental Health
Bethesda, ML, U.S.A.

John C. Morris (Chapter 10)
Department of Neurology and Neurological Surgery
Washington University in St. Louis
St. Louis, MO, U.S.A.

Robin G. Morris (Chapter 1)
Department of Psychology
Institute of Psychiatry
London, England

Eugene H. Rubin (Chapter 10)
Department of Psychiatry
Washington University in St. Louis
St. Louis, MO, U.S.A.

David P. Salmon (Chapter 5)
Department of Neurosciences
University of California School
San Diego School of Medicine
San Diego, CA, U.S.A.

Martha Storandt (Chapter 10)
Department of Psychology
Washington University in St. Louis
St. Louis, MO, U.S.A.

Preface

Dementia diseases constitute the most common cause of severe mental deterioration in the world today, and expected changes in the population structure will inevitably result in that gradually more people become demented. A pronounced memory dysfunction is one of the earliest signs, and is considered a cardinal symptom of dementia. Knowledge about the ways in which dementia diseases affect memory (e.g., which memory functions are most severely implicated, and which are relatively well preserved) not only advances our thinking about the relationship between brain structures and memory functions; it is also imperative for early clinical diagnosis, and forms a basis for sound behavioral and pharmacological intervention.

Despite the invariability of memory impairment in dementia, and although this clinical symptom has been known for more than two thousand years, the nature of this impairment is not completely understood. Not until quite recently research on memory functioning in demented patients has utilized theoretical and methodological advances from basic cognitive psychology. This volume gives a comprehensive treatment of this new and increasingly growing field of inquiry.

The volume is organized into five sections, the number of chapters in each section roughly reflecting the amount of research activity taking place in the respective areas. In the first section focused on episodic memory, Morris reviews current research on short-term memory in Alzheimer's disease, indicating that different components of short-term memory may be differentially affected by dementia. Becker and Lopez propose that the episodic memory deficit in Alzheimer's disease has multiple origins, and also discuss the neuroanatomical basis for different types of memory disturbances in dementia. The chapter by Kopelman is concerned with forgetting, and provides evidence that Alzheimer's disease may not influence rate of forgetting once the information is consolidated in memory. Herlitz, Lipinska, and Bäckman discuss recent demonstrations from experimental and intervention research that Alzheimer patients are able to utilize various forms of cognitive support to improve episodic memory.

Contributions in the second section are concerned with different kinds of non-episodic memories. Salmon, Heindel, and Butters review work indicating that semantic memory and several forms of priming are impaired in Alzheimer's disease, although certain types of skill learning remain relatively intact. Martin applies a model of knowledge representation to object naming, arguing that Alzheimer patients' semantic memory deficits are largely due to a degradation of the semantic network. Reviewing research on memory for motor acts, Dick finds evidence that various forms of motor memory may be relatively well preserved in Alzheimer's disease.

The third section deals with research comparing Alzheimer patients with other groups of patients with memory disturbances. Beatty argues that there are important differences between the ways in which Alzheimer's disease and different types of subcortical dementias affect both explicit and implicit memory. Emery proposes that deficits in language and memory functioning in dementia and depression are best understood in terms of a continuum ranging from normal aging through depression to dementia.

The fourth section is devoted to progression of dementia. In a report from an 11-year longitudinal study, Storandt, Morris, Rubin, Coben, and Berg observe that most of the demographic, behavioral, and biological variables examined, failed to predict the rate of neuropsychological decline in Alzheimer's disease. Diesfeldt reports on a comprehensive follow-up of two Alzheimer patients showing rather different loci of semantic memory impairment, thereby demonstrating the variable nature of Alzheimer's disease.

In the final section, Jorm reviews research using subjective information to assess memory in demented individuals. Jorm concludes that instruments based on reports from informants are reliable and useful for screening purposes, although less useful for more detailed analyses of how dementia affects memory.

I am indebted to several colleagues at the Stockholm Gerontology Research Center for their help in various stages of the editorial process: Agneta Herlitz, Beata Lipinska, Maria Larsson, and Gunilla Rudander. My largest measure of gratitude in this regard goes to my colleague Åke Wahlin. Åke's skillful assistance concerning many conceptual and technical aspects related to the preparation of the book has been inestimable. A very special thanks goes to my wife Agneta and my children Daniel and Hannes. They have all, in different ways, made the editing more pleasant than it would otherwise have been.

Stockholm,
October 1991

Lars Bäckman

Section I

EPISODIC MEMORY IN
ALZHEIMER'S DISEASE

1 Patterns of Short-Term Memory Impairment in Alzheimer's Disease

Robin G. Morris

Institute of Psychiatry, London

Introduction

A hallmark of research into memory is the fractionation of functionally distinct mnemonic processes, thus providing a framework on which to base investigations of memory disorders (Roediger & Craik, 1989). This chapter concerns short-term memory (STM), memory for events that have just been experienced, or what the 19th Century psychologist William James referred to as "an elementary memory" that makes us aware of "the just past." It is distinguished from long-term memory (LTM) where retention of material must last for much longer periods, minutes, hours, or even days. A series of experiments reviewed below have established that STM is impaired in Alzheimer-type Dementia (AD), but then have gone on to establish more clearly the nature of the impairment (cf. Morris, 1991a; Morris & Kopelman, 1986). The chapter reviews the purpose and characteristics of STM in normal subjects and how recent models of STM functioning have been brought to bear on patients with AD. Finally, some of the underlying neurobiological mechanisms for STM are considered in relation to the neuropathological impairment in AD.

The Function of Short-Term Memory

The need to retain small amounts of information in STM so that it can be processed more fully is undisputed (cf. Baddeley, 1986). Clearly, much incoming sensory information is redundant beyond a short period. This is illustrated by studies of memory for prose, where it is shown that the literal surface structure of a sentence is held for a brief period of time, contrasting with the meaning, which decays much less rapidly (Kintsch & Buschke, 1969).

The STM system enables a person to backtrack in situations where the meaning of the sentence is not easily understood (Caplan & Waters, 1990; McCarthy & Warrington, 1987). With tasks such as mental arithmetic, information has to be retained only where it is still relevant to the task in hand. Likewise, in the visuo-spatial domain, moving within an enclosed and unfamiliar environment (such as a room) requires a memory system that will provide an accurate but short-lasting representation of where the person has been (Farah, 1988).

Models of Short-Term Memory

In the 1940's Hebb proposed that the underlying mechanism for STM was a temporary activation of neuronal circuits (Hebb, 1945). This activation declines very rapidly, but a longer lasting memory trace can be laid down by permanent changes in memory structures. In support of this model, it has been observed that the characteristics of STM appear very different from LTM. First, only a small amount of material is retained at any one time (Shiffrin, 1976). For example, on average a person can remember only seven digits in serial order with immediate recall following a single presentation. Although the quantity can be increased by structuring material into meaningful "chunks" (for example, sentences), the capacity limitations are severe (Miller, 1956; Simon, 1974). Second, there is considerable modular specificity in terms of the coding of material (Crowder, 1982). With verbal information, material appears to be stored in phonological form, the sound form of the material. A prominent type of error on STM for verbal material is to produce an item that is phonologically confusable (Conrad, 1964). Similarly, phonologically confusable material (such as the words *mad, cap, map,* and *cat*) is much harder to recall in STM when presented together (Baddeley, 1966; Conrad & Hull, 1964). Third, material recalled from STM is lost very rapidly unless it is processed continuously. Even small amounts of information (for example, three words) can be lost after a period of 20 seconds if the subject is distracted by a subsidiary task such as mental arithmetic (Peterson & Peterson, 1959). In terms of Hebb's (1945) model, material in STM is only retained if the neuronal circuits remain active.

Since Hebb (1945) proposed his model the concept of a STM system has developed considerably. Initially it was seen as a unitary system that stored information before it was transferred for long-term storage. The most influential model, proposed by Atkinson and Shiffrin (1968) was a limited capacity store that was used to process information. The store served as the "workspace" for information processing, receiving information from the senses, and transmitting it to and from LTM. Although other approaches exist, for example "levels of processing" (e.g., Craik, Morris, & Gick, 1990) it has become increasingly clear that the characteristics of STM are explained more easily by postulating not one but a number of interactive storage systems that function in a synchronous fashion (e.g., Baddeley & Hitch, 1974; Friedrich, 1990; Monsell, 1984). More recent formulations have fractionated the short-term store into a cluster of storage systems, rehearsal mechanisms and control processes reflecting a richer understanding of the complexity of the system (Baddeley, 1986; Shallice & Vallar, 1990). For example, it has been possible to differentiate articulatory rehearsal as a specific mechanism for refreshing and updating the memory trace when remembering verbal material (Baddeley, Lewis, & Vallar, 1984; Baddeley, Thomson, & Buchanan, 1975). In addition, the role of control systems in directing the flow of information through short-term memory and determining what processes become active has been recognized more fully (Baddeley, 1990). There is also the suggestion that separate storage systems exist for visuospatial information (Baddeley & Lieberman, 1980; Farah, 1988). Studies of patients with selective impairments of short-term memory have helped to differentiate these subsystems in even further detail and have also challenged the notion that material must pass through a STM system to reach LTM (Baddeley et al., 1984; Shallice & Vallar, 1990; Shallice & Warrington, 1970).

Exploring Short-Term Memory in Alzheimer's Disease

A series of investigations have explored the nature of the STM deficit in AD. These have focused around four main areas, which are elaborated on below: (1) the small reduction in what is referred to as the "recency effect," the ability to recall the last few items in a list of words more easily than the previous items; (2) a consistent reduction in memory span, or STM capacity, using a range of materials; (3) a substantial impairment on any STM task that involves dividing the attention of the subject; and (4) changes in the rate at which material is lost from STM in AD.

The Recency Effect

If subjects are required to recall a list of words (for example, the names of 15 common objects) immediately after presentation, the last few words are recalled more frequently. This so-called recency effect has been interpreted as showing the words are still held in STM at the time of recall, hence their memorability (Glanzer & Cunitz, 1966; Waugh & Norman, 1965). The initial and middle items are thought to be held in LTM and are therefore less accessible. According to this interpretation measuring the size of the recency effect is an indirect measure of STM.

Several studies have examined free recall in AD patients. The frequency of retrieval of each item can be plotted for each item in a list, producing a serial position curve (see Figure 1.1). One method is to measure memory performance on the last few items in a list (3-5 items). Using this method, Miller (1971) found a mild reduction in the recency component of free recall in AD, but this deficit was not found in a subsequent experiment in the same study. Spinnler, Della Sala, Bandera, and Baddeley (1988) adopted the Waugh and Norman (1965) measure in which level of performance is corrected over the middle part of the serial position curve, yielding a STM score. AD patients did not show a reduced corrected recency score in comparison to matched controls. However, if an uncorrected scoring system is used, there does appear to be a slight impairment in recency, albeit with a greater impairment in recalling earlier items (see Figure 1.1).

Other studies have employed Tulving and Colotla's (1970) scoring method which relies on recording the order that items are recalled. Material is assigned to a "STM component" if they have been recalled with seven or fewer intervening items between their presentation and retrieval. Wilson, Bacon, Fox, and Kaszniak (1983) found a very slight deficit on this measure of STM, contrasting with a moderate impairment in recall of the remaining items. Likewise, A. Martin, Brouwers, Cox, and Fedio (1985) reported a small impairment on both the STM measure and the items recalled from long-term memory. The essential result is a very slight reduction in the size of the recency effect using different procedures and methods of scoring. Discrepancies in results may be related to the severity of dementia. Pepin and Eslinger (1989) have recently shown that the shape of the serial position curve changes with dementia severity. Mildly demented patients tend to show a normal recency and primacy effect, but more moderately impaired patients show an overall reduction in performance.

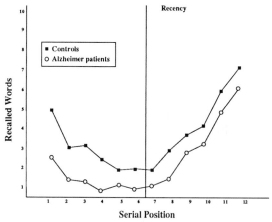

Figure 1.1 . Serial position effects for free recall of words of Alzheimer patients and age-matched controls.

The relative preservation of recency in AD is consistent with the finding that the effect appears to be impervious to various forms of brain damage, including those associated with amnesia (Baddeley & Warrington, 1970) and head injury (Brooks, 1975) and to a range of stressors, such as attentional distraction (Murdock, 1967) and drugs such as alcohol (Baddeley, 1981). Recency has also been thought of as reflecting an ordinal retrieval strategy, which facilitates remembering, starting with material or events that have been encountered most recently (Baddeley, 1986; Baddeley & Hitch, 1977). Nevertheless, this differing interpretation of recency does not negate the notion that the last few items in a list or words are retained in STM storage, but rather specifies the mechanism of retrieval. A decline in the recency effect may therefore be interpreted as either a deficit in STM or a more specific impairment in retrieval strategy.

Memory Span

The capacity of STM can be measured using a simple procedure, termed "memory span," in which a list of items is presented, which must be recalled immediately in serial order. Memory span is taken as the maximum number of items that can be recalled correctly (Miller, 1956). With memory span the deficit in AD patients is consistent across a range of procedures and materials. Thus, memory span for digits is moderately impaired in studies conducted by Corkin (1982), Kaszniak, Garron, and Fox (1979), Kopelman (1985), Morris (1986, 1987a, 1987b); so too is memory span for letters (Morris, 1984) and words (Miller, 1973; Morris, 1984; Spinnler et al., 1988). Only two studies report no deficit, but these include patients at the very early stages of AD (A. Martin et al. 1985; Weingartner, Grafman, Boutelle, Kaye, & D. Martin, 1983). This impairment contrasts with pure amnesic syndromes where memory span is essentially normal (Baddeley & Warrington, 1970).

AD patients also show impairment on the Corsi block span test - a spatial analogue of verbal span - in which patients observe the experimenter tapping out a sequence on an array of blocks and have to repeat the sequence. A study by Cantone, Orsini, Grossi, and De Michele (1978) suggested that Corsi block span is more impaired than auditory-verbal span in AD. They took this to indicate that right hemisphere functioning may be more impaired, since spatial abilities are normally more dominant in the right hemisphere. However, other studies using the Corsi span task have not reported a gross discrepancy between auditory-verbal and spatial span (Corkin, 1982; Spinnler et al., 1988). For example, Spinnler et al. (1988) found a decrement of 23% in verbal span and 22% in spatial span in AD patients compared to a matched control group.

The locus of the deficit in STM capacity. A series of studies by Morris (1984, 1987a, 1987b; Morris & Baddeley, 1988) have investigated the deficit in STM span in relation to verbal memory. As indicated above, verbal material is encoded primarily in phonological form in STM, accounting for the phonological-similarity effect (Conrad, 1964). This finding gives rise to the notion of a phonological store that maintains verbal material for a short period. Studies of normal subjects and neuropsychological patients have separated out this store into two subcomponents, a *phonological short-term store* and an *articulatory rehearsal mechanism* which recycles material in STM in an active fashion (Vallar & Baddeley, 1984). The role of articulatory rehearsal has been demonstrated using a technique called articulatory suppression. If a subject articulates irrelevant verbal material during the memory task (such as saying the word 'the' continuously), this leads to a substantial decrease in memory span for verbal material. Memory span is also reduced when longer words are used in a memory task (the so-called "word-length effect") suggesting that span performance is related to the extra time taken to recycle more lengthy verbal material. The link between these two findings was established when it was observed that the word-length effect disappears under conditions of articulatory suppression (Baddeley et al., 1975).

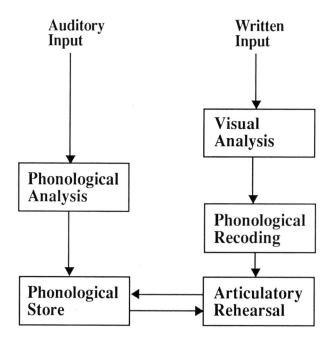

Figure 1.2. Model of processes involved in short-term memory for auditorily and visually presented verbal material. Adapted from "Articulation and short-term memory: Evidence from anarthria" by G. Vallar and S. F. Cappa, 1987, *Cognitive Neuropsychology, 4,* p. 72. Copyright 1987 by Erlbaum. Adapted by permission.

The relationship between these subcomponents has been explored in detail, leading to the model shown in Figure 1.2. Essentially, if material is presented in auditory form it passes directly into the phonological short-term store. This material can then be recycled to update the short-term store in a continuous fashion. Visually presented verbal information only gains access to the phonological store by being cycled through the articulatory rehearsal mechanism. The support for this model comes from the finding that articulatory suppression can cause the phonological-similarity effect to disappear if material is presented visually, but not if it is presented auditorily (Baddeley et al., 1984; Levy, 1971). Thus, with visual presentation, suppressing articulatory rehearsal prevents access to the phonological store and abolishes the effect.

The characteristics of STM in AD have been explored by using the standard variables of phonological similarity, word length, and articulatory suppression. To investigate the functioning of the phonological store, Morris (1984) measured the size of the phonological similarity effect using immediate memory for lists of phonologically similar (*B, C, D, V, G, P*) or dissimilar (*E, H, J, R, W, Y*) letters. A span procedure was employed to avoid the problem of floor or ceiling effects in the patients and control subjects. With both auditorily and visually presented letters the phonological similarity effect was undiminished in the AD group, despite an overall decline in memory span. Repeating the result found with normal subjects (Baddeley et al., 1984), the phonological similarity effect was suppressed using concurrent articulation with visually, but not auditorily presented letters. These results can be interpreted as showing that the phonological store is not impaired in AD, because the size of the phonological similarity effect was not reduced.

Morris (1984) also investigated the size of the word-length effect as an indirect measure of the efficiency of articulatory rehearsal. Following the procedure used by Baddeley et al. (1975), memory span was measured using either monosyllabic words (*sun, hate, harm, wit, bond, yield, worst, twice*) or five-syllabic words (*association, opportunity, representative, organization, considerable, immediately, university, individual*). A pronounced word-length effect in AD patients was found, indicating that the articulatory rehearsal mechanism was functioning normally. The robustness of this effect in AD is illustrated in a more recent study by Morris, Bradley, and Welch (1991) using two sets of pictures of objects with names that varied in word-length. The task involved viewing sequentially a set of cards showing the objects and then recalling the names of the objects in the same serial order (see Figure 1.3). Again, the size of the word-length effect was undiminished in AD, indicating that the subjects can recode the visual information into verbal form and make use of articulatory rehearsal for retention of the names of the objects.

These experiments suggest that both phonological storage and articulatory rehearsal are unimpaired in AD. Further support for this finding was obtained by Morris (1987a, 1987b). The degree to which concurrent articulation reduces memory span can be used to assess the contribution of articulatory rehearsal in memory span performance. In Morris (1987a, 1987b), digit

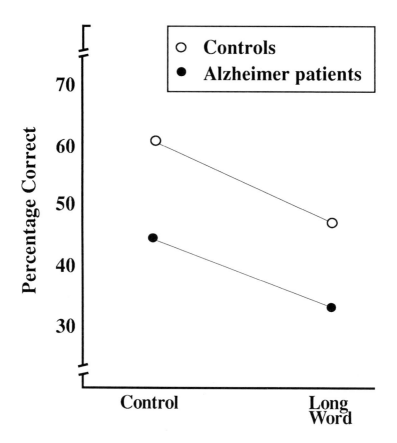

Figure 1.3. The effect of word length on memory performance on a test of object memory in AD patients and control subjects. From "Visual short-term memory in Alzheimer-type dementia" by R. G. Morris, V. Bradley, and J. Welch, 1991.

span was compared with or without concurrent articulation, and results showed that the reduction was the same in AD patients and controls. This was the case whether or not the concurrent articulation was paced by the experimenter or unpaced. The rate of articulatory rehearsal can be assessed by requiring subject to read a series of random digits as rapidly as possible. A reduction in rate may result in a reduced memory span because less material can be recycled over a given period of time to update the phonological store, yet there was no such reduction in the AD patients studied by Morris (1987a).

Taken together, these results indicate that reduction in verbal STM is not caused by an impairment in the phonological store or the articulatory rehearsal mechanism. These findings suggest that the explanation lies in damage to some other parts of the system. One candidate, explored in the next section, is a deficit in the "control processes" of STM that function to coordinate STM functioning. A hint that these processes are impaired came from an incidental finding from the Morris (1984) study. In normal subjects concurrent articulation fails to suppress the word-length effect when material is presented visually (Baddeley et al., 1975). As in all the experiments described above, concurrent articulation is only required at the presentation stage of the memory task. Listening to auditory material and articulatory repetition are highly compatible and these subjects are able to make use of articulatory rehearsal when recalling the material (Baddeley et al., 1984). In AD patients, concurrent articulation at the presentation stage was sufficient to suppress the word-length effect suggesting that AD patients were unable to make use of articulatory rehearsal at the recall stage. The inability of AD patients to engage in a strategy to enhance STM points towards some higher order deficit in information processing as discussed in the next section.

Divided Attention

Short-term forgetting and divided attention. Some investigators have explored retention of material in AD when attention is divided by using variations on a task developed by Peterson and Peterson (1959). The subject is presented with three words or consonants to remember after delays of up to 30 seconds. During the delay the subject is distracted by a subsidiary task such as simple arithmetic. This task is particularly sensitive to the memory deficit in AD patients, who show little impairment if tested separately on the components of the task, but substantial impairment when they are combined. This result holds when a variety of distractor tasks are used, such as a simple tapping task, recurrent articulation of a single word (see Figure 1.4), digit reversal and digit addition, and counting backwards by three's from 100 (Corkin, 1982; Kopelman, 1985; Morris, 1986; Sullivan, Corkin, & Growdon, 1986).

Corkin (1982) reported that even patients at the early stages of AD are moderately or severely impaired on this task. Kopelman (1985) used a version which involved remembering three monosyllabic words whilst counting backwards from 100 by two's or three's. Korsakoff patients were only slightly impaired on this task, whilst AD patients were severely impaired. Of significant interest are the type of errors made in completing the task. Whilst Korsakoff patients tended to recall items from earlier attempts (intrusion errors), AD patients tended to make no response at all (omission errors). In the Corkin (1982) study the extent of the Peterson and Peterson deficit correlated with the severity of dementia, whilst in the Kopelman (1985) study it was greater in younger patients.

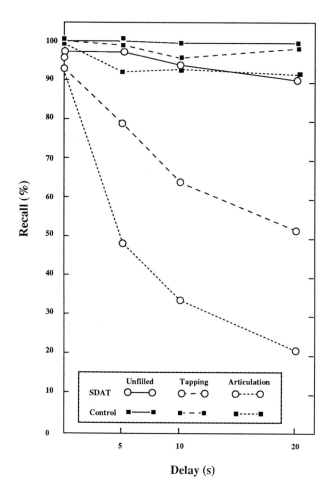

Figure 1.4. Short-term forgetting on the Peterson and Peterson task with no distractor task, or tapping and articulation as distractor tasks in AD patients and controls. From "Short-term forgetting in senile dementia of the Alzheimer's type" by R. G. Morris, 1986, *Cognitive Neuropsychology, 3,* p. 90. Copyright 1986 by Erlbaum. Adapted by permission.

The central executive system and STM functioning. It has been proposed that the deficit on the Peterson and Peterson task reflects an impairment in the control processes that coordinate the different aspects of STM (Morris, 1984, 1986; Morris & Baddeley, 1988). The concept of flexible control processes involving rules and strategies has been incorporated into more recent models of STM (Baddeley, 1986; Shallice & Vallar, 1990). The studies described below were conducted in the framework of Baddeley's Working Memory Model (Baddeley, 1986, 1990; Baddeley & Hitch, 1974), which includes a Central

Executive System (CES) that coordinates and schedules the various operating processes and strategies involved in STM. This system has limited resources such that performance on more attentionally demanding tasks will break down if the resources are exceeded. The evidence for an impairment in these processes comes from a series of studies examining STM, based on the notion that the cognitive operations involved in simultaneous tasks compete for the resources of the CES. An impairment in the CES would make it much more difficult for AD patients to coordinate multiple tasks.

Baddeley, Logie, Bressi, Della Sala, and Spinnler (1986) administered a series of dual-tasks to AD patients. The primary task used was pursuit tracking which requires the subject to maintain a lightpen over a moving stimulus on a Visual Display Unit. By varying the speed of the moving stimulus they were able to obtain a baseline for each subject in which the light pen was over the target for 60% of the time. They then combined tracking with three subsidiary tasks to investigate the effects of divided attention. These were (a) counting from 1 to 5 repeatedly; (b) detecting tones and responding by pressing a footswitch; and (c) recalling strings of digits equivalent to the subject's memory span. The effect of concurrent articulation was to produce a very slight decrease in tracking accuracy in the AD patients and none at all in matched control subjects. This result is to be expected, because articulatory rehearsal is a relatively automatic process that makes minimal demands on attentional resources (Vallar & Baddeley, 1982). The effect of tone detection and tracking performance and vice versa was substantially greater in the AD patients. This result, however, was complicated by the fact that the AD patients were performing worse on the tone detection task when presented alone, thus accounting for the greater effect on tracking when combined. The combination of tracking and digit span was the most salient condition because the difficulties of *both* tasks had been titrated for each subject, individually. Here there was a substantially larger divided attention effect in the AD patients.

A similar dual-task paradigm was used by Morris (1986), based on the Peterson and Peterson (1959) task, with memory for consonant trigrams over delays of up to 15 seconds as the primary task and four subsidiary tasks, namely, tapping on the testing table with one hand, articulating the word "the" continuously, reversing a series of digit-pairs, and adding a series of single digits together. It was predicted that the deficit in AD patients would rise with the difficulty of the subsidiary tasks. This is because the more demanding subsidiary tasks would use up a greater proportion of the already diminished resources of the CES. With no subsidiary task there was no forgetting either for the AD patients or controls. With tapping or articulation there was substantial forgetting for the AD patients, but none for the controls (see Figure 1.4). The extent of the deficit increased further with the digit addition and digit reversal tasks. The finding that even the simple subsidiary tasks produced substantial forgetting indicates the extent of the impairment of control processes in AD.

In normal subjects, these tasks take up so little capacity that they have no effect on the subject's ability to remember the consonant trigrams (Vallar & Baddeley, 1982). In AD patients, the capacity of control processes is so reduced that even a small demand on the system produces a striking deficit in performance. It might be argued that this would have predicted a differential effect of divided attention when combining tracking and articulation in the task employed by Baddeley et al. (1986). Morris and Baddeley (1988) pointed out that there was a tendency in this disruption, which did not reach statistical significance. Also, tracking was adjusted to be just within the subject's capabilities, reducing the control processing load of the two tasks.

Other studies have explored the ability of AD patients to divide their attention between simultaneous inputs. Mohr, Cox, Williams, Chase, and Fedio (1990) and Grady et al. (1989) found that AD patients were very impaired on a dichotic listening task in which simultaneous lists of items were presented to the subject for subsequent recall. This impairment is not due to a problem in processing degraded auditory information, since AD patients were not substantially impaired in repeating degraded words presented monotonically (Grady et al., 1989). It is clear from these studies that AD patients show substantial impairment on a range of dual tasks, even if the difficulty of the individual tasks is controlled.

Structural interference and the complexity hypothesis. There are alternative ways of explaining the increased divided attention effect in AD, some of which are considered below. For example, it has been argued that impairment on dual tasks simply reflects an impairment on individual tasks which is magnified by placing two tasks together (Somberg & Salthouse, 1982). This may be an explanation for some of the divided attention effects observed in AD, but does not explain the result obtained when combining tracking with memory span where the difficulty of the tasks was adjusted to suit the capabilities of the subject (Baddeley et al., 1986).

Another possibility is that dual-tasks produce abnormal structural interference. In other words, AD patients may be impaired on tasks that involve similar mental processes other than the CES. An impairment within a specific processing module would produce the same type of divided attention deficit with two tasks competing for the same resources. Indeed, some of the tasks described above are likely to involve a high degree of structural interference, for example, the combination of remembering consonant trigrams and articulation (Morris, 1986) and attending to two strings of digits in the dichotic listening task (Grady et al., 1989; Mohr et al., 1990). Nevertheless, other tasks such as the combination of tracking and verbal memory span (Baddeley et al., 1986) and remembering consonant trigrams and tapping (Baddeley et al., 1986; Morris, 1986) specifically minimize this type of interference, yet still produce a large deficit in divided attention performance among AD patients.

Finally, divided attention effects in STM in normal older adults have been interpreted as a reflection of overall task complexity (Salthouse, 1985). Could this explanation apply to patients with AD? The notion arises from studies of response times in older adults, which increase rapidly as a function of task complexity (Cerella, 1985). Although the absolute differences increase between young and old subjects, a meta analysis indicates that the proportionate differences remain the same. Task complexity may indeed explain some of the effects of division of attention on STM tasks and clearly more carefully controlled studies will address this question. Note, however, that the procedure used by Baddeley et al. (1986), which controls for complexity, still produces a larger effect of divided attention in AD patients when digit span is combined with tracking. In summary, there may be multiple sources of increased forgetting when distraction occurs, and which operate depending on the type of task used (Morris, Craik, & Gick, 1990).

Rates of Forgetting from Short-Term Memory

Performance on the Peterson and Peterson (1959) task can also provide information concerning how rapidly material is forgotten from STM. By varying the delay between presentation and recall it is possible to investigate the rate at which performance decreases as the delay increases. It should be noted that on the Peterson and Peterson task a "zero" delay condition is used, which if included in the analysis does indicate a greater rate of forgetting in AD. However, as Morris (1986) has pointed out, the zero delay condition is essentially different from the other conditions in that there is by definition no distractor task. It also leads to ceiling effects that distort the pattern of performance in AD patients and controls. For this reason, the zero delay condition should be excluded from the analysis. If this is done, there is no evidence for an increased forgetting rate in AD despite an overall reduction in performance (Corkin, 1982; Kopelman, 1985; Morris, 1986; Sullivan et al., 1986). An alternative way of measuring rates of forgetting for verbal material has been explored by Morris (1991b) using the Wickelgren (1968) task. Here, the subject is presented with a list of eight two-digit numbers. At the end of the list a further two-digit number is presented which is either the same or different from the initial one. By varying the position of the matching number in the list it is possible to alter the number of intervening items between presentation and recall. Figure 1.5 shows that there is a substantial deterioration in performance of AD patients in this task, but no increased rate of forgetting. A signal detection analysis was also conducted on the data, indicating that AD patients had a disproportionate increase in the number of false positive responses.

A feature of both the Peterson and Peterson (1959) and the Wickelgren (1968) task is that measurement of the rate of forgetting is confounded by either interference by competing material (other digits in the list) or by the effects of the distractor task. Sullivan et al. (1986) and Morris (1986) have used versions of the Peterson and Peterson task with no distractor task. These studies indicate that very little material is forgotten without distraction, with both controls and AD patients. A non-verbal analogue of this task has been

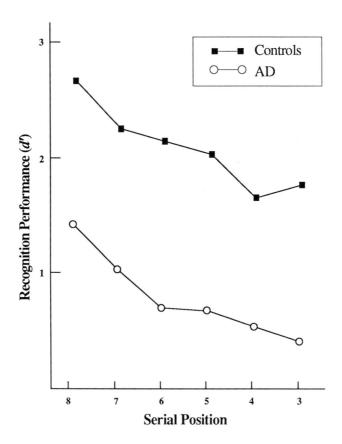

Figure 1.5. Short-term forgetting on the Wickelgren task, in AD patients and controls. From "Response bias in short-term recognition memory in Alzheimer-type dementia" by R. G. Morris, 1991.

developed by Sullivan et al. (1986) in which tapping a sequence of up to 3 blocks on the Corsi block span test is used instead of consonant trigrams. This task showed increased forgetting in AD patients even without distraction. Similarly, Sahakian et al. (1988; see also Morris, Evenden, Sahakian, & Robbins, 1987) have used a version of the delayed-matching to sample task in which the to-be-remembered material is an abstract shape. This is replaced after an un-filled delay by four choice stimuli, including the one that has been shown be-fore. AD patients showed faster rates of forgetting on this task between 4 and 16 seconds compared to controls.

A difficulty with these studies in measuring rates of forgetting is that the controls and patients are still performing at or near ceiling levels with the shorter delays. Where ceiling effects are avoided the initial level of performance along the forgetting curve is not matched, a necessity for an accurate comparison of decline in performance across time (Slamecka & McElree, 1983). Dannenbaum, Parkinson, and Inman (1988) have attempted to avoid ceiling levels of performance and match initial levels by measuring memory for digits with list lengths equal to the span of each subject. They used a single delayed condition which required the subject to recall the digits after counting a number of squares presented in three arrays. Rates of forgetting were estimated from the percentage reduction in performance after the filled delay, indicating a faster forgetting rate in AD patients. A flaw in this study is that the delay interval for the subjects is not fixed. The AD patients, who inevitably have greater difficulty in counting the squares, have to remember the digits for a longer period. Thus, even if the rate of forgetting was not increased for the AD patients, the results would falsely indicate a greater rate.

Encoding Processes in Short-Term Memory

Earlier accounts of the STM impairment in AD have indicated an impairment in encoding material. If material is not encoded sufficiently well, then this will produce a more generalized reduction in memory performance. Wilson et al. (1983) have proposed an encoding deficit that is secondary to an impairment in attention. This has been proposed on the basis of the deficit in free recall in AD in which patients make omission rather than intrusion errors (Wilson et al., 1983). A similar result was observed on the Peterson and Peterson task by Kopelman (1985), contrasting with Korsakoff patients who showed the opposite pattern of results. It is argued that omission errors indicate that the information has not been encoded in the first place. Alternatively, A. Martin et al. (1985) have suggested that AD patients fail to encode the attributes of stimulus material because of impairment in other aspects of information processing such as language. For example, faulty processing of the semantic attributes of words would make them more difficult to recall. Given the widespread intellectual impairment in AD this is an attractive explanation, but does not necessarily account for the all of the STM deficits in these patients. With verbal memory span, the subject relies mainly on phonological coding of material and not on semantic processing as indicated in previous sections.

Neuropsychological Mechanisms

Overall, the evidence points to a pattern of STM memory impairment in AD which is as follows: (1) a preservation of articulatory rehearsal and phonological storage, as indicated by a normal articulation rate, word-length effect, and phonological similarity effects; and (2) an impairment in the control processes associated with STM, indicated by the difficulties that AD patients have on a range of dual tasks, involving tests of memory functioning. Other areas, such as visuospatial memory (Farah, 1988; Hanley, Young, & Pearson, 1991), have yet to be explored in greater detail. Nevertheless, initial studies do appear to indicate abnormal forgetting of visuospatial material from STM in AD (Sahakian et al., 1988; Sullivan et al., 1986).

Comparisons With Aphasic Patients

The pattern of results detailed above can be considered in relation to the neuropathological and neurochemical changes associated with AD. First, a comparison can be made with patients who have a selective deficit in auditory-verbal STM (Shallice & Vallar, 1990; Shallice & Warrington, 1970). These patients show a reduced auditory verbal memory span and a reduced phonological similarity effect (with visual presentation). The word-length effect is reduced with auditorily presented words, but the rate of articulation is normal. In terms of the model presented in Figure 1.2, this has been interpreted as showing a defective phonological store. Patients can only use this store when material is presented auditorily, where material gains obligatory access without the need for phonological recoding. The word-length effect is reduced with auditory presentation because the subjects do not adopt a strategy of passing material through the phonological store to the articulatory rehearsal mechanism (Shallice & Vallar, 1990). Clearly, all these processes are unimpaired in AD, with the exception that AD patients appear unable to use articulatory rehearsal to enhance memory performance at the recall stage of a STM test with visual presentation of material (Morris, 1984).

A review of patients with selective deficits of auditory-verbal STM indicates that the lesions are usually in the perisylvian or temporal parietal regions of the left hemisphere (Shallice & Vallar, 1990). Because the site of the lesion is not precisely localized, it is premature to speculate what area of the brain must show relative preservation in AD. A second comparison can be made with a group of patients with conduction aphasia, who like the patients described above have an impairment in auditory-verbal short-term memory, but with preserved spontaneous language (Damasio & Damasio, 1980). They typically show damage to the posterior portion of the left perisylvian region, which is thought to isolate the two primary language center, Broca's and Wernickes areas (Benson et al., 1973). Again, the relative preservation of the processes associated with auditory-verbal STM in AD points towards these areas of the brain showing minimal damage, although it is not possible to specify the precise structures involved. Studies of the pattern of language impairment in AD point towards a double dissociation, with patients showing fluent spontaneous language, normal phonology and articulation, but impaired naming and comprehension (Morris, 1992). This pattern most closely resembles transcortical motor aphasia, usually associated with left posterior impairment, but sparing of such structures as the arcuate fasciculus and anterior language production areas (Cummings, Benson, & Hill, 1985).

Neurobiological Explanations for the Divided Attention Impairment

In contrast to patients with selective STM deficits, AD patients have a diffuse neuropathology, but with greater damage to the association cortex. The highest density of neuropathological markers, such as neuritic plaques and neurofibrillary tangles, and a greater degree of neurochemical changes occur in association areas of the temporal, parietal and frontal lobes (Pearson, Esiri, Hiorns, Wilcock, & Powell, 1985; Rossor, 1987). Various theories have been proposed that link diffuse neuropathological and neurochemical changes to the impairment in the CES in AD. A simple model that might apply to AD, was originally proposed by Kinsbourne (1980) to explain the effects of normal aging on divided attention performance. His view was that mental operations are more likely to interfere with each other because of the inability to maintain a "functional distance" between tasks. At a physiological level, there is more mutual interference between similar mental processes because they share the same physiological substrate. This view has been considered in the context of AD by Morris (1989, 1991b), where the neurophysiological changes are more pronounced, and there is the possibility of the breakdown of inhibitory processes that separate mental processes. However, it should be noted that even disparate tasks, such as tracking a target with a light pen and remembering a string of digits, results in a pronounced impairment in divided attention in AD (Baddeley et al., 1986).

Becker and his colleagues (Becker, Bajulaiye, & Smith, in press; Becker, Huff, Nebes, Holland, & Boller, 1988) have recently identified patients with AD who appear to have a specific impairment in Central Executive Functioning, as indicated by a deficit in problem solving, cognitive resource allocation, and shifting mental sets. They relate this impairment to a "mass action" effect, in which widespread cerebral lesions combine to produce the cognitive deficit (Chapman & Wolff, 1959). A similar account has been proposed earlier by Morris (1987a; Morris & Baddeley, 1988), based on the notion that control processes are likely to reflect the interaction between cognitive subsystems rather than the functioning of separate processing modules (Barnard, 1985). Very subtle changes in the synchrony of interaction could produce more substantial impairments in these processes. Morris (1987a; Morris & Baddeley, 1988) has also suggested that subcortical nuclei such as the nucleus basalis of Meynert (nbM), which sends cholinergic projections to the neocortex (Candy, Perry, Perry, Biggins, & Thomson, 1983; Ezrin-Waters & Resch, 1986), and is particularly impaired in AD, may fail to play a normal regulatory role in these patients' cognitive processing (Arendt, Bigl, Arendt, & Tennstedt, 1983). This is supported by studies indicating that lesions in the nbM in rats cause a memory deficit that is consistent with an impairment in STM tasks involving divided attention (Kesner, Crutcher, & Measom, 1986).

Mechanisms of Forgetting

In both the verbal and visuospatial memory tasks described above there is a long-term component that contributes to memory performance. For example, with verbal STM, material that is not actively rehearsed or is lost from the phonological store may nevertheless be retrieved from a longer-term store (Morris et al., 1990). Similarly, visuo-spatial STM memory is thought to depend on a store that is associated with the temporary storage of material. Longer-term memories have to be encoded in a more permanent fashion and retrieved later on (a process termed "generation"; Farah, 1984; Kosslyn, 1991).

Impairment in this longer-term element of STM would also contribute to the deficit on tests of STM and be associated with neuropathological changes in the temporal lobes. In AD, there appears to be specific damage to the subiculum and entorinal cortex of the temporal lobes (Hyman, VanHoesen, Damasio et al., 1984), effectively dissociating the hippocampal formation from other brain regions. In non-human primates it has been found that damage to the inferotemporal cortex, amygdala, or hippocampus is associated with a disruption on a delayed matching to sample test (Mishkin, 1982; Sahgal & Iversen, 1978). This task is analogous to the one used by Moss, Albert, Butters, and Payne (1986) and by Sahakian et al. (1988) that demonstrated more rapid decline in the ability to recognize objects over short delays in AD. Similarly, damage to the nbM which provides diffuse projections to the hippocampus also produces a delay-dependent impairment on a modified delayed non-matching to sample test (Dunnett, 1989).

Conclusions

In this chapter studies of short-term memory functioning of groups of AD patients have been reviewed. The theoretical implications of these studies are that diffuse degeneration of the neocortex does not impair short-term phonological storage or articulatory rehearsal, in contrast to the effects of the more circumscribed lesions in patients with a selective impairment in STM. In contrast, the control processes that guide and direct the flow of information processing in STM are impaired. This in itself may indicate something about the underlying neurobiological substrate for mental processes that have been referred to variously as control processes, attentional or processing resources or the functioning of the Central Executive System (Baddeley, 1986; Craik et al., 1990; Norman & Bobrow, 1975; Norman & Shallice, 1986). A fuller appreciation of the mechanisms involved is needed to understand the precise nature of this deficit.

A second consideration is the heterogeneity of AD patients that is obscured by group studies, but presents a promising area for future investigation. For example, some patients with AD have a severe language deficit, with other areas of cognition relatively preserved (Becker et al., 1988; Diesfeldt, this volume; A. Martin et al., 1986). Becker et al. (in press) have put forward the notion of some patients with predominately Central Executive System impairment and others with a predominate memory deficit. This underlines the need not only to fractionate STM into it's different component processes, but applying these models to different subgroups of patients with AD, at different stages of the disorder.

References

Arendt, T., Bigl, V., Arendt, A., & Tennstedt, A. (1983). Loss of neurons in the Nucleus Basalis of Meynert in Alzheimer's Disease, Paralysis Agitans, and Korsakoff's Disease. *Acta Neuropathologica, 61*, 101-108.

Atkinson, R. C., & Shiffrin, R. M. (1968). Human memory: A proposed system and its control processes. In K. W. Spence & J. T. Spence (Eds.), *The psychology of learning and motivation: Advances in research and theory* (Vol. 2). New York: Academic Press.

Baddeley, A. D. (1966). Short-term memory for word sequences as a function of acoustic, semantic, and visual similarity. *Quarterly Journal of Experimental Psychology, 18*, 362-365.

Baddeley, A. D. (1981). The cognitive psychology of everyday life. *British Journal of Psychology, 72*, 257-269.

Baddeley, A. D. (1986). *Working memory*. Oxford: Oxford University Press.

Baddeley, A. D. (1990). *The psychology of memory*. New York: Basic Books.

Baddeley, A. D., & Hitch, G. (1974). Working memory. In G. H. Bower (Ed.), *The Psychology of Learning and Motivation* (Vol. 8). New York: Academic Press.

Baddeley, A. D., & Hitch, G. J. (1977). Recency re-examined. In S. Dornic (Ed.), *Attention and Performance*, (Vol. 8). Hillsdale, NJ: Erlbaum.

Baddeley, A. D., Lewis, V. J., & Vallar, G. (1984). Exploring the articulatory loop. *Quarterly Journal of Experimental Psychology, 26*, 233-252.

Baddeley, A. D., & Lieberman, K. (1980). Spatial working memory. In R. Nickerson (Ed.), *Attention and Performance* (Vol. 8). Hillsdale, NJ: Erlbaum.

Baddeley, A. D., Logie, R., Bressi, S., Della Sala, S., & Spinnler, H. (1986). Dementia and working memory. *Quarterly Journal of Experimental Psychology, 38A*, 603-618.

Baddeley, A. D., Thomson, N., & Buchanan, M. (1975). Word length and the structure of short-term memory. *Journal of Verbal Learning and Verbal Behavior, 14*, 575-589.

Baddeley, A. D., & Warrington, E. K. (1970). Amnesia and the distinction between long- and short-term memory. *Journal of Verbal Learning and Verbal Behavior, 9*, 176-189.

Barnard, P. (1985). Interacting cognitive subsystems: A psycholinguistic approach to short-term memory. In A. Ellis (Ed.), *Progress in the psychology of language*, (Vol. 2). Hillsdale, NJ: Erlbaum.

Becker, J. T., Bajulaiye, O., & Smith, C. (in press). Longitudinal analysis of a two component model of the memory deficits in Alzheimer's disease. *Psychological Medicine*.

Becker, J. T., Huff, F. J., Nebes, R. D., Holland, A., & Boller, F. (1988). Neuropsychological functioning in Alzheimer's disease: Pattern of impairment and rates of progression. *Archives of Neurology, 45*, 263-268.

Benson, D. F., Sheremata, W. A., Bouchard, R., Segarra, J. M., Price, D. L., & Geschwind, N. (1973). Conduction aphasia: A clinico-pathological study. *Archives of Neurology, 28*, 339-346.

Brooks, D. N. (1975). Long- and short-term memory in head injured patients. *Cortex, 11*, 329-340.

Candy, J. M., Perry, R. H., Perry, E. K., Biggins, J. A., & Thomson, B. E. (1983). Pathological changes in the nucleus of Meynert in Alzheimer's and Parkinson's disease. *Journal of Neurological Science, 59*, 277-289.

Cantone, G., Orsini, A., Grossi, D., & De Michele, G. (1978). Verbal and spatial memory span in dementia (an experimental study of 185 subjects). *Acta Neurologica (Naples), 33*, 175-185.

Caplan, D., & Waters, G. S. (1990). Short-term memory and language comprehension: A critical review of the neuropsychological literature. In G. Vallar & T. Shallice (Eds.), *Neuropsychological impairments of short-term memory*. New York: Cambridge University Press.

Cerella, J. (1985). Information processing rates in the elderly. *Psychological Bulletin, 98*, 67-83.

Chapman, L. F., & Wolff, H. G. (1959). The cerebral hemispheres and the highest integrative functions of man. *Archives of Neurology, 1*, 357-424.

Conrad, R. (1964). Acoustic confusion in immediate memory. *British Journal of Psychology, 55*, 75-84.

Conrad, R. & Hull, A. J. (1964). Information, acoustic confusion, and memory span. *British Journal of Psychology, 55*, 429-432.

Corkin, S. (1982). Some relationships between global amnesias and the memory impairments in Alzheimer's disease. In S. Corkin, K. L. Davis, J. H. Growdon, E. Usdin, & R. J. Wurtman (Eds.), *Alzheimer's disease: A report of research in progress*. New York: Raven Press.

Craik, F. I. M., Morris, R. G., & Gick, M. (1990). Adult age differences in working memory. In G. Vallar & T. Shallice (Eds.), *Neuropsychological impairments of short-term memory*. New York: Cambridge University Press.

Crowder, R. G. (1982). The demise of short-term memory. *Acta Psychologica, 50*, 291-323.

Cummings, J. L, Benson, D. F., & Hill, M. A. (1985). Aphasia in dementia of the Alzheimer's type. *Neurology, 35*, 394-396.

Damasio, A. R., & Damasio, H. (1980). The anatomical basis of conduction aphasia. *Brain, 103*, 337-350.

Dannenbaum, S. E., Parkinson, S. R., & Inman, V. W. (1988) Short-term forgetting: Comparisons between patients with dementia of the Alzheimer's type, depressed, and normal elderly. *Cognitive Neuropsychology, 5*, 213-233.

Dunnett, S. B. (1989). Anatomical and behavioral consequences of cholinergic-rich grafts to the neocortex of rats with lesions of the nucleus basalis magnocellularis. *Annals of the New York Academy of Sciences, 495*, 415-429.

Ezrin-Waters, C., & Resch, L. (1986). The nucleus basalis of Meynert. *Canadian Journal of Neurological Science, 13*, 8-14.

Farah, M. J. (1984). The neural basis of mental imagery. *Trends in Neurosciences, 12*, 395-399.

Farah, M. J. (1988). Is visual imagery really visual? Overlooked evidence from neuropsychology. *Psychological Review, 95*, 307-317.

Friedrich, F. J. (1990). Multiple phonological representations and verbal short-term memory. In G. Vallar & T. Shallice (Eds.), *Neuropsychological impairments of short-term memory*. New York: Cambridge University Press.

Glanzer, M., & Cunitz, A. R. (1966). Two storage mechanisms in free recall. *Journal of Verbal Learning and Verbal Behavior, 5*, 351-360.

Grady, C. L., Grimes, A. M., Partronas, N. Sunderland, T., Foster, N. L., & Rapoport, S. I. (1989). Divided attention as measured by dichotic speech performance in dementia of the Alzheimer type. *Archives of Neurology, 46,* 317-320.

Hanley, J. R., Young, A. W., & Pearson, N. A. (1991). Impairment of the visuo-spatial sketch pad. *Quarterly Journal of Experimental Psychology, 43,* 101-125.

Hebb, D. O. (1945). *The organization of behavior.* New York: Wiley.

Hyman, B. T., Van Hoesen, G. W., Damasio, A. R., et al. (1984). Alzheimer's disease: Cell specific pathology isolates the hippocampal formation. *Science, 225,* 1168-1170.

Kaszniak, A. W., Garron, D. C., & Fox, J. H. (1979). Differential aspects of age and cerebral atrophy upon span of immediate recall and paired associate learning in older patients with suspected dementia. *Cortex, 15,* 285-295.

Kesner, R. P., Crutcher, K. A., & Measom, M. O. (1986). Medial septal and nucleus basalis magnocellularis lesions produce order memory deficits in rats which mimic symptomatology of Alzheimer's disease. *Neurobiology of Aging, 7,* 287-295.

Kintsch, W., & Buschke, H. (1969). Homophones and synonyms in short-term memory. *Journal of Experimental Psychology, 80,* 403-407.

Kinsbourne, M. (1980). Attentional dysfunction in the elderly: Theoretical models and research perspectives. In L. W. Poon, J. L. Fozard, L. S. Cermak, D. Arenberg, & L. W. Thompson (Eds.), *New directions in memory and aging.* Hillsdale, NJ: Erlbaum.

Kopelman, M. D. (1985). Rates of forgetting in Alzheimer-type dementia and Korsakoff's syndrome. *Neuropsychologia, 23,* 623-638.

Kosslyn, S. M. (1991). A cognitive neuroscience of visual cognition. In R. Logie & M. Denis (Eds.), *Mental images in human cognition.* Amsterdam: Elsevier.

Levy, B. A. (1971). The role of articulation in auditory and visual short-term memory. *Journal of Verbal Learning and Verbal Behavior, 10,* 123-132.

Martin, A., Brouwers, P., Cox, C., & Fedio, P. (1985). On the nature of the verbal memory deficit in Alzheimer's disease. *Brain and Language, 25,* 323-341.

Martin, A., Brouwers, P., Lalonde, F., Cox, C., Teleska, P., Fedio, P, Foster, N. L., & Chase, T. N. (1986). Towards a behavioral typology of Alzheimer's patients. *Journal of Clinical and Experimental Neuropsychology, 8,* 594-610.

McCarthy, R. A., & Warrington, E. K. (1987). Double dissociation of short-term memory for lists and sentences. *Brain, 110,* 1545-1563.

Miller, E. (1971). On the nature of the memory disorder in presenile dementia. *Neuropsychologia, 9,* 75-81.

Miller, E. (1973). Short- and long-term memory in presenile dementia (Alzheimer's Disease). *Psychological Medicine, 3,* 221-224

Miller, G. A. (1956). The magical number seven, plus or minus two: Some limits on our capacity for processing information. *Psychological Review, 63,* 81-97.

Mishkin, M. (1982). A memory system in the monkey. *Philosophical Transactions of the Royal Society of London B, 298,* 85-95.

Mohr, E., Cox, C., Williams, J., Chase, T. N., & Fedio, P. (1990). Impairment of central auditory function in Alzheimer's Disease. *Journal of Clinical and Experimental Neuropsychology, 12,* 235-246.

Monsell, S. (1984). Components of working memory underlying verbal skills: A "distributed capacities" view. In H. Bouma & D. G. Bouwhuis (Eds.), *Attention and Performance,* (Vol. 10). Hillsdale, NJ: Erlbaum.

Morris, R. G. (1984). Dementia and the functioning of the articulatory loop system. *Cognitive Neuropsychology, 1,* 143-157.

Morris, R. G. (1986). Short-term forgetting in senile dementia of the Alzheimer's type. *Cognitive Neuropsychology, 3,* 77-97.

Morris, R. G. (1987a). Articulatory rehearsal in Alzheimer-type dementia. *Brain and Language, 30,* 351-362.

Morris, R. G. (1987b). The effect of concurrent articulation on memory span in Alzheimer-type dementia. *British Journal of Clinical Psychology, 26*, 233-234.

Morris, R. G. (1989). Neuropsychological aspects of dementia. *Current Opinions in Psychiatry, 2*, 66-71.

Morris, R. G. (1991a). Neuropsychological studies of memory functioning in Alzheimer-type dementia. In J. Weinmann & J. Hunter (Eds.), *Memory: Neurochemical and abnormal perspectives.* London: Harwood.

Morris, R. G. (1991b). *Response bias in short-term recognition memory in Alzheimer-type dementia.* Unpublished manuscript.

Morris, R. G. (1992). Language dysfunction in the dementias. In R. E. Asher & M. Y. Simpson (Eds.), *Encyclopedia of language and linguistics.* Aberdeen: Pergamon and Aberdeen University Press.

Morris, R. G., & Baddeley, A. D. (1988). Primary and working memory in Alzheimer-type dementia. *Journal of Clinical and Experimental Neuropsychology, 10*, 279-296.

Morris, R. G., Bradley, V. A., & Welch, J. L. (1991). *Visual short-term memory in Alzheimer-type dementia.* Unpublished manuscript.

Morris, R. G., Craik, F. I. M., & Gick, M. (1990). Age differences in working memory tasks: The role of secondary memory and the central executive. *Quarterly Journal of Experimental Psychology, 42A*, 67-86.

Morris, R. G., Evenden, J. L., Sahakian, B. J., & Robbins, T. W. (1987). Computer-aided assessment of dementia: Comparative studies of neuropsychological deficits in Alzheimer-type dementia and Parkinson's disease. In S. M. Stahl, S. D. Iversen, & E. C. Goodman (Eds.), *Cognitive neurochemistry,* Oxford: Oxford University Press.

Morris, R. G., & Kopelman, M. D. (1986). The memory deficits in Alzheimer-type dementia: A review. *Quarterly Journal of Experimental Psychology, 38*, 575-602.

Moss, M. B., Albert, M. S., Butters, N., Payne, M. (1986). Differential patterns of memory loss among patients with Alzheimer's disease, Huntington's disease, and alcoholic Korsakoff's syndrome. *Archives of Neurology, 43*, 239-246.

Murdock, B. B. (1967). Recent developments in short-term memory. *British Journal of Psychology, 58*, 421-433.

Norman, D. A., & Bobrow, D. G. (1975). On data-limited and resource-limited processes. *Cognitive Psychology, 7*, 44-64.

Norman, D. A., & Shallice, T. (1986). Reflections on cognition and parallel distributed processing. In J. L. McClelland & D. E. Rumelhart (Eds.), *Parallel distributed processing: Exploration of the microstructure of cognition.* (Vol. 2). Cambridge, MA: MIT Press.

Pearson, R. C. A., Esiri, M. M., Hiorns, R. W., Wilcock, G. K., & Powell, T. P. S. (1985). Anatomical correlates of the distribution of the pathological changes in the neocortex in Alzheimer disease. *Proceedings of the National Academy of Science, USA, 82*, 4531-4534.

Pepin, E. P., & Eslinger, P. J. (1989). Verbal memory decline in Alzheimer's disease: A multiple process deficit. *Neurology, 39*, 1477-1482.

Peterson, L. R., & Peterson, M. J. (1959). Short-term retention of individual verbal items. *Journal of Experimental Psychology, 58*, 93-198.

Roediger, H. L., & Craik, F. I. M. (Eds.). (1989). *Varieties of consciousness: Essays in honour of Endel Tulving.* Hillsdale, NJ: Erlbaum.

Rossor, M. (1987). The neurochemistry of cortical dementias. In S. M. Stahl, S. D. Iversen, & E. C. Goodman (Eds.), *Cognitive neurochemistry,* Oxford: Oxford University Press.

Sahgal, A., & Iversen, S. D. (1978). Categorization and retrieval after selective inferotemporal lesions in monkeys. *Brain Research, 146*, 341-350.

Sahakian, B. J., Morris, R. G., Evenden, J. L., Heald, A., Levy, R., Philpot, M., & Robbins, T. W. (1988). A comparative study of visuospatial memory and learning in Alzheimer-type dementia and Parkinson's disease. *Brain, 111*, 698-718.

Salthouse, T. A. (1985). Speed of behaviour and its implications for cognition. In J. E. Birren & K. W. Schaie (Eds.), *Handbook of the psychology of aging* (2nd Ed.), New York: Van Nostrand.

Shallice, T., & Vallar, G. (1990). The impairment in auditory-verbal short-term storage. In T. Shallice & G. Vallar (Eds.). *Neuropsychological impairments of short-term memory*. New York: Cambridge University Press.

Shallice, T., & Warrington, E. K. (1970). Independent functioning of verbal memory stores: A neuropsychological study. *Quarterly Journal of Experimental Psychology, 22,* 261-273.

Shiffrin, R. M. (1976). Capacity limitations in information processing, attention, and memory. In W. K. Estes (Ed.), *Handbook of learning and cognitive processes*, (Vol. 4). Hillsdale, NJ: Erlbaum

Simon, H. A. (1974). How big is a chunk? *Science, 183,* 482-488.

Slamecka, N. J., & McElree, B. (1983). Normal forgetting of verbal lists as a function of their degree of learning. *Journal of Experimental Psychology: Learning, Memory, & Cognition, 9,* 384-397.

Somberg, T. A., & Salthouse, T. A. (1982). Divided attention abilities in young and old adults. *Journal of Experimental Psychology: Human Perception and Performance, 8,* 651-663.

Spinnler, H., Della Sala, S., Bandera, R., & Baddeley, A. D. (1988). Dementia, aging, and the structure of human memory. *Cognitive Neuropsychology, 5,* 193-211.

Sullivan, E. V., Corkin, S., & Growdon, J. H. (1986). Verbal and nonverbal short-term memory in patients with Alzheimer's disease and in healthy elderly subjects. *Developmental Neuropsychology, 2,* 387-400.

Tulving, E., & Colotla, V. A. (1970). Free recall of trilingual lists. *Cognitive Psychology, 1,* 86-98.

Vallar, G., & Baddeley, A. D. (1982). Short-term forgetting and the articulatory loop. *Quarterly Journal of Experimental Psychology, 34,* 53-60.

Vallar, G., & Baddeley, A. D. (1984). Fractionation of working memory: Neuropsychological evidence for a phonological short-term store. *Journal of Verbal Learning and Verbal Behavior, 23,* 151-161.

Vallar, G., & Cappa, S. F. (1987). Articulation and short-term memory: Evidence from anarthria. *Cognitive Neuropsychology, 4,* 55-78.

Waugh, N. C., & Norman, D. A. (1965). Primary memory. *Psychological Review, 72,* 89-104.

Weingartner, H., Grafman, J., Boutelle, W., Kaye, W., & Martin, P. R. (1983). Forms of memory failure. *Science, 221,* 380-382.

Wickelgren, W. A. (1968). Sparing of short-term memory in an amnesic patient: Implications for strength theory of memory. *Neuropsychologia, 6,* 235-244.

Wilson, R. S., Bacon, L. D., Fox, J. H., & Kaszniak, A. W. (1983). Primary memory and secondary memory in dementia of the Alzheimer-type. *Journal of Clinical Neuropsychology, 5,* 337-344.

2

Episodic Memory in Alzheimer's Disease: Breakdown of Multiple Memory Processes

James T. Becker and Oscar L. Lopez

University of Pittsburgh

Lord Emsworth had an eccentric memory. It was not to be trusted an inch as far as the events of yesterday or the day before were concerned. Even in the small matter of assisting him to find a hat which he had laid down somewhere five minutes ago, it was nearly always useless.

The crime wave at Blandings, P.G. Wodehouse (1937)

Introduction

General

Patients diagnosed with Probable Alzheimer's Disease (McKhann et al., 1984) or Primary Degenerative Dementia (American Psychiatric Association, 1987) suffer from a devastating progressive loss of memory. At the earlier stages of the illness, the patient may be as Wodehouse (1937) described Lord Emsworth's loss of day-to-day memories: The inability to recall where money has been placed, whether bills have been paid, or even the day of the week, which significantly impairs an individual's activities of daily living. The failure to establish and retrieve these memories corresponds to the loss of *episodic memory* as first described by Tulving (1972). The loss of these personally-relevant, context-dependent memories is one of the hallmarks of AD and is the focus of this review.

Episodic Memory

Episodic memory is responsible for the encoding, storage, and retrieval of temporally and spatially defined events, and the temporal and spatial relationships among them (Tulving, 1984). The investigation of these kinds of engrams has, and probably will remain, the focus of most research on memory (Tulving, 1972) and memory disorders. By contrast, semantic memory is described as the memory of information necessary for language, a "mental thesaurus" including not only lexical information (i.e., word meaning and concepts) but also facts and general world knowledge (e.g., the capital of Pennsylvania is Harrisburg). Tulving (1983, 1984) has carefully compared and contrasted the two systems in terms of the kind of information stored, the nature of the cognitive operations performed on this information, and the applications or uses that these different types of memories may serve. The present chapter focuses on the nature of the episodic memory defect in AD, and the discussion of semantic memory is taken up elsewhere (Nebes, 1989).

There are, of course, a variety of other systems used to describe the nature of human memory generally, and the nature of memory loss in amnesic and demented patients, in particular (e.g., Cohen & Squire, 1980; Schacter, 1987; Weiskrantz, 1987). However, it is not the purpose of this chapter to debate the relative merits of these systems. Each has their own strengths and weaknesses, and only time and data will decide which best accounts for the most evidence. It is worth noting, however, that these different systems all appear to agree that learning rules and skills is *not* a function of the systems responsible for either episodic- or semantic-type memories.

Although Tulving (1987) argues that episodic and semantic memory are functionally independent, others suggest that while these concepts are useful heuristic devices, the evidence that they are independent functional systems is less compelling (Baddeley, 1986). Nevertheless, for the sake of this discussion, we assume that these are functionally distinct systems, and that their *dysfunction* in AD results from the breakdown of independent anatomical systems. Further, we will review evidence to suggest that it is also possible to observe patterns of memory loss in AD patients reminiscent of patients with unilateral temporal lobe excisions (e.g., Milner, 1968, 1971).

Episodic Memory in Alzheimer's Disease

General

Studies of AD patients have frequently shown that the earliest symptoms of the disease are characterized by an impairment in episodic memory (i.e., recalling day to day events, e.g., Kaszniak, Poon & Riege, 1988; Kopelman, 1985a). As the disease progresses, patients develop impairments in the ability to perform tasks which reflect on the functions of lexical and semantic systems. The ability to name common objects and to generate lists of words using different types of cues (e.g., letters, categories) is decreased. Both retrieval and storage dynamics appear responsible for this semantic memory loss (Martin & Fedio, 1983; Ober, Dronkers, Koss, Dellis, & Friedland, 1986), but basic

linguistic processes, such as knowledge of syntax, is not related to performance.

Nature of the Memory Loss

When an individual over the age of 50 years presents for evaluation because of "memory lapses," frequently they are unaware that they occur, or they
minimize their significance and attribute them to normal aging. However,
careful neuropsychological evaluation of the patient reveals just how devastated
memory can be. Word list learning is impaired, and delayed recall (e.g., 20
minutes after presentation) can be nil (McCarthy, Ferris, Clark, & Crook, 1981;
Miller, 1973). Verbal free recall is impaired, first by a decrease in the primacy
effect (reflecting secondary memory impairment) and later by a decrease in the
recency effect (reflecting an impairment in primary memory, Martin, Brouwers,
Cox, & Fedio, 1985; Miller, 1971; Pepin & Eslinger, 1989). Figure 2.1 shows a
plot of the recall of 12-item word lists by AD patients, plotted as a function of
the position of the words in the original list. Among the patients, it is clearly
the case that both the primacy and recency effects are diminished or absent
relative to those of the control subjects.

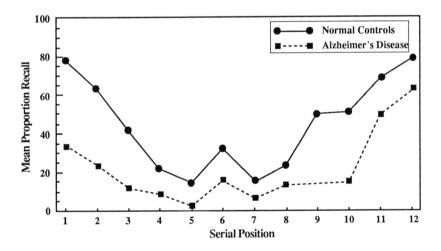

Figure 2.1. Serial position curves for verbal free recall in normal old adults and patients with
a mild to moderate Alzheimer's disease.

Primary memory probably plays an important limiting role in the secondary memory of AD patients (Martin, Brouwers et al., 1985; Martin, Cox,
Brouwers, & Fedio, 1985; R. S. Wilson, Bacon, Fox, & Kaszniak, 1983), and

defects in stimulus encoding may affect subsequent recall (Becker, Boller, Saxton, & McGonigle-Gibson, 1987; Helkala, Laulumaa, Soininen, & Riekkinen, 1988). For example, Figure 2.2 shows the performance of 194 AD patients on the copy, and immediate and delayed recall of a modified Rey-Osterreith figure (Becker et al., 1987). The patients were impaired in their copy of the figure, reflecting the well-documented visual-constructional defects in AD patients. The immediate recall by the patients, however, was significantly *worse* than would be expected based on the extent of the impaired copy; that is, there was a significant group (patient vs. control) by condition (copy vs. immediate recall) interaction.

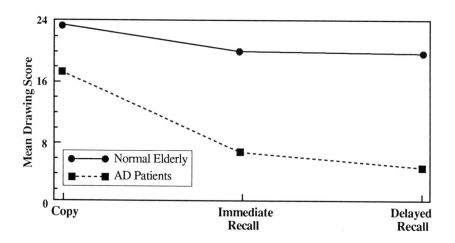

Figure 2.2. The performance of AD patients and normal elderly subjects in the Copy and Recall (Immediate and Delayed) of a simplified Rey-Osterreith figure. Adapted from "Normal rates of forgetting of verbal and non-verbal material in Alzheimer's disease" by J. T. Becker, F. Boller, J. Saxton, and K. McGonigle-Gibson, 1987, *Cortex, 23,* p. 67. Copyright 1987 by Masson Italia Periodici. Adapted by permission.

As described above, AD patients present for evaluation with profound impairments in encoding, storage, and retrieval of episodes from secondary memory. However, in spite of quantitative differences between patients and normal elderly individuals, there are few qualitative differences between patients and controls. That is, the dynamics of human memory appear preserved in AD patients even if their ability to capitalize on those processes is impaired. The goal of much memory research, therefore, has been to describe the nature and extent of the information processing limitations in AD patients.

Studies that qualitatively evaluated episodic memory of AD patients and other dementias or with amnesic syndromes have produced a variety of results. Some researchers find that intrusion errors, defined as inappropriate recurrence of a response from a preceding test, is a useful discriminator for AD (Fuld, Katzman, Davies, & Terry, 1982; Kramer et al., 1988), whereas others dispute the specificity of intrusion errors in AD in relation to normal aging or other dementias (Butters, Granholm, Salmon, Grant, & Wolfe, 1986; Kopelman, 1985b). Butters et al. (1986) studied episodic memory in AD, Huntington's disease (HD), and Korsakoff syndromes (KS) patients. When asked to recall a short passage, AD patients remembered few facts and made numerous prior-story and extra-story intrusion errors, suggesting an increased sensitivity to proactive interference. However, KS patients also produced intrusion errors and showed an increased sensitivity to proactive interference.

In addition, both AD and KS patients manifested perseverative errors on a letter fluency test. HD patients were not prone to intrusion and perseverative errors. The parallel performance of AD and KS patients led the authors to propose a common anatomical structure affected in both diseases. They suggested that the basal forebrain, specifically the Nucleus Basalis of Meynert, which is affected in 47% of KS patients, might be that structure (Arendt, Bigl, Arendt, & Tennstedt, 1983). However, senile (neuritic) plaques and neurofibrillary tangles in the mammillary bodies, hypothalamus, and dorsomedial nucleus of the thalamus have been found in 95% of AD patients (Grossi, Lopez, & Martinez, 1989). These are the main structures affected in KS patients (Mair, Warrington, & Weiskrantz, 1979; Victor, Adams, & Collins, 1971). These findings suggest that subcortical structures involved in memory processes also play an important role in the memory loss of AD patients, and that the common neuropathological lesion of AD and KS may be other than the basal forebrain.

Several reports of performance on verbal recognition memory tasks support the hypothesis that poor initial encoding and the severity of language impairment may account for some of the deficit in verbal memory in AD patients (R. S. Wilson, Bacon, Kramer, Fox, & Kaszniak, 1983; Kaszniak et al., 1986). These findings indicate that language deficits limit the verbal encoding and make a significant contribution to the word recognition impairment. By contrast, face recognition performance seemed not to be affected by language deficits (R. S. Wilson, Kaszniak, Bacon, Fox, & Kelly, 1982). Recognition memory for non-verbal stimuli (e.g., visual forms) (Diesfeldt, 1990) as well as complex figure recall (Becker et al., 1987; Martin, Cox et al., 1985) have been evaluated in AD patients. These visual stimuli are less prone to be verbalized, and constitute an adequate counterpart of the verbal stimuli. Nevertheless, other cognitive deficits may limit the examination of non-verbal memory. It has been demonstrated that visuospatial deficits are responsible in part, for deficient face recognition memory (Diesfeldt, 1990), and visuoconstructional deficits limit the memory for complex figures (Martin, Cox, et al., 1985). Furthermore, AD patients show no specific qualitative feature that could be used to differentiate the pattern of memory deficits from normal controls (Becker et al., 1987; Diesfeldt, 1990; Martin, Brouwers et al., 1985).

Evidence from studies in non-demented subjects has demonstrated that there is a tendency in human memory to encode verbally pictorial material. Visual images can be consolidated in memory and subsequently retrieved by *either* verbal or visual clues (see Paivio 1986, for review). Experiments carried out comparing the effect of verbal mediators on the pictorial memory of AD, KS, HD, and right-hemisphere-damaged patients have provided additional evidence of visual memory deficits in AD (Butters et al., 1983). AD and KS patients failed in the ability to use both verbal material (stories linking figures to the background scenes) and visual context (relationships among pictures, figures, and objects) as an aid in visual recognition memory. These findings strengthen the concept of encoding deficits in AD patients as limiting subsequent memory.

Multiple-Component Breakdown

Our analysis of the episodic memory deficits focuses mainly on evidence derived from study of functional subgroups within the larger population of AD patients. These subgroups, to use the term suggested by Jorm (1985), represent individuals with islands of preserved functions in the context of a syndrome which meets the criteria for Probable AD. The importance of this type of analysis has been discussed in detail by Martin (1990), and will not be reviewed here. However, we take as a starting point the position that it is possible to identify AD patients with specific patterns of neuropsychological dysfunction, that these patterns are not simply the result of random co-occurrences of cognitive defects, and that they relate to the underlying neuroanatomical disruption caused by the disease.

Although the cognitive dysfunction associated with AD is often described as generalized, it is perhaps more accurate and meaningful to describe it as multi-focal. By that we do not mean that the syndrome resembles that of, for example, multi-infarct dementia, with its stepwise progression and patchwork quilt of behavioral change. Rather, the development of CNS dysfunction in AD appears to progress such that different cognitive systems are more or less affected than others. While in the past this has been interpreted as reflecting different disease states (e.g., senile vs. presenile dementia, Brion, 1966; Sjögren, 1951; Sourander & Sjögren, 1970), more recent studies have demonstrated that AD is a single entity (Thal, Grundman, & Klauber, 1988), which may have multiple risk modifiers. Thus, it is reasonable to assume that at various points during the progression of the disease, the neuropsychological profile will reflect the relative impairments and sparing of cognitive functions. These patterns of impairments should, and do, follow the "natural fracture lines of behavior" (Thomas, Hostetter, & Barker, 1968), reflecting the way in which normal memory processes are organized.

Morris and Kopelman (1986), in their excellent review, make the point that the memory loss in AD is the result of multiple system breakdown. They argued that the breakdown was consistent with known models of information processing (see below) consistent with a syndrome like that of focal amnesic patients, plus an additional information processing defect. Further work by Kopelman (1989), confirmed the dissociation of function, and also suggested that the amnesia-like component of the memory loss in AD may be the result of the well documented cholinergic deficiency (Kopelman & Corn, 1988; Whitehouse, Price, Clark, Coyle, & Delong, 1981).

The Working Memory Model

Further investigations of the nature of the additional information processing defect in AD report data which are consistent with the hypothesis that AD patients suffer from a defect in Working Memory (Baddeley, 1986). Working Memory was originally described by Baddeley and Hitch (1974) as memory which does work. Their attention was focused on the dynamics of primary memory, and they concluded that a system which included active processors for the encoding and retrieval of information over short delays was tenable, and also posited the existence of a Central Executive System to oversee the operations. The Working Memory (WM) model suggested that there are two verbal subsystems, and a system dedicated to the processing of non-verbal, imagery-based information. The verbal subsystems, the Articulatory Loop and Phonological Input Store, are thought of as relatively automatic processors which can function without much direct control. Similarly, the Visuospatial Scratchpad was thought of as the nonverbal analog of these two slave systems. Neuropsychogical data suggest that these systems are, indeed, independent and interactive (Baddeley & B. A. Wilson, 1988; Farah, Gazzaniga, Holtzman, & Kosslyn, 1985; Shallice & Warrington, 1970; Vallar & Baddeley, 1984).

The Central Executive System of Working Memory is quite important to our understanding of the system itself, and as we will argue below, for understanding the memory defect in AD patients. The CES bears many similarities to a model of attention described by Norman and Shallice (1980). Of importance to the WM model is the notion that much action or behavior can proceed automatically, but that problems can develop with the system from time to time due to conflicting demands. The Norman and Shallice model then invokes a Supervisory Attentional System not unlike the CES. This system, and by implication the CES, is involved in tasks which require planning or decision-making, situations where the automatic processes cannot function normally or come into conflict, where new situations are to be encountered, or where previously learned associations must be modified or extinguished.

Given the role of the CES in behavior, its failure would produce symptoms not unlike those seen following lesions in the frontal lobes. Baddeley and B. A. Wilson (1988) have identified patients with CES defects, but always in the context of lesions which could directly affect the functions of the frontal lobes. It seems reasonable to argue, therefore, that one consequence of frontal lobe damage is an impaired CES (see also Stuss & Benson, 1987).

Working Memory in AD

This long introduction about Working Memory is important because it permits a rational framework for understanding the patterns of symptoms observed. Furthermore, as the Working Memory model continues to be actively developed, the extent to which data from AD patients can address the model, strengthens the theoretical underpinnings.

In terms of the verbal slave systems of Working Memory, they appear to function normally in AD patients. Although these patient's performance is clearly poorer than that of controls, the qualitative aspects of performance suggest that the same factors which influence normal performance influence that of AD patients. Thus, the Phonological Input Store and Articulatory Loop appear intact in AD patients (Morris & Baddeley, 1988; see also Morris, this volume; Morris & Kopelman, 1986, for review).

The CES, by contrast, does *not* appear to function normally in AD. Baddeley, Bressi, Della Salla, Logie, and Spinnler (1986) compared the performance of AD patients with that of old and young normal control subjects on concurrent tasks. The subjects were required first to demonstrate a stable level of performance on a manual tracking task, and a verbal repetition task. After having established the baseline performance, the subjects were then required to perform the two tasks concurrently. While the older control subjects were less competent than the younger controls, they were nevertheless able to perform. By contrast, the AD patients were dramatically impaired. Their performance on both the tracking and repetition tasks fell dramatically, and there was no evidence that they shifted their attention to only one task to perform it well. The authors interpreted these data to suggest that the AD patients were suffering from a CES defect.

Based on these data and the previous suggestions by Morris and Kopelman (1986), we decided to evaluate a specific model of the memory defect in AD. Specifically, we argued that AD patients suffer from two independent syndromes, an "amnesic syndrome" identical to that seen in patients with focal amnesic syndromes, and a "dysexecutive syndrome" resulting from a defective CES (Becker, 1988). We further argued that based on the patterns of impairment of AD patients, we should be able to identify individual patients with "focal" amnesic and dysexecutive syndromes in the context of probable AD. In the original analysis of 86 patients participating in the Alzheimer Research Program (ARP) at the University of Pittsburgh, we found two patients who met the criteria for (relatively) focal impairment - one with a dysexecutive syndrome and one with an amnesic syndrome.

We have subsequently analysed the performance of all 194 ARP AD patients on measures of verbal fluency (Benton, 1968), verbal similarities (Wechsler, 1945), card sorting (Weigl, 1927), and letter cancellation (Diller et al., 1974) relative to their performance on secondary episodic memory tasks (paired-associate learning and free recall). Figure 2.3 shows a scatterplot of the performance of the AD patients expressed in terms of the Memory and Executive composite scores. At baseline, we were able to identify eight patients with dysexecutive syndromes and 24 with amnesic syndromes, confirming our original observation that this functional dissociation is possible. Baddeley, Della Sala, and Spinnler (in press) independently identified patients with relatively focal impairments in memory or executive function. This study also demonstrated that these dissociations were not merely the result of the random assortment of symptoms, but rather did appear to follow the predictions of the two-component model.

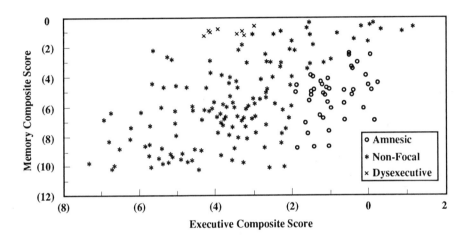

Figure 2.3. The performance of 194 AD patients expressed as composite scores of Memory and Executive functions.

Secondary Episodic Memory

General

What of the "amnesic component" of the memory loss in AD? In describing normal human memory, a distinction is drawn between primary (or Working) memory and secondary memory. Primary memory is limited in both time and information load, and items to-be-remembered must be rehearsed to be maintained. By contrast, secondary memory is long-lived and does not require frequent maintenance rehearsal. Delayed recall of words, stories, or drawings all require secondary memory, and the primacy effect in immediate free recall is also presumably supported by secondary memory. In patients with focal amnesic syndromes, for example medial temporal lobe excisions or herpes simplex encephalitis, measures of primary memory, including digit and word spans, and immediate free recall, are relatively normal. By contrast, delayed recall is nil, leading to the suggestion that this pattern of impairment (i.e., normal immediate recall and impaired delayed recall) is diagnostic of an amnestic syndrome. The neuroanatomical bases of these amnestic syndromes include the hippocampal system and related structures in the temporal lobe, and midline diencephalic structures including the dorsal medial nucleus of thalamus and the mammillary bodies (see Weiskrantz, 1985, 1987, for reviews). Depending on the extent of damage, material-specific defects can also be observed (e.g., Dusoir, Kapur, Byrnes, McKinstry, & Hoare, 1990), with relative preservation of either verbal or non-verbal material.

Secondary Memory Defects in AD

It is clear that AD patients have impaired secondary memory. As was described earlier, the primacy effect in free recall is virtually abolished (Pepin & Eslinger, 1989), and even recognition memory can be reduced to chance levels of performance if there is any sort of delay between stimulus presentation and the test trial (Moss, Albert, Butters, & Payne, 1986).

One hypothesis about the nature of memory loss associated with lesions to the temporal lobe, as would be the case in AD (Hyman, Van Hoesen, & Damasio, 1990; Hyman, Van Hoesen, Kromer, & Damasio, 1986; Hyman, Damasio, Van Hoesen, & Barnes, 1984), suggests that patients with these brain lesions have an abnormally rapid rate of decay of information from secondary memory (Huppert & Piercy, 1979). However, this observation has not been borne out in two separate studies of AD patients. In the first (Kopelman, 1985b), AD patients were given the same recognition memory test used to evaluate the amnesic patient H.M. The performance of the patients was compared with that of normal controls immediately after presentation of the list of photographs. The exposure to the pictures was adjusted (i.e., lengthened) so that the AD patients performed as well as the controls at the short interval, and their recognition memory was re-evaluated up to 24 hours later. Under these conditions, the rate of decay of information from secondary memory was normal.

In a related study of free recall, we examined the ability of AD patients and controls to remember a short, 18-item story, and a modified, 24-item Rey-Osterieth complex figure (Becker, et al., 1987). Figure 2.4 shows the performance of the patients and controls in the immediate and delayed recall of the story, and Figure 2.2 the copy, and recall of the figure for all 194 AD patients and 103 normal controls in the ARP study cohort. The rate of decay of information from immediate to delayed recall did not differ between the patients and controls; although the AD patients remembered less overall, they nevertheless did not have an abnormally rapid rate of forgetting (Becker et al., 1987).

Thus, at least some of the difficulty that AD patients have with secondary episodic memory must be due to processing defects earlier in the chain of events. Two lines of evidence support this conclusion. First, R. S. Wilson, Bacon,

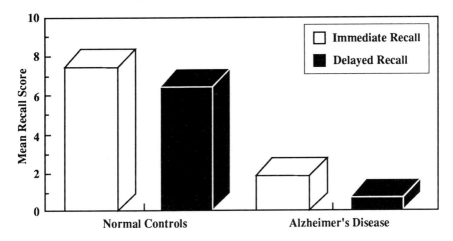

Figure 2.4. The performance of AD patients and normal elderly control subjects on the immediate and delayed recall of a short story. Adapted from "Normal rates of forgetting of verbal and non-verbal material in Alzheimer's disease" by J. T. Becker, F. Boller, J. Saxton, and K. McGonigle-Gibson, 1987, *Cortex, 23*, p. 65. Copyright 1987 by Masson Italia Periodici. Adapted by permission.

Fox et al., (1983) demonstrated that unlike control subjects, AD patient's secondary memory was significantly correlated with their primary memory capacity. That is, the ability (or inability) of the patients to maintain information in primary memory appeared to limit their performance on the secondary memory component of the task. Second, Morris and Kopelman (1986) reached a similar conclusion that AD patients suffer from a defect in the ability to transfer information from primary memory into secondary memory due, at least in part, to an abnormally rapid rate of decay from primary memory.

Subgroups of Amnesic AD Patients

To the extent that the episodic memory loss in AD patients is due to a functional isolation of the hippocampal system from association cortex (Hyman et al., 1984; Hyman et al., 1990; Hyman et al., 1986), then the performance of the "amnesic" AD patients should closely resemble that of patients with focal temporal lobe lesions. However, given that only 10-12% of all AD patients in the ARP cohort appeared "amnesic," the ability to complete prospective studies is limited. However, when attention was paid to the pattern of performance in mildly demented AD patients, important studies have been possible (Haxby et al.,1990; Martin, 1990).

We were interested in learning whether our ability to dissociate patterns of impairment across cognitive domains would also work within a specific domain. That is, based on the results and predictions of the work of Martin (1987) and colleagues (Martin et al., 1986), would it be possible to identify patients with relatively focal impairments in memory for verbal or nonverbal material, but not both? Again, careful examination of the data from the ARP suggests that these patients do exist (Becker, Lopez & Wess, 1991). The performance of the AD patients on the immediate recall of a story and figure (see above) were classified relative to the 5th percentile of the normal control subjects as either "normal" or "abnormal." Although the vast majority of the patients were impaired on both tasks, 25/194 (12.9%) were classified as impaired on *only one* of the tasks - 13 with a verbal memory impairment, and 12 with a nonverbal memory impairment. Of particular importance to the present discussion was the finding that these two groups of patients could not be distinguished in terms of other, non-mnemonic tasks. Put another way, these patients met the criteria for Probable AD, and still had *spared* memory for particular kinds of information. Thus, as had been predicted (Martin, Cox et al., 1985), these patients appeared as if they had focal unilateral temporal lobe lesions.

On the Neuroanatomical Basis of the Episodic Memory Loss

It is also worth considering briefly the nature of the neuropathological changes which might be responsible for the episodic memory loss in AD. It is clearly the case that medial temporal structures are affected in AD and play a critical role in the formation of memories. However, more functional systems than these are affected in AD, and more are involved in the formation and retrieval of memories. Much attention has focused, for example, on the cholinergic projections arising from the basal forebrain, specifically the nucleus basalis of Meynert (Whitehouse et al., 1981). Lesions in the homologous regions of animal brains can produce memory impairment (Mishkin & Appenzeller, 1987), and this line of research has also increased the focus of attention on cholinergic modulation in the treatment of symptoms of AD (e.g., Kopelman, & Corn, 1988). However, in one series of AD patients, 95% of the brains were found to have neuropathological changes in the diencephalon, including the mammillary bodies, hypothalamus, and dorsal medial nucleus of the thalamus (Grossi et al., 1989). Since all of these areas are known to be involved in memory function, this suggests multiple functional loci which, if affected, could result in memory loss, and which may play distinct roles in the formation and recall of information (e.g., Weiskrantz, 1987).

The focus of the neuropathological abnormalities which are responsible for the CES defect must, by definition, be directed towards the frontal cortex. However, it is worth considering an alternative explanation. As has been noted before (Chapman & Wolff, 1959), symptoms of frontal lobe dysfunction can also arise as a result of large cortical lesions. Whether due to mass action, or the fact that the frontal cortex occupies such a large area of the brain, larger CNS lesions invariably result in "frontal lobe" symptoms and signs. Therefore, it may be the case that the dysexecutive syndrome observed in our AD patients may result from a similar mechanism; that is, large areas of the brain whose function is disrupted enough to create the impaired executive functions, but not so much that the dementia is severe. Consistent with that hypothesis is our observation that after a one year follow-up we did *not* observe the development of dysexecutive syndromes while we did observe new cases with amnesic syndromes (Becker et al., 1991). Thus, the dysexecutive syndrome in AD may arise from a generalized abnormality in the CNS and not a specific abnormality in the frontal cortex.

Conclusions

The data presented above were intended to demonstrate that the episodic memory defect in AD patients is the result of a multiple system breakdown. Components of Working Memory and of secondary memory are affected, and they each contribute to the syndrome in different ways. The multiple process breakdown may arise as a result of multiple neuroanatomical system dysfunction, including the medial temporal cortex and the diencephalon. It is possible to demonstrate functional dissociation both between and within cognitive domains. The careful analysis of these dissociations reveals that the neurobehavioral characteristics of AD patients are not unique, and are consistent with the known sequelae of CNS lesions. AD may, therefore, be a useful system for the study and verification of theories and models of brain-behavior relationships.

Acknowledgments

Preparation of this chapter was supported in part by funds from the National Institute on Aging (AG05133) and the National Institute of Mental Health. D. Pulkowski kindly provided secretarial support.

J. T. Becker & O. L. Lopez

References

American Psychiatric Association. (1987). *Diagnostic and statistical manual of mental health disorders.* (3rd ed. rev.). Washington, DC: American Psychiatric Association.

Arendt, T., Bigl, V., Arendt, A., & Tennstedt, A. (1983). Loss of neurons in the nucleus basalis of Meynert in Alzheimer's disease, Paralysis Agitans, and Korsakoff's disease. *Acta Neuropathologica, 61,* 101-108.

Baddeley, A. D. (1986). *Working memory.* Oxford: Oxford University Press.

Baddeley, A. D., Bressi, S., Della Salla, S., Logie, R., & Spinnler, H. (1986). Senile dementia and working memory. *Quarterly Journal of Experimental Psychology, 38A,* 603-618.

Baddeley, A. D., Della Salla, S., & Spinnler, H., (in press). The two-component hypothesis of memory deficit in Alzheimer's disease. *Journal of Clinical and Experimental Neuropsychology.*

Baddeley, A. D., & Hitch, G. J. (1974). Working memory. In G. Bower (Ed.), *Recent advances in learning and motivation.* (Vol. 8). New York: Academic Press.

Baddeley, A. D., & Wilson, B. A. (1988). Frontal amnesia and dysexecutive syndrome. *Brain and Cognition, 1,* 212-230.

Becker, J. T. (1988). Working memory and secondary memory deficits in Alzheimer's disease. *Journal of Clinical and Experimental Neuropsychology, 6,* 739-753.

Becker, J. T., Boller, F., Saxton, J., & McGonigle-Gibson, K. (1987). Normal rates of forgetting of verbal and non-verbal material in Alzheimer's disease. *Cortex, 23,* 59-72.

Becker, J. T., Lopez, O. L., & Wess, J. A. (1991). *Modality specific memory loss in probable Alzheimer's disease.* Manuscript submitted for publication.

Benton, A. L., (1968). Differential behavioral effects in frontal lobe disease. *Neuropsychologia, 6,* 53-60.

Brion, S. (1966). Démence par atrophie cérébrale primitive. *Concurs Medical, 88,* 313-324.

Butters, N., Albert, M. S., Sax, D. S., Miliotis, P., Nagode, J., & Sterste, A. (1983). The effect of verbal mediators on the pictorial memory of brain damaged patients. *Neuropsychologia, 21,* 307-323.

Butters, N., Granholm, E. L., Salmon, D. P., Grant, I., & Wolfe, J. (1986). Episodic and semantic memory: A comparison of amnesic and demented patients. *Journal of Clinical and Experimental Neuropsychology, 9,* 479-497.

Chapman, L. F., & Wolff, H. G., (1959). The cerebral hemispheres and the highest integrative functions of man. *Archives of Neurology, 1,* 357-424.

Cohen, N. J., & Squire, L. R. (1980). Preserved learning and retention of pattern analyzing skill in amnesia: Dissociation of knowing how and knowing that. *Science, 232,* 207-209.

Diesfeldt, H. F. A. (1990). Recognition memory for words and faces in primary degenerative dementia of the Alzheimer type and normal old age. *Journal of Clinical and Experimental Neuropsychology, 12,* 931-945.

Diller, L., Ben-Yishay, Y., Gerstman, L. J., Goodkin, R., Gordon, W., & Weinberg, A. (1974). *Studies in cognition and rehabilitation in hemiplegia* (Rehabilitation Monograph No. 50). New York University.

Dusoir, H., Kapur, N., Byrnes, D. P., McKinstry, S., & Hoare, R. D. (1990). The role of diencephalic pathology in human memory disorder: Evidence from a penetrating paranasal brain injury. *Brain, 113,* 1695-1706.

Farah, M. J., Gazzaniga, M. S., Holtzman, J. D., & Kosslyn, S. M. (1985). A left-hemisphere basis for visual imagery. *Neuropsychologia, 23,* 115-118.

Fuld, P. A., Katzman, R., Davies, P., & Terry, R. D. (1982). Intrusions as a sign of Alzheimer's dementia: Chemical and pathological verification. *Annals of Neurology, 11,* 155-159.

Grossi, D., Lopez, O. L., & Martinez, A. J. (1989). The mammillary bodies in Alzheimer's disease. *Acta Neurologica Scandinavica, 80,* 41-45.

Haxby, J. V., Grady, C. L., Koss, E., Horwitz, B., Hexton, L., Schapiro, M., Friedland, R. P., & Rapoport, S. I. (1990). Longitudinal study of cerebral metabolic asymmetries and associated neuropsychological patterns in early dementia of the Alzheimer type. *Archives of Neurology, 47,* 753-760.

Helkala, E. L., Laulumaa, V., Soininen, H., & Riekkinen, P. J. (1988). Recall and recognition memory in patients with Alzheimer's disease and Parkinson's disease. *Annals of Neurology, 24,* 214-217.

Huppert, F. A., & Piercy, M. (1979). Dissociation between learning and remembering in organic amnesia. *Quarterly Journal of Experimental Psychology, 275,* 317-318.

Hyman, B. T., Damasio, A. R., Van Hoesen, G. W., & Barnes, C. L. (1984). Alzheimer's disease and cell specific pathology isolates the hippocampal formation. *Science, 225,* 1168-1170.

Hyman, B. T., Van Hoesen, G. W., & Damasio, A. R. (1990). Memory-related neural systems in Alzheimer's disease: An anatomic study. *Neurology, 40,* 1721-1730.

Hyman, B. T., Van Hoesen, G. W., Kromer, L. J., & Damasio, A. R. (1986). Perforant pathway changes and the memory impairment of Alzheimer's disease. *Annals of Neurology, 20,* 472-481.

Jorm, A. F. (1985). Subtypes of Alzheimer's dementia: A conceptual analysis and critical review. *Psychological Medicine, 15,* 543-553.

Kaszniak, A. W., Poon, L. W., & Riege, W. (1986). Assessing memory deficits: An information-processing approach. In L. W. Poon (Ed.), *Handbook for clinical memory assessment of older adults.* Washington: American Psychological Association.

Kopelman, M. D. (1985a). Multiple memory deficits in Alzheimer-type dementia: Implications for pharmacotherapy. *Psychological Medicine, 15,* 527-541.

Kopelman, M. D. (1985b). Rates of forgetting in Alzheimer-type dementia and Korsakoff's syndrome. *Neuropsychologia, 23,* 623-638.

Kopelman, M. D. (1989). Remote and autobiographical memory, temporal context memory and frontal atrophy in Korsakoff and Alzheimer patients. *Neuropsychologia, 27,* 437-460.

Kopelman, M. D., & Corn, T. H. (1988). Cholinergic "blockade" as a model for cholinergic depletion: A comparison of the memory deficits with those of Alzheimer-type dementia and the alcoholic Korsakoff syndrome. *Brain, 111,* 1079-1110.

Kramer, J. H., Delis, D. C., Blusewitz, M. J., Brandt, J., Ober, B. A., & Strauss, M. E. (1988). Verbal memory errors in Alzheimer's and Huntington's dementias. *Developmental Neuropsychology, 4,* 1-15.

Mair, W. P., Warrington, E. K., & Weiskrantz, L. (1979). Memory disorders in Korsakoff's psychosis: A neuropathological and neuropsychological investigation of two cases. *Brain, 102,* 749-783.

Martin, A. (1987). Representation of semantic and spatial knowledge in Alzheimer's patients: Implications for models and preserved learning amnesia. *Journal of Clinical and Experimental Neuropsychology, 9,* 191-224.

Martin, A. (1990). Neuropsychology of Alzheimer's disease: The case for subgroups. In M. F. Schwartz (Ed.), *Modular deficits in Alzheimer's-type dementia.* Cambridge: Bradford/MIT.

Martin, A., Brouwers, P., Cox, C., & Fedio, P. (1985). On the nature of the verbal memory deficit in Alzheimer's disease. *Brain and Language, 25,* 323-341.

Martin, A., Brouwers, P., Lalonde, F., Cox, C., Teleska, P., & Fedio, P. (1986) Towards a behavioral typology of Alzheimer's patients. *Journal of Clinical and Experimental Neuropsychology, 8,* 594-610.

Martin, A., Cox, C., Brouwers, P., & Fedio, P. (1985). A note on different patterns of impaired and preserved cognitive abilities and their relation to episodic memory deficits in Alzheimer's patients. *Brain and Language, 26,* 181-185.

Martin, A., & Fedio, P. (1983). Word production and comprehension in Alzheimer's disease: The breakdown of semantic knowledge. *Brain and Language, 19,* 124-141.

McCarthy, M., Ferris, S. H., Clark, E., & Crook, T. (1981). Acquisition and retention of categorized material in normal aging and senile dementia. *Experimental Aging Research, 7,* 127-135.

McKhann, G., Drachman, D. A., Folstein, M. F., Katzman, R., Price, D. L., & Stadlan, E. (1984). Clinical diagnosis of Alzheimer's disease: Report of the NINCDS-ADRDA Work Group under the auspices of the Department of Health and Human Services Task Force on Alzheimer's disease. *Neurology, 34,* 939-944.

Miller, E. (1971). On the nature of the memory disorder in presenile dementia. *Neuropsychologia, 9,* 75-81.

Miller, E. (1973). Short and long-term memory in presenile dementia (Alzheimer's disease). *Psychological Medicine, 3,* 221-224.

Milner, B. (1968). Visual recognition and recall right after temporal lobes excision in man. *Neuropsychologia, 6,* 191-209.

Milner, B. (1971). Interhemispheric differences in localization of psychological processes in man. *Medical Bulletin, 27,* 272-277.

Mishkin, M., & Appenzeller, T. (1987). The anatomy of memory. *Scientific American, 146,* 80-84.

Morris, R. G., & Baddeley, A. D. (1988). Primary and working memory functioning in Alzheimer's type dementia. *Journal of Clinical and Experimental Neuropsychology, 10,* 279-296.

Morris, R. G., & Kopelman, M. D. (1986). The memory deficits in Alzheimer-type dementia: A review. *The Quarterly Journal of Experimental Psychology, 38A,* 575-602.

Moss, M. B., Albert, M. S., Butters, N., & Payne, M. (1986). Differential patterns of memory loss among patients with Alzheimer's disease, Huntington's disease, and Alcoholic Korsakoff's syndrome. *Archives of Neurology, 43,* 239-246.

Nebes, R. D. (1989). Semantic memory in Alzheimer's disease. *Psychological Bulletin, 106,* 377-394.

Norman, D. A., & Shallice, T. (1980). *Attention to action: Willed and automatic control of behavior* (CHIP Report No. 99). San Diego: University of California.

Ober, B. A., Dronkers, N. F., Koss, E., Delis, D. C., & Friedland, R. P. (1986). Retrieval from semantic memory in Alzheimer-type dementia. *Journal of Clinical and Experimental Neuropsychology, 8,* 75-92.

Paivio A. (1986). *Mental representations: A dual coding approach.* New York : Oxford University Press.

Pepin, E. P., & Eslinger, P. J. (1989). Verbal memory decline in Alzheimer's disease: A multiple-process deficit. *Neurology, 39,* 1477-1482.

Schacter, D. L. (1987). Implicit expressions of memory in organic amnesia: Learning of new facts associations. *Human Neurobiology, 6,* 107-118.

Shallice, T., & Warrington, E. K. (1970). Independent functioning of verbal memory stores: A neuropsycholgical study. *Quarterly Journal of Experimental Psychology, 22,* 261-273.

Sjögren, H. (1951). Clinical analysis of morbus Alzheimer and morbus Pick. *Acta Psychiatria et Neurologica Scandinavica, 82,* 68-115.

Sourander, P., & Sjögren, H. (1970). The concept of Alzheimer's disease and its clinical implications. In O. E. W. Wolsteinholme and M. O'Connors (Eds.), *Alzheimer's disease and related conditions.* London: Churchhill.

Stuss, D. T., & Benson, D. F. (1987). *The frontal lobes.* New York: Raven.

Thal, L. J., Grundman, M., & Klauber, M. R. (1988). Dementia: Characteristics of a referral population and factors associated with progression. *Neurology, 8,* 594-610.

Thomas, G., Hostetter, G., & Barker, D. J. (1968). Behavioral function of the limbic system. In E. Stellar & J.M. Sprague (Eds.), *Progress in physiological psychology,* (Vol. 2). New York: Academic Press.

Tulving, E. (1972). Episodic and semantic memory. In E. Tulving & W. Donaldson (Eds.), *Organization of memory*. New York: Academic Press.

Tulving, E. (1983). *Elements of episodic memory*. Oxford: Oxford University Press.

Tulving, E. (1984). Relations among components and processes of memory. *Behavioral and Brain Sciences, 1*, 257-268.

Tulving, E. (1987). Multiple memory systems and consciousness. *Human Neurobiology, 6*, 67-80.

Vallar, G., & Baddeley, A. D. (1984). Fractionation of working memory: Neuropsychological evidence for a phonological short-term store. *Journal of Verbal Learning and Verbal Behavior, 23*, 151-161.

Victor, M., Adams, R. D., & Collins, G. H. (1971). *The Wernicke-Korsakoff syndrome*. Philadelphia: Davis.

Wechsler, D. (1945). A standardized memory scale for memory use. *Journal of Psychology, 19*, 87-95.

Weigl, E. (1927). On the psychology of so-called processes of abstraction. *Journal of Abnormal and Social Psychology, 36*, 3-33.

Weiskrantz, L. (1985). On issue and theories of the human amnesic syndrome. In N. M. Weinberger, J. L. McGaugh, & G. Lynch (Eds.), *Memory systems of the brain: Animal and human cognitive processes*. New York: Guilford Press.

Weiskrantz, L. (1987). Neuroanatomy of memory and amnesia: A case for multiple memory systems. *Human Neurobiology, 6*, 93-103.

Whitehouse, P., Price, D. L., Clark, A. W., Coyle, J. T., & DeLong, M. R. (1981). Alzheimer's disease: Evidence form selective loss of cholinergic neurons in the Nucleus Basalis. *Annals of Neurology, 10*, 122-126.

Wilson, R. S., Bacon, L. D., Fox, S. H., & Kaszniak, A. W. (1983). Primary memory and secondary memory in dementia of the Alzheimer type. *Journal of Clinical and Experimental Neuropsychology, 5*, 337-344.

Wilson, R. S., Bacon, L. D., Kramer, R. L., Fox, S. H., & Kaszniak, A. W. (1983). Word frequency effect and recognition memory in dementia of the Alzheimer type. *Journal of Clinical and Experimental Neuropsychology, 5*, 97-104.

Wilson, R. S., Kaszniak, A. W., Bacon, L. D., Fox, S. H. & Kelly, M. P. (1982). Facial recognition memory in dementia. *Cortex, 18*, 329-336.

Wodehouse, P. G. (1937). *The crimewave at Blandings*. New York: The Book League of America.

Memory Functioning in Dementia – L. Bäckman (Editor)

3   **Storage, Forgetting, and Retrieval in the Anterograde and Retrograde Amnesia of Alzheimer Dementia**

Michael D. Kopelman

St Thomas's Hospital, London

Introduction

Conventional wisdom suggests that dementia may involve accelerated forgetting and a failure of memory storage in both anterograde and retrograde memory:

"The proper and peculiar place assigned and allotted for Memory is the Brayne, the mansion and dwelling house of Wit and all the Senses: which being affected or ... discrased, all the functions and offices of Nature are ... passioned: insomuch that ... there steppeth in place ... *forgetfulness*, amazednesse, dotage, foolishness, lack of right wits, doltishnes, and idiocie." [C. Levinus Lemnius (1561)]

"The *progressive destruction of memory* follows a logical order - a law ... it begins with the most recent recollections which, being ... rarely repeated and ... having no permanent associations represent organization in its feeblest form." [K. T. Ribot (1882)]

The first quotation suggests that Lemnius viewed accelerated forgetting as the essence of the memory impairment in dementia; and the second quotation indicates that Ribot believed that a progressive destruction of memory stores produces retrograde amnesia. In a disorder such as Alzheimer's disease, in which there is a widespread loss of neurons and synaptic connections (Katzman et al., 1988; Masliah, Terry, DeTeresa, & Hansen, 1989), it is easy to conceive how the (distributed) neural networks presumed to underlie memories should come to be destroyed. On the other hand, a sizeable body of research in recent years has examined the nature of the memory deficits in dementia (and organic amnesia) in terms of encoding, storage and forgetting, and retrieval processes. Such studies suggest that, despite appearances, accelerated forgetting and a destruction of memory stores may not be the underlying basis of the memory impairment in mild and moderate dementia.

The purpose of the present chapter is to review such evidence with respect to both the anterograde and retrograde amnesia in Alzheimer's disease.

It is conventional to consider rates of forgetting in terms of "short- term" and "long-term" forgetting, and this distinction will be employed in the present chapter. In addition, brief reference will be made to what might be labelled (somewhat inelegantly) as "intermediate-term" forgetting. Finally, the nature of the deficit in the retrograde amnesia of Alzheimer dementia will be considered, with particular reference to autobiographical memory.

Short-Term Forgetting

Verbal Memory

Short-term forgetting has most commonly been assessed using the so-called Brown-Peterson task. In this task, small quantities (usually triads) of verbal material (consonants or words) are presented visually or orally to a subject; and retention is measured over delays of approximately 0 to 30 sec, during which the subject performs a distractor task (usually counting backwards) to prevent rehearsal (Brown, 1958; Peterson & Peterson, 1959). As is well known, findings in Korsakoff's syndrome on this test have been variable, with some studies reporting no impairment (Baddeley & Warrington, 1970; Warrington, 1982), some finding only mild or varying degrees of impairment (Kopelman, 1985; Mayes, Meudell, Mann, & Pickering, 1988), and others obtaining severe impairment (Butters & Cermak, 1980; Cermak, Butters, & Goodglass, 1971). In the Mayes et al. (1988) study, substantial impairment was found in one patient, and no impairment in another patient until a 15 sec delay. Similar variability was reported by Kopelman (1985) in 16 Korsakoff patients.

Corkin (1982) reported the first study of Brown-Peterson performance in Alzheimer patients. She used auditory presentation of the stimuli, finding severe impairment in her Alzheimer groups at all delays between 3 sec and 30 sec, the degree of impairment being broadly correlated with a clinical rating of the severity of the dementia. By contrast, a group of five "global amnesic" patients showed intact performance up to 9 sec delay, and severe impairment at 15 sec and beyond.

Kopelman (1985) also found severe impairment in a group of mildly to moderately impaired Alzheimer patients between 2 and 20 sec delay, following visual presentation of words (see Figure 3.1). In this study, Korsakoff patients generally showed only a mild (non-significant) degree of impairment, although their curve was beginning to deviate from that of healthy controls at 20 sec delay. The Alzheimer patients showed a predominance of omission errors, but did not differ significantly from the healthy controls or Korsakoff patients in terms of intrusion errors or acoustic, visual, or semantic confusions. The clinical validity of the test was demonstrated by the fact that, whereas younger, healthy subjects of high IQ performed best at this test, younger, Alzheimer patients, in whom neuropathological and neurochemical changes are most likely to have been severe (Bondareff, Mountjoy, & Roth, 1982; Mann, Yates, & Marcyniuk, 1984) performed particularly poorly. The correlation with intelligence was maintained in the Alzheimer group despite their much lower general level of IQ, i.e., the most demented patients performed worst. Furthermore, there were consistent correlations with two measures of the degree of cortical atrophy on CT scan, such that patients with more severe atrophy or larger ventricles performed worse on this test (see also Kopelman, in press).

VERBAL SHORT-TERM FORGETTING

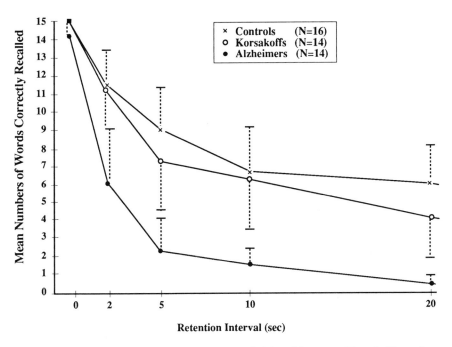

Figure 3.1. Mean number of words correctly recalled by Alzheimers, Korsakoffs, and controls on the Brown-Peterson test (± *SD*). Adapted from "Rates of forgetting in Alzheimer-type dementia and Korsakoff's syndrome" by M. D. Kopelman, 1985, *Neuropsychologia, 23*, p. 627. Copyright 1985 by Pergamon Press. Adapted by permission.

Morris (1986) used differing distractor tasks in the Brown-Peterson test to examine the effect of varying the processing load involved in performing this test. There was an "unfilled" condition (no distractor task), a motor tapping task, an "articulation" task (saying "the, the, the..." repetitively), a "digit addition" task (adding two digits), and a "digit reversal" task (repeating two digits in the reverse order). During 20 sec delay, the Alzheimer group showed only a minimal (non-significant) trend towards impairment in the unfilled condition, but Alzheimer patients were significantly impaired in all the remaining conditions, more so in the articulation condition than the motor tapping condition, and somewhat more so in the digit addition and reversal conditions than in the articulation condition. Morris interpreted this "abnormal forgetting" in terms of a reduction in central processing resources which results in a breakdown of the maintenance rehearsal of verbal material.

Dannenbaum, Parkinson, and Inman (1988) employed a version of the Brown-Peterson test in which they "titrated" the memory load to be remembered according to letter span in order to equate group performances for immediate recall as closely as possible. By so doing, these authors appeared to show markedly accelerated forgetting in Alzheimer patients over a delay of approximately 6.3 sec, relative to depressed patients and healthy subjects. Their data also appear to replicate Kopelman's (1985) finding of a predominance of omission errors, rather than intrusions in the Alzheimer group, although this aspect of their findings was not commented upon. However, despite the use of their procedure, it is by no means clear that Dannenbaum et al. avoided the problems of a ceiling effect at immediate recall, and forgetting was measured at only a single delay interval.

Non-Verbal Memory

Sullivan, Corkin, and Growdon (1986) developed a non-verbal analogue of the Brown-Peterson test, requiring delayed retention of Corsi block sequences. The Corsi blocks are an arrangement of nine black wooden blocks in an irregular pattern on a black baseboard (Corkin, 1982; Smirni, Villardita, & Zappala, 1983). The experimenter tapped between one and three blocks, after which the set of Corsi blocks was covered and the subject required to perform a finger-tapping distractor task for between 3 and 15 sec. There were also unfilled (no distractor) conditions. In brief, the Alzheimer patients were impaired across all conditions, particularly where the distractor task was employed.

Kopelman (in press) employed the same test and distractor task in Alzheimer and Korsakoff patients, requiring subjects to retain either 2 or 3 blocks (titrated against block span) over 2 to 20 sec delay. Figure 3.2 shows that Alzheimer patients were severely impaired in this test, and this was the case whether the scoring was in terms of total blocks recalled in any order or blocks recalled in the correct sequence. Korsakoff patients showed an intermediate (and statistically significant) degree of impairment, relative to healthy controls. The degree of impairment on this test was correlated with two measures of cortical atrophy on CT scan, and also with a measure of right hemisphere dysfunction (errors on the Picture Arrangement subtest, scored according to the McFie and Thompson [1972] criteria). This was interpreted as indicating that right hemisphere atrophy might underlie the deficit on this test, and it was also suggested that left hemisphere atrophy might account for impairment on the (verbal) Brown-Peterson test. If the latter were the case, it would help to explain the inconsistent results previously obtained in Korsakoff and other organic amnesic patients.

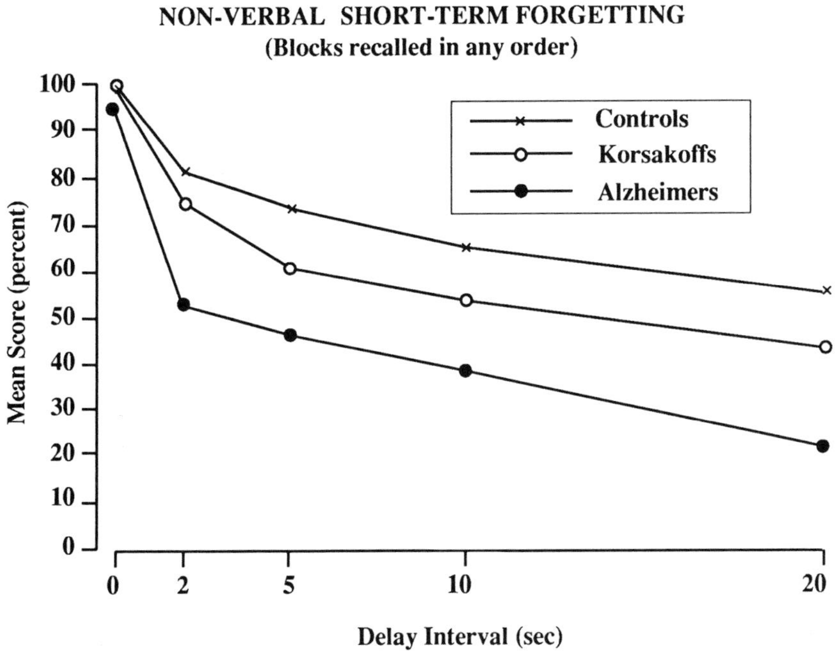

NON-VERBAL SHORT-TERM FORGETTING
(Blocks recalled in any order)

Delay Interval (sec)

Figure 3.2. Mean scores at each delay interval on the non-verbal, short-term forgetting task by healthy controls, Korsakoff patients, and Alzheimer patients. *SDs* (2-20 sec): Controls = 7.8 - 19.1; Korsakoffs = 12.9 - 16.0; Alzheimers = 15.5 - 27.6. From "Non-verbal, short-term forgetting in the alcoholic Korsakoff syndrome and Alzheimer-type dementia" by M. D. Kopelman, in press, *Neuropsychologia.* Copyright 1992 by Pergamon Press. Adapted by permission.

Cholinergic Blockade

Kopelman and Corn (1988) employed verbal and non-verbal versions of the Brown-Peterson test in healthy subjects who had been administered a cholinergic blocker (hyoscine/scopolamine) as a model for the effect of cholinergic depletion in patients. These authors found only minimal (non-significant) impairment on the verbal version of the test which had been administered to patients by Kopelman (1985), but a significant impairment on the verbal test when the distractor task was made more difficult in a manner analogous to that used by Morris (1986). On the non-verbal version of the test used in Alzheimer patients by Sullivan et al. (1986) and Kopelman (in press), cholinergic blockade (at 0.4 mg scopolamine I/V) did indeed produce a significant degree of impairment in a pattern similar to that seen in the patients (see Figure 3.3). In short, this model would suggest that cholinergic depletion within the neo-cortex may contribute in part to the impairments on short-term forgetting tests seen in Alzheimer patients.

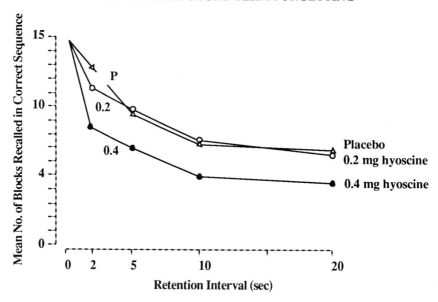

Figure 3.3. Visuospatial short-term forgetting test (block retention test). Distraction = finger-tapping task (see text). Adapted from "Cholinergic 'blockade' as a model for cholinergic depletion: A comparison of the memory deficits with those of Alzheimer-type dementia and the alcoholic Korsakoff syndrome" by M. D. Kopelman and T. H. Corn, 1988, *Brain, 111*, p. 1089. Copyright 1988 by Pergamon Press. Adapted by permission.

Nature of the Impairment

Traditionally, impaired Brown-Peterson performance has been interpreted as demonstrating accelerated short-term forgetting (e.g., Butters & Cermak, 1980), rather than an encoding or retrieval deficit. However, this interpreta-

tion has been queried because it is usually dependent upon intact performance at the zero delay interval (a ceiling effect), and because of a qualitative
difference in the task between immediate recall and after delays involving either rehearsal or distraction (Kinsbourne & Wood, 1975). To demonstrate
unequivocally accelerated forgetting, it is necessary to show a significant group
x interval interaction effect at points beyond the zero delay interval.

Such an interaction effect does not appear to be evident in Corkin's (1982)
study. Kopelman (1985) found an Alzheimer/Control x interval interaction
effect between 2 and 5 sec, which just failed to reach statistical significance,
but otherwise the curves were in parallel. Morris (1986) appears to have found
abnormal forgetting in his articulation conditions between 5 and 20 sec (although the interaction effects were not reported), but there were no significant
group x delay interactions in the digit addition and digit reversal conditions
between 5 and 20 sec, leaving the overall interpretation of these results
somewhat equivocal. As mentioned above, it is by no means clear that
Dannenbaum et al. (1988) circumvented this problem; and, on the non-verbal
tests, both Sullivan et al. (1986) and Kopelman (in press) obtained curves in
their Alzheimer groups which were in parallel to those of the healthy control
(and Korsakoff) groups. In general, these results suggest that the short-term
retention curves of Alzheimer patients lie at a lower level but in parallel with
those of healthy subjects.

Kinsbourne and Wood (1975) argued that such a pattern of performance
is most likely to reflect either an encoding or a retrieval deficit, although the
possibility of very rapidly accelerated decay of the memory trace cannot be
completely excluded. In favour of the Kinsbourne and Wood (1975) interpretation, Money, Kirk, and McNaughton (in press) have recently employed a non-
verbal delayed matching-to-sample test, obtaining a curve in Alzheimer patients
parallel (but at a lower level) to that of healthy controls during delays from 0
to 32 sec. It may be that a reduction in available processing resources (cf. Craik,
1984) in Alzheimer patients produces the encoding/retrieval deficit found in
performance at these tasks (see Kopelman, in press).

Long-Term Forgetting

The Measurement of Forgetting

"Long-term" forgetting refers to the rate of loss from secondary memory,
after learning has been accomplished. The precise method whereby this is
defined varies from study to study, but the great difficulty for investigators of
amnesic or dementing patients is to ensure that adequate learning has been
accomplished before measuring forgetting rates. It is, of course, ideal to try to
"match" the initial learning by a patient group to that of healthy subjects in
order to avoid the difficulties which arise in measuring forgetting rates if this
is not done (Loftus, 1985; Slamecka, 1985).

An example of the problems which arise in doing this is seen in a study by Inglis (1959), assessing the relative contribution of impairments in learning and retention (forgetting) in a group of patients diagnosed as having senile dementia. He used a paired-associate learning test, consisting of nine word-pairs of varying degrees of difficulty, results for the completely new pairs being the most pertinent. He concluded that there is indeed a severe learning deficit in these patients and that "retention processes" are also affected. However, in order to obtain this result, healthy subjects had to be given between 10 and 14 learning trials to acquire the new pairs, whereas the patients had to be given a mean of 54.8 and 59.2 learning trials (in two different groups) with a ceiling being imposed at 60 learning trials. At 30 min delay, the healthy subjects required a mean of 3.9 trials to relearn the pairs, whereas the patients required a mean of 56.8 trials (ceiling = 60) to relearn the pairs. In short, even after far more exposures to the word-pairs than the healthy controls, it cannot be claimed that the dementing patients had learned them to the same degree, because a substantial proportion of the patients must have reached the ceiling number of acquisition trials without obtaining learning to criterion.

Huppert and Piercy (1978) described a picture recognition test which appeared to circumvent this problem. They exposed photographic slides of pictures taken from magazines for four to eight times as long to amnesic patients as to healthy controls, and thereby managed to match their groups' initial recognition scores on a yes-no task administered at 10 min delay. As is well known, they found that, the forgetting rate of Korsakoff patients over the course of a week was the same as that of their controls, a finding subsequently replicated by Squire (1981), Kopelman (1985), and Martone, Butters, and Trauner (1986). In addition, Huppert and Piercy (1979) claimed that a bitemporal lobectomy patient (HM) forgot faster than either controls or Korsakoff patients, suggesting that the temporal lobes may mediate long-term retention, an argument also put forward by others on the basis of findings in ECT, post-head injury concussed patients, and encephalitic patients (Levin, High, & Eisenberg, 1988; Parkin & Leng, 1988; Squire, 1981). However, Huppert and Piercy's (1979) finding in HM was not replicated in a more detailed study by Freed, Corkin, and Cohen (1987).

Alzheimer Studies

Kopelman (1985) took the opportunity to use the Huppert-Piercy test to investigate long-term forgetting in Alzheimer (and Korsakoff) patients. Alzheimer patients show extensive pathology within the hippocampi and the temporal lobes, implying that these patients would show accelerated forgetting if Huppert and Piercy's (1979) hypothesis was correct. Using exposure times approximately 14 times as long in Alzheimer and Korsakoff patients as in healthy controls, the Alzheimer group's recognition memory performance at 10 min was matched to that of the Korsakoff group, and only a little below that of the healthy control subjects. Figure 3.4 shows that the rate of forgetting over 24 hours and a week (indicated by the slopes of the curves) was the same in the Alzheimer group as in the other two groups. This was true whether scoring was in terms of percent correct scores, recognition scores as a proportion of scores at 10 min, or d'.

LONG-TERM FORGETTING

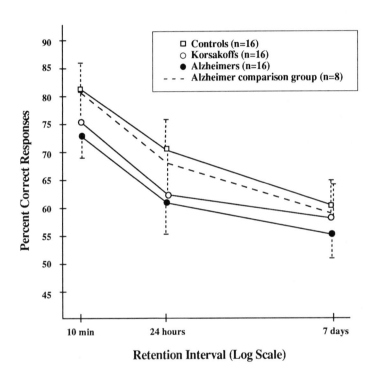

Figure 3.4. Mean percentage of pictures correctly identified as target or distractor (true positive + true negative) by Alzheimers, Korsakoffs, and controls on the Huppert-Piercy test (± 1 *SD*). Adapted from "Rates of forgetting in Alzheimer-type dementia and Korsakoff's syndrome" by M. D. Kopelman, 1985, *Neuropsychologia, 23*, p. 631. Copyright 1985 by Pergamon Press. Adapted by permission.

The only differences between the groups were that (a) the Alzheimer patients produced a significantly higher number of false positive responses than the other two groups, and (b) whereas older subjects performed worse in the control and Korsakoff groups, this age correlation was obliterated in the Alzheimer group, presumably because younger Alzheimer patients commonly have a more severe pathology. Taken together with the Freed et al. (1987) finding, this result indicates that in Alzheimer dementia, as in organic amnesia, the principal problem is in acquiring (or retrieving) new information rather than in its retention, and that temporal lobe pathology is not especially conducive to accelerated forgetting. In this connection, it should be mentioned that Huppert and Kopelman (1989) did find a slight increase in the forgetting rate of elderly healthy subjects, compared with younger subjects on this test; they suggested that a mild cerebral metabolic decrement, rather than any structural damage, might have produced this pattern of performance in healthy older subjects.

Hart, Kwentus, Taylor, and Harkins (1987) used a test involving the recognition of line drawings to investigate forgetting rates in Alzheimer, depressed, and healthy subjects. Their procedure was designed to match the subject groups at 90 sec delay (see below), but it appears that forgetting rates from 10 min to 48 hours were essentially in parallel between the groups, consistent with the Kopelman (1985) finding.

Freed, Corkin, Growdon, and Nissen (1989) used a forced-choice version of the Huppert-Piercy test to compare forgetting rates of Alzheimer patients and healthy controls at intervals of 10 min, 24 hours, and 72 hours. Using exposure times 4 to 16 times as long in the Alzheimer group as in the controls, initial recognition scores were somewhat lower in the Alzheimer than the control group, but the overall rate of forgetting over 72 hours was the same in the two groups, consistent with the Kopelman (1985) finding. However, further analysis of the pattern of performance suggested that there were two subgroups of Alzheimer patients; in the first, there was a steady decline in recognition scores at the 10 minute, 24 hour, and 72 hour delay intervals. In the second group, there was a substantial decline between 10 min and 24 hours, but then a "rebound" effect, whereby Alzheimer patients were performing as well at 72 hours as at 10 min. (In the Kopelman [1985] data, only 2 out of 16 Alzheimer patients showed any degree of rebound between 24 hours and a week, and this was a relatively weak effect.) The rebound effect is difficult to explain, but Freed et al. argued that it might result from an impairment of attentional focusing in the rebound subgroup, perhaps related to locus coeruleus pathology, and they provided some evidence consistent with this interpretation.

In summary, these three studies do not provide any evidence that forgetting rates are accelerated in Alzheimer patients on a picture recognition test, once learning has been accomplished for as long as 10 min. Consistent with this, Kopelman and Corn (1988) employed the Huppert-Piercy test in healthy subjects who had been administered a cholinergic antagonist (hyoscine/scopolamine) as a model for the effect of cholinergic depletion in Alzheimer patients. By prolonging exposure time (to 1.5 sec per slide), subjects who saw the slides after cholinergic blockade were matched at 10 min to the performance of a placebo group (who viewed the slides for 0.5 sec each). Figure 3.5 shows that their rates of forgetting over 2 hours and 40 min and 48 hours' delays were virtually identical. On the other hand, a cholinergic blockade group

(0.5 sec per slide) who did not have a prolonged exposure time, relative to the placebo group, showed a significantly impaired level of performance at 10 min delay, indicative of an acquisition or learning deficit, with a subsequent forgetting curve parallel to that of the placebo group. Figure 3.5 also shows that a group who received the cholinergic antagonist only after viewing the slides and performing the initial recognition test also showed a forgetting curve parallel to that of the placebo group, indicating that there is no retrograde effect of the drug. In short, this result indicates that cholinergic blockade produced a pattern of impairment on this test identical to that seen in Alzheimer dementia (or the Korsakoff syndrome), that is, an acquisition deficit (as determined by scores at 10 min in the 0.5 sec scopolamine group), but no effect on the subsequent rate of long-term forgetting.

CHOLINERGIC BLOCKADE: LONG-TERM FORGETTING

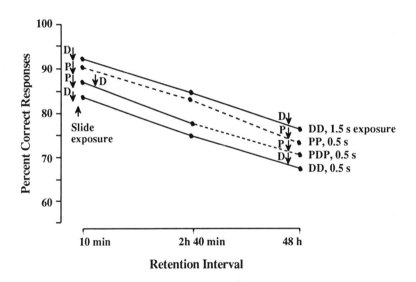

Figure 3.5. Long-term forgetting test (Huppert-Piercy Recognition Test). Three groups viewed the slides for 0.5 s each, and the fourth group for a mean of 1.5 s per slide. Group PP and both DD groups received an initial infusion at 0 min on day 1 and a "shot" of placebo 60 min later (5 to 7 min after the end of recognition test 1). Group PDP received a placebo infusion at 0 min on day 1, an infusion of 0.4 mg hyoscine 1 h later, and placebo on day 2. Continuous line = drug/ hyoscine; broken line = placebo. Adapted from "Cholinergic 'blockade' as a model for cholinergic depletion: A comparison of the memory deficits with those of Alzheimer-type dementia and the alcoholic Korsakoff syndrome" by M. D. Kopelman and T. H. Corn, 1988, *Brain, 111,* p. 1095. Copyright 1988 by Pergamon Press. Adapted by permission.

Intermediate-Term Forgetting

There have been a number of studies in which forgetting rates have been investigated either during intervals which fall between what are conventionally regarded as short-term and long-term forgetting, or in which a period of retention encompasses aspects of both short-term and long-term memory.

Moss, Albert, Butters, and Payne (1986) presented a series of 16 words five times to groups of Alzheimer, Korsakoff, Huntington, and healthy subjects. Word recall was tested at 15 sec and 2 min delay. Alzheimer patients appeared to show faster forgetting between 15 sec and 2 min than the other subject groups, although this finding was qualified by the fact that they also manifested lower initial levels of performance, and there was no attempt to match initial learning.

Hart et al. (1987), reported accelerated forgetting rates in Alzheimer patients between a 90-sec and a 10-min delay, relative to depressed patients and healthy controls. However, a much briefer (and potentially easier) test was given to the subjects at 90 sec than at 10 min or subsequent delays (2 hours and 48 hours). Testing at 90 sec required that Alzheimer patients reached a criterion score of 13 out of 16 correct on a subsample of just 8 (6.15%) repeated slides and 8 distractor slides from a total series of 130 slides, which were shown repeatedly to the Alzheimer patients until that criterion was reached. At 10 min and subsequent intervals, a much more substantial battery of 36 target slides and 36 distractor slides was used, making the memory load at these later intervals much greater. In short, the task at 90 sec was by no means analogous to that at the subsequent delays, and consequently the claim that forgetting was accelerated between 90 sec and 10 min cannot be substantiated from these data.

Becker, Boller, Saxton, and McGonicle-Gibson (1987) examined immediate and delayed (30 min) recall of a story and immediate and delayed (30 min) recall of the Rey-Osterreith figure, finding no evidence of accelerated forgetting in Alzheimer patients relative to normal elderly subjects. However, there was no attempt to match the initial performance of the Alzheimer group on these tasks to that of the healthy elderly subjects, and the findings for story recall may have been confounded by a floor effect in the Alzheimer group.

Somewhat similarly, Butters et al (1988) compared the "savings scores" (delayed recall/immediate recall x 100) of Alzheimer, organic amnesic, and Huntington patients with those of healthy controls on four subtests from the Wechsler Memory Scale - Revised: Logical memory, visual reproduction, and verbal and visual paired-associates. The Alzheimer patients did not appear to show accelerated forgetting on either of the paired associate tests, relative to healthy controls, and their forgetting rate on logical memory and visual reproduction did not differ significantly from the organic amnesic group. Similarly, when the organic amnesic group was subdivided into eleven Korsakoff patients and five patients with hippocampal lesions, there were no significant differences in savings scores across any of the four tests. However, the results in this study are confounded by the absence of any matching procedures for initial learning across the subject groups, and the probable presence of floor effects in many of the tests.

In short, the findings from these four studies are inconclusive. The results obtained by Moss et al. (1986) and Hart et al. (1987) suggest that there might be an accelerated rate of forgetting in Alzheimer patients between approximately 15 sec delay and 10 min delay, but the results obtained by Becker et al. (1987) and Butters et al. (1988), encompassing aspects of both primary and secondary memory, generally find no differences in forgetting rate between the groups. However, all these four studies are confounded by the absence of proper matching procedures for initial learning. Given that studies of both short-term and long-term forgetting appear to indicate an acquisition and/or retrieval deficit, it appears unlikely that accelerated forgetting will be found in the intervening delay intervals, when proper matching procedures have been used. However, that possibility remains, if such delays are critical for some physiological process of memory consolidation.

Retrograde Amnesia and Autobiographical Memory

Possible Nature of the Deficit

The above studies suggest that anterograde amnesia does not produce an accelerated forgetting of newly acquired memories, once adequate learning has been accomplished for as long as 10 min. If that is the case, it appears less likely that there is an accelerated forgetting of old or remote memories, a destruction of memory storage. However, this remains a possibility and, according to Ribot's (1882) law of regression quoted above, the progressive destruction of memories from the most recent to the most distant would predict a marked temporal gradient, that is, a relative sparing of the earliest memories.

Traditionally, two alternative hypotheses have been put forward with regard to this issue. The first is that there is a generalized retrieval deficit, which was formerly thought to imply a uniform, "flat" loss of remote memories across all earlier time periods (Albert, Butters, & Brandt, 1981; Sanders & Warrington, 1971). Second, the apparent loss of earlier memories may, in fact, reflect the progressive onset of an anterograde impairment, producing a steep temporal gradient to the memory loss, that is, a relative sparing of the earliest memories (Albert et al., 1981; Cohen & Squire, 1981). However, there has been increasing recognition that the situation may not be as simple as this dichotomy implies; if early memories are especially well rehearsed or salient, they may be relatively well preserved even in the presence of a retrieval deficit (Cermak, 1984; Weiskrantz, 1985). A number of studies have now examined the remote memory curves of Alzheimer patients in an attempt to shed light on this issue, some using tests of public information and others using measures of autobiographical memory.

Tests of Public Information

R. S. Wilson, Kaszniak, and Fox (1981) employed a "famous faces" test, and a recall test asking questions about people and events, to assess remote memory in senile dementia patients. Although the patients were severely impaired compared with healthy elderly subjects, their curves remained in parallel with those of the control group, leading Wilson and colleagues to conclude that there was a uniform loss of remote memories across all earlier time periods. The only exception to this was that, on the famous faces test, the patients failed to show the slight recency effect for the last ten years found in the healthy subjects. By contrast, Moscovitch (1982), using the same test, obtained a steep temporal gradient in 10 memory-disordered patients, nine of whom were considered to have early Alzheimer dementia. In fact, the gradient in this memory-disordered group was such that these subjects actually performed better than healthy elderly subjects for memories of 30 to 40 years earlier; this pattern of results is very difficult to interpret.

However, more recent studies have produced more consistent results on tests of this type. Beatty, Salmon, Butters, Heindel, and Granholm (1988) used the same famous faces test in groups of Alzheimer and Huntington patients and healthy controls. In conditions of free and cued recall, the Alzheimer patients showed a gentle temporal gradient, with relative sparing of memories from 30 to 40 years earlier. Sagar, Cohen, Sullivan, Corkin, and Growdon (1988) constructed a "famous scenes" test for use in North America, consisting of pictures of news events from the 1940s to the 1980s, in which subjects were asked to recall the event depicted and to perform a 3-choice recognition test. There were four items per decade. On the recall of events, Alzheimer patients (and also demented Parkinson patients) showed severe impairment, the results suggesting a gentle gradient, whereby the deficit was greatest for the most recent decades. Similarly, the Alzheimer patients showed a significant degree of impairment across all decades on the recognition version of this test with a suggestion of a gentle temporal gradient, although the demented Parkinson patients were intact in terms of recognizing the events depicted on this version of the test.

Kopelman (1989) constructed a British version of the famous scenes test, which he called the Famous News Events test. In this case, the test covered events from the 1930s to the 1980s; there were ten items per decade, and there were five choices in the recognition version of the test. Figures 3.6 and 3.7 show a severe impairment in Alzheimer patients with a gentle temporal gradient, this time clearly demonstrated by significant group x decade interaction effects, in both the recall (Figure 3.6) and recognition (Figure 3.7) versions of this test.

In this study, Korsakoff patients showed a significantly steeper temporal gradient than the Alzheimer patients on the recall version of the test, and their impairment relative to healthy controls extended back 20 to 30 years from the time of testing. As the mean duration of the illness (and time hospitalized) in this Korsakoff group was 5.75 years, this implies a retrograde component to their amnesia of 15 to 25 years.

NEWS EVENTS TEST: AGE-MATCHED COMPARISON

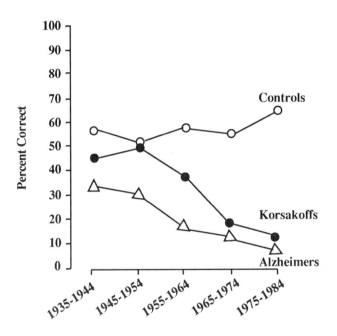

Figure 3.6. News events test (recall): Age-matched comparison. Results obtained from the six oldest Korsakoff patients (mean age = 62.8 ± 2.0), an age-matched sub-sample of the Alzheimer group (*n* = 8) (mean age = 64.5 ± 4.1), and normal controls (mean age = 61.75 (± 13.1). Adapted from "Remote and autobiographical memory, temporal context memory, and frontal atrophy in Korsakoff and Alzheimer patients" by M. D. Kopelman, 1989, *Neuropsychologia, 27,* p. 447. Copyright 1989 by Pergamon Press. Adapted by permission.

NEWS EVENTS TEST: RECOGNITION VS RECALL

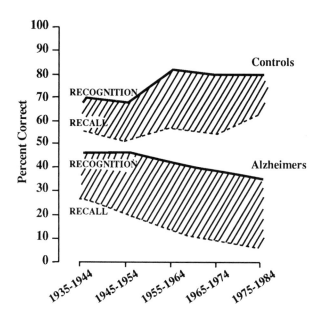

Figure 3.7. News events test: Recognition vs recall (Alzheimer patients and healthy controls). *N* = 16 in each group. The shaded area represents improved performance on recognition relative to recall testing. *SDs* (recognition): Controls = 14.8 - 16.9; Alzheimers = 16.7 - 21.0. (From "Remote and autobiographical memory, temporal context memory, and frontal atrophy in Korsakoff and Alzheimer patients" M. D. Kopelman, 1989, *Neuropsychologia, 27,* p. 448. Copyright 1989 by Pergamon Press. Adapted by permission).

Autobiographical Memory

Autobiographical memory refers to the recall of incidents or events from a subject's own past life as opposed to memory for famous faces, personalities, or news events. It has most commonly been assessed by the so called Crovitz technique (Crovitz & Schifmann, 1974) derived from Galton's (1879) experiments. In this test, the subject is given a cue-word and asked to think of an event or incident from his or her personal memory relating to that word, to describe it, and to specify when and where the event occurred. Scoring is in terms of the descriptive richness of the memories produced, and their specificity in time and place. Using this technique, Zola-Morgan, Cohen, and Squire

(1983) found that Korsakoff patients were able to produce such memories, on prompting, but that they had to delve much further back into their remote past (mean = 30.4 years) than did comparison groups of non-Korsakoff alcoholic (mean = 20.1 years) and healthy controls (mean = 12.7 years). Baddeley and B. A. Wilson (1986) obtained a closely similar result in two Korsakoff patients, but found that some patients with focal frontal lobe pathology produced florid confabulation to the cues, whereas other patients with frontal lesions demonstrated impoverished (non-fluent) retrieval of autobiographical memories.

Sagar et al. (1988) used this technique in Alzheimer and Parkinson patients, incorporating a cueing procedure, with non-specific prompts. They found that Alzheimer patients showed severe impairment, relative to both Parkinson patients and healthy controls, using either an uncued or cued technique. Moreover, when tested again after 24 hours, the Alzheimer patients produced a much lower proportion of their memories from the first day to the same cues than did the other two groups of subjects. On analysis of the age of the memories recalled, all the groups tended to recall most frequently from the most recent five-year period, although this tendency was least marked in the Alzheimer group. Moreover, the most demented patients (according to the Newcastle [Blessed] Dementia Scale) tended to retrieve a higher proportion of their recalled memories from the most distant decades, although the significance of this tendency was somewhat clouded by a floor effect. The authors concluded that this pattern of results was broadly consistent with the existence of a temporal gradient, that is, a relative sparing of the most distant memories in the most demented patients.

Kopelman, B. A. Wilson, and Baddeley (1989, 1990) described and published an Autobiographical Memory Interview, designed to give a more sensitive measure of the temporal gradient in autobiographical memory than the Crovitz test. It consists of a semi-structured interview asking about specific items from three broad "time-bands" - namely childhood, early adult life, and the most recent period. Moreover, it distinguishes between memory for events (which are termed autobiographical incidents) and memory for facts about a subject's past life (the latter being referred to as personal semantic memory). Confabulation does not appear to be a major problem in administering and scoring this test (Kopelman et al., 1990). Using this test, it has proved possible to plot patterns of retrograde memory loss in amnesic and demented patients with a variety of different diagnoses, severe impairment and some degree of temporal gradient being found in most cases. For example, patients with vascular dementia were found to have a relatively flat temporal gradient, and patients who have suffered herpes simplex encephalitis were the most severely impaired on these schedules (Kopelman et al., 1989).

Kopelman (1989) administered the Autobiographical Memory Interview, alongside the News Events Test, to Alzheimer and Korsakoff patients. In this study, strenuous efforts were taken to validate the responses obtained by checking the findings with the next-of-kin and with current care staff, by scrutiny of medical records, and by examining the responses for inconsisten-

cies. Figures 3.8 and 3.9 show that, on the recall of both autobiographical incidents (events) and personal semantic memories (facts), Alzheimer patients
manifested a relatively gentle temporal gradient, compared with healthy controls, whereas Korsakoff patients showed a significantly steeper temporal
gradient.

AUTOBIOGRAPHICAL INCIDENTS

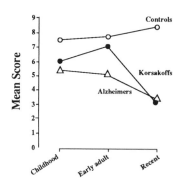

Figure 3.8. Autobiographical Incidents. *SDs:* Controls = 1.2 - 1.5; Korsakoffs = 1.25 - 2.1;
Alzheimers = 2.1 - 2.4. Adapted from "Remote and autobiographical memory, temporal
context memory, and frontal atrophy in Korsakoff and Alzheimer patients" M. D. Kopelman,
1989, *Neuropsychologia, 27,* p. 450. Copyright 1989 by Pergamon Press. Adapted by permission.

PERSONAL SEMANTIC MEMORY

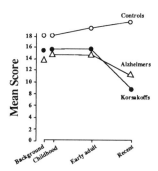

Figure 3.9. Personal semantic memory. Max score = 21. *SDs:* Controls = 1.0 - 2.9; Korsakoffs
= 2.0 - 4.7; Alzheimers = 3.6 - 4.25. Adapted from "Remote and autobiographical memory,
temporal context memory, and frontal atrophy in Korsakoff and Alzheimer patients" by M.
D. Kopelman, 1989, *Neuropsychologia, 27,* p. 447. Copyright 1989 by Pergamon Press.
Adapted by permission.

The difference in the temporal gradient of the two groups occurred between early adult life and recent events/facts, and both the clinical groups showed some degree of impairment even for the childhood period - a pattern broadly consistent with that obtained on the News Events Test (see Figure 3.6). Within the Alzheimer group, there were sizeable and statistically significant correlations between the performance on these two schedules and performance on the recall and recognition components of the News Events Test. In the Korsakoff group, these two schedules correlated significantly with each other, but not with performance on the News Events Test (which showed a significant correlation with IQ).

Dall'Ora, Della Sala, and Spinnler (1989) developed a somewhat similar schedule for use in Italian subjects, which they administered to Alzheimer patients and to amnesic patients who, on the basis of CT scan and clinical evidence, were thought to have either widespread or focal cortical damage. Their schedule, which asked about memory for autobiographical incidents (rather than personal semantic facts) had been very thoroughly standardized in a sample of 157 healthy, elderly subjects (Borrini, Dall'Ora, Della Sala, Marinelli, & Spinnler, 1989). Like Kopelman et al. (1990) these authors found that confabulation was not a serious difficulty in administering or scoring their test. However, although they found pronounced impairment in all three patient groups, they failed to find any clear evidence of a temporal gradient. This is almost certainly the result of the fact their most recent period covered memories from the age of 40 till two years before testing, whereas in the Kopelman et al. (1989, 1990) interview, recent memories are constrained to a period of one year before testing (or for some items five years). When a similar technique was used by the Italians, they also obtained a temporal gradient (Della Sala, personal communication). Dall'Ora et al. (1989) also made the interesting observation that autobiographical memory appeared to be more severely impaired in those amnesic patients who had widespread brain damage than in those who had more local damage, although their precise criteria for widespread damage were not entirely clear. However, such a finding was not obtained in the Kopelman (1989) study, in which the correlations between overall retrograde memory performance and two CT scan measures of cortical atrophy were small and non-significant ($r = -0.18$ and $r = -0.14$; see Kopelman, 1991).

Storage or Retrieval Deficit ?

Taken together, these various studies of the more semantic and the autobiographical components of retrograde memory indicate that Alzheimer patients show severe impairment across the tasks with a gentle temporal gradient, that is, with some degree of sparing of early memories. However, the temporal gradient is not as steep as that seen in Korsakoff or other organic amnesic patients. Kopelman (1989) suggested that there might be relative sparing of early memories in the Alzheimer group because these are particularly salient and well-rehearsed, and the steeper gradient in the Korsakoff group might result from an additional, progressive anterograde impairment arising from their period of heavy drinking. There are two reasons for supposing that the retrograde loss in the Alzheimer group might result, at least in part, from a retrieval deficit or a disruption of the organization of the retrieval processes, rather than from a destruction of memory storage.

First, a striking feature of the Alzheimer group's performance on the News Events Test was their remarkably good response to recognition testing, compared with their very poor recall performance. The shaded areas in Figure 3.7 show the differences between recognition and recall performance on this test in the healthy control and Alzheimer groups, respectively. In terms of recognition minus recall scores, the Alzheimer patients showed a significantly greater improvement on recognition testing across all decades than did the healthy controls ($F(1,30) = 6.23$, $p < .025$). The Korsakoff group also showed a marked improvement on recognition testing (not shown here), which was significantly greater than the healthy controls ($F(1,30) = 6.04$, $p < .025$). Weiskrantz (1985) pointed out that a marked response to cueing or recognition testing for memories long preceding the onset of an illness must be indicative of a retrieval component to the retrograde amnesia, whatever the slope of a remote memory curve. Hirst et al. (1986) have attributed the disproportionate impairment of amnesic patients in recall relative to recognition performance on anterograde tests to a failure of reflective activity in encoding the intrinsic and extrinsic contextual relations of learned material; a failure to make use of contextual cues might be one aspect of the retrieval deficit in retrograde memory (Baddeley, 1982; Kopelman, 1989).

Second, there were generally low and non-significant correlations between the severity of anterograde amnesia and performance on the various tests of retrograde amnesia (Kopelman, 1989; Parkin, Montaldi, Leng, & Hunkin, 1990; cf. Shimamura & Squire, 1986). Moreover, cholinergic blockade, which mimicked many of the salient aspects of anterograde amnesia (see above), did not produce any retrograde effect, suggesting that cholinergic depletion contributes to the anterograde but not to the retrograde loss in Alzheimer dementia (Kopelman & Corn, 1988). In order to investigate this issue further, Kopelman (1991) conducted a more detailed statistical analysis of the results of his (1989) retrograde amnesia study. For this purpose, a retrograde memory quotient (RMQ) was constructed on the basis of the means and standard deviations of the control group's performance across five retrograde tests; an anterograde memory quotient (AMQ) was determined on the basis of published norms for four anterograde tests; and an R/A difference score was determined by subtracting AMQ from RMQ, a positive score indicating relative sparing of retrograde memories. Data were also available from 16 Alzheimer and 16 Korsakoff patients for performance on eight measures of frontal function (FAS verbal fluency, FAS scores corrected for verbal IQ, alternating birds and colors fluency, a modified Weigl test, the Nelson Card Sorting scores for categories and perseverations, cognitive estimates, and picture arrangement error scores).

Table 3.1
Correlations Between Frontal Tests and RMQ, AMQ and R/A Difference Scores: Total Patient Sample (N = 32)

Frontal Tests	RMQ	AMQ	R/A DIFFERENCE
FAS Verbal Fluency	.52**	.27	.36*
Miller Correction	.10	-.24	.29
Birds and Colors	.59***	.26	.43**
Modified Weigl	.33*	.08	.29
Card-sorting categories	.51**	-.00	.56***
Card-sorting % perseverations	-.40	-.02	-.42**
Cognitive estimates	-.64***	-.48**	-.32*
Picture Arrangement errors	-.21	-.22	-.06

Note. From "Frontal dysfunction and memory deficits in the alcoholic Korsakoff syndrome and Alzheimer-type dementia" by M. D. Kopelman, 1991.
* $p < .05$; ** $p < .01$; *** $p < .001$.

Table 3.1 shows that, whereas six out of eight of the frontal tests correlated significantly with RMQ and five out of eight with the R/A difference score, only one out of eight frontal tests correlated significantly with AMQ.

Table 3.2
Correlations Between Individual Retrograde (Remote Memory) Tests and Individual Frontal Tests: Total Patient Sample (N = 32)

	News event recognition	News event recall	Famous personalities	Personal semantic schedule	Autobiographical incidents schedule
FAS Verbal Fluency	.41**	.45**	.39*	.34*	.36*
Miller Correction	.23	.14	.00	-.01	.07
Birds and Colors	.43**	.43**	.19	.38*	.62***
Modified Weigl	.16	.27	.04	.31*	.38*
Card-sorting categories	.41*	.47**	.09	.33*	.49**
Card-sorting % perseverations	-.43**	-.27	-.15	-.30*	-.24
Cognitive Estimates	-.51**	-.49**	-.59***	-.50**	-.36*
Picture Arrangement errors	-.15	-.19	-.18	-.20	-.15

Note. From "Frontal dysfunction and memory deficits in the alcoholic Korsakoff syndrome and Alzheimer-type dementia" by M. D. Kopelman, 1991.
* $p < .05$; ** $p < .01$; *** $p < .001$.

Moreover, Table 3.2 shows that this pattern of correlations held good across four individual measures of retrograde memory (News Events recognition and recall scores, Personal Semantic memory scores, and Autobiographical Incidents scores). The only test in which the pattern was much less evident was a Famous Personalities test (Stevens, 1979), which required subjects to make only familiarity judgments as to whether they recognized each name as famous or not. Finally, whereas AMQ predicted only 21% of the variance in RMQ scores, a regression equation based on three of the frontal tests accounted for 57% of the variance in Alzheimer patients, 68.5% in Korsakoff patients, and 64% in the total group.

This finding led Kopelman (1991) to suggest that the *combination* of frontal dysfunction and limbic-diencephalic pathology produces the temporally-extensive retrograde loss seen in Alzheimer and Korsakoff patients, but which is not found in some amnesic patients who have pathology confined to the limbic circuits (Dusoir, Kapur, Byrnes, McKinstry, & Hoare, 1990; Graff-Radford, Tranel, Van Hoesen, & Brandt, 1990; Hodges & Ward, 1989; Squire, Amaral, Zola-Morgan, Kritchevsky, & Press, 1989; Winocur, Oxbury, Roberts, Agnetti, & Davis 1984; Zola-Morgan, Squire, & Amaral, 1986). Although Kopelman (1991) argued that combined frontal and limbic-diencephalic pathology produces an extensive retrograde amnesia, Baddeley and B. A. Wilson (1986) have reported impoverished retrieval of autobiographical memories in some patients with apparently isolated frontal lesions and disorganized, confabulated retrieval in other frontal patients - a finding which has recently been replicated in a group of radiologically confirmed frontal patients by Spinnler (1991). It seems likely that frontal lesions produce this extensive retrograde loss by a disruption of the organization of retrieval processes (Baddeley & B. A. Wilson, 1986; Kopelman, 1991; Stuss & Benson, 1986).

Conclusions

It appears likeliest that the disruption of neural circuitry and of distributed networks, which must inevitably result from the loss of neurons and synaptic connections in Alzheimer's disease, produces a severe encoding or learning deficit and a disruption of retrieval processes, rather than accelerated forgetting or a destruction of memory storage, in the early stages of the disorder. Studies of verbal and non-verbal short-term forgetting have revealed forgetting curves in Alzheimer groups which have usually been parallel to those of healthy controls. Such a pattern of impairment is best interpreted as reflecting either an encoding or a retrieval deficit, possibly itself the consequence of diminished processing resources, rather than accelerated forgetting (Kinsbourne & Wood, 1975; Kopelman, in press). Studies of long-term forgetting have also produced parallel forgetting curves in Alzheimer patients and controls, consistent with the pattern which cholinergic blockade studies suggest would occur in cholinergic depletion. This is most likely to have resulted from a severe acquisition deficit, such as has also been postulated in organic amnesic syndromes (Huppert & Piercy, 1978; Kopelman, 1985). Those studies which have examined intermediate forgetting, or have encompassed aspects of both short-term and long-term forgetting, have generally produced equivocal results. Although the intermediate delays require further investigation, such studies do not as yet indicate that we should overrule the main conclusion of the more tightly controlled investigations of short-term and long-term forgetting, namely that forgetting curves in Alzheimer patients are equivalent or parallel to those of healthy controls.

Investigations into memory for remote public information and the autobiographical component of retrograde memory have indicated that these deficits correlate poorly with the degree of impairment on tests of anterograde amnesia, suggesting some independent basis for these aspects of the disorder. A recent study has suggested that the marked frontal atrophy and frontal dysfunction, seen in even relatively early Alzheimer patients, may produce a disruption of the organization of retrieval processes, resulting in the temporally-extensive retrograde loss. A gentle temporal gradient has been found in most of the recent retrograde amnesia studies in Alzheimer patients, and this is consistent with the present theory on the assumption that early memories are better rehearsed and more salient than more recent memories, thereby giving them some protection against the retrieval deficit. The present theory also predicts that varying patterns of retrograde loss may be found in different dementia patients, dependent upon the degree of involvement of pathology in the frontal lobes.

Donald Hebb (1945) argued that "no-one has proved that any single form of normal behavior is dependent on ... [the] frontal poles." However, the present theory emphasizes their role in maintaining our access to personal memories about our past as well our knowledge of the world. Consequently, their involvement in the pathology of Alzheimer's disease produces the personal devastation of dementia.

References

Albert, M. S., Butters, N., & Brandt, J. (1981). Patterns of remote memory in amnesic and demented patients. *Archives of Neurology, 38,* 495-500.

Baddeley, A. D. (1982). Domains of recollection. *Psychological Review, 89,* 708-729.

Baddeley, A. D., & Wilson, B. A. (1986). Amnesia, autobiographical memory, and confabulation. In D. C. Rubin (Ed.), *Autobiographical memory.* Cambridge: Cambridge University Press.

Baddeley A. D., & Warrington, E. K. (1970). Amnesia and the distinction between long- and short-term memory. *Journal of Verbal Learning and Verbal Behavior, 9,* 176-189.

Beatty, W. W., Salmon, D. P., Butters, N., Heindel, W. C., & Granholm, E. L. (1988). Retrograde amnesia in patients with Alzheimer's disease or Huntington's disease. *Neurobiology of Aging, 9,* 186-86.

Becker, J. T., Boller, F., Saxton, J., & McGonicle-Gibson, K. L. (1987). Normal rates of forgetting of verbal and non-verbal material in Alzheimer's disease. *Cortex, 23*, 59-72.

Bondareff, W., Mountjoy, C. Q., & Roth, M. (1982). Loss of neurons of origin of the adrenergic projection to the cerebral cortex (nucleus locus ceruleus) in senile dementia. *Neurology, 32*, 164-168.

Borrini, G., Dall'Ora, P., Della Sala, S., Marinelli, L, & Spinnler, H. (1989). Autobiographial memory: Sensitivity to age and education of a standardized enquiry. *Psychological Medicine, 19*, 215-224.

Brown, J. (1958). Some tests of the decay theory of immediate memory. *Quarterly Journal of Experimental Psychology, 10*, 12-21.

Butters, N., & Cermak, L. S. (1980). *Alcoholic Korsakoff's syndrome: An information-processing approach to amnesia.* New York and London: Academic Press.

Butters, N., Salmon, D. P., Munro Cullum, C., Cairns, P., Tröster, A. I., & Jacobs, D. (1988). Differentiation of amnesic and demented patients with the Wechsler Memory Scale - Revised. *Clinical Neurologist, 2*, 133-148.

Cermak, L. S. (1984). The episodic-semantic distinction in amnesia. In L. R. Squire & N. Butters (Eds.), *The neuropsychology of memory* (1st ed.). New York and London: Guilford Press.

Cermak, L. S., Butters, N., & Goodglass, H. (1971). The extent of memory loss in Korsakoff patients. *Neuropsychologia, 9*, 307-315.

Cohen, N. J., & Squire, L. R. (1981). Retrograde amnesia and remote memory impairment. *Neuropsychologia, 19*, 337-356.

Corkin, S (1982). Some relationships between global amnesias and the memory impairments in Alzheimer's disease. In S. Corkin, K. L. Daivs, J. H. Growdon, E. Usdin, & R. J. Wurtman (Eds.), *Alzheimer's Disease: A report of research in progress.* New York: Raven Press.

Craik, F. I. M. (1984). Age differences in remembering. In L. R. Squire, & N. Butters (Eds.), *The neuropsychology of memory.* New York and London: Guilford Press.

Crovitz, H. F., & Schifmann, H. (1974). Frequency of episodic memories as a function of their age. *Bulletin of the Psychonomic Society, 4*, 517-518.

Dall'Ora, P., Della Sala, S., & Spinnler, H. (1989). Autobiographical memory: Its impairment in amnesic syndromes. *Cortex, 25*, 197-217.

Dannenbaum, S. E., Parkinson, S. R., & Inman, V. W. (1988). Short-term forgetting: Comparisons between patients with dementia of the Alzheimer-type, depressed, and normal elderly. *Cognitive Neuropsychology, 5*, 213-233.

Dusoir, H., Kapur, N., Byrnes, D. P., McKinstry, S., & Hoare, R. D. (1990). The role of diencephalic pathology in human memory disorder: Evidence from a penetrating paranasal injury. *Brain, 113*, 1695-1706.

Freed, D. M., Corkin, S., & Cohen, N. J. (1987). Forgetting in H.M.: A second look. *Neuropsychologia, 25*, 461-472.

Freed, D. M., Corkin, S., Growdon, J. H., & Nissen, M. J. (1989). Selective attention in Alzheimer's disease: Characterizing cognitive subgroups of patients. *Neuropsychologia, 27*, 325-339.

Galton, F. (1879). Psychometric experiments. *Brain, 2*, 149-162.

Graff-Radford, N. R., Tranel, D., Van Hoesen, G. W., & Brandt, J. P. (1990). Diencephalic amnesia. *Brain, 113*, 1-25.

Hart, R. P., Kwentus, J. A., Taylor, J. R., & Harkins, S. W. (1987). Rate of forgetting in dementia and depression. *Journal of Consulting and Clinical Psychology, 55*, 101-105.

Hebb, D. O. (1945). Man's frontal lobes: A critical review. *Archives of Neurology and Pathology, 54*, 10-24.

Hirst, W., Johnson, M. K., Kim, J. K., Phelps, E. A., Risse, G., & Volpe, B. T. (1986). Recognition and recall in amnesics. *Journal of Experimental Psychology: Learning, Memory, and Cognition, 12*, 445-451.

Hodges, J. R., & Ward C. D. (1989). Observations during transient global amnesia: A behavioral and neuropsychological study of five cases. *Brain, 112*, 595-620.

Huppert, F. A., & Piercy, M. (1978). Dissociation between learning and remembering in organic amnesia. *Nature, 275*, 317-318.

Huppert F. A., & Piercy, M. (1979). Normal and abnormal forgetting in organic amnesia: Effect of locus of lesion. *Cortex, 15*, 385-390.

Huppert, F. A., & Kopelman, M. D. (1989). Rates of forgetting in normal aging: A comparison with dementia. *Neuropsychologia, 27*, 849-860.

Inglis, J. (1959). Learning, retention, and conceptual usage in elderly patients with memory disorder. *Journal of Abnormal and Social Psychology, 59*, 210-215.

Katzman, R., Terry, R. D., Deteresa, R., Brown, T., Davies, P., Fuld, P. A., Renbing, X., & Peck, A. (1988). Clinical pathological, and neurochemical changes in dementia: A subgroup with preserved mental status and numerous neocortical plaques. *Annals of Neurology, 23*, 138-144.

Kinsbourne, M., & Wood, F. (1975). Short-term memory processes and the amnesic syndrome. In D. Deutsch & J. A. Deutsch (Eds.), *Short-term memory*. New York: Academic Press.

Kopelman, M. D. (1985). Rates of forgetting in Alzheimer-type dementia and Korsakoff's syndrome. *Neuropsychologia, 23*, 623-638.

Kopelman, M. D. (1989). Remote and autobiographical memory, temporal context memory, and frontal atrophy in Korsakoff and Alzheimer patients. *Neuropsychologia, 27 ,* 437-460.

Kopelman, M. D. (1991). Frontal dysfunction and memory deficits in the alcoholic Korsakoff syndrome and Alzheimer-type dementia. *Brain, 114*, 117-137.

Kopelman, M. D. (in press). Non-verbal, short-term forgetting in the alcoholic Korsakoff syndrome and Alzheimer-type dementia. *Neuropsychologia.*

Kopelman, M. D., & Corn, T. H. (1988). Cholinergic 'blockade' as a model for cholinergic depletion: A comparison of the memory deficits with those of Alzheimer-type dementia and the alcoholic Korsakoff syndrome. *Brain, 111*, 1079-1110.

Kopelman, M. D., Wilson, B. A., & Baddeley, A. D. (1989). The Autobiographical Memory Interview: A new assessment of autobiographical and personal semantic memory in amnesic patients. *Journal of Clinical and Experimental Neuropsychology, 11*, 724-744.

Kopelman, M. D., Wilson, B. A., & Baddeley, A. D. (1990). *The Autobiographical Memory Interview* (Manual). Bury St Edmunds: Thames Valley Test Company.

Lemnius, C. L. (1561). The touchstone of complexions. Translated and reprinted in R. Hunter & I. Macalpine (Eds.), *Three Hundred Years of Psychiatry: 1535-1860*. London: Oxford University Press (1963).

Levin, H., High, W. M., & Eisenberg, H. M. (1988). Learning and forgetting during post-traumatic amnesia in head-injured patients. *Journal of Neurology, Neurosurgery, and Psychiatry, 51*, 14-20.

Loftus, G. R. (1985). Observations - evaluating forgetting curves. *Journal of Experimental Psychology: Learning, Memory, and Cognition, 11*, 397-406.

Mann, D. M. A., Yates, P. O., & Marcyniuk, B. (1984). Alzheimer's presenile dementia, senile dementia of Alzheimer type, and Down's syndrome in middle age form: An age-related continuum of pathological changes. *Neuropathology and Applied Neurobiology, 10*, 185-207.

Martone, E., Butters, N., & Trauner, D. (1986). Some analyses of forgetting of pictorial material in amnesic and demented patients. *Journal of Clinical and Experimental Neuropsychology, 8*, 161-178.

Masliah, E., Terry, R. D., DeTeresa, R. M., & Hansen, L. A. (1989). Immunohistochemical quantification of the synapse-related protein synpatophysin in Alzheimer disease. *Neuroscience Letters, 103*, 234-239.

Mayes, A. R., Meudell, P. R., Mann, D., & Pickering, A. (1988). Location of lesions in Korsakoff's syndrome: Neuropsychological and neuropathological data on two patients. *Cortex, 24,* 367-388.

McFie, J., & Thompson, J. A. (1972). Picture arrangement: A measure of frontal lobe function? *British Journal of Psychiatry, 121,* 547-552.

Money, E. A., Kirk, R. C., & McNaughton, N. (in press). Alzheimer's dementia produces a loss of discrimination but no increase in rate of memory decay in delayed matching to sample. *Neuropsychologia*

Morris, R. G. (1986). Short-term forgetting in senile dementia of the Alzheimer's type. *Cognitive Neuropsychology, 3,* 77-97.

Moscovitch, M. (1982). A neuropsychological approach to perception and memory in normal and pathological aging. In F. I. M. Craik & S. Treub (Eds.), *Aging and cognitive processes.* New York: Plenum Press.

Moss, M. B., Albert, M. S., Butters, N., & Payne, M. (1986). Differential patterns of memory loss among patients with Alzheimer's disease, Huntington's disease, and alcoholic Korsakoff's syndrome. *Archives of Neurology, 43,* 239-246.

Parkin, A. J., & Leng, N. R. C. (1988). Comparative studies of human amnesia: Syndrome or syndromes? In H. Markowitsch (Ed.), *Information processing by the brain.* Toronto: Hans Huber.

Parkin, A. J., Montaldi, D., Leng, N. R. C., & Hunkin, N. M. (1990). Contextual cueing effects in the remote memory of alcoholic Korsakoff patients and normal subjects. *The Quarterly Journal of Experimental Psychology, 42A,* 585-596.

Peterson, L. R., & Peterson, M. J. (1959). Short-term retention of individual items. *Journal of Experimental Psychology, 58,* 193-198.

Ribot, K. T. (1882). *Diseases of memory.* New York: Appleton.

Sagar, H. J., Cohen, N. J., Sullivan, E. V., Corkin, S., & Growdon, J. H. (1988). Remote memory function in Alzheimer's disease and Parkinson's disease. *Brain, 111,* 185-206.

Sanders, H., & Warrington, E. K. (1971). Memory for remote events in amnesic patients. *Brain,*   *94,* 661-668

Shimamura, A. P., & Squire, L. R. (1986). Korsakoff's syndrome: A study of the relation between anterograde amnesia and remote memory impairment. *Behavioral Neuroscience, 100,* 165-170.

Slamecka, N. J. (1985). Observations on comparing rates of forgetting: Comment on Loftus (1985). *Journal of Experimental Psychology: Learning, Memory, and Cognition, 11,* 812-816.

Smirni, P., Villardita, C., & Zappala, G. (1983). Influence of different paths on spatial memory performance in the Block-Tapping Test. *Journal of Clinical Neuropsychology, 5,* 355-359.

Spinnler, H. (1991). Autobiographical memory. In F. Boller and F. Forette (Eds.), *Mémoire et vieillissement* [Memory and Aging]. Paris: Fondation Nationale de Gerontologie,

Squire, L. R. (1981). Two forms of human amnesia: An analysis of forgetting. *Journal of Neuroscience, 1,* 635-640.

Squire, L. R., Amaral, D. G., Zola-Morgan, S., Kritchevsky, M., & Press, G. (1989). Description of brain injury in the amnesic patient N.A. based on magnetic resonance imaging. *Experimental Neurology, 105,* 23-35.

Stevens, M. (1979). Famous personality test: A test for measuring remote memory. *Bulletin of the British Psychological Society, 32,* 211.

Stuss, D. T., & Benson, D. F. (1986). *The Frontal Lobes.* New York: Raven Press.

Sullivan, E. V., Corkin, S., & Growdon, J. H. (1986). Verbal and non-verbal short-term memory in patients with Alzheimer's disease and in healthy elderly subjects. *Developmental Neuropsychology, 2,* 387-400.

Warrington, E. K. (1982). The double dissociation of short- and long-term memory deficits. In L. S. Cermak, (Ed.), *Human memory and amnesia.* Hillsdale, NJ: Erlbaum.

Weiskrantz, L. (1985). On issues and theories of the human amnesic syndrome. In N. M. Weinberger, J. L. McGaugh, & G. Lynch (Eds.), *Memory systems of the brain.* New York and London: Guilford Press.

Wilson, R. S., Kaszniak, A. W., & Fox, J. H. (1981). Remote memory in senile dementia. *Cortex, 17,* 41-48.

Winocur, G., Oxbury, S., Roberts, R., Agnetti, V., & Davis, C. (1984). Amnesia in a patient with bilateral lesions to the thalamus. *Neuropsychologia, 22,* 123-143.

Zola-Morgan, S. Cohen, N. J., & Squire, L. R. (1983). Recall of remote episodic memory in amnesia. *Neuropsychologia, 21,* 487-500.

Zola-Morgan, S., Squire, L. R., & Amaral, D. G. (1986). Human amnesia and the medial temporal region: Enduring memory impairment following a bilateral lesion limited to field CA1 of the hippocampus. *Journal of Neuroscience, 6,* 2950-2967.

Memory Functioning in Dementia – L. Bäckman (Editor)

4   Utilization of Cognitive Support for Episodic Remembering in Alzheimer's Disease

Agneta Herlitz, Beata Lipinska, and Lars Bäckman

Karolinska Institute

Introduction

Aging-related deficits in episodic memory functioning are well documented (see Hultsch & Dixon, 1990; Kausler, 1991, for recent reviews). However, many investigators have also noted that normal aging is characterized by a substantial memory plasticity (e.g., Bäckman & Nilsson, 1984, 1985; Craik, 1983). Specifically, older adults typically exhibit sizable performance increments in tasks wherein the intructions, the retrieval information, or the material itself, guide the learner in initiating appropriate memory operations (e.g., Bäckman, 1991; Bäckman, Mäntylä, & Herlitz, 1990; Craik, Byrd, & Swanson, 1987; Light, 1991). Hence, there is strong evidence that healthy aged individuals can utilize cognitive support to enhance episodic remembering. The purpose of the present chapter is to provide a review of empirical work on the ability of patients with Alzheimer's disease (AD) to utilize support for improving episodic memory. Knowledge of whether AD patients can utilize different forms of cognitive support may inform us of preserved and impaired abilities, and thereby of the nature of the episodic memory deficit in this group of patients.

We begin with a definitition of the meaning of the concept of cognitive support, and continue with a presentation of results from studies investigating utilization of support associated with the richness and the amount of exposure to the material among AD patients. Next, we turn to studies investigating utilization of support directly related to semantic memory in AD. In organizing the results on support related to semantic memory, we have ordered the studies according to whether they have investigated effects of elaboration, organization, or prior knowledge on episodic memory (Herlitz, 1991). Finally, in the last part of the chapter we discuss utilization of cognitive support in the context of memory training with AD patients.

In memory research, the term support has been used in a variety of ways. Investigators have used expressions such as contextual support, schematic support, internal support, external support, and cognitive support. We have chosen to adopt a broad definition of the concept of support and used the term cognitive support. According to our definition, cognitive support encompasses contextual, internal, external, and schematic forms of support. Consequently, cognitive support can be found in the material, the encoding conditions, and the retrieval conditions, but also internally in the form of subjects' prior knowledge. When effects of cognitive support are evaluated, a condition involving little support is typically compared to a condition that involves more support. Note that cognitive support may vary not only in terms of type of support, but also in terms of strength of support. For example, it is possible to conceive of different types of encoding support, such as support in the form of semantic activation or motoric activation (cf. Dick, this volume). Similarly, encoding support may vary in strength, as in the case with a word list that is possible to organize, but presented in either an unclustered or a clustered fashion (Herlitz, 1991).

We have divided the research pertaining to utilization of cognitive support in AD into five categories: (a) support associated with the richness of material, (b) support associated with amount of exposure to the material, (c) support associated with elaboration of the material, (d) support associated with organization of the material, and (e) support associated with prior knowledge of the material. Certainly, we do not believe that this classification is the only possible one, or that it covers all examples of cognitive support in the literature. However, we do believe that these five areas represent a substantial proportion of the published work on cognitive support and episodic memory in AD.

Item Richness

It is well known that some types of material are easier to remember than others. Young adults, as well as old adults, typically show effects of type of material on episodic memory. The pattern of data for AD patients differs from what is normally seen with healthy elderly adults.

In contrast to healthy aged individuals, AD patients perform equally well with words and faces (R. S. Wilson, Kaszniak, Bacon, Fox, & Kelly, 1982), rare and common words (R. S. Wilson, Bacon, Kramer, Fox, & Kaszniak, 1983), they show no picture superiority effect (Rissenberg & Glanzer, 1986), and they are able to make relatively less use of imagery in recognition memory compared to normal older adults (Hart, Smith, & Swash, 1985; Kaszniak, R. S. Wilson, & Fox, 1981). Moreover, Butters et al. (1983) varied the amount of contextual support provided during encoding of pictorial and spatial information, but this manipulation did not enhance memory performance in AD patients.

The insensitivity to manipulations of materials in AD has been extended so as to cover materials and tasks in which there is motoric activation at encoding. In the subject-performed task (SPT), subjects are instructed to perform series of simple, concrete motor actions for purposes of later recall (Cohen, 1981). Dick, Kean, and Sands (1989a) investigated free recall performance of patients with a mild to moderate AD and normal controls for SPTs and the verbal descriptions of SPTs. These investigators replicated earlier research in that normal older adults showed higher recall for SPTs than for the verbal control tasks (Bäckman, 1985; Bäckman & Nilsson, 1984), although the AD patients failed to exhibit such an improvement.

In a related study by Karlsson et al. (1989), mildly, moderately, and severely demented AD patients were either asked to perform a series of SPTs, or presented with the same verbal commands visually and auditorily. Items were categorizable into five semantic categories and, following a free recall test, subjects received the category names as retrieval cues. Despite performing at an overall lower level, mildly, moderately, and severely demented patients exhibited an improvement that was comparable to that of the normal older adults in cued recall as compared to free recall in the SPT task, but not in the verbal control task. Comparing the results of Dick et al. (1989a) with those of Karlsson et al. (1989), it appears that it may be necessary to provide retrieval cues in order to obtain effects of richness of the material in AD.

A follow-up study (Herlitz, Adolfsson, Bäckman, & Nilsson, 1991) was conducted in order to evaluate what factors in the SPT task that are critical to AD patients' performance increment. Categorizable lists of words or objects were presented under five different encoding conditions: (a) nouns, (b) objects, (c) objects with a semantic orienting question, (d) objects with self-generated motoric acts, and (e) objects with experimenter-instructed motoric acts (SPTs). Subjects were asked to memorize the items for free recall, and were subsequently provided with the category names in cued recall. As in Karlsson et al. (1989), mildly, moderately, and severely demented AD patients, and a group of normal older adults participated. Results showed that normal older adults and mildly demented AD patients were able to utilize cues to improve memory performance in all conditions. Moderately demented patients utilized cues in all conditions except in the verbal condition, whereas severely demented patients utilized cues only in the motoric condition. Thus, the results again showed that SPTs provided an effective encoding in AD patients, but also that the ability to utilize category cues following a motoric encoding may be preserved later in AD than the ability to utilize cues following a semantic encoding.

Another exception to the negative results on studies investigating effects of item richness on memory in AD comes from a study by Rissenberg and Glanzer (1987). This study demonstrated an effect of concrete versus abstract words in a free recall task among AD patients. Similarly, Hart et al. (1985) found a higher rate of false positives in recognition for very common words compared with more uncommon ones in both normal older adults and AD patients, the effect being somewhat greater for the patients. However, in both these studies the results were interpreted to mean that AD patients did not show "true" effects of item concreteness, but rather demonstrated a deficiency in verbal ability and contextual memory.

Although there seem to be exceptions to the general rule that AD patients are unable to benefit from increasing richness of materials, it is clear that they show a different pattern as compared to normal older adults. In contrast to what is true in normal aging, providing support also at retrieval appears to be necessary for AD patients to utilize a rich stimulus input for improving memory.

Item Exposure

Studies investigating effects of rate of presentation and number of study trials are reviewed in this subsection. This manipulation is often done in order to equate performance levels for different groups (e.g., young/old, normal old/ AD patients), and is frequently used in studies investigating rate of forgetting. By manipulating presentation rate, some investigators (e.g., Arenberg, 1965; Kinsbourne & Berryhill, 1972) have found that older adults benefit selectively from decreasing task pacing with respect to recall of different types of material. Others have reported that altering presentation rate affects young and old adults in a similar manner (e.g., Craik & Rabinowitz, 1985). The latter pattern of data was obtained in a recent study by Huppert and Kopelman (1989) on rate of forgetting. This study showed that increasing presentation rate from 0.5 to 1.0 sec for the elderly group resulted in comparable baseline perform-ance for young and old adults.

In AD, it also appears that a prolonged presentation rate may boost memory performance. Corkin et al. (1984), and Kopelman (1985) extended the presentation rate from approximately 1-2 sec for normal older adults to 16 sec for mildly to moderately demented AD patients, thereby obtaining comparable results for the demented and non-demented individuals in recall and recog-nition after a 10-min retention interval. Similarly, Huppert and Piercy (1979) reported comparable recognition performance for normal old subjects and AD patients, when exposure time for pictoral stimuli was adjusted. These studies provide indirect evidence that AD patients are capable of improving perform-ance when item exposure is prolonged.

Varying the number of study trials, several investigators (e.g., Cohen, Sandler, & Scroeder, 1987; Crew, 1977) have found that normal older adults benefit substantially in recall of both words and SPTs as a function of increased exposure to the to-be-remembered (TBR) items. Moscovitch, Winocur, and McLahlan (1986) demonstrated that normal older adults improved recognition of sentences over sessions, whereas AD patients did not show such a pattern of data. McFarland, Warren, and Crockard (1985) reported the occurrence of a generation effect (i.e., an advantage of subject-generated words over experi-menter provided words) in normal older adults as a function of number of study trials. The same results were found in a study by Dick, Kean, and Sands (1989b), in which normal older adults demonstrated a generation effect only after they had already experienced the generated items on a previous trial. In contrast to their healthy counterparts, moderately demented AD patients showed little evidence of a generation effect regardless of number of study trials. However, performance on a word completion task improved across study trials for both normal older adults and for the AD patients, indicating an effect of item exposure.

Thus, a prolonged presentation rate appears to improve AD patients's memory performance. Hence, it would seem logical that also an increased number of study trials would improve memory performance in demented subjects. However, as noted the results are not as clearcut regarding an increased number of study trials as with an increased presentation rate.

In the next three sections we will discuss utilization of semantic support for episodic memory in AD. The tasks that have been used in this research differ in many respects, but can be divided into three broad categories according to whether they require (a) elaboration of the meaning of items, (b) organization of items into semantic categories, or (c) utilization of item-specific prior knowledge.

Item Elaboration

Craik and Lockhart (1972) suggested that memory strength is determined by how "deeply" a stimulus is processed, with the deepest level of processing being concerned with aspects of stimulus meaning. Studies on the effects of elaboration of TBR items in AD have been concerned with levels-of-processing (Corkin, 1982; Martin, Brouwers, Cox, & Fedio, 1985) and with the generation effect (Dick et al., 1989b; Lipinska, Bäckman, Mäntylä, & Viitanen, 1992; Mitchell, Hunt, & Schmitt, 1986).

Studies on levels-of-processing in AD have yielded somewhat conflicting results. Corkin (1982) used a traditional levels-of-processing paradigm in which she encouraged groups of mildly, moderately, and severely demented AD patients, and normal older adults to process the items at either of three different levels: A sensory (e.g., Does a man/woman say the word?), a phonemic (e.g., Does the word rhyme with ___?), or a semantic level (e.g., Is the word a type of ___?). In a verbal recognition test, normal older adults showed the expected beneficial effect of the semantic orienting question in comparison with the sensory or rhyme questions. This was, however, not true for the AD patients, who performed at the same level irrespective of orienting question. Martin et al. (1985) presented mildly demented AD patients and normal older adults with four lists of nouns. In the first, "free" encoding condition, subjects were merely shown the items with instructions to remember them. In the other three encoding conditions, subjects were either asked to generate a rhyme for each noun, to tell where the item could be found, or to pantomime an action involving the item. The two latter encoding conditions were thought to require subjects to process the items with respect to their meaning (semantic encoding). In contrast to the study by Corkin (1982), the mildly demented patients, similar to the normal older adults, recalled more words from the two lists requiring semantic elaboration of the TBR items than from the rhyme condition. The pattern of data was the same irrespective of whether subjects were tested by means of free recall, or by selectively cuing subjects with their own responses to words that they could not recall.

Another form of elaborative encoding has been studied by Dick et al. (1989b) and Mitchell et al. (1986). The question of potential differences in recall of internally generated and externally provided information was investigated in these studies. Internally generated information is known to be remembered better than externally provided information in normal controls. This effect has been termed the generation effect (Slamecka & Graf, 1978). The mildly to moderately demented AD patients in the study by Mitchell et al. (1986) were asked to study sentences following the basic form "The (subject) (verb) the (object)." Half the sentences were read by the subject and half required that an object was generated to complete the sentence. At test, participants were presented with the subjects of the sentences and were asked to recall the corresponding objects. Results showed higher recall for generated than for read objects in normal older adults, whereas the AD patients failed to demonstrate a significant advantage for the generated words. In an extensive study, Dick et al. (1989b) obtained similar results. They found that moderately demented subjects showed no generation effect under conditions of free recall, cued recall, and recognition. However, when the patient group was subdivided on the basis of their scores on the Mini-Mental State Exam (MMSE; Folstein, Folstein, & McHugh, 1975), a different pattern of data emerged: Mildly demented patients showed a superiority in recognition of generated over read words, whereas moderately demented patients did not. Dick et al. concluded that the generation effect is not totally absent in mildly demented patients, although it does not approach the size seen in normal older adults.

A similar pattern of results was obtained in a recent study from our own laboratory (Lipinska et al., 1992). Mildly demented AD patients and normal older adults were presented with 20 stimulus words. For each word, subjects were asked to generate one idiosyncratic property that, according to their own experience, constituted an appropriate description of the word. All stimulus words belonged to a unique taxonomic category. Following an immediate (AD patients) or delayed (normal older adults) unexpected free recall test, subjects were provided with their self-generated cues for half the words, and with the taxonomic cues for the remaining words. As can be seen in Figure 4.1, both normal older adults and AD patients benefited from both types of retrieval cues. In addition, for both groups the self-generated cues were more effective than the taxonomic cues. These results suggest that manipulations designed to support the encoding by actively involving the subject in the production of stimulus information may be beneficial for patients with a mild AD.

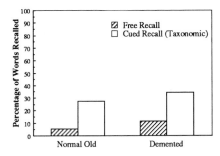 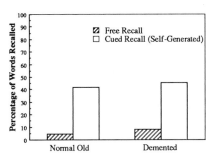

Figure 4.1. Mean percentage of words free and cued recalled by normal older adults (one week after study) and AD patients (immediately after study). From "Effectiveness of self-generated cues in normal aging and Alzheimer's disease" by B. Lipinska, L. Bäckman, T. Mäntylä, and M. Viitanen, 1992.

This pattern of results is somewhat different from that obtained by Mitchell et al. (1986). In the Mitchell et al. (1986) study, subjects were required to remember the generated words, whereas Lipinska et al. (1992) provided subjects with the generated words as an aid in recalling the TBR words. Thus, in the study by Mitchell et al. (1986) subjects were more restricted in their self-generation activity and had to remember the whole specific context in the recall test. Conceivably, this is a more effortful cognitive activity than just recalling the TBR word, which should penalize AD patients to a greater extent than normal older adults. Another factor that may contribute to the different results is that Mitchell et al. (1986) used a more impaired group of AD patients. Variations in severity of dementia determined whether AD patients showed a generation effect in the study by Dick et al. (1989b). Thus, the differences in results between these studies may be due to differences in cognitive demands and degree of dementia.

Item Organization

The next category of utilization of semantic memory concerns the ability to benefit from a categorized or categorizable materials. It involves studies in which subjects are expected to benefit from the inherent organization of the material (Cushman, Como, Booth, & Caine, 1988; Herlitz & Viitanen, 1991; Weingartner et al., 1981; Weingartner et al., 1982) and studies in which subjects are instructed to organize the material (Buschke, 1984; Diesfeldt, 1984).

Weingartner et al. (1981; Weingartner et al., 1982) presented mildly demented AD patients with three lists of words for immediate free recall. The first list consisted of randomly selected words; the second of words drawn from two superordinate categories presented randomly intermixed; and the third of words drawn from two superordinate categories, with the words presented clustered into categories. Normal older adults improved recall as the list went from random, through unclustered, to clustered. This was not true for the AD patients, who showed no differences in performance between the related and unrelated word lists. A study by Cushman et al. (1988) also demonstrates AD patients' inability to benefit from an inherent semantic organization. They used a paradigm known as release from proactive interference (PI). In this task, subjects study several word lists with instructions to recall the words after each list. Words in consecutive lists may belong to the same semantic category, with the exception of the last list. The demonstration of enhanced recall following the change in semantic category in the last list is thought to indicate encoding of semantic aspects of the material. The results of the study by Cushman et al. (1988) demonstrated that normal older adults showed the expected build up of PI over the first four related lists, and a release from PI following a shift to a new semantic category in the fifth list. Neither of these effects were seen in a group of mildly to moderately demented AD patients. This finding again suggests that AD patients' ability to spontaneously utilize semantic information at encoding is impaired.

An interesting question concerns what will happen if AD patients are "forced" to organize the material? Would they then exhibit memory improvement relative to a control condition? A group of moderately to severely demented patients in a study by Diesfeldt (1984) were presented short categorizable word lists under two different encoding conditions. In one condition, the words were presented without informing the subjects of the category structure of the list. In another condition, subjects were asked to categorize the words into two categories as they were presented. These two encoding conditions yielded similar free recall performance. The AD patients were also tested with cued recall, which produced a somewhat different pattern of data. Category cuing increased AD patients' recall when subjects had organized the material during study, but did not increase recall following the uninformed encoding condition. That is, recall was significantly better when explanation about the category structure was combined with category cues at recall, as compared to all other conditions. A similar result was obtained by Buschke (1984) in a study using a search procedure at encoding. Subjects were asked to identify the "tool," the "animal" etc. in a set of visually presented TBR pictures. Free recall was assessed and subjects were also cued with the category names for those items they did not retrieve in free recall. Although AD patients' free recall performance was far below that of normal older adults, their cued recall performance reached the level of normal older adults. In an attempt to replicate these data, Cushman et al. (1988) found that AD patients performed far below normal older adults in both free and cued recall, although they showed increased performance following the provision of cues.

In a recent study (Herlitz & Viitanen, 1991), we sought to further investigate potential differences between normal older adults and mildly and moderately demented AD patients in the ability to utilize semantic organization for improving episodic remembering. In one experiment, groups of mildly and moderately demented patients and a group of normal older adults were presented with two lists of words: (a) a list of semantically unrelated words, and (b) a list of words from four semantic categories presented randomly intermixed. Free recall was assessed and, following the organizable word list, subjects also received a cued recall test with the category names serving as cues.

As can be seen in Figure 4.2, the normal controls, as opposed to the mildly and moderately demented AD patients, performed at a higher level in the organizable list as compared to the random list. However, the normal older adults and the mildly demented AD patients showed an increase from free to total recall (the total recall score is based on the number of words recalled in free recall together with new words recalled in cued recall) in the organizable word list. This was not true for the moderately demented AD patients.

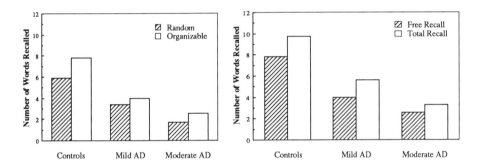

Figure 4.2. Mean free recall in the random and organizable list (leftmost panel), and mean free and total recall performance in the organizable list (rightmost panel) by normal older adults and patients with mild and moderate AD. Adapted from "Semantic organization and verbal episodic memory in patients with mild and moderate Alzheimer's disease" by A. Herlitz and M. Viitanen, 1991, *Journal of Clinical and Experimental Neuropsychology, 13*, pp. 564-565. Copyright 1991 by Swets & Zeitlinger. Adapted by permission.

In a second experiment we explored whether a stronger semantic support at encoding would result in higher recall and cue utilization, particularly for the moderately demented patients. New groups of mildly and moderately demented patients and a group of normal controls were again presented with two word lists: (a) words from four semantic categories presented randomly intermixed, and (b) words from four semantic categories presented clustered, together with information about the organization of the list.

As can be seen in Figure 4.3, normal older adults again showed that they were able to utilize the semantic organization provided at encoding, performing at a higher level in the clustered as compared to the organizable word list. In addition, the results of the first experiment were replicated and extended in that both normal older adults and mildly demented patients performed at a higher level in total as compared to free recall in the organizable word list, and also in the clustered word list. For the moderately demented patients, this effect was present only in the clustered word list.

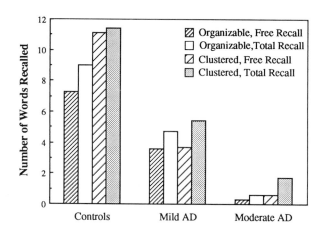

Figure 4.3. Mean free and total recall performance in the organizable and clustered lists by normal older adults and patients with mild and moderate AD. From "Semantic organization and verbal episodic memory in patients with mild and moderate Alzheimer's disease" by A. Herlitz and M. Viitanen, 1991, *Journal of Clinical and Experimental Neuropsychology, 13,* p. 569. Copyright 1991 by Swets & Zeitlinger. Adapted by permission.

Besides indicating that there are conditions under which memory facilitation from semantic organization may be obtained in AD patients, this study supports the notion that AD patients show a deficit in utilizing semantic knowledge as an aid for episodic remembering. The tasks used in the present study can be viewed as instances on a continuum, with the random, the organizable, and the clustered list reflecting increasing levels of semantic support at encoding. At retrieval, the free and total recall scores differ with respect to level of retrieval support provided, the latter score giving an estimate of the sum of supportive conditions at encoding and retrieval. It thus appears that patients with a moderate AD are more severely affected than patients with a mild AD with respect to the ability to utilize semantic organization. AD patients require more semantic support than normal older adults to improve memory, and the level of support required seems to increase as a function of increasing severity of dementia.

Item Knowledge

The last category of utilization of semantic memory concerns the use of prior knowledge as an aid for episodic remembering. It has been found that the availability of task-relevant prior knowledge improves memory in normal aging and may reduce or eliminate age differences in memory performance (e.g., Bäckman, Herlitz, & Karlsson, 1987; Hultsch & Dixon, 1983).

Typically, studies investigating prior knowledge and memory have focused on comparisons between the remote and recent past, with Ribot's (1882) law as a point of departure. According to this law, the probability of forgetting an event is inversely related to the time elapsed since the occurrence of the event. This implies that, among older adults, memories from early adulthood should be better preserved than memories dating just a few years back. In studies addressing this issue, the test materials have typically been pictures of famous individuals who attained their fame during different time periods. Results have been quite straightforward: AD patients show a consistent deficit in free recall, cued recall, and recognition of major public events and famous individuals from the remote and recent past in comparison with normal older adults (Beatty, Salmon, Butters, Heindel, & Granholm, 1988; Kopelman, 1989; Sagar, Cohen, Corkin, & Growdon, 1985; Sagar, Cohen, Sullivan, Corkin, & Growdon, 1988; R. S. Wilson, Kaszniak, & Fox, 1981). More interestingly, most studies have shown that AD patients remember major public events and famous individuals from the 1930s, 1940s, and 1950s better than those from today; that is, they show a temporal gradient in their semantic memory (see Kopelman, this volume).

Similar findings have been obtained in research on autobiographical memory. In these studies, subjects are encouraged to produce a memory of a particular incident prompted with a cue which is either specific or unspecific in time. Results show that AD patients tend to produce more memories from early than from late adulthood both spontaneously and with unspecific cues (Sagar et al., 1988). AD patients also remember events from early adulthood in a more detailed and vivid form than from late adulthood (Kopelman, 1989).

It thus seems clear that AD patients, like normal older adults, have better prior knowledge of episodic and semantic information dating from the remote past compared to recent information. Similar results have been found in case studies. Martin (1987) showed that a patient with AD who had excellent premorbid drawing skills was able to draw descriptive pieces of art quite proficiently late in the disease process, and Crystal, Grober, and Masur (1989) demonstrated preserved musical ability in a musicologist with AD. To account for these findings, it has been suggested that an anterograde memory deficit might be responsible for the inferior performance of AD patients in recalling items from the recent past; that is, they show a progressively impaired ability to encode or retain new information (R. S. Wilson et al., 1981).

We have conducted two studies specifically investigating the effects of prior knowledge on episodic memory in AD (Bäckman & Herlitz, 1990; Lipinska, Bäckman, & Herlitz, in press). In the study by Bäckman and Herlitz (1990) mildly demented AD patients and normal older adults participated. Photographs of famous individuals were presented for purposes of later episodic recognition. Half of the famous individuals attained their fame during the 1940s, and the other half consisted of individuals who are famous today. Following an episodic recognition test, subjects were asked to (a) indicate, by answering yes or no, whether they were familiar with the face presented before they arrived at the laboratory, and (b) to select the correct name for each face from a set of four names. These two tests were conducted to assess subjects' prior knowledge of the material.

Replicating prior research, normal older adults perceived more faces as familiar than the AD patients, and both groups of subjects perceived more dated than contemporary faces as familiar (see Figure 4.4). The name recognition task revealed exactly the same pattern of data, and it was concluded that both groups had knowledge of more dated than contemporary famous faces. Most interesting, the episodic face recognition task indicated better performance for the dated than for the contemporary faces for the normal older adults, but not for the AD patients (see Table 4.1). These results suggest that AD is associated with a deficit in utilizing prior knowledge in episodic memory.

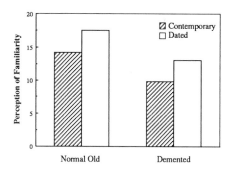 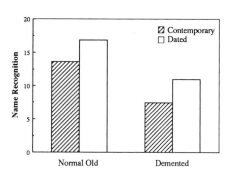

Figure 4.4. Mean number of contemporary and dated famous individuals perceived as familiar (leftmost panel) and correctly identified in the name recognition task (rightmost panel) by normal older adults and patients with AD. Adapted from "The relationship between prior knowledge and face recognition memory in normal aging and Alzheimer's disease" by L. Bäckman and A. Herlitz, 1990, *Journal of Gerontology: Psychological Sciences, 45,* p. 96. Copyright 1990 by The Gerontological Society of America. Adapted by permission.

In a follow-up study (Lipinska et al., in press), we explored whether a stronger semantic activation at encoding would result in beneficial effects of prior knowledge on face recognition memory also for AD patients. In comparison with the procedure used by Bäckman and Herlitz (1990), the increase of semantic activation was accomplished by (a) having subjects generate statements concerning the famous individuals during study, and (b) providing the names of the famous individuals along with the pictures at both study and test. The generation of statements and the provision of names were assumed to increase the activation of the underlying knowledge structure, thus facilitating the elaboration of the TBR information.

Table 4.1
Mean episodic face recognition performance of normal older adults and patients with AD as a function of type of face

	Type of Face						
	Contemporary				Dated		
Group	Hit rate	False alarm rate	d'		Hit rate	False alarm rate	d'
Normal old	.87	.04	2.88		.94	.01	3.88
Demented	.66	.32	.88		.74	.37	.97

Note. Adapted from "The relationship between prior knowledge and face recognition memory in normal aging and Alzheimer's disease" by L. Bäckman and A. Herlitz, 1990, *Journal of Gerontology: Psychological Sciences, 45,* p. 97. Copyright 1990 by The Gerontological Society of America. Adapted by permission.

New groups of mildly demented AD patients and normal older adults were presented with dated and contemporary famous faces with name tags for later recognition, and were asked to generate unique statements about each face, during one min per picture. In a subsequent unexpected self-paced recognition test, the target faces were presented along with distractors and subjects were asked to make yes/no recognition judgments for each presented face.

Subjects' level of prior knowledge for the TBR pictures was determined by counting the total number of unique statements each subject generated about the presented faces. As can be seen in Figure 4.5, results showed that both groups of subjects possessed more prior knowledge of the dated than of the contemporary individuals.

However, in contrast to the results of the Bäckman and Herlitz (1990) study, both groups performed better with the dated than with the contemporary faces in the episodic recognition test. Thus, as the level of semantic activation at encoding increased, AD patients were able to utilize their task-relevant prior knowledge to enhance episodic remembering (see Table 4.2).

In sum, both normal older adults and AD patients show the same pattern of performance in tasks assessing prior knowledge in that both groups recall and recognize more episodic and semantic knowledge from the remote past than from more recent decades. But in contrast to normal older adults,

AD patients have difficulties in effectively accessing the semantic information, and may fail to utilize prior knowledge to improve episodic memory performance. However, when the level of semantic activation is high, also mild AD patients are able to utilize prior knowledge to enhance episodic remembering.

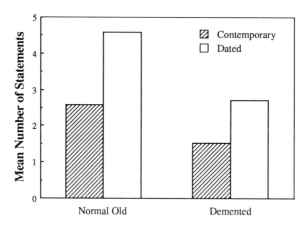

Figure 4.5. Mean number of statements generated by normal older adults and patients with AD for contemporary and dated famous individuals. Adapted from "When Greta Garbo is easier to remember than Stefan Edberg: Influences of prior knowledge on recognition memory in Alzheimer's disease" by B. Lipinska, L. Bäckman, and A. Herlitz, in press, *Psychology and Aging*. Copyright 1992 by the American Psychological Association. Adapted by permission.

Table 4.2
Mean episodic face recognition performance of normal older adults (one week after study) and patients with AD (15 min after study) for contemporary and dated famous individuals

	Type of Face						
	Contemporary				Dated		
Group	Hit rate	False alarm rate	*d′*		Hit rate	False alarm rate	*d′*
Normal old	.89	.07	3.14		.93	.07	3.59
Demented	.69	.11	2.15		.81	.10	2.85

Note. From "When Greta Garbo is easier to remember than Stefan Edberg: Influences of prior knowledge on recognition memory in Alzheimer's disease" by B. Lipinska, L. Bäckman, and A. Herlitz, in press, *Psychology and Aging*. Copyright 1992 by the American Psychological Association. Adapted by permission.

Memory Training

The research reviewed in this chapter suggests that AD patients can utilize support for remembering, although they may require more support than
their healthy aged counterparts in order to show memory facilitation. Providing support also at retrieval appears to be particularly important for detecting
effects of various kinds of encoding manipulations in AD. In most memory
training research, tasks involving relatively little retrieval support (e.g., free
recall, paired-associate learning) are used to evaluate potential gains (see Poon,
Walsh-Sweeney, & Fozard, 1980; Yesavage, Lapp, & Sheikh, 1989, for reviews).
In addition, and perhaps paradoxically, memory training procedures typically
involve strategies and techniques (e.g., imagery, the method of loci, face-name
mnemonics) that put rather severe demands on memory. Although normal
older adults have been found to benefit from a variety of different types of
memory training (e.g., Bäckman, 1989; Kliegl, Smith, & Baltes, 1989; Roberts,
1983), recent research indicates that the magnitude of improvement from
training in healthy aged people is positively correlated with global cognitive
functioning as measured by the MMSE (Hill, Yesavage, Sheikh, & Friedman,
1989). The study by Hill et al. (1989) showed no gains from training in face-
name mnemonics and the method of loci in nondemented older adults with a
mild cognitive impairment. Given this state of affairs, it is not surprising that
gains have been small or nonexistant when traditional memory training procedures have been used in intervention research with demented individuals
(e.g., Beck et al., 1985; Brinkman et al., 1982; Bäckman, Josephsson, Herlitz,
Stigsdotter, & Viitanen, 1991; Yesavage, 1982; Yesavage, Westphal, & Rush,
1981; Zarit, Zarit, & Reever, 1982).
    There are, however, some exceptions to this negative pattern of outcome.
In the following, we will discuss these exceptions with the aim of delineating
salient characteristics of the approaches adopted. In a case study, Hill,
Evankovich, Sheikh, and Yesavage (1987) showed that an imagery-based
mnemonic increased reliably the duration of face-name associations in an AD
patient. The authors suggested that this positive result may partly be due to
that they used retention duration rather than number of faces and names
recalled as the criterion variable. However, in an attempt to replicate the Hill
et al. (1987) data in a larger sample, Bäckman et al. (1991) failed to find any
effects of the mnemonic in seven out of eight demented patients. Thus, it appears that the initial data of Hill et al. have limited generalizability. To determine potential common features of those AD patients who respond to this type
of memory training remains an important avenue for future investigation.
    Quayhagen and Quayhagen (1989) tested the efficacy of an extensive
home-based memory-training program involving practice in several everyday
memory activities (e.g., recall of facts and daily schedules, visualizing spatial
routes, planning trips, recognizing faces from photos). The program ran for eight
months (six hours per week), and performance in a variety of memory tasks

was assessed prior to training, four months after the training started, and after the completion of the training program. Results showed that trained AD patients maintained their baseline performance level across testing occasions, whereas control patients deteriorated across time. In addition, caregivers to trained patients maintained their well being, life satisfaction, depression level, and perceieved burden, although caregivers to controls experienced deterioration in all these health-related measures over the eight-month period.

Camp and collaborators (e.g., Camp, 1989; Camp & McKitrick, in press; McKitrick & Camp, 1989; Stevens & Camp, 1990) have examined the effects of a modified version of the spaced-retrieval technique (Landauer & Bjork, 1978) on the duration of face-name and object-location associations in AD patients. The spaced-retrieval technique involves retrieval of the same target information at increasingly longer intervals. If a retrieval failure occurs, the subject receives feedback and the retention interval is reduced to a previous interval at which successful retrieval occurred. The studies by Camp and colleagues have demonstrated quite impressive training gains in demented patients (see also, Moffat, 1989). It has been speculated that spaced retrieval may involve the use of implicit memory processes (Camp & McKitrick, in press). Given this possibility, it is interesting to note that although some studies indicate implicit memory deficits in AD (e.g., Heindel, Salmon, Shults, Walicke, & Butters, 1989; Shimamura, Salmon, Squire, & Butters, 1987), other research suggests that, under some conditions, implicit memory may be well preserved in this disease (e.g., Grosse, R. S. Wilson, & Fox, 1990; Ober & Shenaut, 1988).

Most procedures used in memory training studies with demented individuals draw on abilities that are severely impaired in dementia (e.g., organization, imagery). As suggested when comparing the outcome of these studies with that of the spaced-retrieval studies, a more profitable approach may be to use training methods that enable the use of abilities that are less affected by the disease process (Bäckman et al., 1991). It has been demonstrated that AD patients show preserved learning of motor procedures (Eslinger & Damasio, 1986; Heindel et al., 1989) and a generation effect in the retention of psychomotor information (Dick, Kean, & Sands, 1988). In addition, motor action at encoding has been found to boost verbal episodic memory in AD patients at different levels of severity of impairment (Herlitz et al., 1991; Karlsson et al., 1989). On the basis of these findings, Bäckman et al. (1991) speculated that motor activity might be a useful component in memory training programs designed for AD patients (see also Dick, this volume; B. A. Wilson, 1989).

In a recently completed study, Josephsson, Bäckman, Borell, Nygård, and Bernspång (1991) examined whether training in various task-relevant motor procedures would result in improved performance of different everyday activities (e.g., brushing teeth, doing the table) in mildly to moderately demented AD patients who had started experiencing decline in the activity in question. To optimize interest and motivation among the participants, activities were selected on the basis of patients' preferences. Preliminary data indicate that most patients showed improved performance after training, provided that external guidance (e.g., hints, signs) was provided during task performance. In addition, some patients at mild stages exhibited performance gains also when external reminders were withdrawn.

The study on training of everyday activities as well as the studies on spaced retrieval discussed above are designed such that an acceptable performance level in the criterion tasks may be accomplished without taxing cognitive skills that are grossly impaired in AD. Related examples of this strategy of enhancing performance in dementia are found in intervention research in which features of the physical environment are changed and reinforcement contingencies are implemented. Such modifications have been found to reduce undesirable communication behaviors like agressive outbursts (Spayd & Smyer, 1988), negative accusations (Green, Linsk, & Pinkston, 1986), and paranoid speech (Carstensen & Fremouw, 1981) in demented patients. Much work within this tradition is conducted within the realm of reality orientation therapy, and involves the use of different types of external memory aids (e.g., diaries, signposts, concrete reminders). Specific reality orientation procedures have been found to improve demented patients' orientation and memory for personal facts (Hanley, 1981) as well as memory for appointments (Hanley & Lusty, 1984). In a recent home-based study, Bourgeois (1990) showed that the use of an external memory aid resulted in greatly improved conversation behaviors in three AD patients. Conceivably, the high degree of retrieval support and the low demands on self-initiated cognitive operations constitute important factors for the efficacy of training procedures based on utilization of external memory aids.

In the remainder of this chapter we will pinpoint prominent features of the training procedures employed in studies demonstrating gains in demented patients. First, it is apparent that most of these programs are rather extensive. For example, the training program used in the Quayhagen and Quayhagen (1989) study ran for 8 months, and in many of the other studies reviewed the training lasted for several weeks. This might be an important factor for the successful outcomes, given that AD patients appear to be able to benefit from more study time in memory tasks (e.g., Corkin et al., 1984).

Second, training studies on (a) face-name and object-location retention duration involving implicit memory processes, (b) everyday activities involving motor memory functions, and (c) external memory aids involving utilization of retrieval support, illustrate the importance of arranging the training situation such that relatively well preserved cognitive skills can be used to perform the tasks in question. Third, in many of the reviewed studies family members have been involved in the training. The active participation of caregivers may serve at least two important purposes. On the one hand, it may reduce the patient's level of anxiety in a demanding and stressful situation (cf. Cavanaugh et al., 1989) and, on the other, it may facilitate the continuation of the training once the program is formally terminated.

Fourth, a factor that is particularly salient in research on the use of external memory aids is the high degree of retrieval support. Arranging a learning situation in which there is a high level of environmental support reduces the importance of self-initiated cognitive processes, and perhaps even make them redundant. To this end, there is an interesting similarity between the basic experimental work and the intervention research in that studies from both domains indicate the importance of supporting both encoding and retrieval, if the goal is to improve memory in AD. However, an observed performance increment in a task that is simply due to the patient following the instructions on a sign, calls into question whether the patient actually has learned something new. In other words, it is questionable whether such an improvement reflects a change in any underlying cognitive process. Although such improvements may be of limited theoretical interest, they may nevertheless be both easier to accomplish and more clinically relevant compared to those seen after training of self-initiated memory processes.

In sum, traditional approaches to memory training are typically ineffective in dementia. The few cases in which such approaches have been successful have involved rather extensive programs and the active participation of caregivers. Training approaches based on the use of relatively well preserved memory skills have generally been more effective in this group of patients. Still, it should be pointed out that, in comparison with normal older adults (a) training gains in demented patients (when they are observed) are typically smaller, (b) demented patients often require more training in order to show gains, (c) there is considerable interindividual variability with respect to susceptibility to memory training in dementia, and (d) gains observed in demented patients are often characterized by maintaining a certain level of skill, rather than by an actual performance increment. Keeping these caveats in mind, the training-related improvements observed may have both a theoretical value indicating a cognitive reserve capacity in dementia, and a clinical value improving the patient's everyday functioning.

Summary

It is abanduntly clear that AD patients, irrespective of degree of dementia, perform at a lower level than normal older adults in episodic memory tasks. However, given that support is provided at retrieval, it is possible to detect utilization of encoding support in AD patients. When degree of dementia is taken into consideration, it appears that the amount of support required to show memory improvement increases with increasing dementia severity. That is, mildly demented AD patients are able to utilize the same type of cognitive support at encoding as normal older adults, provided that retrieval support is present. Moderately demented AD patients, however, need a stronger support at encoding, in addition to the retrieval support, in order to utilize the cognitive support. For severely demented patients, it is unclear whether further increases in the strength of encoding support is sufficient to improve memory. However, the quality of the encoding support appears to be of some importance for severely demented patients. This is indicated by the fact that only a motoric activation at encoding, together with cuing at retrieval has been found to enhance memory in this group of patients (see Herlitz, 1991). The intervention literature is consistent with these findings, indicating the importance of providing support at both encoding and retrieval in order to demonstrate training-related gains in AD.

Acknowledgments

Preparation of this chapter was supported by grants from The Bank of Sweden Tercentenary Foundation, and The Swedish Council for Social Research to Lars Bäckman.

References

Arenberg, D. (1965). Anticipation interval and age differences in verbal learning. *Journal of Abnormal Psychology, 70,* 419-425.

Bäckman, L. (1985). Further evidence for the lack of adult age differences on free recall of subjects-performed tasks: The importance of motor action. *Human Learning, 4,* 79-85.

Bäckman, L. (1989). Varieties of memory compensation by older adults in episodic remembering. In L. W. Poon, D. C. Rubin, & B. A. Wilson (Eds.), *Everyday cognition in adulthood and late life.* New York: Cambridge University Press.

Bäckman, L. (1991). Recognition memory across the adult life span: The role of prior knowledge. *Memory & Cognition, 19,* 63-71.

Bäckman, L., & Herlitz, A. (1990). The relationship between prior knowledge and face recognition memory in normal aging and Alzheimer's disease. *Journal of Gerontology: Psychological Sciences, 45,* 94-100.

Bäckman, L., Herlitz, A., & Karlsson, T. (1987). Pre-experimental knowledge facilitates episodic recall in young, young-old, and old-old adults. *Experimental Aging Research, 13,* 89-91.

Bäckman, L., Josephsson, S., Herlitz, A., Stigsdotter, A., & Viitanen, M. (1991). The generalizability of training gains in dementia: Effects of an imagery-based mnemonic on face-name retention duration. *Psychology and Aging, 6,* 489-492.

Bäckman, L., Mäntylä, T., & Herlitz, A. (1990). The optimization of episodic remembering in old age. In P. B. Baltes & M. M. Baltes (Eds.), *Successful aging: Perspectives from the behavioral sciences.* New York: Cambridge University Press.

Bäckman, L., & Nilsson, L.-G. (1984). Aging effects in free recall: An exception to the rule. *Human Learning, 3,* 53-69.

Bäckman, L., & Nilsson, L.-G. (1985). Prerequisites for lack of age differences in memory performance. *Experimental Aging Research, 11,* 67-73.

Beatty, W. W., Salmon, D. P., Butters, N., Heindel, W. C., & Granholm, E. L. (1988). Retrograde amnesia in patients with Alzheimer's disease or Huntington's disease. *Neurobiology of Aging, 9,* 181-186.

Beck, C. K., Heacock, P., Thatcher, R., Mercer, S. O., Sparkman, C., & Roberts, M. A. (1985, July). *Cognitive skills remediation with Alzheimer's patients.* Paper presented at the 13th International Congress of Gerontology, New York.

Bourgeois, M. S. (1990). Enhancing conversation skills in patients with Alzheimer's disease using a prosthetic memory aid. *Journal of Applied Behavior Analysis, 23,* 29-42.

Brinkman, S. D., Smith, R. C., Meyer, J. S., Vroulis, G., Shaw, T., Gordon, J. R., Allen, R. H. (1982). Lecithin and memory training in suspected Alzheimer's disease. *Journal of Gerontology, 37,* 4-9.

Buschke, H. (1984). Cued recall in amnesia. *Journal of Clinical Neuropsychology, 6,* 433-440.

Butters, N., Albert, M. S., Sax, D. S., Miliotis, P., Nagode, J., & Sterste, A. (1983). The effect of verbal mediators on the pictorial memory of brain-damaged patients. *Neuropsychologia, 21,* 307-323.

Camp, C. J. (1989). Facilitation of new learning in Alzheimer's disease. In G. Gilmore, P. Whitehouse, & M. Wykle (Eds.), *Memory and aging: Research, theory, and practice.* New York: Springer.

Camp, C. J., & McKitrick, L. A. (in press). Memory interventions in DAT populations: Methodological and theoretical issues. In R. L. West & J. D. Sinnott (Eds), *Everyday memory and aging: Current research and methodology.* New York: Springer.

Carstensen, L., & Fremouw, W. J. (1981). The demonstration of a behavioral intervention for late life paranoia. *The Gerontologist, 21,* 329-333.

Cavanaugh, J. C., Dunn, N. J., Mowery, D., Feller, C., Niederehe, G., Frugé, E., & Volpendesta, D. (1989). Problem-solving strategies in dementia patient-caregiver dyads. *The Gerontologist, 29,* 156-158.

Cohen, R. L. (1981). On the generality of some memory laws. *Scandinavian Journal of Psychology, 23,* 267-282.

Cohen, R. L., Sandler, S. P., & Scroeder, K. (1987). Aging and memory for words and actions events: Effects of item repetion and list length. *Psychology and Aging, 2,* 280-285.

Corkin, S. (1982). Some relationships between global amnesias and the memory impairments in Alzheimer's disease. In S. Corkin, K. L. Davies, J. H. Growdon, E. Usdin, & R. J. Wurtman (Eds.), *Alzheimer's Disease: A report of progress.* New York: Raven Press.

Corkin, S., Growdon, J. H., Nissen, M. J., Huff, F. J., Freed, D. M., & Sagar, H. J. (1984). Recent advances in the neuropsychological study of Alzheimer's disease. In R. J. Wurtman, S. Corkin, & J. H. Growdon (Eds.), *Alzheimer's disease: Advances in basic research and therapies.* Cambridge, MA: Center for Brain Sciences and Metabolism-Trust.

Craik, F. I. M. (1983). On the transfer of information from temporary to permanent memory. *Philosophical Transactions of The Royal of Society London, 302,* 341-359.

Craik, F. I. M., Byrd, M., & Swanson, J. M. (1987). Patterns of memory loss in three elderly samples. *Psychology and Aging, 2,* 79-86.

Craik, F. I. M., & Lockhart, R. A. (1972). Levels of processing: A framework for memory research. *Journal of Verbal Learning and Verbal Behavior, 11,* 671-684.

Craik, F. I. M., & Rabinovitz, J. C. (1985). The effects of presentation rate and encoding task on age-related memory deficits. *Journal of Gerontology, 40,* 309-315.

Crew, F. F. (1977). *Age differences in retention after varying study and test trials.* Unpublished Master's thesis, Georgia Institute of Technology.

Crystal, H. A., Grober, E., & Masur, D. (1989). Preservation of musical memory in Alzheimer's disease. *Journal of Neurology, Neurosurgery, and Psychiatry, 52,* 1415-1416.

Cushman, L. A., Como, P. G., Booth, H., & Caine, E. D. (1988). Cued recall and release from proactive interference in Alzheimer's disease. *Journal of Clinical and Experimental Neuropsychology, 10*, 685-692.

Dick, M. B., Kean, M.-L., & Sands, D. (1988). The preselection effect on the recall facilitation of motor movements in Alzheimer-type dementia. *Journal of Gerontology: Psychological Sciences, 43*, 127-135.

Dick, M. B., Kean, M.-L., & Sands, S. (1989a). Memory for action events in Alzheimer-type dementia: Further evidence of an encoding failure. *Brain and Cognition, 9, 71-87*.

Dick, M. B., Kean, M.-L., & Sands, S. (1989b). Memory for internally generated words in Alzheimer-type dementia: Breakdown in encoding and semantic memory. *Brain and Cognition, 9*, 88-108.

Diesfeldt, H. F. A. (1984). The importance of encoding instructions and retrieval cues in the assessment of memory in senile dementia. *Archives of Gerontology and Geriatrics, 3*, 51-57.

Eslinger, P. J., & Damasio, A. R. (1986). Preserved motor learning in Alzheimer's disease: Implications for anatomy and behavior. *Journal of Neuroscience, 6*, 3006-3009.

Folstein, M. F., Folstein, S. E., & McHugh, P. R. (1975). "Mini-mental state:" A practical method for grading the cognitive state of patients for the clinician. *Journal of Psychiatric Research, 12*, 189-198.

Green, G. R., Linsk, N. L., & Pinkston, E. M. (1986). Modification of verbal behavior of the mentally retarded impaired elderly by their spouses. *Journal of Applied Behavioral Analysis, 19*, 329-336.

Grosse, D. A., Wilson, R. S., & Fox, J. H. (1990). Preserved word-stem completion priming of semantically encoded information in Alzheimer's disease. *Psychology and Aging, 5*, 304-306.

Hanley, I. G. (1981). The use of signposts and active training to modfiy ward disorientation in elderly patients. *Journal of Behavioral Therapy and Experimental Psychiatry, 12*, 241-247.

Hanley, I. G., & Lusty, K. (1984). Memory aids in reality orientation: A single-case study. *Behavior Research Therapy, 22*, 709-712.

Hart, S. A., Smith, C. M., & Swash, M. (1985). Recognition memory in Alzheimer's disease. *Neurobiology of Aging, 6*, 287-292.

Heindel, W. C., Salmon, D. P., Shults, C. W., Walicke, P. A., & Butters, N. (1989). Neuropsychological evidence for multiple memory systems: A comparison of Alzheimer's, Huntington's, and Parkinson's patients. *Journal of Neuroscience, 9*, 582-587.

Herlitz, A. (1991). *Remembering in Alzheimer's Disease: Utilization of cognitive support.* Doctoral dissertation, University of Umeå, Umeå.

Herlitz, A., Adolfsson, R., Bäckman, L., & Nilsson, L.-G. (1991). Cue utilization following different forms of encoding in mildly, moderately, and severely demented patients with Alzheimer's disease. *Brain and Cognition, 15*, 119-130.

Herlitz, A., & Viitanen, M. (1991). Semantic organization and verbal episodic memory in patients with mild and moderate Alzheimer's disease. *Journal of Clinical and Experimental Neuropsychology, 13*, 559-574.

Hill, R. D., Evankovich, K. D., Sheikh, J. I., & Yesavage, J. A. (1987). Imagery mnemonic training in a patient with primary degenerative dementia. *Psychology and Aging, 2*, 204-205.

Hill, R. D., Yesavage, J. A., Sheik, J. I., & Friedman, L. (1989). Mental status as a predictor of response to memory training in older adults. *Educational Gerontology, 51*, 633-639.

Hultsch, D. F., & Dixon, R. A. (1983). The role of pre-experimental knowledge in text processing in adulthood. *Experimental Aging Research, 9*, 17-22.

Hultsch, D. F., & Dixon, R. A. (1990). Learning and memory in aging. In J. E. Birren & K. W. Schaie (Eds), *Handbook of the psychology of aging.* San Diego: Academic Press.

Huppert, F. A., & Kopelman, M. D. (1989). Rates of forgetting in normal aging: A comparison with dementia. *Neuropsychologia, 27,* 849-860.

Huppert, F. A., & Piercy, M. (1979). Normal and abnormal forgetting in organic amnesia: Effects of locus of lesion. *Cortex, 15,* 385-390.

Josephsson, S., Bäckman, L., Borell, L., Nygård, L., & Bernspång, B. (1991, July). *Training of ADL activities and procedural skills in dementia.* Paper presented at the International Conference on Memory, Lancaster, England.

Karlsson, T., Bäckman, L., Herlitz, A., Nilsson, L.-G., Winblad, B., & Österlind, P.-O. (1989). Memory improvement at different stages of Alzheimer's disease. *Neuropsychologia, 27,* 737-742.

Kaszniak, A. W., Wilson, R. S., & Fox, J. H. (1981). Effects of imagery and meaningfulness on free recall and recognition memory in presenile and senile dementia. *International Journal of Neuroscience, 12,* 264.

Kausler, D. H. (1991). *Experimental psychology, cognition, and human aging* (2nd ed.). New York: Springer-Verlag.

Kinsbourne, M., & Berryhill, J. L. (1972). The nature of the interaction between pacing and the age decrement in learning. *Journal of Gerontology, 27,* 471-477.

Kliegl, R., Smith, J., & Baltes, P. B. (1989). Testing-the-limits and the study of adult age differences in cognitive plasticity of mnemonic skill. *Developmental Psychology, 25,* 247-256.

Kopelman, M. D. (1985). Rates of forgetting in Alzheimer-type dementia and Korsakoff's syndrome. *Neuropsychologia, 23,* 623-638.

Kopelman, M. D. (1989). Remote and autobiographical memory, temporal context memory, and frontal atrophy in Korsakoff and Alzheimer patients. *Neuropsychologia, 27,* 437-460.

Landauer, T. K., & Bjork, R. A. (1978). Optimal rehearsal patterns and name learning. In M. Gruneberg, P. Morris, & R. Snykes (Eds.), *Practical aspects of memory.* London: Academic Press.

Light, L. L. (1991). Memory and aging: Four hypotheses in search of data. *Annual Review of Psychology, 42,* 333-376.

Lipinska, B., Bäckman, L., & Herlitz, A. (in press) When Greta Garbo is easier to remember than Stefan Edberg: Influences of prior knowledge on recognition memory in Alzheimer's disease. *Psychology and Aging.*

Lipinska, B., Bäckman, L., Mäntylä, T., & Viitanen, M. (1992). *Effectiveness of self-generated cues in normal aging and Alzheimer's disease.* Unpublished manuscript.

Martin, A. (1987). Representation of semantic and spatial knowledge in Alzheimer's patients: Implications for models of preserved learning in amnesia. *Journal of Clinical and Experimental Neuropsychology, 9,* 191-224.

Martin, A., Brouwers, P., Cox, C., & Fedio, P. (1985). On the nature of the verbal memory deficit in Alzheimer's disease. *Brain and Language, 25,* 323-341.

McFarland, C. E., Jr., Warren, L. R., & Crockard, J. (1985). Memory for self-generated stimuli in young and old adults. *Journal of Gerontology, 40,* 205-207.

McKitrick, L. A. & Camp, C. J. (1989, August). *Name and location learning in SDAT with spaced-retrieval.* Paper presented at the annual convention of the American Psychological Association, New Orleans, LA.

Mitchell, D. B., Hunt, R. R., & Schmitt, F. A. (1986). The generation effect and reality monitoring: Evidence from dementia and normal aging. *Journal of Gerontology, 41,* 79-84.

Moffat, N. J. (1989). Home-based cognitive rehabilitation with the elderly. In L. W. Poon, D. C. Rubin, & B. A. Wilson (Eds.), *Everyday cognition in adulthood and late life.* New York: Cambridge University Press.

Moscovitch, M., Winocur, G., & McLahlan, D. (1986). Memory as assessed by recognition and reading time in normal and memory impaired people with Alzheimer's disease and other neurological disorders. *Journal of Experimental Psychology: General, 115*, 331-347.

Ober, B. A., & Shenaut, G. K. (1988). Lexical decision and priming in Alzheimer's disease. *Neuropsychologia, 26*, 273-286.

Poon, L. W., Walsh-Sweeney, L., & Fozard, J. L. (1980). Memory skill training for the elderly: Salient issues on the use of imagery mnemonics. In L.W. Poon, J. L. Fozard, L. S. Cermark, D. Arenberg, & L.W. Thompson (Eds.), *New directions in memory and aging.* Hillsdale, NJ: Erlbaum.

Quayhagen, M. P., & Quayhagen, M. (1989). Differential effects of family-based strategies on Alzheimer's disease. *The Gerontologist, 29*, 150-155.

Ribot, K. T. (1882). *Diseases in memory.* New York: Appleton.

Rissenberg, M., & Glanzer, M. (1986). Picture superiority in free recall: The effects of normal aging and primary degenerative dementia. *Journal of Gerontology, 41*, 64-71.

Rissenberg, M., & Glanzer, M. (1987). Free recall and word finding ability in normal aging and senile dementia of the Alzheimer's type: The effect of item concreteness. *Journal of Gerontology, 42*, 318-322.

Roberts, P. (1983). Memory strategy instructions with the elderly: What should memory training be the training of? In M. Pressley & J. E. Levin (Eds.), *Cognitive strategy research: Psychological foundations.* New York: Springer.

Sagar, H. J., Cohen, N. J., Corkin, S., & Growdon, J. H. (1985). Dissociations among processes in remote memory. *Annals of the New York Academy of Sciences, 444*, 533-535.

Sagar, H. J., Cohen, N. J., Sullivan, E. V., Corkin, S., & Growdon, J. H. (1988). Remote memory function in Alzheimer's disease and Parkinson's disease. *Brain, 111*, 185-206.

Shimamura, A. P., Salmon, D. P., Squire, L. R., & Butters, N. (1987). Memory dysfunction and word priming in dementia and amnesia. *Behavioral Neuroscience, 101*, 347-351.

Slamecka, N. J., & Graf, P. (1978). The generation effect: Delineation of a phenomenon. *Journal of Experimental Psychology: Human Learning and Memory, 4*, 592-604.

Spayd, C. S., & Smyer, M. A. (1988). Interventions with agitated, disoriented, or depressed residents. In M. A. Smyer, M. D. Cohn, & D. Brannon (Eds.), *Mental health consultation in nursing homes.* New York: New York University Press.

Stevens, A. B., & Camp, C. J. (1990). Spaced-retrieval: A memory intervention for dementia of the Alzheimer's type (DAT). *Clinical Gerontologist, 10*, 58-61.

Weingartner, H., Kaye, W., Smallberg, S. A., Cohen, R., Ebert, M. H., Gillin, J. C., & Gold, P. (1982). Determinants of memory failures in dementia. In S. Corkin, K. L. Davies, J. H. Growdon, E. Usdin, & R. J. Wurtman (Eds.), *Alzheimer's disease: A report of progress.* New York: Raven Press.

Weingartner, H., Kaye, W., Smallberg, S. A., Ebert, M. H., Gillin, J. C., & Sitaram, N. (1981). Memory failures in progressive idiopathic dementia. *Journal of Abnormal Psychology, 80*, 187-196.

Wilson, B. A. (1989). Designing memory-therapy programs. In L.W. Poon, D. C. Rubin, & B. A. Wilson (Eds.), *Everyday cognition in adulthood and late life.* New York: Cambridge University Press.

Wilson, R. S., Bacon, L. D., Kramer, R. L., Fox, J. H., & Kaszniak, A. W. (1983). Word frequency effect and recognition memory in dementia of the Alzheimer type. *Journal of Clinical Neuropsychology, 5*, 97-104.

Wilson, R. S., Kaszniak, A. W., Bacon, L. D., Fox, J. H., & Kelly, M. P. (1982). Facial recognition memory in dementia. *Cortex, 18*, 329-336.

Wilson, R. S., Kaszniak, A. W., & Fox, J. H. (1981). Remote memory in senile dementia. *Cortex, 17*, 41-48.

Yesavage, J. A. (1982). Degree of dementia and improvement with memory training. *Clinical Gerontologist, 1*, 77-81.

Yesavage, J. A., Lapp, D., & Sheikh, J. I. (1989). Mnemonics as modified for use by the elderly. In L. W. Poon, D. C. Rubin, & B. A. Wilson (Eds.), *Everyday cognition in adulthood and late life.* New York: Cambridge University Press.

Yesavage, J. A., Westphal, J., & Rush, L. (1981). Senile dementia: Combined pharmacologic and psychologic treatment. *Journal of the American Geriatrics Society, 29*, 164-171.

Zarit, S. H., Zarit, J. M., & Reever, K. E. (1982). Memory training for severe memory loss: Effects on senile dementia patients and their families. *The Gerontologist, 4*, 373-377.

Section II

NON-EPISODIC FORMS OF MEMORY IN ALZHEIMER'S DISEASE

Memory Functioning in Dementia – L. Bäckman (Editor)
© 1992 Elsevier Science Publishers B.V. All rights reserved.

5   Semantic Memory, Priming, and Skill Learning in Alzheimer's Disease

David P. Salmon, William C. Heindel, and Nelson Butters

San Diego School of Medicine

Introduction

The preponderance of our knowledge about the memory dysfunction associated with Alzheimer's disease (AD) emanates from studies which explicitly assess the ability of these patients to learn and retain new information (i.e., episodic memory). Numerous investigations have shown that AD patients suffer profound deficits in episodic memory, and that such deficits are an early and ubiquitous feature of AD (for review see, Nebes, in press). Indeed, it is largely from these studies that memory impairment has been adopted as a defining characteristic of AD, and of dementia in general, in current diagnostic schemes (e.g., DSM III-R).

In addition to this long-standing interest in the episodic memory impairment of AD, the status of other forms of memory in this disorder has recently become the focus of research attention. For example, a number of investigations have examined the structure and organization of semantic memory in patients with AD. As defined by Tulving (1983), semantic memory comprises general knowledge, rules, and procedures which are highly overlearned and essentially context free. It includes such information as knowledge of the alphabet, rules of arithmetic, and the words that make up one's vocabulary. Semantic memory is distinct from episodic memory which consists of information for events and episodes that remain tightly linked to the temporal and spatial context in which they were originally acquired.

Semantic and episodic memory also differ in that the two forms of memory are differentially affected in patients with circumscribed amnesia. Amnesic patients are especially impaired in their attempts to acquire new episodic information (i.e., anterograde amnesia), while their semantic memory appears to be relatively intact. Although unable to remember a short list of words or a name and address for more than a few minutes, amnesic patients retain knowledge of arithmetical, geographic, and historical facts, and are able to name objects, orally generate exemplars from semantic categories and use rules of syntax and grammar in a normal fashion. This dissociation indicates that semantic memory is not dependent upon the same medial temporal (e.g., hippocampus) or diencephalic brain structures which are damaged in amnesic patients and thought to underlie their episodic memory deficits (Cermak, 1984; Squire, 1987). Rather, semantic memory may be critically dependent upon neocortical association areas which are presumed to store semantic representations. Thus, recent studies of semantic memory in patients with the more extensive cortical damage associated with AD are of particular theoretical and empirical interest.

In the majority of studies of episodic and semantic memory in AD patients, retention of information has been explicitly assessed. That is, the patient was told to consciously attempt to learn and retain some bit of new information (i.e., episodic memory), or was told to try to recall some bit of information from a long-standing preexisting store (i.e., semantic memory). Recently, however, a number of studies have focused upon AD patients' implicit memory abilities. Implicit memory refers to information that does not require conscious recollection; rather, it is knowledge that is expressed indirectly through the performance of the specific operations comprising a task (Graf & Schacter, 1985, 1987; Schacter, 1987). Implicit memory may be expressed through the unconscious facilitation of a subject's performance on some task due to prior exposure to stimulus materials (i.e., priming), or through improvement in performance on a particular motor or cognitive task with repeated practice (i.e., procedural learning).

As with episodic and semantic memory, explicit and implicit memory are differentially affected in patients with circumscribed amnesia (Squire, 1987). Although patients with amnesia exhibit severe deficits in explicit memory, these same patients demonstrate preserved implicit memory. For example, amnesic patients who are profoundly impaired on recall or recognition memory tests retain the ability to benefit from the prior presentation of information on priming tasks (Cermak, Talbot, Chandler, & Wolbarst, 1985; Gardner, Boller, Moreines, & Butters, 1973; Graf, Squire, & Mandler, 1984; Shimamura, 1986; Shimamura & Squire, 1984; Warrington & Weiskrantz, 1968, 1970). Similarly, amnesic patients demonstrate normal learning and retention of new visuomotor and cognitive based skills (Brooks & Baddeley, 1976; Cermak, Lewis, Butters, & Goodglass, 1973; Cohen & Squire, 1980; Corkin, 1968), despite being unable to remember any of the learning episodes or the specific stimuli used in these tasks. These demonstrations of preserved implicit memory in even profoundly amnesic patients provided the impetus for studying this form of memory in AD patients. How the extensive cognitive and neurological deficits of AD affect these potentially preserved memory processes has been examined in recent investigations.

The present chapter will describe some of the recent research concerning non-episodic forms of memory in patients with AD, and discuss the implications of this research for our understanding of the organization of memory in the brain. Specifically, the first part of the chapter will review several studies which examine the effect of AD on the structure and organization of semantic memory. This will be followed by a discussion of long-term (i.e., over the course of minutes) priming in AD patients, and an examination of a possible relationship between these patients' priming and semantic memory abilities. The subsequent section will describe a number of possible mechanisms underlying the priming performance of AD patients. Finally, studies examining the ability of AD patients to acquire and retain motor and cognitive skills (i.e., procedural memory) will be briefly reviewed.

Semantic Memory

While deficits in explicit memory are a hallmark of AD that have been described in great detail (e.g., Nebes, in press), a number of studies have demonstrated that these patients also have impaired semantic memory (for review, see Nebes, 1989). One line of evidence of semantic memory impairment in AD patients is provided in studies which require these patients to orally generate words that are members of restricted phonemic or semantic categories. In one such study, Butters and his colleagues (Butters, Granholm, Salmon, Grant, & Wolfe, 1987) examined the verbal fluency of AD, Huntington's disease (HD), and amnesic alcoholic Korsakoff (AK) patients using both letter (i.e., F, A, and S) and category (i.e., animals) fluency tasks. In these tasks, subjects orally generated for one minute words beginning with a particular letter or exemplars from a particular semantic category. Although the subjects in the various patient groups were matched for overall severity of dementia with the Dementia Rating Scale (DRS) (Mattis, 1976), the performance of the early AD patient group on the fluency tests was distinguishable from those of the other two patient groups. The HD and AK patients demonstrated severe and moderate deficits, respectively, on both fluency tasks, presumably due to a general retrieval deficit produced by the frontal lobe dysfunction inherent in these neurologic disorders. In contrast, the early AD patients were impaired *only* on the category fluency task. The disproportionately severe fluency impairment exhibited by AD patients when generating exemplars from a specific semantic category (e.g., animals) as compared to generating words that begin with a particular letter is most likely a reflection of the different demands the two tasks place upon the organization of the semantic network. Whereas the letter fluency task can be performed using phonemic cues to search a very extensive set of appropriate exemplars, category fluency requires the generation of words from a much smaller set of exemplars within a single abstract semantic category. Successful performance on the category fluency tasks requires the individual to know the attributes that define the category and to be able to use this knowledge to locate specific category exemplars.

In related studies, Martin and Fedio (1983) and Tröster and his colleagues (Tröster, Salmon, McCullough, & Butters, 1989) examined the types of responses produced by AD patients on a semantically-based category fluency task from the DRS in which subjects must orally generate items that can be found in a supermarket. Both of these studies demonstrated that AD patients generated significantly fewer specific items (e.g., carrot) per superordinate category (e.g., vegetables) than did normal control subjects, as well as a larger ratio of superordinate category names to total words produced. These findings seem to reflect a disruption in the organization of semantic memory that is characterized by an initial loss of the most specific attributes of a semantic category with relative preservation of more general superordinate knowledge. If the semantic representations of objects and categories are viewed as being organized in a hierarchical fashion with the most general aspects at the top and more specific features at the bottom, then AD patients demonstrate a progressive "bottom-up" breakdown in the hierarchical organization of semantic knowledge and memory (Chertkow & Bub, 1990; Martin, 1987; Martin & Fedio, 1983; Tröster et al., 1989).

Further evidence of impaired semantic memory in AD patients is provided by numerous demonstrations of these patients' deficits on tests of object naming (for review, see Hart, 1988). Patients with AD are much more likely than normal control subjects or patients with other dementing disorders to produce superordinate and within category associative errors on confrontation naming tasks (Bayles & Tomoeda, 1983; Huff, Corkin, & Growdon, 1986; Smith, Murdoch, & Chenery, 1989; Hodges, Salmon, & Butters, in press). For example, Hodges and his colleagues recently compared the performance of AD, HD and normal control (NC) subjects on a modified version of the Boston Naming Test, and performed a comprehensive classification of error types produced on the test. The results of this detailed analysis revealed that NC subjects made predominantly semantic-category and circumlocutory errors. Patients with HD differed from NC subjects only in that they produced a significantly greater proportion of visually based errors. The AD patients, on the other hand, made a significantly greater proportion of semantically-based errors (i.e., semantic-superordinate and semantic-associative errors) than did the NC and HD subjects, even though the AD and HD patients were matched for overall naming ability. These results suggest that naming deficits in Huntington's disease initially involve primarily a disruption of perceptual analysis, whereas in AD such naming impairments reflect a breakdown in semantic processes. The increased prevalence of semantic-superordinate errors in the naming performance of AD patients is consistent with a "bottom-up" breakdown in their semantic knowledge.

Whether the semantic memory deficit of AD patients is the result of impaired access to relatively intact semantic memory, or due to an actual loss of semantic knowledge, remains an important theoretical issue. To address this question, two recent studies have evaluated the nature of the semantic memory impairment in AD patients in light of the criteria developed by Warrington and

Shallice (1979; Shallice, 1987) to distinguish between semantic storage and semantic access disorders. The Warrington and Shallice criteria assume that if a particular item has been permanently lost from semantic memory, then a patient should: (1) demonstrate consistent failure in accessing that item across different tests and test sessions; (2) demonstrate a loss of detailed knowledge along with relatively preserved superordinate knowledge about the item; (3) derive no benefit from semantic cueing in accessing that item.

In the first study to directly assess this notion, Chertkow and Bub (1990) administered picture-naming and word-to-picture matching tests to AD patients who had been carefully screened to ensure that they had no visual perceptual deficits. Each test was composed of the same 150 pictorial stimuli. On the naming task, the AD patients were shown each stimulus and asked to simply name the item pictured. On the matching task, subjects were shown each target stimulus with four distractor pictures from the same semantic category, and asked to point to the picture that corresponded to the verbal label. Patients with AD were markedly impaired on the naming task relative to control subjects, correctly naming only 72% of the pictures. Semantic cueing provided very little benefit on the naming test with only 13% of the unnamed pictures correctly identified after presentation of a semantic cue. A similar marked impairment in the AD patients was observed on the matching task, and a remarkable consistency was shown between the items correctly completed or failed on the naming and matching tasks. That is, 85% of the items correctly identified on the matching test were also correctly identified on the naming task, whereas only 21% of the items incorrectly identified on the matching test were named correctly.

When the same picture naming task was readministered to the AD patients approximately one month later, 92% of the items that were initially missed were again failed. In addition, AD patients were found to be significantly impaired in their ability to answer probe questions concerning perceptual, functional, and contextual aspects of items from the naming task, but had no difficulty identifying superordinate category membership. Such sparing of superordinate information about items misnamed on confrontation naming testing has also been noted by other investigators (Huff et al., 1986; Hodges et al., in press).

Chertkow and Bub (1990) also asked AD patients to generate as many exemplars as possible from the same eight semantic categories used in the picture naming test. Subjects were allowed to generate items for sixty sec for each category. As expected, AD patients generated significantly fewer words than did normal control subjects in all eight categories. Furthermore, fewer than 7% of all the items generated on this task were items that the patients had previously been unable to name. The remarkable consistency in the particular items failed across the naming, matching and fluency tasks strongly indicated that there is an actual loss of semantic knowledge in AD rather than a deficiency in accessing semantic information.

Further evidence for a true loss of semantic knowledge in AD is provided in a recent study by Hodges and his colleagues (Hodges, Salmon, & Butters, 1991). These investigators evaluated semantic memory in a group of 22 AD patients using a battery of tests designed to probe for knowledge of a particular item across different modes of access. The various tests in the battery all employed the same 48 stimulus items which were exemplars from three categories of living items (i.e., land animals, birds, and water creatures) and three categories of non-living items (i.e., household items, vehicles, and musical instruments). Knowledge of the items was first assessed with fluency tasks in which subjects were asked to generate as many exemplars as possible from each of the six semantic categories. Subjects were given sixty sec to generate exemplars from each category. A confrontational naming test employing the 48 items was administered next. The naming task was followed by a sorting task which was designed to test superordinate and subordinate knowledge about each item in a non-verbal fashion. Subjects first sorted all 48 items at the highest superordinate level (i.e., living versus non-living), then at an intermediate superordinate level in the living (i.e., land animals vs. water animals vs. birds) and non-living domains (i.e., household items vs. vehicles vs. musical instruments), and finally at a subordinate level (e.g., land animals sorted on the basis of size vs. habitat vs. fierceness). Following the sorting task, subjects were administered a word-to-picture matching test in which they were asked to point to the picture of the item named by the examiner from an array of six exemplars from the same category (e.g., land animals). Finally, a vocabulary task was administered in which patients were asked to define words which were a subset of the items used in the previous semantic memory tests.

The results of Hodges et al.'s study indicated that the AD patients were impaired relative to normal control subjects on all measures of semantic memory. Furthermore, the AD patients demonstrated a disproportionately severe deficit when knowledge of subordinate information was tested on the fluency, sorting, and vocabulary tasks. This pattern of relatively preserved superordinate knowledge on the sorting and vocabulary tests, in conjunction with the disproportionate reduction in the generation of exemplars from lower order categories, suggests a loss of semantic knowledge in AD patients, rather than a disorder of semantic access. This conclusion is strengthened by the analysis of item-to-item correspondence in errors produced on a number of tests used in this study. The AD patients showed a significant correspondence between the items they were unable to name and those that were missed on the word-to-picture matching task. There was similar correspondence in errors between the naming and sorting, and between the naming and vocabulary tests. Also, items that were not named correctly on the naming test were very rarely produced spontaneously on the verbal fluency tasks using the same semantic categories. The striking correspondence in items missed across tasks designed to access semantic knowledge through different modes of input and output in this and other studies (Chertkow & Bub, 1990; Huff, Mack, Mahlmann, & Greenberg, 1988) offers compelling evidence of actual semantic memory loss in AD. It should be noted, however, that evidence for a true loss of semantic knowledge in AD patients has not been found by some investigators (Abeysinghe, Bayles, & Trosset, 1990; Bayles, Tomoeda, Kaszniak, & Trosset, in press), and that the nature of the semantic memory impairment in Alzheimer's disease remains an important area for future research.

Implicit Memory: Priming

Another form of memory that has been recently investigated in patients with AD is priming. Priming refers to the unconscious facilitation of a subject's performance on some task simply through prior exposure to the stimulus materials used in the task. The dissociation of this form of implicit memory from traditional explicit memory is demonstrated by its preservation in profoundly amnesic patients. For example, in a study by Graf and colleagues (Graf et al., 1984), amnesic patients demonstrated as strong a tendency (relative to chance) as normal control subjects to complete three-letter word stems (e.g., *MOT*) with previously presented words (e.g., *MOTEL*), despite the amnesic patients' failure to recall or recognize these words on standard memory tests. Amnesic patients apparently treat the stem-completion task as a word puzzle and report that the words seem to "pop" into mind in response to the stems even though the words are not recognized as familiar.

Two recent studies (Shimamura, Salmon, Squire, & Butters, 1987; Salmon, Shimamura, Butters, & Smith, 1988) compared the lexical priming performance of patients with AD, HD and AK, as well as normal control subjects, on the word-stem completion task previously used by Graf et al. (1984). Subjects were first exposed to a list of 10 target words (e.g., MOTEL, ABSTAIN) and asked to rate each word in terms of its "likability." Following two presentations and ratings of the entire list, the subjects were shown three-letter stems (e.g., MOT, ABS) of words that were and were not on the presentation list and asked to complete the stems with the "first word that comes to mind." Half of the stems could be completed with previously presented words, while the other half were used to assess baseline guessing rates. Other lists of words were used to assess the subjects' ability at free recall and recognition.

Although all three patient groups were severely and equally impaired on free recall and recognition of presented words, the AK and HD patients exhibited intact stem-completion priming. In comparison to the AK and HD patients, the AD patients showed little or no tendency to complete the word stems with previously presented words. That is, for the AD patients the presentation-rating procedure failed to generate the transient memory traces needed for this form of implicit memory. Similar deficits in the stem-completion priming performance of AD patients have been reported by Keane and colleagues (Keane, Gabrieli, Fennema, Growdon, & Corkin, 1991) and by Randolph (1991).

Salmon and his colleagues (Salmon et al., 1988) also compared the priming performance of AD, HD, and intact control subjects on a semantic priming test which employed a paired-associate procedure. In this task, subjects were first asked to judge categorically or functionally related word pairs (e.g., BIRD-ROBIN, NEEDLE-THREAD) and later to "free-associate" to the first words of the previously presented pairs and to words that were not presented as part of the paired-associates. The results with this priming task showed that AD patients were significantly less likely to produce the second word of the semantically-related pair than were the other two subject groups. In fact, the priming score for the AD patients did not differ from baseline guessing rates.

A similar free-association procedure was used by Brandt, Spencer, McSorley, and Folstein (1988) to assess verbal priming in AD patients. These investigators first read a list of 10 stimulus words to AD and NC subjects. After a short delay, an unrelated free-association task was administered in which the subject was asked say a word in response to a probe word read by the experimenter. For half of the probe words, a previously presented stimulus word was the third most common associate according to normative data. The other half of the probe words were not associated with any of the 10 stimulus words. Priming of the stimulus words was demonstrated in the NC subjects by their increased tendency to produce the previously presented stimulus words as the primary associate in the free-association task. Patients with AD also showed a slightly increased tendency to produce the previously presented words, but this priming was impaired relative to that of the NC subjects.

The priming impairment exhibited by AD patients appears not to be limited to the verbal domain. Heindel and his colleagues (Heindel, Salmon, & Butters, 1990) used a picture fragment test to compare the priming and cued recall performances of AD and HD patients, and intact control subjects. On this pictorial priming task, subjects were asked to say "the first thing you think of" when shown incompletely drawn pictures. Half of the pictures had been shown to the subject in an unrelated naming task, and half were novel pictures. The NC and HD subjects demonstrated priming through their increased ability to identify fragmented versions of previously seen pictures relative to novel pictures. Patients with AD were impaired relative to both the HD and NC subject groups on this pictorial priming task.

The studies of priming in AD patients described above were among the first to demonstrate significant deficiencies in long-term priming in any neurologically impaired patient group, and suggest that priming may be mediated by neural substrates that are selectively disrupted in AD. Since AD patients, and not HD or amnesic patients, evidence marked pathology in temporal, parietal and frontal association cortices (Brun, 1983; Terry & Katzman, 1983), impaired priming may be the result of damage to those neocortical association areas which are presumed to store the representations of semantic memory. This cortical damage in AD patients may result in a breakdown in the organization of semantic knowledge that is necessary to support priming. That is, the hierarchical associative network underlying semantic knowledge may have deteriorated sufficiently in the AD patients to greatly limit the capacity of available cues to activate traces of previously presented stimuli. For example, the cue "bird" may not evoke an unconscious activation of the categorical associate "robin" on the semantic priming task because the association between the two words has been greatly weakened. Similarly, the association in semantic memory between the word stem MOT and the word MOTEL on the lexical priming task may have been sufficiently disrupted to negate the facilitating effect of the word's presentation. The impaired performance of AD patients on the pictorial priming task can also be interpreted in terms of a disruption of semantic memory if, as some investigators (Anderson & Bower, 1974; Nelson, Reed, & McEvoy, 1977) have proposed, pictures and words both access a common semantic memory store.

Priming and Semantic Memory

If the priming deficits described above reflect a deterioration in the structure of semantic knowledge, then a relationship should exist between performance on these tests of priming and performance on traditional measures of semantic knowledge (e.g., object naming, verbal fluency). Only a weak relationship, at best, should exist between priming performance and performance on tests assessing other "non-semantic" neuropsychological processes (e.g., tests of episodic memory, attention). To address this issue, stem-completion and paired-associate priming scores of 30 mildly to moderately demented AD patients were compared with their scores on traditional neuropsychological tests of episodic and semantic memory, language, attention, and visuospatial processes (Salmon, Heindel and Butters, in preparation). Correlational analyses revealed that the stem-completion priming score was not significantly related to any other neuropsychological measure, including scores on tests of semantic memory (e.g., Boston Naming Test, Number Information Test, Letter and Category Fluency Tests, Vocabulary Subtest from the Wechsler Adult Intelligence Scale). To further examine the relationship among these variables, the priming scores and the scores on these other neuropsychological tests were subjected to a principal components factor analysis with varimax rotation. Five factors emerged from this analysis: A semantic knowledge factor, an attention/memory factor, a general dementia factor, a memory factor, and a priming factor. The priming score loaded heavily only on the priming factor (and notably not on the semantic knowledge factor). Similar results were obtained in correlational and principal components factor analyses of paired-associate priming scores and other neuropsychological test scores.

The results of these factor analyses cast doubt upon the notion that the priming deficit of AD patients is mediated by the disruption of their semantic memory. Indeed, other investigators have noted that AD patients exhibit normal priming under some conditions, and that their semantic memory deficit is apparent only on "effortful" (e.g., free recall, recognition) memory tasks. In a study by Nebes and colleagues (Nebes, Martin, & Horn, 1984), a given word was preceded (by approximately 500 msec) either by a semantically related word (primed trials) or by an unrelated word (unprimed trials), and priming was measured by the difference in naming latencies between primed and unprimed trials. The results of this study showed that both the AD patients and control subjects had a slight and equivalent facilitation in naming latency when a word was preceded by a semantic associate (i.e., semantic priming). Based on these data, Nebes et al. concluded that AD patients' semantic memory is normal when it is assessed with techniques which rely solely upon automatic information processing. Nebes (1989) has reviewed additional evidence supporting his conclusion about AD patients' semantic processing problems.

Possible Mechanisms Underlying the Priming Deficit of AD Patients

The results of the study by Nebes et al. (1984), in conjunction with the failure to find a significant relationship between the AD patient's stem-completion and paired-associate priming deficits and their impairment on traditional tests of semantic memory, suggests that the deficits in long-term priming exhibited by AD patients may be due to, or at least influenced by, some factor other than the breakdown of semantic memory. One possible alternative explanation may be that AD patients fail to process the target words at a semantic level during the initial orienting phase of the long-term priming task. To examine this alternative, Grosse, Wilson, and Fox (1990) administered a stem-completion priming task to AD patients in which the encoding demands were increased at the time of initial word presentation.

These investigators employed a sentence frame task for stimulus presentation. In this presentation format subjects were required to complete sentence frames (e.g., "He hit the nail with a ____.") with the single best fit word (e.g., "hammer"). In the test phase, three letter word stems of the best fit words and distractor words were presented in a stem-completion task. The authors proposed that this sentence completion task more effectively ensures that target stimuli are fully and elaboratively processed at a semantic level than in the "likability-judgment" or naming tasks used in previous studies. On the stem-completion task, AD patients correctly completed 36% of targets that they had accessed during the stimulus presentation task, while correctly completing only 18% of the distractor items (baseline performance). Similarly, the NC subjects correctly completed 34% of targets during the stem-completion task, and 20% of the distractor items. Thus, there was no significant difference between the groups in stem-completion priming. However, the degree of priming exhibited by the control subjects in this study is considerably less than that observed in other studies that have used the stem-completion procedure. In Grosse et al.'s study the NC and AD subjects' priming was only 14% and 18% above baseline completion levels, respectively. While the level of priming exhibited by the AD patients is comparable to the 16% increase above baseline noted by Heindel, Salmon, Shults, Walicke, and Butters (1989), and similar to the increases reported by Shimamura et al. (1987) and Salmon et al. (1988), the 14% increase for NC subjects is far below the 40% to 50% increase for NC subjects reported in other studies of stem-completion priming (Graf et al., 1984; Heindel et al., 1989; Shimamura et al., 1987; Salmon et al., 1988). Thus, rather than improving the stem-completion performance of AD patients, the elaborative encoding procedure employed by Grosse et al. appears to have reduced the priming of NC subjects to an impaired level.

Partridge and colleagues (Partridge, Knight, & Feehan, 1990) also recently examined this alternative explanation by changing the nature of the orienting task in the stem-completion paradigm to a task which would increase the likelihood of semantic processing of the target words. Rather than judging the likability of the target words during the presentation phase of the task (as in the studies by Shimamura et al. and Salmon et al.), AD patients were required to supply the meaning of each word, thus ensuring that the semantic properties of the words had been analyzed. With this procedure, Partridge et al. observed normal levels of stem-completion priming in AD patients. Unfortunately, the 'likability judgment' and 'semantic processing' orienting tasks were not directly compared in this study, so alternative explanations for the differences in Partridge et al.'s results and those of Shimamura et al. (1987) and Salmon et al. (1988) (e.g., subject differences) can not be ruled out.

Another possible mechanism underlying the priming deficit of AD patients is a generalized disturbance in attention, arousal, or activation which could lead to an inability to activate an otherwise intact representation in semantic memory to a level that would be sufficient to support long-term priming. Traces may still be sufficiently activated, however, to manifest intact priming over the very short (e.g., 500 msec) delay intervals used in the Nebes et al. (1984) paradigm. The demonstration that priming performance improves in AD patients as the semantic processing demands at time of encoding are increased does not completely rule out this possibility, since the amount of attentional resources allocated to the task most likely increase as well. Indeed, Partridge et al. (1990) pointed out that one major difference between their "definition" orientation task and the "liking" orientation task used by Salmon et al. (1988) is the level of attentional processing required.

Although not as extensively studied as other cognitive functions, attentional disturbances appear to be relatively common in patients with AD. Cossa, Della Sala, and Spinnler (1989), employing an automated visual search task, found that normal control subjects improved their performance when cues were available to direct attention (either actively or passively), whereas AD patients did not. Nebes and Brady (1989) found that AD patients showed greater difficulty distributing attention across increasingly larger arrays of stimuli than did normal controls, although their focused attention ability appeared relatively intact. Grady et al. (1989), using a dichotic listening task, also found divided attention impairments in AD patients that could not be attributed to a perceptual processing deficit. Finally, Freed, Corkin, Growdon, and Nissen (1989) found that a subgroup of AD patients demonstrated anomalous performance on a task involving the covert orientation of visual attention.

Freed et al. (1989) also suggested that the selective attention impairments seen in some AD patients may be the behavioral manifestation of noradrenergic deficits resulting from damage to the locus coeruleus (LC). LC neuropathology has been observed in a subset of AD patients at autopsy (Mann, Yates, & Marcyniuk, 1986; Marcyniuk, Mann, & Yates, 1986; Tomlinson, Irving, & Blessed, 1981; Zweig et al., 1988), and both animal and human studies have implicated noradrenaline in selective attention processes (Clark, Geffen, & Geffen, 1989; Sara, 1985a, 1985b). In a review of the literature, Posner and Petersen (1990) concluded that the noradrenergic system is primarily concerned with maintaining vigilance and alertness, and provides critical support for the involvement of the posterior parietal system in visual orientation and selective attention. Sara (1985a) has similarly suggested that the LC modulates selective attention by enhancing "cortical tonus," and therefore increasing the signal-to-noise ratio of cortical information processing. In this view, noradrenergic deficits in AD patients could lead to an inability to activate an otherwise intact representation in semantic memory at a level that would be sufficient to support priming.

Despite the evidence reviewed above, it is still possible that the verbal priming deficits of AD patients are strongly related to their deficits in semantic memory, but that this relationship is overshadowed by the variability contributed by some other cognitive process involved in performing the priming tasks. Several investigators (e.g., Keane et al., 1991; Tulving & Schacter, 1990) have suggested that most priming tasks involve both a semantic and a pre-semantic perceptual processing component, but that the relative contribution of each component varies across tasks. Because of their verbal nature, the stem-completion and paired-associate priming tasks appear to be more heavily weighted towards the semantic than the perceptual processing component. Although control subjects are able to perform these tasks using their intact semantic memory system, AD patients may be forced to rely upon their relatively preserved perceptual abilities since their semantic system is impaired. For the AD patient, the relative contribution of perceptual processes to stem-completion priming may be greater than that of semantic processes. Thus, the AD patients' verbal priming deficit may still be fundamentally due to their semantic memory impairment, but the variability that is seen in these patients' residual priming performance is now related more to their perceptual than to their semantic abilities.

This interpretation of the AD patients' stem-completion and paired-associate priming deficits, and the lack of correlation between these deficits and semantic memory dysfunction, is dependent upon a relative preservation of pre-semantic perceptual priming ability in these patients. Initial evidence for preserved perceptual priming in AD patients was provided by Moscovitch,

Winocur, and McLahlan (1986) who found normal repetition effects on AD patients' speed of reading geometrically transformed script. Further evidence in support of this notion is found in a recent study by Keane and her colleagues (Keane et al., 1991) which examined both stem-completion and perceptual priming in the same AD patients. In the perceptual priming task, subjects were required to identify briefly presented words, half of which had been presented previously in an unrelated reading task. Priming was reflected in the shorter exposure time necessary to identify previously presented words relative to words not previously seen. The stem-completion task was similar to that employed by Shimamura et al. (1987). Consistent with previous reports, Keane et al. found impaired stem-completion priming in AD patients. Despite this deficit, these same patients demonstrated preserved perceptual priming ability.

Implicit Memory: Skill Learning

In contrast to the lexical and semantic priming deficits exhibited by patients with AD, the ability to acquire and retain motor and cognitive based skills (i.e., procedural learning) appears to be preserved in these patients. Eslinger and Damasio (1986) demonstrated that AD patients were able to acquire the motor skills underlying a pursuit rotor task as easily as were age-matched normal control subjects. In this task, subjects learned to maintain contact between a hand-held stylus and a rotating metallic disk.

Heindel and his colleagues (Heindel, Butters, & Salmon, 1988) also examined the ability of AD patients to learn the pursuit rotor task, and compared their performance to those of patients with HD and circumscribed amnesia, as well as to normal control subjects. The pursuit rotor task was chosen for this comparison because it has the advantage that initial levels of performance can be equated by manipulating the difficulty (i.e., speed of rotation of the disk) of the task. Equating initial performance ensures that group differences in skill acquisition cannot be attributed to ceiling or floor effects. As Eslinger and Damasio (1986) found, patients with AD evidenced rapid and extensive motor learning over practice sessions that was equivalent to the learning exhibited by amnesic patients and normal control subjects. The HD patients, in contrast, were impaired in learning this motor skill, which suggests that this form of implicit memory may be mediated by a corticostriatal system that is severely compromised in HD (Bruyn, Bots, & Dom, 1979). As suggested by Heindel et al., the neostriatal damage suffered by HD patients may lead to a deficiency in developing the motor programs that are necessary to perform the pursuit rotor task. In learning a motor skill, appropriate movements comprising the target skill must be combined in a correct temporal sequence (i.e., a motor program). In the early stages of learning a motor skill, an elementary closed-loop negative feedback system is employed in which new motor commands are generated in direct response to visually perceived errors. As motor programs are acquired and modified through practice, a sequence of movements can be organized in advance of their performance (rather than simply responding to errors) and smooth, coordinated motor performance ensues. Since the neostriatal damage in the HD patients precludes their developing motor programs, these patients may demonstrate some improvement in the early stages of motor skill acquisition by relying upon their error-correction mode of performance. However, their inability to generate new motor programs would prevent them from adopting the more effective predictive mode of performance utilized by AD patients, amnesics and normal control subjects.

Another form of procedural memory that is preserved in patients with circumscribed amnesia is classical adaptation-level effects observed in a weight judgment task (Benzig & Squire, 1990). This form of perceptual biasing was recently examined in patients with dementia (Heindel, Salmon, & Butters, 1991). In this weight judgment task, AD and HD subjects were first exposed to either a relatively heavy (heavy bias) or a relatively light (light bias) set of weights, and were later asked to rate the heaviness of a standard set of 10 weights using a 9-point scale. Patients with AD and intact NC subjects both perceived the standard set of weights as heavier following the light bias trials and lighter following the heavy bias trials, despite the AD patients' poor explicit memory for the initial biasing session. In contrast, the weight judgments of the HD group was not significantly influenced by prior exposure to relatively heavy or light weights. These results are of particular interest since the weight biasing task may involve the modification of programmed movement parameters. A number of studies (for review, see Jones, 1986) have demonstrated that the perception of weight is normally mediated by centrally generated motor commands rather than by peripheral sensory information. The sensation of heaviness is then influenced by discrepancies between the intended, or programmed, force and the actual force needed to lift an object. Prior exposure to relatively heavy or light weights (i.e., the biasing trials) may result in an increase or decrease in the amount of force programmed for lifting weights, which would then lead to an illusory decrease or increase in the perceived heaviness of the standard set of weights. Thus, the impaired weight biasing performance of the HD patients, like their skill learning deficits shown with the pursuit rotor task, may be due to a motor programming deficit resulting from neostriatal dysfunction.

Procedural memory in demented patients has been further examined with a serial reaction procedure developed by Nissen and Bullemer (1987). The serial reaction time task is a four-choice procedure in which a subject must respond as quickly as possible to the illumination of one of four lights, each located immediately above a corresponding response key. During the first four blocks of trials, the stimuli are presented in a particular 10-item sequence that is repeated 10 times in each block. The stimuli are presented in a new random sequence during the fifth block of trials. Procedural learning is reflected in a reduction in response latency over the first four blocks of trials as the subject benefits from the sequence repetition. An increase in response time is anticipated on the fifth block of trials (i.e., the new random sequence) if the initial response time decline is due to learning of the stimulus sequence rather than to learning non-specific aspects of the task. Amnesic AK patients demonstrate a normal decline in response latency over the first four blocks of this task, and a normal increase in response latency during the random sequence trial (Nissen & Bullemer, 1987). The decline in response latency on the repeated sequence suggests that these amnesic patients learned and retained the sequence despite an inability to recall it explicitly.

Two recent studies have examined the performance of AD and HD patients on this serial reaction time task. In the first study (Knopman & Nissen, 1987), patients with AD were found to respond generally slower than NC subjects on this task, but demonstrated the same rate of decline in response latency over the blocks of trials with a repeating sequence, and a normal increase in response latency when a random sequence was presented. In contrast to the AD patients' normal procedural learning on this task, Knopman & Nissen (1990) found that HD patients were impaired. The HD patients demonstrated significantly less decline in response latency than age matched controls over the repeating sequence trials, and showed less increase in response latency than controls during the block of trials in which a new random stimulus sequence was presented.

The results of these studies of procedural learning and memory in AD, HD, and amnesic patients suggest that the ability to acquire motor and some cognitive based skills is not dependent upon the medial temporal, diencephalic or cortical association areas affected in AD or circumscribed amnesia. Rather, these abilities appear to be critically dependent upon the neostriatal structures damaged in Huntington's disease and perhaps other subcortically based dementing disorders (e.g., Parkinson's disease).

Furthermore, these studies of procedural memory, in conjunction with the studies of priming described previously, suggest that a dissociation may exist between AD and HD patients in their patterns of impaired and preserved implicit memory functions. Patients with AD are impaired on tests of long-term priming which are performed normally by HD patients. In contrast, HD patients are impaired on skill learning tasks which are easily mastered by AD patients. To directly examine this issue within a single investigation, Heindel and his colleagues (Heindel et al., 1989) compared the performance of patients with circumscribed amnesia, AD, HD, and Parkinson's disease (PD) on two forms of implicit memory, skill learning and verbal priming. Motor skill learning was assessed with the pursuit rotor task and long-term verbal priming was evaluated in the same patients with the stem-completion procedure used by Salmon et al. (1988). Although amnesics performed normally on both tasks, a double dissociation was observed between AD and HD patients on the two implicit memory tasks. The AD patients were severely impaired on verbal priming but showed normal acquisition of the pursuit rotor skill; the HD patients showed the opposite relationship. The performance of the PD patients was dependent upon whether they were demented or not. Demented PD patients were impaired on both implicit memory tasks whereas the nondemented PD patients were intact on both tests. For both the HD and PD patients, their impairments on the motor skill learning task correlated with their degree of dementia, not with the severity of their motor deficits (i.e., chorea, bradykinesia, rigidity, tremor).

The studies of implicit memory in demented and amnesic patients reviewed above have some important implications for the neurologic basis of memory systems which are usually preserved in amnesic patients. Although both verbal priming and motor skill learning remain unimpaired in amnesic patients, the double dissociation between HD and AD patients on the verbal priming and pursuit rotor tasks suggests that various forms of implicit memory depend upon different neuroanatomical substrates. While the HD patients' impairment on the pursuit rotor task is certainly consistent with the proposed association between the acquisition of motor skills and the neostriatum, the AD patients' deficiencies on verbal priming (and semantic memory in general) may be attributable to the neocortical damage associated with this disorder.

Conclusions

Even in the earliest stages of dementia, AD patients' exhibit deficiencies in semantic memory which are sufficiently severe as to result in marked failures on tests of category fluency and confrontation naming. Recent evidence suggests that the semantic memory deficit of AD may reflect a true loss of semantic knowledge in which representations of concepts are actually lost. Furthermore, this loss of semantic knowledge may proceed in "bottom-up" manner with specific features of a concept lost before its more general features. In addition, AD patients are impaired on tests of lexical, semantic, and pictorial priming which are performed normally by patients with Huntington's disease or circumscribed amnesia.

Despite these deficits in priming, and in contrast to HD patients and perhaps patients with other forms of basal ganglia dementia (i.e., Parkinson's disease), patients with AD maintain the ability to acquire and retain motor skills. Thus, it appears that different forms of implicit memory depend upon quite distinct neurological structures. Lexical, semantic, and pictorial priming (i.e., impaired in AD) may be mediated by the temporal or parietal association cortices affected in AD, whereas motor (and perhaps visuomotor and cognitive) skill learning requires the integrity of the basal ganglia (Butters, Heindel, & Salmon, 1990).

Clearly, recent investigations of different forms of non-episodic forms of memory in patients with AD have begun to delineate the extent of these patients' impaired and preserved memory capacities. In addition to furthering our knowledge about the neuropsychological deficits associated with Alzheimer's disease, these studies may lead to important information about the necessary and sufficient conditions for the normal operation of semantic and implicit memory.

Acknowledgments

The preparation of this manuscript was supported in part by NIA grants AG-05131 and AG-08204 to the University of California at San Diego.

References

Abeysinghe, S. C., Bayles, K. A., & Trosset, M. W. (1990). Semantic memory deterioration in Alzheimer's subjects: Evidence from word association, definition, and associate ranking tasks. *Journal of Speech and Hearing Research, 33*, 574-582.

Anderson, J. R., & Bower, G. H. (1974). A propositional theory of recognition memory. *Memory and Cognition, 2*, 406-412.

Bayles, K. A., & Tomoeda, C. K. (1983). Confrontation naming impairment in dementia. *Brain and Language, 19*, 98-114.

Bayles, K. A., Tomoeda, C. K., Kaszniak, A. W., & Trosset, M. W. (in press). Alzheimer's disease effects on semantic memory: Loss of structure or impaired processing? *Journal of Cognitive Neuroscience.*

Benzig, W. C., & Squire, L. R. (1989). Preserved learning and memory in amnesia: Intact adaptation-level effects and learning of stereoscopic depth. *Behavioral Neuroscience, 103*, 538-547.

Brandt, J., Spencer, M., McSorley, P., & Folstein, M. F. (1988). Semantic activation and implicit memory in Alzheimer disease. *Alzheimer's Disease and Associated Disorders, 2*, 112-119.

Brooks, D. N., & Baddeley, A. D. (1976). What can amnesic patients learn? *Neuropsychologia, 14*, 111-122.

Brun, A. (1983). An overview of light and electron microscopic changes. In B. Reisberg (Ed.), *Alzheimer's Disease.* New York: The Free Press.

Bruyn, G. W., Bots, G., & Dom, R. (1979). Huntington's chorea: Current neuropathological status. In T. Chase, N. Wexler, & A. Barbeau (Eds.), *Advances in Neurology, Vol. 23: Huntington's Disease.* New York: Raven Press.

Butters, N., Granholm, E. L., Salmon, D. P., Grant, I., & Wolfe, J. (1987). Episodic and semantic memory: A comparison of amnesic and demented patients. *Journal of Clinical and Experimental Neuropsychology, 9*, 479-497.

Butters, N., Heindel, W. C., & Salmon, D. P. (1990). Dissociation of implicit memory in dementia: Neurological implications. *Bulletin of the Psychonomic Society, 28*, 359-366.

Cermak, L. S. (1984). The episodic-semantic distinction in amnesia. In L. R. Squire and N. Butters (Eds.), *Neuropsychology of memory.* New York: Guilford Press.

Cermak, L. S., Lewis, R., Butters, N., & Goodglass, H. (1973). Role of verbal mediation in performance of motor tasks by Korsakoff patients. *Perceptual and Motor Skills, 37*, 259-262.

Cermak, L. S., Talbot, N., Chandler, K., & Wolbarst, L. R. (1985). The perceptual priming phenomenon in amnesia. *Neuropsychologia, 23,* 615-622.

Chertkow, H., & Bub, D. N. (1990). Semantic memory loss in dementia of Alzheimer's type. *Brain, 113,* 397-417.

Clark, C., Geffen, G., & Geffen, L. (1989). Catecholamines and the covert orientation of attention in humans. *Neuropsychologia, 27,* 131-139.

Cohen, N. J., & Squire, L. R. (1980). Preserved learning and retention of pattern analyzing skills in amnesia: Dissociation of knowing how and knowing that. *Science, 210,* 207-210.

Corkin, S. (1968). Acquisition of motor skill after bilateral medial temporal lobe excision. *Neuropsychologia, 6,* 255-265.

Cossa, F., Della Sala, S., & Spinnler, H. (1989). Selective visual attention in Alzheimer's and Parkinson's patients: Memory- and data-driven control. *Neuropsychologia, 27,* 887-892.

Eslinger, P. J., & Damasio, A. R. (1986). Preserved motor learning in Alzheimer's disease: Implications for anatomy and behavior. *Journal of Neuroscience, 6,* 3006-3009.

Freed, D. M., Corkin, S., Growdon, J. H., & Nissen, M. J. (1989). Selective attention and Alzheimer's disease: Characterizing cognitive subgroups of patients. *Neuropsychologia, 27,* 325-339.

Gardner, H., Boller, F., Moreines, J., & Butters, N. (1973). Retrieving information from Korsakoff patients: Effects of categorical cues and reference to the task. *Cortex, 9,* 165-175.

Grady, C. L., Grimes, A. M., Partronas, N., Sunderland, T., Foster, N. L., & Rapoport, S. I. (1989). Divided attention, as measured by dichotic speech performance, in dementia of the Alzheimer type. *Archives of Neurology, 46,* 317-320.

Graf, P., & Schacter, D. L. (1985). Implicit and explicit memory for new associations in normal and amnesic subjects. *Journal of Experimental Psychology: Learning, Memory, and Cognition, 11,* 501-518.

Graf, P., & Schacter, D. L. (1987). Selective effects of interference on implicit and explicit memory for new associations. *Journal of Experimental Psychology: Learning, Memory, and Cognition, 13,* 45-53.

Graf, P., Squire, L. R., & Mandler, G. (1984). The information that amnesic patients do not forget. *Journal of Experimental Psychology: Human Learning and Memory, 10,* 164-178.

Grosse, D. A., Wilson, R. S., & Fox, J. H. (1990). Preserved word-stem-completion priming of semantically encoded information in Alzheimer's disease. *Psychology and Aging, 5,* 304-306.

Hart, S. A. (1988). Language and dementia: A review. *Psychological Medicine, 18,* 99-112.

Heindel, W. C., Butters, N., & Salmon, D. P. (1988). Impaired learning of a motor skill in patients with Huntington's disease. *Behavioral Neuroscience, 102,* 141-147.

Heindel, W. C., Salmon, D. P., & Butters, N. (1990). Pictorial priming and cued recall in Alzheimer's and Huntington's disease. *Brain and Cognition, 13,* 282-295.

Heindel, W. C., Salmon, D. P., & Butters, N. (1991). The biasing of weight judgments in Alzheimer's and Huntington's disease: A priming or programming phenomenon? *Journal of Clinical and Experimental Neuropsychology, 13,* 189-203.

Heindel, W. C., Salmon, D. P., Shults, C. W., Walicke, P. A., & Butters, N. (1989). Neuropsychological evidence for multiple implicit memory systems: A comparison of Alzheimer's, Huntington's, and Parkinson's disease patients. *Journal of Neuroscience, 9,* 582-587.

Hodges, J. R., Salmon, D. P., & Butters, N. (in press). The nature of the naming deficit in Alzheimer's and Huntington's disease. *Brain.*

Hodges, J. R., Salmon, D. P., & Butters, N. (1991). *Semantic memory impairment in Alzheimer's disease: Failure of access or degraded knowledge?* Manuscript submitted for publication.

Huff, F. J., Corkin, S., & Growdon, J. H. (1986). Semantic impairment and anomia in Alzheimer's disease. *Brain and Language, 28,* 235-249.

Huff, F. J., Mack, L., Mahlmann, J., & Greenberg, S. (1988). A comparison of lexical-semantic impairments in left-hemisphere stroke and Alzheimer's disease. *Brain and Language, 34,* 262-278.

Jones, L. A. (1986). Perception of force and weight: Theory and research. *Psychological Bulletin, 100,* 29-42.

Keane, M. M., Gabrieli, J. D. E., Fennema, A. C., Growdon, J. H., & Corkin, S. (1991). Evidence for a dissociation between perceptual and conceptual priming in Alzheimer's disease. *Behavioral Neuroscience, 105,* 326-342.

Knopman, D. S., & Nissen, M. J. (1987). Implicit learning in patients with probable Alzheimer's disease. *Neurology, 37,* 784-788.

Knopman, D. S., & Nissen, M. J. (1990). Procedural learning is impaired in Huntington's disease: Evidence from the serial reaction time test. *Neuropsychologia, 29,* 245-254.

Mann, D. M. A., Yates, P. O., & Marcyniuk, B. (1986). A comparison of nerve cell loss in cortical and subcortical structures in Alzheimer's disease. *Journal of Neurology, Neurosurgery, and Psychiatry, 49,* 310-312.

Marcyniuk, B., Mann, D. M. A., & Yates, P. O. (1986). The topography of cell loss from locus coeruleus in Alzheimer's disease. *Journal of Neurological Science, 76,* 335-345.

Martin, A. (1987). Representation of semantic and spatial knowledge in Alzheimer's patients: Implications for models of preserved learning in amnesia. *Journal of Clinical and Experimental Neuropsychology, 9,* 191-124.

Martin, A., & Fedio, P. (1983). Word production and comprehension in Alzheimer's disease: The breakdown in semantic knowledge. *Brain and Language, 19,* 124-141.

Mattis, S. (1976). Mental status examination for organic mental syndrome in the elderly patient. In L. Bellack & T. Karasu (Eds.), *Geriatric Psychiatry,* New York: Grune & Stratton.

Moscovitch, M., Winocur, G., & McLachlan, D. (1986). Memory as assessed by recognition and reading time in normal and memory-impaired people with Alzheimer's disease and other neurological disorders. *Journal of Experimental Psychology: General, 115,* 331-347.

Nebes, R. D. (1989). Semantic memory in Alzheimer's disease. *Psychological Bulletin, 106,* 377-394.

Nebes, R. D. (in press). Cognitive dysfunction in Alzheimer's disease. In F. I. M. Craik & T. Salthouse (Eds.), *Handbook of aging and cognition.* Hillsdale, NJ: Erlbaum.

Nebes, R. D., & Brady, C. B. (1989). Focused and divided attention in Alzheimer's disease. *Cortex, 25,* 305-315.

Nebes, R. D., Martin, P. R., & Horn, L. C. (1984). Sparing of semantic memory in Alzheimer's disease. *Journal of Abnormal Psychology, 93,* 321-330.

Nelson, D. L., Reed, V. S., & McEvoy, C. L. (1977). Learning to order pictures and words: A model of sensory and semantic encoding. *Journal of Experimental Psychology: Human Learning and Memory, 3,* 485-497.

Nissen, M. J., & Bullemer, P. (1987). Attentional requirements of learning: Evidence from performance measures. *Cognitive Psychology, 19,* 1-32.

Partridge, F. M., Knight, R. G., & Feehan, M. (1990). Direct and indirect memory performance in patients with senile dementia. *Psychological Medicine, 20,* 111-118.

Posner, M., & Petersen, S. (1990). The attention system of the human brain. *Annual Review of Neuroscience, 13,* 25-42.

Randolph, C. (1991). Implicit, explicit and semantic memory functions in Alzheimer's disease and Huntington's disease. *Journal of Clinical and Experimental Neuropsychology, 13,* 479-494.

Salmon, D. P., Shimamura, A. P., Butters, N., & Smith, S. (1988). Lexical and semantic priming deficits in patients with Alzheimer's disease. *Journal of Clinical and Experimental Neuropsychology, 10,* 477-494.

Sara, S. (1985a). The locus coeruleus and cognitive function: Attempts to relate noradrenergic enhancement of signal/noise in the brain to behavior. *Physiological Psychology, 13,* 151-162.

Sara, S. (1985b). Noradrenergic modulation of selective attention: Its role in memory retrieval. *Annals of the New York Academy of Sciences, 444,* 178-193.

Schacter, D. L. (1987). Implicit memory: History and current status. *Journal of Experimental Psychology: Learning, Memory and Cognition, 13,* 501-517.

Shallice, T. (1987). Impairments of semantic processing: Multiple dissociations. In M. Coltheart, G. Sartori, & R. Job (Eds.), *The cognitive neuropsychology of language.* London: Erlbaum.

Shimamura, A. P. (1986). Priming effects in amnesia: Evidence for a dissociable memory function. *Quarterly Journal of Experimental Psychology, 38A,* 619-644.

Shimamura, A. P., Salmon, D. P., Squire, L. R., & Butters, N. (1987). Memory dysfunction and word priming in dementia and amnesia. *Behavioral Neuroscience, 101,* 347-351.

Shimamura, A. P., & Squire, L. R. (1984). Paired-associate learning and priming effects in amnesia: A neuropsychological study. *Journal of Experimental Psychology: General, 113,* 556-570.

Smith, S. R., Murdoch, B. E., & Chenery, H. J. (1989). Semantic abilities in dementia of the Alzheimer type: 1. Lexical semantics. *Brain and Language, 36,* 314-324.

Squire, L. R. (1987). *Memory and brain.* New York: Oxford University Press.

Terry, R. D., & Katzman, R. (1983). Senile dementia of the Alzheimer type. *Annals of Neurology, 14,* 497-506.

Tomlinson, B. E., Irving, D., & Blessed, G. (1981). Cell loss in the locus coeruleus in senile dementia of the Alzheimer type. *Journal of Neurological Science, 11,* 205-242.

Tröster, A. I., Salmon, D. P., McCullough, D., & Butters, N. (1989). A comparison of the category fluency deficits associated with Alzheimer's and Huntington's disease. *Brain and Language, 37,* 500-513.

Tulving, E. (1983). *Elements of Episodic Memory.* Oxford: Oxford University Press.

Tulving, E., & Schacter, D. L. (1990). Priming and human memory systems. *Science, 247,* 301-306.

Warrington, E. K., & Shallice, T. (1979). Semantic access dyslexia. *Brain, 102,* 43-63.

Warrington, E. K., & Weiskrantz, L. (1968). New method of testing long-term retention with special reference to amnesic patients. *Nature, 217,* 972-974.

Warrington, E. K., & Weiskrantz, L. (1970). Amnesic syndrome: Consolidation or retrieval? *Nature, 228,* 628-630.

Zweig, R., Ross, C., Hedreen, J., Steele, C., Cardillo, J., Whitehouse, P., Folstein, M. F., & Price, D. L. (1988). The neuropathology of aminergic nuclei in Alzheimer's disease. *Annals of Neurology, 24,* 233-242.

Memory Functioning in Dementia – L. Bäckman (Editor)
1992 Elsevier Science Publishers B.V.

119

6

Semantic Knowledge in Patients With Alzheimer's Disease: Evidence For Degraded Representations

Alex Martin

National Institute of Mental Health

Introduction

A common consequence of damage to the neocortex is an inability to perform tasks that are dependent on previously acquired knowledge and skills. Simply stated, patients who have sustained cortical injury seem to no longer know what they used to know and appear to be unable to do what they previously could do. As a result, it has often been implicitly assumed that the deficit is a reflection of an actual loss of some previously acquired knowledge or skill rather than an inability to simply retrieve or gain access to an intact store of knowledge. The particular type of deficit that occurs is, of course, largely dependent on the location of damage within the cerebral hemispheres. Thus, the extensive literature on the myriad disorders of recognition (the agnosias), language (the aphasias), and action (the apraxias) appear to provide compelling evidence that different types of knowledge are stored or represented in relatively discrete regions of the cerebral cortex.

The hypothesis that knowledge is actually stored in cerebral cortex is supported by the fact that bilateral damage limited to the hippocampus and other structures of the medial temporal lobe results in a profound inability to explicitly recall and recognize all types of recently presented material (global amnesia), while having little or no effect on the retrieval and utilization of knowledge and skills acquired in the more distant past. For example, amnesic patients can perform normally on tests of object naming and visuospatial skill. In marked contrast, patients with Alzheimer's disease (AD) often present with a global amnesia plus deficits in a variety of other cognitive domains including object naming and visuospatial ability. As would be expected, this combination of impairments is due to the fact that the characteristic pathology of AD is most common and most severe in the medial temporal region (especially the entorhinal cortex, hippocampus, and amygdala; Hyman, Van Hoesen, &

Damasio, 1990) and in the association regions of the cerebral cortex (especially posterior temporal and parietal zones; Brun & Gustafson, 1976).

Object naming deficits and other word-finding difficulties are particularly common and disabling problems for patients with AD. Although there is good evidence to believe that this deficit is due primarily to involvement of the left posterior temporal cortex, the underlying cause of this deficit has not been adequately characterized. In fact, contrary to the commonly held view noted above, there has been recent debate concerning whether naming deficits and other "knowledge" impairments are best understood as resulting from an actual loss or degradation of a specific knowledge system versus impaired access to an intact semantic store (Shallice, 1988). In this chapter I will first briefly review evidence both in support and against the hypothesis that AD patients have an actual loss or degradation of knowledge. I will then outline a model of normal semantic representations of objects based on the premise that semantically related items are represented by specific, but overlapping neuronal networks. The argument will be made that the types of deficits seen in AD patients on effortful as well as on more automatic measures of semantic knowledge are consistent with the expected outcome of damage to this type of representation. The implications of these degraded representations for object naming and word-finding ability will then be discussed.

Evidence for Degraded Knowledge Representations

As I have argued previously (Martin, 1987; Martin & Fedio, 1983), the pattern of word-finding impairments in AD seems to be most consistent with the degraded store hypothesis. This argument was based on several related observations and findings. First, as often seen following damage to association cortex, the deficits in AD are not complete or total. Rather, as a rule, these patients exhibit some knowledge about the meaning of words and about the functions and other characteristics of objects. For example, AD patients will often provide accurate, but incomplete definitions of words on vocabulary tasks and provide accurate but incomplete descriptions of objects that they are unable to name. Second, in addition to providing some descriptive information, their object naming errors often consist of the name of an object from the same semantic category as the item presented or the name of the category to which the target object belongs (e.g., Bayles & Tomoeda, 1983; Huff, Corkin, & Growden, 1986; Martin & Fedio, 1983). Third, these patients have marked difficulty generating lists of items that belong to the same semantic category, and this category fluency deficit can be disproportionately severe in comparison to performance on fluency tasks that are more dependent on lexical than semantic search (Butters, Granholm, Salmon, Grant, & Wolfe, 1987; Shuttleworth and Huber, 1988; Weingartner et al., 1981; but see Ober,

Dronkers, Koss, Delis, & Friedland, 1986; and Rosen, 1980, for negative find-ings). Fourth, when asked to generate a list of items that have a more general relation to each other (e.g., items found in a supermarket) AD patients, like normal elderly controls, tend to sample from a variety of categories (e.g., fruits, vegetables), but produce fewer examples from each category. They also tend to produce an abnormally large ratio of category labels to specific item names (Martin & Fedio, 1983; Nebes & Brady, 1990; Ober et al., 1986; Tröster, Salmon, McCullough, & Butters, 1989). Finally, when their knowledge about specific objects is directly probed, AD patients often make accurate judgments con-cerning superordinate (e.g., living versus manmade) and more specific category membership (e.g., tools versus foods versus animals). However, these patients have difficulty answering simple yes/no questions concerning specific object attributes (e.g., "is it used to hold things?," "is it used to cut things?," "does it have moving parts?," for tools). Moreover, this tendency to make attribute errors occurs most often with objects that the patients are unable to name (Chertkow, Bub & Seidenberg, 1989; Martin, 1987; Martin & Fedio, 1983; Warrington, 1975).

This pattern of results has been interpreted as suggesting that semantic knowledge about objects is hierarchically organized proceeding from knowledge of specific attributes to more global, superordinate information (Warrington, 1975). Furthermore, we have argued that AD, and perhaps other disorders affecting posterior regions of the left temporal lobe (see, for example, Whitehouse, Caramazza, & Zurif, 1978), results in a loss of knowledge of those attributes that distinguish closely related objects within the same semantic category (Martin, 1987; Martin & Fedio, 1983). If so, then in response to ei-ther a picture of an object or presentation of the object's name, AD patients may be forced to rely on a semantic representation that is abnormally underspecified due to a lack of critical, object-specific attributes (i.e., those attributes that serve to distinguish similar objects within the same semantic category). It should be readily appreciated that an under-specified represen-tation with regard to object-specific features is also an overgeneralized repre-sentation in relation to other, closely related objects within the same seman-tic category. If this were in fact the case, then it could be assumed that essen-tially the same semantic representation would be elicited in response to the presentation of objects that bore a close semantic relationship to each other.

This type of degraded representation explanation is appealing because it seems to account for many of the features enumerated above concerning the performance of AD patients on semantic tasks. For example, when confronted with an object, an over-generalized representation should lead to the normal activation of knowledge that is specific for the category to which the object belongs. This representation should be perfectly adequate for eliciting correct, but incomplete object descriptions and for making judgments concerning superordinate and more specific category memberships. However, it should be insufficient for making judgments about object-specific attributes or fea-tures, or for consistently providing the object's name on category fluency and object naming tests.

The finding that AD patients could correctly answer questions concerning category membership but not object-specific attributes (Martin & Fedio, 1983) and, most importantly, that attribute knowledge was most impaired for objects that the patients could not name (Martin, 1987) were critical pieces of evidence in support of the degraded store hypothesis. These findings, which were obtained using a procedure developed by Warrington (1975), were subsequently replicated by Chertkow et al., (1989); see also Chertkow and Bub (1990). However, other investigators, using different paradigms, have reported data that appear to be at odds with the notion of a loss of attribute knowledge in AD. For example, Grober, Buschke, Kawas, and Fuld (1985) found that AD patients could accurately distinguish those attributes associated with an object from those that were not, although their judgment of the relative importance or saliency of these attributes was abnormal. More recently, Bayles, Tomoeda, and Trosset (1990) reported evidence suggesting that category knowledge may actually be more impaired than attribute knowledge, and Nebes and Brady (1988, 1990), using reaction time procedures, have found evidence suggesting intact knowledge and organization of both semantic attributes and category relationships.

These findings have, in part, lead to the suggestion that the word finding difficulty experienced by patients with AD may not be due a semantic deficit per se, but rather to the disruption of other processes deemed necessary for accurate and efficient lexical search and retrieval. As correctly noted by Nebes (e.g., Nebes, Martin, & Horn, 1984) most of the evidence in support of the semantic deficit hypothesis in AD was derived from impaired performance on effortful, attention demanding tasks. Might the performance of AD patients on these tasks be reflecting impairments of attentional and/or retrieval processes rather than a true deterioration of knowledge?

On-Line Semantic Priming

To address this possibility, Nebes and colleagues decided to utilize a procedure that they believed would reflect the status of the semantic system while placing minimum demands on attentional and retrieval processes. The task they chose was an on-line semantic priming task. The main assumption underlying this procedure is that the presentation of either a word or a picture of an object will automatically activate its representation in semantic memory. It is further assumed that this activation will spread to semantically related concepts, thus momentarily increasing their accessibility. Typically, when normal individuals are required to process a word (the target), either by reading it or judging whether it is a real word or a nonword (the lexical decision task), the time to perform this operation on the target item is decreased when it is immediately preceded by a semantically related word (the semantic prime) relative to when it is preceded by a semantically unrelated item. For example, the time to read "hammer" will be faster if the preceding item is "screwdriver" (the semantically related prime) in comparison to when the preceding item is "dog" (the unrelated prime). Nebes and colleagues reasoned that, if the semantic system is disrupted in AD, then semantic activation should be substantially reduced, or absent in these patients. However, contrary to this expectation, the AD patients showed a normal amount of semantic priming. Based on this and other findings, Nebes (1989, in press) has argued that the semantic system or network may be essentially intact in AD and that their poor performance on other more effortful and demanding tasks of semantic knowledge may be due to a defect in the intentional search of semantic memory. Nebes thus views the difficulties on object naming and verbal fluency tasks as primarily a reflection of impaired access to, or deficient search of, a generally intact semantic store.

Subsequent studies of semantic priming have tended to confirm Nebes initial observation. In fact, the majority of recent studies have found that, not only do AD patients show semantic priming or facilitation, they actually show significantly greater facilitation, or *hyperpriming* in comparison to normal elderly controls (Balota & Duchek, 1991; Chertkow et al., 1989; Hartman, 1991; Nebes, Boller, & Holland, 1986; Nebes, Brady, & Huff, 1989). In all of these studies, the time needed to read a word or to decide whether a letter string represented a real word, was reduced to a significantly greater degree by semantic primes (relative to unrelated primes) in the AD patients in comparison to control subjects. Thus, the AD patients seem to be *more sensitive* to the semantic prime than are normal individuals.[1]

Most investigators have interpreted hyper-normal semantic priming as indicating that the semantic system of these patients is essentially intact (although see Chertkow & Bub, 1990, for a different interpretation). The critical question, however, is whether hyperpriming is inconsistent with the type of degraded store model previously described. If patients with AD are restricted to an over-generalized semantic representation, then what would be the expected outcome on a semantic priming task? To answer this question we must specify a set of assumptions about normal semantic representations.

A Model of Semantic Representations of Objects

For illustrative purposes we will restrict our discussion to the processes assumed to be critical for object naming. Most current models of object vision maintain that, when presented with an object, the visual system first creates a viewer-center representation based on the pattern of light that impinges on the retina. This low-level representation is so-named because it is totally dependent on the position of the viewer in relation to the object. To support object recognition, this representation must be transformed into an object-centered representation; that is, a representation that is invariant across retinal translations. It is this object-centered representation that allows us to recognize an object as the same object when viewed from different locations or in different orientations (see Humphreys & Bruce, 1989, for review). Studies with nonhuman primates indicate that the creation of these object-centered representations is dependent on the functioning of a hierarchically organized occipital inferior-temporal system (see Desimone & Ungerleider, 1989, for review). This object-centered representation would then automatically activate a semantic-object representation consisting of our stored knowledge about the object in question, including knowledge of both physical and functional features or attributes. In man, it is further assumed that this semantic representation would also activate the appropriate lexical entry for naming.

A critical property of an object-centered representation is that it must be specific enough to allow us to visually discriminate different versions of the same type of object. That is, the object-centered representation must be sufficiently detailed to allow us, for example, to easily distinguish one type of chair from another type of chair due to differences in physical form. In contrast, the semantic representation of both of these objects must be general enough to represent the concept of "chair," yet specific enough to represent only "chair" and not other objects that may share many of the same attributes (e.g., "desk"). We will further assume that this semantic representation is instantiated in brain as a distributed network of neuronal connections that represent the features and properties of the object in question. Thus, in response to a picture of an object or an object's name, a specific neuronal network is activated. Because this network represents the specific attributes associated with the object, semantically related objects (e.g., chairs and desks) must be normally represented by overlapping networks, with the degree of overlap being equal to the number of shared attributes. Now, what would be the outcome of damage to these neuronal networks? Remember that, by definition, semantically similar objects share a large number of attributes, and thus are assumed to be represented by largely overlapping networks. If so, then any random pathological process (e.g., the development of plaques and tangles in the posterior temporal lobe) should tend to make these representations *more similar*. Over time, as the degree of pathology increases, so should the inability to distinguish, on a semantic level, objects from the same category, as long as they have more than 50% of their attributes in common.[2] As a result, it is assumed that when an AD patient is confronted with an object, the semantic representation that is activated is no longer specific enough to activate only the object's name, but rather will activate a number of lexical entries (i.e., the names of all of the objects consistent with the the patients under-specified, and thus, over-generalized representation). For evidence consistent with over-generalized representations in monkeys following damage to posterior temporal cortex the reader may consult Dean (1982) and Gaffan, Harrison and Gaffan (1986).

Now, returning to the semantic priming paradigm, if this formulation is correct, then, for the AD patient, the presentation of a prime that bears a close semantic relationship to the target (semantic priming) should approach the degree of activation that occurs when the identical object is presented as both the prime and target (repetition priming). Thus, to the extent that direct repetition of a word or object normally produces a greater degree of facilitation than the presentation of a semantically related prime, then the presentation of semantically related primes to AD patients should produce greater facilitation or *hyperpriming*, in comparison to normal controls.

Evidence in Support of Degraded Semantic Representations of Objects

We have recently obtained evidence in support of just this possibility (Martin, Lalonde, Wertheimer, & Sunderland, 1991). As reviewed above, studies of semantic priming in AD patients, as well as the overwhelming majority of studies with normal subjects, have used words as stimuli. However, because our main goal is to understand object naming difficulty, we decided to test predictions of the model using pictures of objects rather than words. The paradigm we chose was an object decision task because, in our experience, AD patients have little difficulty making this type of global judgement (i.e., real versus novel object). On each trial subjects were presented with either a picture of a real object (from the Snodgrass & Vanderwart, 1980 set) or a picture of a meaningless, novel construction or "nonobject" (from the Kroll & Potter, 1984 set) presented on a computer screen. Subjects were required to respond as quickly as possible by key press if the picture was of a real object (i.e., something that exists in the world) and to refrain from responding if the object was not real. Each target object and nonobject was preceded by the presentation of a prime consisting of either a neutral stimulus (a grid of intersecting lines), a nonobject, an unrelated real object, or the exact same object. In addition, two types of semantic primes were used. These consisted of closely and distantly related items based on previously determined category typicality ratings (Battig & Montague, 1969). For example, for the target picture of a bed the closely related item was a picture of a table and the distantly related item was a picture of a vase. The prime was presented for 150 msec and the subjects were told to attend to the picture but not to respond. The prime was then followed by the presentation of the target stimulus which remained visible until the subject responded or until two seconds had elapsed. Depending on the experiment, the time interval between the onset of the prime and the onset of the target (the stimulus onset asynchrony or SOA) varied from 250 to 2000 msec. Based on the above discussion, it was predicted that AD patients would show normal priming when the prime was the same object as the target and greater than normal activation when the prime was semantically related to the target.

Our preliminary data have been highly supportive of these predictions, but only under certain conditions. As illustrated in Figure 6.1 A, using an SOA of 250 msec the AD patients showed robust facilitation when the target object was preceded by the brief presentation of the same object (repetition or identity priming) relative to the neutral prime condition. Moreover, the relative amount of repetition priming was equivalent for the patients and age-matched normal controls. However, the patients showed no evidence of semantic facilitation when the target was preceded by the semantically-related prime. This experiment was repeated at a later time under the identical conditions except for the use of a longer SOA (750 msec). Under this condition, the patients again showed normal repetition priming. Moreover, in support of the degraded representation model, they also showed significantly greater semantic priming than did the normal subjects (see Figure 6.1 B). As can be seen in the figure, with an SOA of 750 msec the relative difference between repetition and semantic priming was substantially smaller for the AD patients than for the elderly controls. Hyperpriming thus appears to be specific for semantically mediated activation.

We have replicated this set of findings in an essentially identical study except that the SOA was randomly varied from 250 to 2000 msec from trial to trial. Under this condition, the AD patients showed no semantic facilitation at an SOA of 250 msec, normal facilitation at an SOA of 500 msec, significantly increased semantic facilitation or hyperpriming at 1000 msec, and no semantic priming at an SOA of 2000 msec (see Figure 6.2). The degree of facilitation that occurred when the same object served as the prime and target continued to be robust and equivalent for the patients and controls at SOAs of 1000 and 2000 msecs.

Although these findings are consistent with the degraded store model, the objection might be raised that the so-called hyperpriming phenomenon may be simply an artefact of an overall slowing of response times. This, however, is unlikely to be the case for several reasons. First, our analyses were based on percent change from baseline rather than on the absolute difference in RT which might have artificially inflated between-group differences. Second, the AD patients were abnormally slow at all SOAs, yet showed abnormally large priming effects at some intervals and not others. Third, repetition or identity priming was normal even though the patients responded significantly more slowly than the controls under this condition. Finally, it has recently reported that patients who are slow, but not anomic (i.e., individuals with Parkinson's disease), do not show increased semantic facilitation (Chertkow, in press). Therefore, it cannot be the case that an overall slowing of response times will necessarily result in a significantly greater percent change from baseline. Hyperpriming does not appear to be an artefact of overall slowing, but rather, as argued here, it may well be a direct consequence of degraded representations.

Our data thus replicate and extend previous reports of hyperpriming and in our view are consistent with the hypothesis of degraded, over-generalized semantic representations in patients with AD. Our results further suggest that

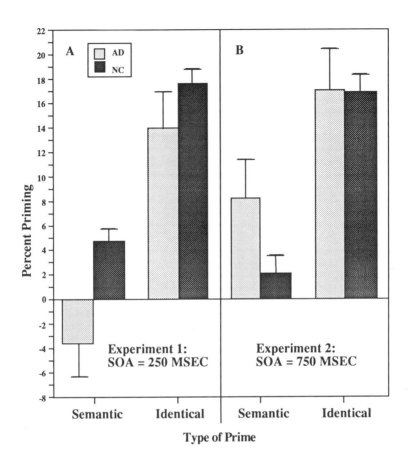

Figure 6.1. Performance by patients with Alzheimer's disease (AD; *N* = 8) and age- and education-matched normal controls (NC; *N* = 13) on an object decision task with primes that were semantically-related or identical to the target object. Bars represent mean percent semantic and direct repetition priming (± SEM), relative to the neutral prime condition. In comparison to controls, the AD patients showed significantly reduced semantic priming at an SOA of 250 msec and significantly increased semantic priming with an SOA of 750 msec. In both studies repetition priming was equivalent for the patients and controls.

semantic activation is a dynamic process and that this process is qualitatively different in AD patients in comparison to normals. In patients with AD it appears that activation of the semantic system develops at an abnormally slow rate. However, once the system is stimulated, the degree of activation seems to be substantially greater than that seen in normal individuals.

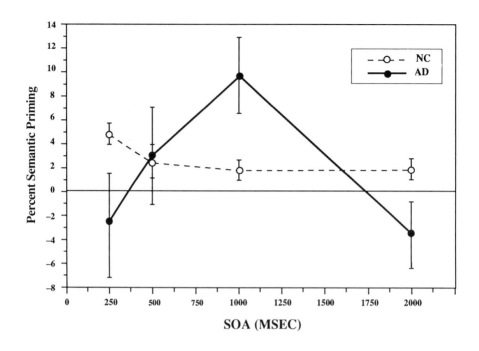

Figure 6.2. Percent semantic priming (±SEM) on the object decision task for AD patients (*N* = 6) and normal controls (*N* = 15) with SOA randomly varied from trial to trial. Semantic activation in AD was highly variable and significantly reduced relative to normal control levels with SOAs of 250 msec and 2000 msec, equivalent to normal at 500 msec, and significantly increased at an SOA of 1000 msec.

It is particularly noteworthy that increased semantic facilitation also can be produced in normal subjects. This can be most readily accomplished by perceptually *degrading* the target stimulus (see Neely, 1991, for review). Under this condition, increased facilitation or hyperpriming occurs because perceptual degradation of the target produces relatively more slowing of response times when the target is preceded by an unrelated prime than when it is preceded by a semantically related prime. Therefore, it appears that, even for normal individuals, semantic activation provides relatively greater aid for processing degraded, than for processing nondegraded, information. I have argued that AD patients have degraded representations, albeit on a semantic, as opposed to a perceptual level. Therefore, it might be expected that AD patients would derive greater than normal benefit from semantically related primes.

In sum, our present findings, although preliminary, suggest that hyperpriming in AD appears to be a reproducible and generalized phenomenon that occurs with both word and picture stimuli. I have argued that this phenomenon does not indicate a normal semantic system but rather is indicative of a system composed of degraded representations. If so, then what are the implications of these degraded representations for our understanding of the performance of AD patients on other types of cognitive tasks?

Implications for Object Naming and Word-Finding Ability

As noted previously, patients with AD often perform poorly on tasks of object naming. Within the context of the present model, naming difficulty and the production of semantic errors occur because degraded representations lead to an over-activation of an intact lexical system. The model of normal semantic activation assumes that the presentation of an object will activate its own semantic representation as well as the representation of closely related objects within the same semantic category. Under normal circumstances, this activation of related representations is assumed to be short-lived so that the lexical entry (name) associated with the target object is specifically activated above some threshold value while alternative labels (the names of semantically related objects) are inhibited. Because, for the AD patients, the semantic representation is no longer precise enough to activate a single lexical entry, competition is assumed to occur among a number of lexical choices. Therefore, within the context of this model, naming failures and errors occur because of the co-activation of several names within the lexical system. AD patients may well suffer from a retrieval "deficit" as suggested by Nebes. However, this retrieval deficit may be a direct consequence of degraded representations rather than an inability to carry out an efficient, directed search of the lexicon.

It should also be noted that, in contrast to one of the criteria for degraded stores specified by Warrington and Shallice (1979), the present model does not predict nor require a consistent patterns of errors over repeated administrations of the same object naming test. The lexical system itself is assumed to be essentially intact, and therefore, AD patients are assumed to have retained the specific names of objects. However, since the correct name as well as the names of semantically related objects are all activated, inconsistent naming could occur and still be due primarily to a degraded representation. Degraded representation are assumed to lead to the activation of a set of lexical entries above some critical retrieval threshold. As a result, the correct name may or may not be retrieved at a particular point in time, dependent, perhaps, on momentary fluctuations in the activation of the lexical entries.

Finally, it would also be predicted that semantic cues should be generally of little help for naming unless they are specific for the object in question, and only for that object. Providing the name of the semantic category that the object belongs to ("a piece of furniture") or more general information ("used for cutting") should not help because it is assumed that it is just this type of knowledge that the patients retain. In contrast, cues specific to the item in question (e.g., phonemic cues that provide the initial sound of the object's name) should help because they narrow down the choice among the several names assumed to have been activated. This prediction is consistent with the frequent observation that on, for example, the Boston Naming Test (Kaplan, Goodglass, & Weintraub, 1983; from which the above examples of semantic cues were taken), AD patients are usually helped to a much greater extent by phonemic cues than by semantic cues.

Conclusions

I have argued that the semantic representations in anomic patients with AD (and, perhaps in other patients with anomia resulting from posterior damage to the left temporal cortex) are abnormally under-specified with regard to the object-specific attributes that distinguish closely related items within the same semantic category. It was also argued that a consequence of these degraded semantic representations would be hyper-facilitation from semantically related, but not identical, primes. Our studies provided support for this possibility and also provided evidence that the magnitude of semantic priming in AD is critically dependent on the duration between between the prime and target.

I have also attempted to infer some of the consequences that these degraded representations may have for explicit measures of object naming and word-finding ability. One could also imagine that this loss of semantic precision would have dire consequences for performance on both explicit and implicit tests of memory (Martin, Mack, Lalonde, & Sunderland, in press). A critical question for future study will be to determine the extent to which this type of degraded storage model can be applied to other types of encoding deficits that play a critical role for episodic memory failures in patients with AD (Bäckman & Herlitz, 1990; Martin, Brouwers, Cox, & Fedio, 1985).

My overall approach in this chapter has been to focus attention on one symptom of impaired memory that commonly occurs in AD. My thinking on this issue has been guided by a model that, although highly speculative, is consistent with some of the known functions and properties of the occipital-temporal lobe object recognition system. The neuropathology of AD is, of course, not limited to temporal cortex. To the contrary, AD is the example, par excellence, of a multi-system disorder that affects a variety of brain regions and neurotransmitter systems. Our understanding of the nature of cognitive dysfunction is these patients is thus ultimately dependent on the ability to understand the interaction of multiple deficits and their consequence for individual pieces of behavior, such as object naming.

Given the relatively wide-spread involvement of both cortical and subcortical regions in AD there is little doubt that these patients often suffer from attentional difficulties, retrieval problems, and other impairments that add to their failure on various tests of object naming and word-finding ability. However, the central question is whether these processing deficits can, in and of themselves, account for the naming failures seen in these patients. My intuition is that they cannot. I would expect that, if we had a drug that could alleviate attentional and other processing deficits, these patients would perform better, but would still have considerable object-naming difficulty.

My position has been that naming deficits in these patients are primarily due to a degradation of knowledge. Moreover, I would suggest that the *nature* (but not extent) of this deficit is affected to a surprisingly small degree by other types of cognitive dysfunction. This is the lesson of modularity, a lesson that for me has been underscored and strengthened by observation and study of AD patients who had relatively focal, and qualitatively distinct patterns of preserved and impaired cognitive abilities (see Martin, 1987, 1990). AD patients with cortical pathology limited largely to the left temporal lobe presented with a cleaner, but qualitatively similar pattern of word-finding and object-naming deficits as that seen in more globally impaired patients. Similarly, AD patients with pathology limited to parietal regions presented with visuospatial problems that were similar to those seen in the globally impaired individuals. Moreover, the patients with relatively focal and severe visuospatial impairments could perform normally on object naming tests thus providing strong evidence that these spatial deficits do not necessarily interfere with object recognition ability. In fact, the visuospatial and construction impairment in one of these patients (Patient C in Martin, 1987, in whom AD has now been confirmed by autopsy) was strikingly limited to novel material. This patient was unable to copy meaningless forms and designs, but could draw objects from memory and copy meaningful objects and scenes with remarkably preserved skill. We have recently studied a similar case who, relative to controls, produced perfectly normal copies of objects, but not of cut-up and rearranged versions of the same objects, and could copy structurally possible, but not impossible versions of the same figures (Kampen & Martin, 1989). Patients like these provide rather strong evidence for a modular-type organization of knowledge and skill systems that can function in relative isolation from each other.

The ability to learn and remember implies that some type of relatively permanent change has occurred in the brain. If this change exists, then it must be modifiable or degradable by injury and disease. If the changes that represent such higher-order cognitions as semantic knowledge of objects do not reside in neocortex, than where do they reside? And if they are not disrupted in patients with AD, then in whom are they disrupted?

Footnotes

[1] Not all studies of on-line semantic priming have found normal or hyper-normal facilitation in AD patients. Ober and Shenaut (1988) found no evidence of semantic priming, whereas Albert and Milberg (1989) reported highly variable performance with some AD patients showing semantic priming and others showing inhibition rather than facilitation (slower performance with semantically-related relative to unrelated primes). It is likely that these and other inconsistent reports will be traceable to important differences in methodology and in the types of patients studied. In fact, the magnitude of semantic priming in normal subjects is critically dependent on a host of experimental variables (see Neely, 1991, for review), and it is well known that, as a group, AD patients may be quite heterogeneous with regard to patterns of preserved and impaired cognitive functions due to individual differences in the distribution of neuropathology (see Martin, 1990, for review).

[2] As a corollary, the semantic representation of objects that share few attributes and features would be expected to become less similar as more pathology develops over time. Once the few shared links in the network (attributes) are disrupted, the connection between these representations should be broken. As a result, one would predict that distantly-related objects would produce less semantic activation in AD than in normal subjects.

Acknowledgments

I would like to thank Dr. Trey Sunderland for providing access to the Alzheimer's patients and for his helpful comments and discussion of a previous version of this manuscript. Thanks also to Dr. François Lalonde and Susan Wertheimer for their assistance with subject testing and data analysis. Some of the material included in this paper appeared in a chapter by A. Martin in Neuropsychology of Memory (2nd Edition), L. R. Squire & N. Butters (Eds.), Guilford Press.

References

Albert, M. S., & Milberg, W. (1989). Semantic processing in patients with Alzheimer's disease. *Brain and Language, 37*, 163-171.
Bäckman, L., & Herlitz, A. (1990). The relationship between prior knowledge and face recognition memory in normal aging and Alzheimer's disease. *Journal of Gerontology: Psychological Sciences, 45*, 94-100.

Battig, W. F., & Montague, W. E. (1969). Category norms for verbal items in 56 categories: A replication and extension of the Connecticut category norms. *Journal of Experimental Psychology Monograph, 80*, (3, Pt. 2).

Bayles, K. A., & Tomoeda, C. K. (1983). Confrontation naming impairment in dementia. *Brain and Language, 19*, 98-114.

Bayles, K. A., Tomoeda, C. K., & Trosset, M. W. (1990). Naming and categorical knowledge in Alzheimer's disease. *Brain and Language, 39*, 498-510.

Balota, D. A., & Duchek, J. M. (1991). Semantic priming effects, lexical repetition effects, and contextual disambiguation effects in healthy aged individuals and individuals with senile dementia of the Alzheimer type. *Brain and Language, 40*, 181-201.

Brun, A., & Gustafson, L. (1976). Distribution of cerebral degeneration in Alzheimer's disease: A clinico-pathological study. *Archives of Psychiatry and Neurological Sciences, 233*, 15-33.

Butters, N., Granholm, E. L., Salmon, D. P., Grant, I., & Wolfe, J. (1987). Episodic and semantic memory: A comparison of amnesic and demented patients. *Journal of Clinical and Experimental Neuropsychology, 9*, 479-497.

Chertkow, H. (in press). Priming changes in dementia of the Alzheimer's type. *Journal of Clinical and Experimental Neuropsychology.*

Chertkow, H., Bub, D. N., & Seidenberg, M. (1989). Priming and semantic memory loss in Alzheimer's disease. *Brain and Language, 36*, 420-446.

Chertkow, H., & Bub, D. N. (1990). Semantic memory in dementia of Alzheimer's type: What do various measures measure? *Brain, 113*, 397-417.

Dean, P. (1982). Analysis of visual behavior in monkeys with inferotemporal lesions. In D. J. Ingle, M. A. Goodale, & R. J. W. Mansfield (Eds.), *Analysis of visual behavior.* Cambridge, MA: MIT Press.

Desimone, R., & Ungerleider, L. G. (1989). Neural mechanisms of visual processing in monkeys. In F. Boller & J. Grafman (Eds.), *Handbook of neuropsychology* (Vol. 2). Amsterdam: Elsevier.

Gaffan, D., Harrison, S., & Gaffan, E. A. (1986). Visual identification following inferotemporal ablation in the monkey. *Quarterly Journal of Experimental Psychology, 38B*, 5-30.

Grober, E., Buschke, H., Kawas, C., & Fuld, P. A. (1985). Impaired ranking of semantic attributes in dementia. *Brain and Language, 26*, 276-286.

Hartman, M. (1991). The use of semantic knowledge in Alzheimer's disease: Evidence for impairments of attention. *Neuropsychologia, 29*, 213-228.

Hyman, B. T., Van Hoesen, G. W., & Damasio, A. R. (1990). Memory-related neural systems in Alzheimer's disease: An anatomic study. *Neurology, 40*, 1721-1730.

Huff, F. J., Corkin, S., & Growdon, J. H. (1986). Semantic impairment and anomia in Alzheimer's disease. *Brain and Language, 28*, 235-249.

Humphreys, G. W., & Bruce, V. (1989). *Visual cognition: Computation, experimental and neuropsychological perspectives.* London: Erlbaum.

Kampen, D., & Martin, A. (1989). The role of object knowledge in constructional skill: A case report. *Journal of Clinical and Experimental Neuropsychology, 11*, 90.

Kaplan, E., Goodglass, H., & Weintraub, S. (1983). *Boston Naming Test.* Philadelphia: Lea & Febiger.

Kroll, J. F., & Potter, M. C. (1984). Recognizing words, pictures, and concepts: A comparison of lexical, object, and reality decisions. *Journal of Verbal Learning and Verbal Behavior, 23*, 39-66.

Martin, A. (1987). Representation of semantic and spatial knowledge in Alzheimer's patients: Implications for models of preserved learning in amnesia. *Journal of Clinical and Experimental Neuropsychology, 9*, 191-224.

Martin, A. (1990). The neuropsychology of Alzheimer's disease: The case for subgroups. In: M. Schwartz (Ed.), *Modular Deficits in Alzheimer-Type Dementia.* Cambridge: Bradford Books/MIT Press.

Martin, A., Brouwers, P., Cox, C., & Fedio P. (1985). On the nature of the verbal memory deficit in Alzheimer's disease. *Brain and Language, 25*, 323-341.

Martin, A., Lalonde, F., Wertheimer, S., & Sunderland, T. (1991). *On-line semantic and repetition priming in patients with Alzheimer's disease and the normal elderly: Evidence for qualitatively distinct patterns of activation.* Unpublished manuscript.

Martin, A., Mack, C., Lalonde, F., & Sunderland, T. (in press). Priming of objects in patients with Alzheimers disease. *Journal of Clinical and Experimental Neuropsychology.*

Martin, A., & Fedio, P. (1983). Word production and comprehension in Alzheimer's disease: The breakdown of semantic knowledge. *Brain and Language, 19*, 124-141.

Nebes, R. D. (1989). Semantic memory in Alzheimer's disease. *Psychological Bulletin, 106*, 377-394.

Nebes, R. D. (in press). Cognitive dysfunction in Alzheimer's disease. In F. I. M. Craik & T. Salthouse (Eds.), *Handbook of cognitive aging.* Hillsdale, NJ: Erlbaum.

Nebes, R. D., Boller, F., & Holland, A. (1986). Use of semantic context by patients with Alzheimer's disease. *Psychology and Aging, 1*, 261-269.

Nebes, R. D., & Brady, C. B. (1988). Integrity of semantic fields in Alzheimer's disease. *Cortex, 24*, 291-299.

Nebes, R. D., & Brady, C. B. (1990). Preserved organization of semantic attributes in Alzheimer's disease. *Psychology and Aging, 5*, 574-579.

Nebes, R. D., Brady, C. B., & Huff, F. J. (1989). Automatic and attentional mechanisms of semantic priming in Alzheimer's disease. *Journal of Clinical and Experimental Neuropsychology, 11*, 219-230.

Nebes, R. D., Martin, D. C., & Horn, L. C. (1984). Sparing of semantic memory in Alzheimer's disease. *Journal of Abnormal Psychology, 93*, 321-330.

Neely, J. H. (1991). Semantic priming effects in visual word recognition: A selective review of current findings and theories. In D. Besner & G. W. Humphreys (Eds.), *Basic processes in reading: Visual word recognition.* Hillsdale, NJ: Erlbaum.

Ober, B. A., Dronkers, N. F., Koss, E., Delis, D. C., & Friedland, R. P. (1986). Retrieval from semantic memory in Alzheimer-type dementia. *Journal of Clinical and Experimental Neuropsychology, 8*, 75-92.

Ober, B. A., & Shenaut, G. K. (1988). Lexical decision and priming in Alzheimer's disease. *Neuropsychologia, 26*, 273-286.

Rosen, W. (1980). Verbal fluency in aging and dementia. *Journal of Clinical Neuropsychology, 2*, 135-146.

Shallice, T. (1988). *From neuropsychology to mental structure.* Cambridge: Cambridge University Press.

Shuttleworth, E. C., & Huber, S. J. (1988). The naming disorder of dementia of Alzheimer type. *Brain and Language, 34*, 222-234.

Snodgrass, J. G., & Vanderwart, M. (1980). A standardized set of 260 pictures: Norms for naming agreement, familiarity, and visual complexity. *Journal of Experimental Psychology: Human Learning and Memory, 6*, 174-215.

Tröster, A. I., Salmon, D. P., McCullough, D., & Butters, N. (1989). A comparison of category fluency deficits associated with Alzheimer's and Huntington's disease. *Brain and Language, 37*, 500-513.

Warrington, E. K. (1975). The selective impairment of semantic memory. *Quarterly Journal of Experimental Psychology, 27*, 635-657.

Warrington, E. K. & Shallice, T. (1979). Semantic access dyslexia. *Brain, 102*, 43-63.

Weingartner, H., Kaye, W., Smallberg, S. A., Ebert, M. H., Gillin, J. C., and Sitaram, N. (1981). Memory failures in progressive idiopathic dementia. *Journal of Abnormal Psychology, 90*, 187-196.

Whitehouse, P., Caramazza, A., & Zurif, E. (1978). Naming in aphasia: Interacting effects of form and function. *Brain and Language, 6*, 63-74.

Memory Functioning in Dementia – L. Bäckman (Editor)

7   Motor and Procedural Memory in Alzheimer's Disease

Malcolm B. Dick

University of California, Irvine

Introduction

"Tell me; I'll forget.
Show me, I may remember.
But involve me, and I'll understand."

Recent research suggests that the memory impairment in Alzheimer's disease (AD) follows the pattern described by this ancient Chinese proverb. Numerous studies examining memory for verbal, visual, and spatial information have shown that AD patients perform at a level far below that of normal older adults. Based on these findings, Martin, Brouwers, Cox, and Fedio (1985), proposed that (a) AD patients fail to encode those meaningful or salient features of a stimulus which increase its memorability, and (b) this impairment extends "across the board" to compromise the encoding of all kinds of information, both verbal and nonverbal. However, the recent discovery that AD patients can learn simple motor movements and skills defies the common assumption that these individuals cannot acquire or retain any new information. The handful of studies performed to date clearly show that AD patients can learn motor- or movement-based information (Dick, Kean, & Sands, 1988) as well as some rather complex perceptual-motor skills such as the rotary pursuit (Corkin et al., 1986; Eslinger & Damasio, 1986; Heindel, Salmon, Shults, Walicke, & Butters, 1989). Consequently, memory for motor information, which by its very nature requires the subject's active participation, may be relatively spared in this impaired population.

In reviewing the limited research on motor memory in AD, this chapter will (a) discuss the importance of studying motor memory, (b) compare memory for motor skills and discrete movements, (c) suggest how knowledge about motor memory may be used in the management, care, and rehabilitation of AD patients, and (d) identify areas for further research.

Why Study Motor Memory in Alzheimer's Disease?

At first glance, it would appear fruitless to investigate memory for movement information in AD. An extensive body of literature suggests that AD patients exhibit a severe memory deficit regardless of the type of material to be remembered (see reviews by Bäckman, Mäntylä, & Herlitz, 1990; Kaszniak, Poon, & Riege, 1986; Morris & Kopelman, 1986). For example, in contrast to normal adults, studies comparing memory for words and faces (Wilson, Kaszniak, Bacon, Fox, & Kelly, 1982), rare and common words (Wilson, Bacon, Kramer, Fox, & Kaszniak, 1983), and pictures and words (Rissenberg & Glanzer, 1986) have shown that the performance of AD patients is unaffected by the type of material presented. Based on these and similar findings, Martin et al. (1985) proposed that the encoding problem in AD extends across the board to encompass the encoding of all kinds of information. However, evidence from several divergent sources can be used to argue against this assumption.

First, histological studies have shown that the neural damage in AD is not global. More specifically, the distribution of senile plaques and neurofibrillary tangles is heaviest in the hippocampus and parietotemporal areas of the brain, with the primary motor and sensory areas being relatively spared (Brun & Englund, 1981). Second, neuroimaging studies using positron emission tomography (PET) show a higher level of metabolic activity in the motor and sensory areas of the brain than in the temporal and parietal regions. Third, studies of language suggest that performing a well learned motor program may help the AD patient activate and/or retrieve otherwise inaccessible information from memory. For example, handling an object or having its use demonstrated can facilitate an AD patient's naming ability (Lawson & Barker, 1968).

Finally, from a theoretical perspective, motor and verbal learning may involve separate memory systems. It is thought that memory for movement based information involves "procedural" (Squire, 1987), "implicit" (Graf & Schachter, 1985), or "indirect" (Johnson & Hasher, 1987) learning while memory for words in a list and other types of factual information is governed by "declarative," "explicit," or "direct" learning. Declarative memory requires conscious recollection of a previous experience and is typically assessed explicitly through tests of recall and recognition. In comparison, procedural memory is demonstrated when information from a previous experience alters or facilitates an individual's performance on a task. For example, procedural learning occurs when performance on a motor skill, such as riding a bicycle, is facilitated by practicing the skill itself.

Types of Motor Memory

Memory for Motor Skills

At this point, memory for motor skills appears to be one of the few forms of procedural learning spared in AD. The discovery that amnestic patients can learn a variety of new procedural skills while being unable to acquire declarative information (Graf, Squire, & Mandler, 1984) prompted researchers to investigate whether the same dissociation exists in AD. Both amnestics and AD patients show a severe deficit in declarative memory while retaining some procedural learning abilities. However, in comparison to amnestics, who are able to perform a wide range of procedural learning tasks at near normal levels (Cohen & Squire, 1980), AD patients demonstrate this form of memory in only a limited number of situations. While AD patients retain the ability to learn motor-based skills (Eslinger & Damasio, 1986; Heindel, Butters, & Salmon, 1988; Heindel et al., 1989) and simple serial reaction time tasks (Grafman et al., 1990; Knopman & Nissen, 1987), research is inconclusive regarding the preservation of other kinds of procedural learning such as word-stem completion priming (Corkin et al., 1986; Grosse, Wilson, & Fox, 1990; Heindel et al., 1989; Partridge, Knight, & Feehan, 1990; Salmon, Shimamura, Butters, & Smith, 1988; Shimamura, Salmon, Squire, & Butters, 1987) and pattern analysis (Corkin et al., 1986; Crystal, Grober, & Masur, 1989). AD patients appear to have difficulty with tasks involving complex perceptual abilities and/or access to semantic memory, but are capable of acquiring forms of procedural knowledge involving motor skills.

Several case studies have documented the preservation of premorbid skills which rely heavily on motor functioning. For example, musical (Beatty et al., 1989; Crystal et al., 1989), artistic (Cummings & Zarit, 1987; Martin, 1987), and athletic (Schacter, 1983) skills have been retained by AD patients for many years following the onset of the disease. These reports, which are concerned with the retention of skills that were highly developed prior to onset, demonstrate a form of "retrograde" procedural learning.

To the surprise of many researchers, mildly to moderately demented AD patients also demonstrate an ability to learn novel motor-based skills which do not rely on premorbid experiences. The small number of experimental studies performed to date have focused primarily on the ability of AD patients to learn the rotary pursuit task (Eslinger & Damasio, 1986; Heindel et al., 1988; Heindel et al., 1989). In the rotary pursuit task, the subject uses a hand-held pointer to track a small target located on the rim of a rotating disk. The amount of time a subject is able to keep the pointer in contact with the target is recorded across learning trials. The results of these studies clearly indicate that AD patients can significantly improve their time on target when given multiple practice trials. For example, in a study by Eslinger and Damasio (1986), AD patients showed approximately 150% improvement in time on target, almost three times as much as that shown by normals over the same training period.

When given comparable amounts of practice at learning a short list of words, these AD patients demonstrated little improvement, only 6% in comparison to the 50% or more shown by healthy older adults. While AD patients show essentially a flat learning curve for verbal information, their learning curve on the rotary pursuit task is similar to that found in normal older adults (Eslinger & Damasio, 1986; Heindel et al., 1988).

Memory for Discrete Movements

Researchers have used the term "motor memory" in a generic fashion to refer to the processes underlying performance on a diverse assortment of motor tasks. Within the construct of motor memory, a distinction can be made between memory for motor skills and memory for movements. Memory for motor skills can be differentiated from memory for movements in that (a) motor skills are acquired slowly through repeated practice, (b) conscious recollection of a previous experience with the task is unnecessary, and (3) learning is demonstrated implicitly through performance. For example, learning on the rotary pursuit task is measured indirectly via improvement in tracking performance across trials. While memory for motor skills appears to tap primarily procedural kinds of learning, memory for movements places a greater emphasis on declarative memory. More specifically, memory for movement involves the explicit recall or reproduction of a previously learned movement, or some attribute of that movement.

A series of studies was conducted by this author to investigate various aspects of memory for movements in AD. To date, no other research exists in this area. These experiments contrasted memory for motor and verbal information with parallel tasks. This strategy was used to test (a) the common assumption that the cognitive impairment in AD compromises the encoding of all kinds of information, and (b) the degree to which verbal and motor memory are isomorphic, that is, affected by similar processes and governed by the same general laws.

Some researchers argue for a single parsimonious memory system, with a unitary set of laws that can be applied across the verbal and motor domains. As evidence, this school of thought cites a number of similar phenomena in both domains, including release from proactive inhibition (Dickinson & Higgins, 1977), incidental learning (Dickinson, 1977), levels of processing (Ho & Shea, 1979), context (Shea & Zimny, 1983) and serial position (Magill & Dowell, 1977) effects, as well as differences between recall and recognition (Wallace & McGhee, 1979). An opposing school of thought contends that the verbal and motor domains are governed by different sets of rules and involve separate, independent memory stores (Adams, 1983). For example, Engelkamp and Krumnacker (1980) and Saltz and Donnenwerth-Nolan (1981) propose that the motor system is mediated by different mechanisms from those governing the verbal and visual systems, and an individual's performance in the motor domain is not necessarily correlated with performance in the other two.

In studies using a parallel design, poor performance by AD patients on both verbal and motor tasks would support the validity of the encoding limitation hypothesis (Martin et al., 1985) and the unitary nature of the mechanisms underlying memory. However, similar performance by AD patients and normal older adults on the motor tasks would support the existence of separate memory systems and conflict with the assumption that AD patients are impaired in the encoding of all types of information.

Enhancing motor memory in AD. Researchers have demonstrated that the same cognitive process, actively involving the subject in stimulus generation, facilitates both verbal and motor memory in a wide variety of populations, including children, the mentally retarded, and normal older adults. In the verbal domain, this process is called the *generation effect* (Slamecka & Graf, 1978) and refers to the fact that recall is superior when the subject generates the to-be-remembered material compared to merely reading it. In the motor domain, the parallel process has been called the *preselection effect* (Stelmach, Kelso, & Wallace, 1975) and refers to the fact that when a blindfolded subject is allowed to select the end location of a motor movement, recall is more accurate than when the same location is determined by the experimenter. The empirical results of studies investigating the generation and preselection effects in these varied populations are essentially the same: Information that is internally generated by the subject is recalled more accurately than identical information provided by an external source.

Given the impressive effect that subject involvement has on memory in normal adults, several studies have examined whether this same process would enhance retention in individuals with AD. In Dick, Kean, and Sands (1989a), instructions directed subjects to either read a list of words or generate the same material according to a specified rule. Presumably, the act of generating a word from semantic memory results in a deeper or more meaningful encoding of its features than does simply reading it. The results supported this interpretation as both the young and healthy older adults recalled more than twice as many subject-generated words as read words. In contrast, the AD patients showed no recall advantage for internally generated verbal information. The absence of the generation effect under conditions involving free recall and recognition (Dick et al., 1989a), as well as cued recall (Mitchell, Hunt, & Schmitt, 1986), provides converging evidence that this process is impaired in AD patients.

However, a considerably different pattern of results emerged in an analogous preselection task which involved the recall of discrete motor movements made on a linear positioning apparatus (Dick et al., 1988). This task involves positioning of a moveable slide along two parallel rails. The experiment compared the recall accuracy of subject-generated (preselected) movements and experimenter-defined (constrained) movements under conditions excluding all visual input. Preselected movements are considered to be more meaningful and hence processed at a deeper level of analysis than are constrained movements. In the controls and AD patients, preselected movements were recalled more accurately than constrained movements. The ability of the generative process to enhance recall on the motor but not the verbal task suggests that the encoding deficiency in AD may not extend across all types of information. In addition, these results suggest that, at least in the motor domain, efforts to enhance encoding in AD patients can have a facilitative effect on their memory.

Encoding and forgetting in motor memory. Additional studies by this author investigating memory for verbal and motor information in AD used two well known research paradigms. These experiments examined: (a) the rate of forgetting of verbal and motor information from short-term memory (STM) using the Brown-Peterson distractor task, and (b) differences in how verbal and motor information are encoded with the release from proactive interference (RPI) paradigm. If memory for movements is relatively preserved in AD as the preselection study suggested (Dick et al., 1988), it was hypothesized that the pattern of performance found on STM tasks using motor stimuli might also be different from that found in the analogous situation using verbal materials.

Most of the experimental data and theory concerning the STM deficit in AD have come from studies using three types of tasks: (a) digit or word span, (b) the Brown-Peterson distractor task, and (c) immediate free recall of supraspan word lists (cf., Kaszniak et al., 1986). The results of these studies indicate that AD patients suffer from both an encoding deficiency and an accelerated loss of information from the short-term store. While these three tasks have considerably advanced our understanding of the STM deficit in AD, they all suffer from the same limitation of relying on verbal materials for the to-be-remembered stimuli.

A recent experiment by this author examined STM functioning in AD patients using a verbal and "motor analogue" of the Brown-Peterson task (Dick, Kean, & Harris, 1991). By using a motor analogue of the Brown-Peterson task, it is possible to examine the encoding and retention of different aspects of a movement. Memory for both the "distance" and "direction" of a movement were studied as these features appear to be represented by qualitatively different types of memory codes. More specifically, directional information appears to be represented by higher level, conceptual codes while distance information is represented by lower level, perceptual codes (Diewert, 1975; Laabs, 1973).

In this experiment, the verbal version of the Brown-Peterson task involved presenting three words to the subject on each trial, with recall being tested either immediately or after varying delay intervals (5, 10, or 20 seconds) filled with a distracting cognitive activity (i.e., counting backwards aloud). In the motor analogue of this task, the experimenter determined the length and direction of a linear movement which the blindfolded subject then performed using his or her dominant arm. Following 0, 5, 10, or 20 seconds of the interference task (counting aloud), the subject was asked to reproduce the same movement. On each trial, memory for distance was determined by comparing the lengths of the initial and recall movements, and memory for direction by determining the size of the angle separating these two movements. Varying the interval between the initial and recall movements provided information regarding the rate of decay of distance and directional information.

For the most part, the results of the verbal version of the Brown-Peterson task held no surprises and essentially replicated previous research (Corkin, 1982; Kopelman, 1985). Compared to the normal controls, the AD patients showed a very steep gradient of forgetting with almost no memory of the three words after only 5 seconds of the distractor task. In comparison, these same patients were able to recall some aspects of the motor movements even after 20 seconds of the distractor task. Evidently, not all information is lost from STM after only a few seconds in AD, and the shape of the forgetting curve is a function of the type of information being processed. Interestingly, the AD patients exhibited greater difficulty in encoding and retaining information about the movement's direction than its distance. These results suggest that AD patients have more difficulty in encoding the conceptual than the perceptual features of a movement.

The RPI task was used in a follow-up study to further investigate differences in how AD patients encode verbal and motor information. Proactive interference refers to the increasing difficulty subjects have learning later members of a series following the learning of its earlier members. RPI occurs when a shift in the features of the to-be-remembered stimuli results in improved learning and memory. A sensitive test of vulnerability to interference, RPI can be used to determine the effect that changes in the conceptual features of a stimulus have on encoding.

In the verbal RPI task, similar to that used by Cushman, Como, Booth, and Caine (1988), subjects were presented with a series of five word lists with recall being tested immediately after each list. The first four lists consisted of items from the same conceptual category (e.g., occupations). In the "category shift" condition, the fifth list consisted of items from a different category (e.g., clothing). In the "no-shift" control condition, items in all five lists came from the same conceptual category. By manipulating the conceptual features of the words on the critical fifth trial, we determined what attributes of the stimuli were being encoded into memory. In contrast to normal adults, AD patients in both the present experiment and the Cushman et al. (1988) study did not show the expected build-up of proactive interference across lists nor did they show RPI with changes in the conceptual characteristics of the stimulus words. The absence of a RPI effect in the AD patients following a shift from one taxonomic category to another suggests that these individuals are deficient in processing the semantic or meaningful properties of a verbal stimulus.

In an analogous RPI task, blindfolded subjects were presented with a series of five movements of varying lengths to remember. Subjects were asked to recall the movements in the reverse order of presentation so that the last movement in the series was the first one recalled. As directional information appears to be encoded at a meaningful or conceptual level, a change in this attribute, like the category shift in the verbal task, was expected to produce

RPI (Dickinson & Higgins, 1977). In the shift condition, the critical fifth movement in the series was similar to the first four in length but differed from the others in direction. In the no-shift control condition, all five movements were performed in the same direction. Evidence for the RPI phenomenon was obtained by comparing the accuracy of recall for the critical fifth movement in the shift and no-shift conditions.

While only normal adults showed RPI in the verbal task, both AD patients and controls demonstrated (a) a build-up of proactive interference across trials on the motor task, and (b) improved recall following a change in the direction of the last movement in the series. The presence of RPI in the motor but not the verbal domain suggests that AD patients are sensitive to changes in the meaningful characteristics of movements but not words.

Summary of Research on Memory for Movements

In summary, the studies investigating memory for movements in AD have demonstrated that: (a) memory for motor information can be enhanced by actively involving AD patients in the generation of the to-be-remembered movements, (b) motor information may not be lost as rapidly from short-term memory as verbal information, and (c) AD patients have difficulty encoding the meaningful aspects of both motor movements and words.

Subject-Performed Tasks

Memory for motor skills appears to be primarily procedural in nature while the reproduction of discrete movements seems to place a greater emphasis on declarative learning. However, some paradigms, such as subject-performed tasks (SPTs), may involve both a procedural and a declarative memory component. In SPTs, subjects are asked to perform and later recall a series of simple concrete actions such as bouncing a ball and breaking a toothpick. Experiments using SPTs compare memory for a series of performed tasks with memory for verbal descriptors of the same tasks. In the control condition, subjects receive verbal decriptions of the to-be-remembered tasks but no objects are presented and the described activities are not performed motorically. It has been speculated that recall of the verbal descriptors relies on declarative memory whereas the manipulation of the objects at encoding activates well-learned motor programs in procedural memory.

Researchers have used SPTs to investigate the benefits of motoric activation at encoding in AD patients. Two early studies (Dick, Kean, & Sands, 1989b; Karlsson et al., 1989) compared the retention of SPTs and verbal descriptors in AD patients and normal elderly controls. At free recall, the normal older adults in these studies showed better memory for SPTs than the verbal descriptors, while the AD patients failed to exhibit this effect. Despite these negative findings, motoric activation at encoding does appear to benefit the AD patient when cues are provided at recall. In studies by Karlsson et al. (1989) and Herlitz, Adolfsson, Bäckman, and Nilsson (1991), subjects were presented with SPTs from various semantic categories so that category names could be used as retrieval cues. While the advantage for SPTs fails to occur in AD patients at free recall (Dick et al., 1989b; Karlsson et al., 1989), these same individuals show a marked improvement in memory for activities when cues are provided at retrieval. These findings suggest that active motor involvement at encoding along with cuing at retrieval can enhance memory in AD.

Data from the SPT studies illustrate the importance of providing support at both encoding and retrieval in order to optimize memory functioning in AD patients. The relatively intact performance of AD patients on many motor tasks may be related to the high degree of similarity between encoding and retrieval conditions. In studies examining motor learning, the task demands at retrieval are identical to those present at encoding. For example, in the preselection study by Dick et al. (1988), patients were asked to select and perform a movement at encoding and replicate this same movement at time of retrieval.

Practical Applications

Studies investigating motor learning in AD have been reviewed in light of questions about the extent of the encoding deficit in the disease and the nature of memory processes governing various types of information. It could be concluded from this review that evidence of motor learning in AD (a) refutes the common assumption of "across the board" impairment in encoding, and (b) supports the declarative-procedural distinction in memory processes. However, the implications of research findings which demonstrate that motor learning is possible even in the late stages of AD extend beyond description and theoretical development to day-to-day patient care. Knowledge about the nature and extent of preserved abilities in AD can be used to design behavioral management strategies and rehabilitative programs to optimize functioning.

Theories of adaptive behavior and experiential knowledge of care providers both suggest that presenting AD patients with tasks which utilize remaining strengths can reduce problem behaviors and promote maximal functioning. Currently, manipulating the physical, social, and activity-related aspects of the AD patient's environment is considered the cornerstone of effective care and management (Knopman & Sawyer-DeMaris, 1990). Lawton and Nahemow (1973) suggested that adaptive behavior and positive affect are products of an adequate match between environmental demands and individual competence. Consequently, maladaptive behavior and negative affect can be reversed, according to Lawton and Nahemow, by lowering environmental demands or increasing individual competence. To date, patient management strategies in

AD have focused primarily on lowering environmental demands by eliminating confusing items from the environment, adding cues, and modifying task demands (Kemp, 1988). However, in the motor domain, it may also be possible to raise the competency of AD patients through efficient training strategies aimed at developing the preserved ability of these impaired individuals to learn and retain new movement information.

The activities AD patients are asked to engage in - from activities of daily living to recreational activities - constitute part of the environment that can be modified to maximize functioning (Ansello, 1985). To produce adaptive behavior, activities should present the AD patient with limited demands which are sufficiently matched to individual competence. Involving patients in activities which tap and develop relatively intact abilities, such as motor skills, should maximize functioning, reduce problem behaviors, and enhance mood. The effectiveness of modifying task demands as a behavior management strategy remains untested. However, caregivers of dementia patients attending adult day care centers, which provide activities tailored for the cognitively impaired, report that program involvement can improve mood and reduce problem behaviors such as agitation, combativeness, wandering, and sleep disturbance (California Department of Aging, 1987). In a survey of 346 adult day care centers across the United States, activities which utilize motor skills, such as dancing, exercise, and physically active games, were rated as most successful with demented participants (Mace & Rabins, 1984). To date, activity professionals have promoted the use of motor activities with dementia patients based on experiential knowledge of what works (Mace, 1987). Research findings which establish the continued ability of AD patients to acquire motor information now provide an empirical basis for the effectiveness of movement-based activities with these impaired individuals.

To help care providers match task demands to remaining competencies, Levy (1986) recently outlined a downward progression of six cognitive ability levels during dementia and provided suggestions for appropriate motor tasks at each level. For example, at level 4, Levy describes individuals with significant cognitive impairment as appearing less confused while engaged in two- to three-step action-oriented activities such as yardwork or simple household chores. In comparison, highly disorganized individuals at level 2 will be successful only at activities involving one-step, repetitive gross motor actions, such as throwing a ball. At this level, a primary goal of care becomes redirecting unwanted and unsafe movement patterns, such as wandering, into productive motor activities, such as dancing. Care providers working with severely demented patients at levels 1 and 2 must find creative ways to utilize movement in achieving desired ends, such as cooperation in activities of daily living or participation in activity programs. For example, movement therapy has been used to stimulate past memories in severely demented patients (Sandel & Kelleher, 1987). With encouragement, engaging dementia patients in simple, repetitive movements can lead to verbalizations about images associated with those movements. Although problem behaviors such as wandering cannot be alleviated entirely through behavioral management strategies, teaching caregivers to distract patients from unwanted behaviors with activities which utilize preserved motor abilities could significantly reduce the frustration both caregiver and patient may experience when performance demands fail to adequately match competencies.

Further Areas of Exploration

Most of our knowledge about how AD patients learn and retain motor information has come from the handful of recent experiments reviewed in this chapter. As research concerning memory for movement information in AD is very sparse, this area merits further investigation. Several aspects of motor learning in AD have not been examined. These include (a) the acquisition of both fine and gross motor skills, (b) the effects that variations in amount and type of practice have on acquisition of motor skills, (c) the retention of motor skills over long-term delays, (d) the transfer or generalization of motor learning, (e) inter- and intra-individual differences in motor learning, and (f) the effectiveness of applying these research findings to patient management.

Fine versus Gross Motor Skills

The ability of AD patients to learn both "fine" and "gross" motor skills has not yet been examined. Generally speaking, behaviors that involve total body movement and multi-limb movement such as walking, swimming, making a tennis serve, or rolling a ball are considered "gross" motor skills. In contrast, "fine" motor skills involve the manipulation of small objects, tools, or the precise control of machines. Tasks such as typing, handwriting, and operating the rotary pursuit apparatus are considered fine motor skills. It is unknown whether the pattern of relatively normal learning shown by AD patients on fine motor skills, such as rotary pursuit, also characterizes their learning of a well coordinated, gross motor movement such as throwing.

Amount and Type of Practice

Research has failed to address how varying the amount and type of practice influences the learning of both fine and gross motor skills in AD. The ability of AD patients to learn the rotary pursuit task has been demonstrated within short practice periods. However, it is unknown whether providing additional training, which facilitates learning in normal adults, will similarly enhance the performance of AD patients.

Retention of Motor Skills

With the exception of Eslinger and Damasio (1986), who found little for-getting on the rotary pursuit apparatus after a 20-minute delay, researchers have failed to examine whether AD patients can retain this or any other motor skill for longer periods of time. This is surprising as motor skills, once learned, are remarkably resistant to forgetting. For example, normal adults have shown little forgetting of the rotary pursuit task after delays ranging from 10 minutes to 4 weeks (Jahnke & Duncan, 1956), to one year (Bell, 1950). Studies of gross motor skills have found essentially the same patterns of excellent long-term retention as seen with fine motor skills (e.g., Ryan, 1962). While AD patients can acquire new motor skills, it is unknown whether these impaired individuals demonstrate a pattern of long-term retention similar to that of normal adults.

Transfer of Motor Skills

The question of whether AD patients can use a motor skill learned in one task situation to facilitate the learning of a second motor task also remains unanswered. The ability to transfer or generalize a skill across different task situations is a cardinal feature of adaptive functioning. Studies of normal adults show that the transfer of motor skills is an automatic process that usually occurs without conscious awareness (Keele, Cohen, & Ivry, 1990). As automatic types of processing are relatively well maintained in AD (cf., Jorm, 1986), the positive transfer of motor skills from one situation to another may also occur in AD patients.

Inter- and Intra-Individual Differences

While AD patients can acquire new motor skills, not all of these indi-viduals acquire them with equal proficiency, and a small percentage show little or no improvement with practice. The variability between AD patients in motor learning is greater than that found with normal adults and occurs on a wide variety of motor tasks including the rotary pursuit (Eslinger & Damasio, 1986), serial reaction time (Knopman & Nissen, 1987), and preselection (Dick, et al., 1988) tasks. These studies suggest that relatively global measures such as the severity of the patient's cognitive impairment and overall level of intellectual functioning do not appear to account for this variability. At present, our un-derstanding of why some AD patients can acquire a motor task while others cannot is limited to these findings and requires further investigation.

Patient Management

The discovery that motor learning is relatively preserved in AD appears to have many practical applications for patient care. For instance, AD patients may be able to use the relatively preserved procedural memory system which governs motor learning to partially compensate for losses in other cognitive abilities. In addition, the knowledge that AD patients can learn and retain new movement-based information can be used by care providers to develop effective behavioral management strategies. Future research should empirically evaluate the efficacy of applying these new discoveries to Motor Memory behavior management and rehabilitation.

References

Adams, J. A. (1983). On integration of the verbal and motor domains. In R. A. Magill (Ed.), *Memory and control of action*. Amsterdam: North-Holland.

Ansello, E. F. (1985). The activity coordinator as environmental press. *Activities, Adaptation, and Aging, 6*, 87-97.

Bäckman, L., Mäntylä, T., & Herlitz, A. (1990). The optimization of episodic remembering in old age. In P. B. Baltes & M. M. Baltes (Eds.), *Successful aging: Perspectives from the behavioral sciences*. New York: Cambridge University Press.

Beatty, W. W., Zavadil, K. D., Bailly, R. C., Rixen, G. L., Zavadil, L. E., Farnham, N., & Fisher, L. (1988). Preserved musical skill in a severely demented patient. *International Journal of Clinical Neuropsychology, 10*, 158-164.

Bell, H. M. (1950). Retention of pursuit rotor skill after one year. *Journal of Experimental Psychology, 40*, 648-649.

Brun, A., & Englund, E. (1981). Regional patterns of degeneration in Alzheimer's disease: Neuronal loss and histopathological grading. *Histopathology, 5*, 549-564.

California Department of Aging. (1987, September-October). *Report of the caregiver opinion survey* (available from the California Department of Aging, 1600 K Street, Sacramento, California 95814).

Cohen, N. J., & Squire, L. R. (1980). Preserved learning and retention of pattern analyzing skills in amnesia: Dissociation of knowing how and knowing that. *Science, 210*, 207-210.

Corkin, S. (1982). Some relationships between global amnesias and the memory impairments in Alzheimer's disease. In S. Corkin, K. L. Davis, J. H. Growden, E. Usdin, & R. J. Wurtman (Eds.), *Alzheimer's Disease: A report of progress in research*. Raven Press: New York.

Corkin, S., Gabrieli, J. D. E., Stanger, B. Z., Mickel, T., Rosen, T. J., Sullivan, E. V., & Growdon, J. H. (1986). Skill learning and priming in Alzheimer's disease. *Neurology, 36*, 296.

Crystal, H. A., Grober, E., & Masur, D. (1989). Preservation of musical memory in Alzheimer's disease. *Journal of Neurology, Neurosurgery, and Psychiatry, 52*, 1415-1416.

Cummings, J. L., & Zarit, J. M. (1987). Probable Alzheimer's disease in an artist. *Journal of the American Medical Association, 258*, 2731-2734.

Cushman, L. A., Como, P. G., Booth, H., & Caine, E. D. (1988). Cued recall and release from proactive interference in Alzheimer's disease. *Journal of Clinical and Experimental Neuropsychology, 10*, 685-692.

Dick, M. B., Kean, M.- L., & Harris, A. (1991). *Forgetting from short-term motor memory in Alzheimer's disease.* Manuscript submitted for publication.

Dick, M. B., Kean, M.- L., & Sands, D. (1988). The preselection effect on the recall facilitation of motor movements in Alzheimer-type dementia. *Journal of Gerontology, 43,* 127-135.

Dick, M. B., Kean, M.- L., & Sands, D. (1989a). Memory for internally generated words in Alzheimer-Type Dementia: Breakdown in encoding and semantic memory. *Brain and Cognition, 9,* 88-108.

Dick, M. B., Kean, M.- L., & Sands, D. (1989b). Memory for action events in Alzheimer-Type Dementia: Further evidence of an encoding failure. *Brain and Cognition, 9,* 71-87.

Dickinson, J. (1977). Incidental motor learning. *Journal of Motor Behavior, 9,* 135-138.

Dickinson, J., & Higgins, N. (1977). Release from proactive and retroactive interference in motor short-term memory. *Journal of Motor Behavior, 9,* 61-66.

Diewert, G. L. (1975). Retention and coding in motor short-term memory: A comparison of storage codes for distance and location. *Journal of Motor Behavior, 7,* 183-190.

Engelkamp, J., & Krumnacker, H. (1980). Image and motor processes in the retention of verbal materials. *Zeitschrift fur Experimentelle und Angewandte Psychologie, 27,* 511-533.

Eslinger, P. J., & Damasio, A. R. (1986). Preserved motor learning in Alzheimer's disease: Implications for anatomy and behavior. *Journal of Neuroscience, 6,* 3006-3009.

Graf, P., & Schacter, D. L. (1985). Implicit and explicit memory for new associations in normal and amnesic subjects. *Journal of Experimental Psychology: Learning, Memory, and Cognition, 11,* 501-518.

Graf, P., Squire, L. R., & Mandler, G. (1984). The information that amnesic patients do not forget. *Journal of Experimental Psychology: Learning, Memory, and Cognition, 10,* 164-178.

Grafman, J., Weingartner, H., Newhouse, P. A., Thompson, K., Lalonde, F., Litvan, I., Molchan, S., & Sunderland, T. (1990). Implicit learning in patients with Alzheimer's disease. *Pharmacopsychiatry, 23,* 94-101.

Grosse, D. A., Wilson, R. S., & Fox, J. H. (1990). Preserved word-stem-completion priming of semantically encoded information in Alzheimer's disease. *Psychology and Aging, 5,* 304-306.

Heindel, W. C., Butters, N., & Salmon, D. P. (1988). Impaired learning of a motor skill in patients with Huntington's disease. *Behavioral Neuroscience, 102,* 141-147.

Heindel, W. C., Salmon, D. P., Shults, C. W., Walicke, P. A., & Butters, N. (1989). Neuropsychological evidence for multiple implicit memory systems: A comparison of Alzheimer's, Huntington's, and Parkinson's disease patients. *The Journal of Neuroscience, 9,* 582-587.

Herlitz, A., Adolfsson, R., Bäckman, L., & Nilsson, L.- G. (1991). Cue utilization following different forms of encoding in mildly, moderately, and severely demented patients with Alzheimer's disease. *Brain and Cognition., 15,* 119-130.

Ho, L., & Shea, J. B. (1979). Orienting task specificity in incidental motor learning. *Journal of Motor Behavior, 11,* 135-140.

Jahnke, J. C., & Duncan, C. P. (1956). Reminiscence and forgetting in motor learning after extended rest intervals. *Journal of Experimental Psychology, 52,* 273-282.

Johnson, M. K., & Hasher, L. (1987). Human learning and memory. *Annual Review of Psychology, 38,* 631-638.

Jorm, A. F. (1986). Controlled versus automatic information processing in senile dementia: A review. *Psychological Medicine, 16,* 77-88.

Karlsson, T., Bäckman, L., Herlitz, A., Nilsson, L.- G., Winblad, B., & Österlind, P.- O. (1989). Memory improvement at different stages of Alzheimer's disease. *Neuropsychologia, 27,* 737-742.

Kaszniak, A. W., Poon, L. W., & Reige, W. (1986). Assessing memory deficits: An information processing approach. In L. W. Poon (Ed.), *Handbook for clinical memory assessment of older adults*, Washington, D.C: American Psychological Association.

Keele, S. W., Cohen, A. & Ivry, R. (1990). Motor programs. In M. Jeannerol (Ed.), *Attention and performance* (Vol. 13). Hillsdale, NJ: Erlbaum.

Kemp, B. J. (1988). Eight methods family members can use to manage behavioral problems in dementia. *Topics in Geriatric Rehabilitation, 4*, 50-59.

Knopman, D. S. & Nissen, M. J. (1987). Implicit learning in patients with probable Alzheimer's disease. *Neurology, 37*, 784-789.

Knopman, D. S. & Sawyer-DeMaris, S. (1990). A practical approach to managing behavioral problems in dementia patients. *Geriatrics, 45*, 27-35.

Kopelman, M. D. (1985). Multiple memory deficits in Alzheimer type dementia: Implications for pharmacotherapy. *Psychological Medicine, 16*, 379-390.

Laabs, G. J. (1973). Retention characteristics of different reproduction cues in motor short-term memory. *Journal of Experimental Psychology, 100*, 168-177.

Lawson, J. S., & Barker, M. G. (1968). The assessment of nominal dysphasia in dementia: The use of reaction-time measures. *British Journal of Medical Psychology, 41*, 411-414.

Lawton, M. P., & Nahemow, L. (1973). Ecology and the aging process. In C. Eisdorfer & M. P. Lawton (Eds.), *The psychology of adult development and aging*. Washington, D.C.: American Psychological Association.

Levy, L. L. (1986). A practical guide to the care of the Alzheimer's disease victim: The cognitive disability perspective. *Topics in Geriatric Rehabilitation, 1*, 16-26.

Mace, N. L. (1987). Principles of activities for persons with dementia. *Physical and Occupational Therapy in Geriatrics, 5*, 13-27.

Mace, N. L. & Rabins, P. (1984, December). *A survey of day care for the demented adult in the United States*. (Available from the National Council on Aging, 600 Maryland Ave., West Wing 100, Washington, D. C. 20024).

Magill R. A. & Dowell, M. N. (1977). Serial-position effects in in motor short-term memory. *Journal of Motor Behavior, 9*, 319-323.

Martin, A. (1987). Representation of semantic and spatial knowledge in Alzheimer's patients: Implications for models of preserved learning in amnesia. *Journal of Clinical and Experimental Neuropsychology, 9*, 191-224.

Martin, A., Brouwers, P., Cox, C., & Fedio, P. (1985). On the nature of the verbal memory deficit in Alzheimer's disease. *Brain and Language, 25*, 323-341.

Mitchell, D. B., Hunt, R. R., & Schmitt, F. A. (1986). The generation effect and reality monitoring: Evidence from dementia and normal aging. *Journal of Gerontology, 41*, 79-84.

Morris, R. G., & Kopelman, M. D. (1986). The memory deficits in Alzheimer-type dementia: A review. *Quarterly Journal of Experimental Psychology, 38A*, 575-602.

Partridge, F. M., Knight, R. G., & Feehan, M. (1990). Direct and indirect memory performance in patients with senile dementia. *Psychological Medicine, 20*, 111-118.

Rissenberg, M. & Glanzer, M. (1986). Picture superiority in free recall: The effects of normal aging and primary degenerative dementia. *Journal of Gerontology, 41*, 64-71.

Ryan, E. D. (1962). Retention of stabilometer and pursuit rotor skills. *Research Quarterly, 25*, 91-99.

Salmon, D. P., Shimamura, A. P., Butters, N., & Smith, S. (1988). Lexical and semantic priming deficits in patients with Alzheimers disease. *Journal of Clinical and Experimental Neuropsychology, 10*, 501-508.

Saltz, E., & Donnenwerth-Nolan, S. (1981). Does motoric imagery facilitate memory for sentences? A selective interference test. *Journal of Verbal Learning and Verbal Behavior, 20*, 322-332.

Sandel, S. L., & Kelleher, M. (1987). A psychosocial approach to dance-movement therapy. *Activities, Adaptation, and Aging, 9*, 25-39.

Schacter, D. L. (1983). Amnesia observed: Remembering and forgetting in a natural environment. *Journal of Abnormal Psychology, 92*, 236-242.

Shea, J. B., & Zimny, S. T. (1983). Context effects in memory and learning movement information. In R. A. Magill (Ed.), *Memory and control of action.* Amsterdam: North Holland.

Shimamura, A. P., Salmon, D. P., Squire, L. R., & Butters, N. (1987). Memory dysfunction and word priming in dementia and amnesia. *Behavioral Neuroscience, 101*, 347-351.

Slamecka, N. J., & Graf, P. (1978). The generation effect: Delineation of a phenomenon. *Journal of Experimental Psychology: Human Learning and Memory, 4*, 592-604.

Squire, L. R. (1987). *Memory and brain.* New York: Oxford University Press.

Stelmach, G. E., Kelso, J. A. S., & Wallace, S. A. (1975). Preselection in short-term motor memory. *Journal of Experimental Psychology: Human Learning and Memory, 1*, 745-755.

Wallace, S. A., & McGhee, R. C. (1979). The independence of recall and recognition in motor learning. *Journal of Motor Behavior, 11*, 141-151.

Wilson, R. S., Bacon, L. D., Kramer, R. L., Fox, J. H., & Kaszniak, A. W. (1983). Word frequency effect and recognition memory in dementia of the Alzheimer type. *Journal of Clinical Neuropsychology, 5*, 97-104.

Wilson, R. S., Kaszniak, A. W., Bacon, L. D., Fox, J. H., & Kelly, M. P. (1982). Facial recognition memory in dementia. *Cortex, 18*, 329-336.

Section III

ALZHEIMER'S DISEASE AND OTHER CLINICAL POPULATIONS

Memory Functioning in Dementia – L. Bäckman (Editor)
© 1992 Elsevier Science Publishers B.V. All rights reserved.   153

8   **Memory Dysfunction in the
       Subcortical Dementias**

William W. Beatty

University of Oklahoma

Introduction

The term "subcortical dementia" was introduced by Albert, Feldman, and Willis (1974) to describe the intellectual impairment associated with progressive supranuclear palsy (PSP). The dementia of PSP was said to be characterized by slowed information processing (bradyphrenia), impairments in problem solving, planning and the ability to manipulate acquired knowledge, memory disturbances (forgetfulness) believed to arise from difficulties with retrieval, and mood and personality changes (especially apathy and depression) without the aphasia, apraxia, agnosia and more severe amnesia of Alzheimer's disease (AD) and other cortical dementias (e.g., Pick's disease).

In subsequent years, the concept of subcortical dementia has been expanded to include other neurological disorders such as Huntington's disease (HD), Parkinson's disease (PD), Wilson's disease, and multiple sclerosis (MS) (e.g., Cummings & Benson, 1984; Huber & Paulson, 1985; Rao, 1986).

The increasing range of diseases to which the concept of subcortical dementia has been applied provides one measure of the growing interest in this concept. However, the idea that there are two separable dementia syndromes, one subcortical, the other cortical, has been questioned.

On strict anatomical grounds the cortical-subcortical distinction is impossible to defend since cortical changes occur in PD, HD, and MS (e.g., Boller, Mitzutani, Roessman, & Gambetti, 1980; Sandberg & Coyle, 1984), and subcortical pathology is typical of AD (e.g., Katzman, 1986). Nevertheless, the distinction between cortical and subcortical dementia might have clinical validity (see Cummings, 1986, 1988; Whitehouse, 1986, for differing views). For this to be the case, it would be necessary to show that the apparent qualitative differences between dementias cannot be attributed to differences in overall dementia severity.

In a recent and thorough review of the neuropsychological literature on AD, HD and PD, Brown and Marsden (1988) concluded that the concept of distinct subcortical and cortical dementia syndromes lacked empirical confirmation because neither the required similarity in the profiles of cognitive impairment of HD and PD nor the differences between patterns of cognitive disturbance in these diseases and in AD had been established. Instead, they suggested that the similarities in the patterns of cognitive impairment in HD, PD and AD were far greater than the differences.

Since the publication of their paper, two studies have demonstrated differences in the profiles of cognitive impairment of HD and AD patients on relatively simple mental status examinations. Brandt, Folstein, and Folstein (1988) equated groups of AD and HD patients in terms of total score on the Mini-Mental State Examination (MMSE) (Folstein, Folstein, & McHugh, 1975). Patients with AD were more impaired than patients with HD in recalling words after a brief delay, while HD patients were more impaired than AD patients on serial subtraction. These differences were obtained over a broad range of levels of dementia severity. Similar findings were reported by Salmon, Kwo-on Yuen, Heindel, Butters, and Thal (1989) using the Dementia Rating Scale (Mattis, 1976). In groups of HD and AD patients that were equated for total score on the test, they found that the AD patients were more impaired than the HD patients in the Memory subtest, while the HD patients were more impaired than the AD patients on the Initiation subtest. Similar comparisons for other patient groups have not yet been reported. Nevertheless, these findings demonstrate that there are differences in the patterns of cognitive impairment displayed by HD and AD patients which cannot be attributed to differences in dementia severity.

Using a somewhat more elaborate battery, Huber, Shuttleworth, and Freidenberg (1989) were able to differentiate AD and PD patients, equated for overall scores on the MMSE. The AD patients had more serious memory, naming, and orientation problems, while the PD patients did more poorly on tasks requiring rapid information processing. This is similar to the pattern of more severe initiation deficits in the HD patients reported by Salmon, Kwo-on Yuen et al., (1989).

These studies establish that there are differences in the overall cognitive profiles of AD and subcortical patients with dementia, but they do not address the question of whether these differences are qualitative or only quantitative.

In this chapter, I will review recent studies concerned with memory in patients with PD, HD, and MS. Where possible, comparisons of these patient groups with AD patients will be made. Such comparisons are difficult to make because the overall level of cognitive impairment is often not comparable among groups. This is especially true for comparisons of MS and AD patients and to a lesser extent of comparisons of PD and AD patients. Unlike HD and AD, in which dementia inevitably results if the patient survives long enough, cognitive impairments in MS and PD are quite variable. Many investigators have chosen to study only mildly affected patients in the hope of avoiding some of the interpretative difficulties associated with pronounced sensory and motor disability typical of advanced stages of these diseases. This strategy is often useful but it further complicates comparisons of different dementias.

Albert (1978) suggested that "frontosubcortical dementia" might be a more appropriate term to describe the cognitive impairments associated with subcortical diseases. Although this suggestion was never adopted, many investigators have considered the possibility that the cognitive changes that accompany subcortical diseases arise from disruption of frontal lobe circuitry. The relationship between memory disturbances and deficits in problem solving and other "executive" functions usually ascribed to the frontal lobes receives extensive consideration in this review.

Anterograde Memory

Deficits in learning and remembering new information are commonly reported in MS, PD, and HD. Explicit memory tasks, on which subjects consciously try to recall or recognize previously presented material have been studied most often, but there is increasing interest in implicit memory, which does not require conscious recollection.

Short-Term Memory

Clinically, short-term memory (STM) is usually assessed using tests such as digit or word span for verbal STM and block span for non-verbal STM. On such tests, MS patients often perform normally (Heaton, Nelson, Thompson, Burks, & Franklin, 1985; Jambor, 1969; Rao, Hammeke, McQuillen, Khatri, & Lloyd, 1984) but mild deficits have been observed in some studies (Fischer, 1988; Huber et al., 1987; Lyon-Caen et al., 1986). In PD, performance on digit or word span tests may be normal (Asso, 1969; Huber, Shuttleworth, Paulson, Bellchambers, & Clapp, 1986; Lees & Smith, 1983; Taylor, Saint-Cyr, & Lang, 1987) or somewhat impaired (Halgin, Riklan, & Mishiak, 1977; Pirozzolo, Hansch, Mortimer, Webster, & Kusowski, 1982; Riklan, Whelinan & Cullinan, 1976). In HD, digit span is usually impaired (Boll, Heaton, & Reitan, 1974; Brandt et al., 1984; Josiassen, Curry, & Mancall, 1983), except perhaps very early in the course of the disease (Butters, Sax, Montgomery, & Tarlow, 1978). Digit span is generally impaired in AD (Kaszniak, Garron, & Fox, 1979; Kopelman, 1985; Miller, 1975; Wilson, Bacon, Fox, & Kaszniak, 1983), but in a few studies, deficits have not been observed (Pillon, Dubois, Lhermitte, & Agid, 1986; Weingartner et al., 1981).

Findings with the Brown-Peterson paradigm which measures speed of forgetting from STM are basically similar. On this task subjects must remember stimuli (3 or 4 words or letters) for varying intervals (usually 0-30 sec). Rehearsal is prevented by some sort of a distractor task that is performed during the retention interval. With MS patients, findings are mixed. While Grant, McDonald, Trimble, Smith, and Reed (1984) found deficits, many of their patients were tested during periods of active disease. Subsequent studies, which largely avoided this problem, observed no impairments (Litvan et al., 1988; Rao, Leo, & St. Aubin-Faubert, 1989). In our own research we have found impairments in chronic progressive (Beatty, Goodkin, Monson, Beatty, & Hertsgaard, 1988) but not in relapsing remitting (Beatty, Goodkin, Monson, & Beatty, 1989) patients. Deficits were marked, however, only for patients who were mildly demented. Similar results have been reported for PD patients. Impairments are mild among non-demented patients, but more striking among patients with mild dementia (Beatty, Staton, Weir, Monson, & Whitaker, 1989; Tweedy, Langer, & McDowell, 1982).

Performance on the Brown-Peterson task is clearly impaired in HD (Butters et al., 1978; Meudell, Butters, & Montgomery, 1978) and in AD (Kopelman, 1985; Morris, 1986). AD patients, in particular, show very rapid forgetting from STM on the Brown-Peterson test (see Morris, this volume).

Short-term memory in AD and PD patients has also been studied using paradigms adapted from the animal learning literature. On the delayed response task, subjects must remember the location of a target over a brief interval. On the delayed alternation task, subjects must alternate the location of choices over trials. Freedman and Oscar-Berman (1986) found that AD patients were impaired on both tasks, whereas demented PD patients were impaired only on the delayed response task. Non-demented PD patients were not impaired on either task. Using a more difficult delayed response task, Sahakian et al. (1988) found mild impairments in non-demented PD patients and more severe deficits among recently diagnosed AD patients.

In delayed matching to sample, subjects are shown a sample stimulus, and, after a delay, they must select it from an array of other targets. Sahakian et al. (1988) found deficits on delayed matching in both non-demented PD patients and AD patients, but the pattern of impairment was quite different. AD patients performed normally on the simultaneous matching condition and at 0-sec delay, but their performance worsened with increasing delay lengths. This parallels the usual findings with AD patients on the Brown-Peterson test. PD patients, by contrast, were equally impaired on simultaneous matching and at all delay lengths. This result suggests that a perceptual disturbance might explain the PD patients' impairments. While this may be a factor, the PD and AD patients were equally impaired on a pattern recognition test, suggesting that differences in STM may explain the differences between the AD and PD patients' performances on the delayed matching task.

Work by Sagar and colleagues (Sagar, Sullivan, Gabrieli, Corkin, & Growdon, 1988; Sullivan & Sagar, 1989) may help to explain these results. In tests of both verbal and nonverbal recognition memory, they observed that for short delays PD patients exhibited impairments. At longer delays, however, their performance matched that of controls. AD patients did not show this pattern. Their deficits were equally severe at all retention intervals studied.

Long-Term Memory: Recall

When asked to recall newly learned material, patients with subcortical diseases are usually impaired, even when their performance on standard mental status tests is within normal limits. For verbal memory, comparable deficits have been reported for word lists (e.g., Beatty, Goodkin, Monson et al., 1989; Rao et al., 1984; Weingartner, Caine, & Ebert, 1979), paired associates (e.g., Butters et al., 1978; El-Awar, Becker, Hammond, Nebes, & Boller, 1987; Fischer, 1988), and brief prose passages (e.g., Bowen, 1976; Butters, Granholm, Salmon, Grant, & Wolfe, 1987; Rao et al., 1989). Nonverbal recall, usually measured by reproduction of complex designs, is also impaired (Butters et al., 1978; Fischer, 1988; Riklan et al., 1976).

On tests that involve multiple presentations of the same material (e.g., a word list), patients with HD, MS, or PD are typically impaired on the first learning trial, but thereafter improve at an almost normal rate, at least for the first few trials (e.g., Beatty & Butters, 1986; Beatty, Goodkin et al., 1988; Beatty, Staton et al., 1989). Acquisition rates may not be normal if the patients are moderately demented. AD patients, even those who are mildly demented, show little or no learning (Ober, Koss, Friedland, & Delis, 1985; Weingartner et al. 1981). As might be expected, serial position curves for MS, PD, and HD patients are not significantly different from normal (Caine, Bamford, Schiffer, Shoulson, & Levy, 1986; Litvan et al., 1988; Taylor, Saint-Cyr, & Lang, 1986), whereas AD patients show little evidence of a primacy effect (Kaszniak, Wilson, & Fox, 1981).

Since MS, HD, and PD patients are generally impaired on the first learning trial in a free recall test, the possibility that their learning deficits reflect impaired encoding has received extensive experimental attention. For normal subjects, words that are high in imageability are more easily recalled than words that are not. Weingartner et al. (1979) reported that HD patients recalled high and low imagery words equally poorly, but in a subsequent study Beatty and Butters (1986) did not replicate this finding. The HD patients in their study recalled high imagery words better than low imagery words. Other findings indicate that the use of imagery is intact in AD (Ober et al., 1985) as well as in PD and MS (Beatty, Staton et al., 1989; Caine et al., 1986).

Another variable that affects recall is the degree to which the to-be-remembered material is organized at input (e.g., by semantic categories). In contrast to their usual deficits in learning a list of unrelated words, Caine, Ebert, and Weingartner, (1977) found that both HD and PD patients performed normally when the word list was organized into explicit semantic categories. By contrast, mildly demented AD patients showed no benefit from this manipulation; they learned just as poorly as when the list was comprised of unrelated words (Weingartner et al., 1981).

Butters, Albert, Sax, Miliotis, Nagode, and Sterste (1983) found that HD patients were able to use stories to link figures with background scenes on a picture recognition task, but AD patients did not benefit from the addition of stories to the task. In a subsequent study, Granholm and Butters (1988) compared HD and AD patients using an encoding specificity paradigm. Like controls, the HD patients benefited from the provision of either strong or weak semantic cues at both input and retrieval. The AD patients did not show this pattern and their performance indicated that they did not encode the semantic relationship between the test words and the cue words. These findings suggest fundamental differences in the ability of HD and AD patients to encode verbal information semantically.

It should not be concluded, however, that encoding is entirely normal in HD or PD. Although Caine et al. (1977) and Weingartner, Burns, Diebel, and LeWitt (1984) found normal recall by both HD and PD patients with explicitly categorized lists, only the PD patients showed additional increases when recall was cued by providing the category names.

When PD patients are required to learn a list containing words from different categories that are not explicitly grouped they exhibit recall impairments (Tweedy et al., 1982) which are associated with reduced use of semantic clustering (Taylor, Saint-Cyr, & Lang, 1990). A similar pattern has been reported for MS patients (Raymond, Stern, Authelet, & Penney, 1987). This raises the following question: Do MS, PD and HD patients have a normal capacity to encode verbal information semantically?

This question can most easily be answered by measuring release from proactive interference (PI). On this test, subjects receive a series of short-term memory trials on which words from the same semantic class (e.g., articles of clothing) are presented. Performance deteriorates over trials until, without warning, the semantic class of the words is changed. Improvement in memory on the trial after the shift in semantic class is termed release from PI and is taken as an index of capacity for semantic encoding. Although Tweedy et al. (1982) observed modest impairments in release from PI in PD patients, Beatty, Staton et al. (1989) were unable to replicate their findings. They reported that both nondemented and mildly demented PD patients showed normal release from PI. Similar findings have been reported for both HD (Beatty & Butters, 1986; Wilson et al., 1987) and MS (Beatty, Goodkin, Monson, & Beatty, 1989) patients, even those with mild dementia. However, Huber and Paulson (1987) found that HD patients with advanced disease did not show release from PI. Taken together, these findings suggest that most patients with subcortical diseases retain the capacity for normal semantic encoding, although they may not utilize this ability as efficiently as normal controls, perhaps because of difficulties processing information rapidly. The findings of Huber and Paulson (1987) raise the possibility, however, that the capacity for semantic encoding is lost in advanced dementias regardless of whether they are "subcortical" or "cortical" in origin. The issue may be impossible to resolve, because in advanced HD pathology of the frontal cortex is common (Sandberg & Coyle, 1984). In general, the distinction between the cortical and subcortical dementias, at the neuropathological level, becomes increasingly blurred as the diseases progress.

The only published study of release from PI in AD patients was inconclusive. The patients did not exhibit significant build up of PI, making their failure to show release uninterpretable (Cushman, Como, Booth, & Caine, 1988).

Long-Term Memory: Recognition

AD patients exhibit clear deficits on a number of verbal and non-verbal recognition memory tests (e.g., Hart, Smith, & Swash, 1985; Miller, 1975; Moss, Albert, Butters, & Payne, 1986; Salmon, Granholm, McCullough, Butters, & Grant, 1989; Wilson et al., 1983). This highly consistent finding is one line of evidence that these patients have a significant deficit in the initial encoding or storage of information. Conversely, the observation of normal recognition memory and impaired recall would imply that encoding and storage mechanisms are relatively intact, leaving retrieval as the likely site of memory disturbance. To what extent is recognition memory preserved in subcortical disease?

In MS, normal performance on delayed verbal recognition tests has been observed in a number of studies (Beatty, Goodkin, Monson, & Beatty, 1989; Caine et al., 1986; Rao et al., 1989). Mild deficits have also been reported. These are most often observed in chronic progressive patients, especially if they are mildly demented (Beatty & Gange, 1977; Beatty, Goodkin et al., 1988; Rao et al., 1984). For HD patients, the typical finding is that recognition memory is impaired (e.g., Butters, Wolfe, Martone, Granholm, & Cermak, 1985; Caine et al., 1977, 1986), although Martone, Butters, Payne, Becker, and Sax (1984) observed unimpaired performance. Butters et al. (1985) have argued that the recognition deficits of HD patients are less severe than their impairments in recall. The major evidence for this position is that when HD and alcoholic Korsakoff patients were matched for severity of recall impairments, the HD patients performed significantly better on recognition tests.

A number of studies have reported that PD patients are unimpaired on verbal recognition tasks, although they are impaired on free recall of the same material (e.g., El Awar et al., 1987; Taylor et al., 1986; Tweedy et al., 1982; Weingartner et al., 1984). These studies used patients who were not demented. Beatty, Staton et al. (1989) found that nondemented PD patients performed normally on a verbal recognition test, but mildly demented patients were impaired. This raises the possibility that the differences in recognition memory performance between PD and AD patients are entirely the result of differences in the overall level of cognitive functioning. However, work by Helkala, Laulumaa, Soininen, and Riekkinen (1988) suggests that this is not the case. They found that when PD and AD patients were equated for severity of dementia (based on IQ test scores) and for verbal recall, the PD patients performed significantly better on verbal recognition tests.

Although Flowers, Pearce, and Pearce (1984) found that PD patients performed normally on nonverbal (as well as on verbal) recognition memory tests, Taylor et al. (1986) found deficits among nondemented PD patients on the Delayed Recognition Test (Moss et al., 1986), but only for the spatial position component. Recognition span for words and geometric designs was normal. As noted earlier in the section on short-term memory, Sahakian et al. (1988) observed impaired performance by nondemented PD patients on a delayed matching to sample task (one form of nonverbal recognition memory). Sullivan and Sagar (1989), who noted more severe deficits on recognition memory tests by PD patients when retention intervals were short, suggested that Flowers et al. (1984) may have observed normal recognition performance because they used relatively long retention intervals (1-45 min). They suggested that impairments in short-term memory in combination with relative sparing of long-term memory might be related to the clinical phenomenon of bradyphrenia, the slowness of thought that is one suggested characteristic of subcortical dementia. Recent work by Bradley, Welch, and Dick (1989) suggests that during memory tests, PD patients may exhibit greater deficits in the speed of processing visuospatial than verbal information. This difference might explain the somewhat greater vulnerability of nonverbal memory for these patients.

Rates of Forgetting

In most studies of recall, patients and controls are given the same amount of training (e.g., some number of presentation-recall trials). Under these conditions, the terminal level of learning will typically be lower for the patients than the controls. To measure forgetting after a delay, savings scores, which express performance on delay trials as a percentage of performance on the last learning trial, are usually used.

In general, MS patients exhibit normal rates of forgetting (i.e., savings scores) for verbal free recall (Beatty, Goodkin, et al., 1988, 1989) and for brief stories taken from the Wechsler Memory Scale (Rao et al., 1989). For nondemented PD patients, savings scores are normal, while for mildly demented PD patients, savings scores were lower than normal (Beatty, Staton et al., 1989). These findings raise the possibility that forgetting rate may simply reflect the severity of global dysfunction.

Tröster, Jacobs, Butters, Cullum, and Salmon (1989) compared savings scores of HD and AD patients on the revised version of the Wechsler Memory Scale. The patient groups were equated for overall dementia severity. AD patients attained significantly lower savings scores than did the HD patients who, in turn, scored lower than controls. Similar results were obtained for logical memory and visual reproduction, indicating at least quantitative differences in forgetting among dementias of different etiologies.

It should be noted that the rapid forgetting of AD patients on the Brown-Peterson test and on the various tasks described above does not occur under all circumstances. With extensive additional practice, Kopelman (1985) was able to elevate the level of picture recognition memory by AD patients to that of controls at a 10-min delay. Thereafter, their rates of forgetting were comparable to those of controls. Using a different picture recognition task, Hart, Kwentus, Harkins, and Taylor (1988) equated AD patients and controls for initial learning. They observed faster forgetting by the AD patients, but most of the differences occurred during the first 10 min after learning. Considered as a whole, these findings suggest two conclusions: 1) Forgetting rates are related to severity of dementia, and 2) AD patients ordinarily acquire little information and forget rapidly. If by heroic training methods retention can be maintained for at least several minutes, then forgetting is normal.

Implicit Memory

Amnesic subjects, who perform very poorly on recall or recognition tests that make explicit reference to specific events or episodes, may perform normally on tasks that allow retention to be displayed implicitly, without requiring conscious attempts at recollection (Schacter, 1987). Examples of implicit memory tasks include classical conditioning, perceptual and motor skills, various types of verbal and nonverbal priming and, perhaps certain cognitive skills. Although it was initially thought that all of these tasks were organized by a single memory process or system, it is now quite clear that multiple systems are involved. In fact, different verbal priming paradigms (e.g. speed of lexical decision versus stem completion) appear to yield different conclusions about the state of implicit semantic memory in AD patients (for reviews of these issues, see chapters by Dick and Salmon, Heindel, & Butters, this volume).

With respect to acquisition of perceptual and motor skills it seems clear that HD patients are impaired. Martone et al. (1984) first observed deficits in HD on a mirror reading task and Heindel and colleagues (Heindel, Butters, & Salmon, 1988; Heindel, Salmon, Shults, Walicke, & Butters, 1989) extended these findings to pursuit rotor learning, a task which is learned normally by AD patients (Eslinger & Damasio, 1986; Heindel et al., 1988, 1989). A similar dissociation was seen on a weight judgment task in which AD, but not HD, patients showed normal biasing of judgments by prior exposure to a series of heavier weights (Heindel, Salmon, & Butters, 1989).

For PD patients, the experimental results regarding perceptual and motor learning are in conflict. Heindel, Salmon et al (1989) found that nondemented PD patients showed normal pursuit rotor learning, although mildly demented PD patients were as severely impaired as HD patients. In their study, pursuit rotor learning was not correlated with the severity of neurological symptoms. By contrast, Harrington, Haaland, Yeo, and Marder (1990) found impairments in pursuit rotor learning by PD patients which were correlated with the severity of bradykinesia, but not with mental status. The same patients acquired mirror reading and paired-associate learning normally. Finally, Beatty and Monson (in press) observed normal pursuit rotor learning by nondemented and mildly demented PD patients, although both patient groups showed impairment in recall of explicit facts about the task acquired incidentally. Identical results were observed for MS patients (Beatty, Goodkin, Monson, & Beatty, in press).

HD patients have been reported to perform normally on lexical, semantic, and pictorial priming tasks (Heindel et al., 1988, 1989; Heindel, Salmon, & Butters, 1990; Salmon, Shimamura, Butters, & Smith, 1988; Shimamura, Salmon, Squire, & Butters, 1987). On the same tasks, equally demented AD patients exhibited moderate to severe impairment. Again, results with PD patients are inconsistent. Heindel, Salmon, Shults et al. (1989) observed impaired lexical priming by mildly demented PD patients and normal priming by nondemented patients. Using the same materials and nearly identical procedures, Beatty and Monson (in press) were unable to replicate their results. In their study, both nondemented and mildly demented PD patients primed normally. The limited available data indicate that MS patients show normal lexical and semantic priming (Beatty & Monson, 1990a, in press).

The status of cognitive skills such as the 5-disc version of the Tower of Hanoi puzzle as measures of implicit memory is uncertain since amnesic subjects, as well as advanced HD patients do not learn normally (Butters et al., 1985). Saint-Cyr, Taylor, and Lang (1988) designed an easier 4-disc puzzle, called the Tower of Toronto (TT), and administered the task to PD, HD, and amnesic patients. Several measures of explicit recall and recognition were also given. The two amnesic patients performed normally on the TT, but poorly on the explicit memory tests. The PD patients showed exactly the opposite pattern, performing normally on the recall and recognition tests, but poorly on the TT. Thus, they observed a double dissociation between the cognitive skill and explicit memory tasks. The performance of the early stage HD patients complicated the picture as these patients fell into two subgroups: One group resembled the PD patients, while the other resembled the amnesics. Saint-Cyr et al. (1988) stated that their results supported the hypothesis that the neostriatum is part of a circuit essential for acquisition of cognitive procedures. Although this idea has considerable appeal, the inconsistencies in the available data would seem to preclude any definitive conclusion about the role of the neostriatum in the acquisition of either cognitive or motor skills.

Access to Established Memories

Remote Memory

Most investigations of remote memory in patients with subcortical disease have used versions of the remote memory battery devised by Albert, Butters, and Levin (1979) which requires identification of famous people from photographs and recall or recognition of past public events. Studies with this battery have consistently found evidence for a "flat" temporal gradient of retrograde amnesia in these patients; that is, remote memory deficits are equally severe for all past decades. Comparable findings have been reported for HD patients (Albert, Butters, & Brandt, 1981; Beatty, Salmon, Butters, Heindel, & Granholm, 1988), PD patients (Freedman, Rivoira, Butters, Sax, & Feldman, 1984; Huber, Shuttleworth, & Paulson, 1986) and MS patients (Beatty, Goodkin et al, 1988; Beatty, Goodkin, Monson, et al., 1989).

Recently, Beatty (1989) studied remote memory for visuospatial information by having subjects locate places on maps of regions they had lived in at various times in the past. HD patients located fewer places than controls and their deficits were equally severe for knowledge of the region in which they were born and raised and for the region in which they currently resided. Mildly demented MS and PD patients are also impaired on tests of geographical knowledge (Beatty, Goodkin et al., 1988; Beatty & Monson, 1989), but the shape of the temporal gradient is not known. By contrast, Sagar, Cohen, Sullivan, Corkin, & Growdon (1988) reported that the remote memory deficits of their PD patients were less severe for knowledge of the distant than for more recent time periods. The reasons for this discrepancy are not apparent.

Studies of remote memory in AD patients consistently show marked overall deficits with relative preservation of knowledge from the distant past. Evidence for a gentle temporal gradient of retrograde amnesia in AD (superimposed upon a pattern of severe general loss) has now been obtained for tests requiring knowledge of public persons and events, of personal semantic and autobiographical information and of the geography of places lived in at various times in the past (Beatty & Salmon, 1991; Beatty, Salmon et al, 1988; Kopelman, 1989; Sagar, Cohen et al., 1988). However, Wilson, Kaszniak, and Fox (1981) observed only a slight trend for temporally graded RA in their AD patients. The reasons for this discrepancy are unclear, but may relate to the greater overall severity of dementia of their patients.

All studies agree that deficits in remote memory are related to overall mental status. For PD patients, impairments are evident only if patients are mildly demented (Friedman et al., 1984; Huber, Shuttleworth et al., 1986), but for MS patients mild impairments occur on the Albert battery even among patients of normal mental status (Beatty, Salmon et al., 1988). For HD patients, the overall severity of remote memory loss is related to disease duration and severity, but there is no evidence that the pattern of retrograde amnesia evolves from a "flat" to a "sloping" gradient as the disease progresses (Albert et al., 1981).

This observation is important because it suggests that the greater overall cognitive impairment of the AD patients relative to the other patient groups which exists in comparison across studies is probably not responsible for the temporal gradient of retrograde amnesia in AD. Indeed, we have found that the temporal gradient is more easily observed in AD patients whose dementias are mild (Beatty & Salmon, 1991; Beatty, Salmon et al., 1988). Performance by AD patients with more advanced dementias is so poor that it is difficult to avoid floor effects.

Semantic Memory

Verbal fluency tests require subjects to name as many words as possible that begin with a particular letter or are exemplars of a particular semantic category. Because the information is highly overlearned, impairments are likely to reflect difficulties in memory retrieval. Further, if the major cause of memory problems in patients with subcortical diseases is retrieval failure, then deficits should be equally severe for various fluency tasks since a generalized retrieval disturbance should affect various classes of knowledge in a similar manner. On the other hand, a selective impairment of category but not of letter fluency would imply a breakdown in the organization of semantic memory, since normal performance on letter fluency could, in principle, be maintained using phonemic cues.

For MS patients, the available data clearly reveal that performance on both letter and category fluency tasks is impaired, and the degree of impairment is equivalent (Beatty, Goodkin et al., 1988; 1989; Caine et al., 1986; Rao et al., 1989). A deficit on letter fluency is well established in HD and occurs early in the course of the disease (e.g., Butters et al., 1978). Impairment on category fluency was also observed in one study (Butters et al., 1987), but fell short of significance in another (Caine et al., 1986). In PD, impaired fluency is usually observed (e.g., El Awar et al., 1987; Lees & Smith, 1983; Pillon et al., 1986; Taylor et al., 1986), but the deficits are not large unless patients are at least mildly demented (Beatty, Staton et al., 1989). In a few studies (e.g., Huber, Shuttleworth, Paulson et al., 1986; Weingartner et al., 1984) normal fluency performance has been observed. With respect to the relative impairment on letter and category fluency tests in PD the data are mixed. Matison, Mayeaux, Rosen, & Fahn (1982) found impairments on category, but not on letter fluency tasks, whereas Globus, Midworf, and Melamed (1985) obtained the opposite pattern. Gurd and Ward (1989) found that deficits were equally severe on letter and fluency tests.

Patients with AD are impaired on both letter and category fluency tests (e.g., El Awar et al., 1987; Huber, Shuttleworth, Paulson et al., 1986; Martin & Fedio, 1983; Ober, Dronkers, Koss, Delis, & Friedland, 1986). Some evidence indicates that the patients' impairments on category fluency are greater in magnitude than on letter fluency (Butters et al., 1987; Weingartner et al., 1981). Such relative sparing of performance on letter fluency is probably only evident when dementia is mild. Assuming that these findings are reproducible, they are consistent with the idea that early in AD there is an extensive loss of exemplars comprising various semantic categories (see Diesfeldt, this volume).

Memory, Subcortical Disease, and the Frontal Lobes

Because the basal ganglia are connected to the frontal lobes by a complex set of parallel circuits (Alexander, DeLong, & Strick, 1986), it is reasonable to hypothesize that some (or many) of the cognitive disturbances observed in subcortical disease result from disruption of these frontal circuits.

In an important paper, Taylor et al. (1986) proposed that the cognitive impairments in PD result from impairments in the ability to generate efficient strategies when required to rely on self-directed task-specific planning. To the extent that the memory deficits of PD patients are largely the result of difficulties with retrieval, this amounts to proposing that PD patients are unable to devise suitable strategies for efficient memory retrieval.

To test this hypothesis, Beatty, Monson, and Goodkin (1989) used a modified version of the Supermarket Test (Mattis, 1976). As in the original test, subjects were asked to name as many items as possible that might be found in a supermarket. The instructions were modified to encourage (but not explicitly instruct) subjects to use the spatial arrangement of departments (e.g., vegetables, drinks) in a supermarket to form the basis for an efficient search strategy. High search efficiency would occur if subjects named all of the different vegetables they could think of and then moved onto drinks, and so on, whereas low search efficiency would occur if subjects produced exemplars in an unorganized way.

PD patients generated fewer correct examples and attained lower search efficiency scores than controls. Correlational analyses demonstrated that search efficiency scores for the patients were positively related to performance on measures that reflect access to semantic memory (e.g., naming, category fluency), but not to tests of problem solving (i.e., performance on the Wisconsin Card Sorting Test, WCST). To the extent that problem solving might be expected to be related to the ability to formulate an efficient plan for memory retrieval, the results offer no support for the idea that this deficit is responsible for memory failure in PD. Instead, low search efficiency by PD patients seemed to be more a consequence than a cause of impaired access to semantic memory. Comparable results were found for MS patients in the same study. No data are currently available for HD patients.

Temporal Order Memory

Patients with focal lesions of the frontal lobes are impaired in making judgments of relative recency but perform normally on tests of content recognition and these deficits are correlated with poor performance on the WCST, implicating the dorsolateral region of the prefrontal cortex (Milner, Petrides, & Smith, 1985). Recent work by Sagar and colleagues indicates that PD patients have particular difficulty making temporal judgments about events in memory.

Sagar, Cohen et al. (1988) found that PD patients showed impairments in dating events in remote memory although their recognition memories for content of the same information were nearly normal. By contrast, AD patients showed equivalent difficulties on the content and dating tasks.

In subsequent studies Sagar, Sullivan et al. (1988) and Sullivan and Sagar (1989) extended these findings to the anterograde memory domain using a procedure that allowed simultaneous evaluation of content recognition and recency discrimination. On both verbal and nonverbal versions of the test, the PD patients were disproportionately impaired on the recency discrimination, while deficits by the HD patients were equivalent on the two tasks. Sagar and his colleagues attributed their PD patients' difficulties with temporal memory to frontal lobe dysfunction, although they did not actually demonstrate that the impairments in recency judgments were correlated with deficits on other tasks known to be sensitive to frontal lobe lesions.

Beatty and Monson (1991) studied verbal temporal order memory in MS patients using a procedure similar to that used by Sagar and his colleagues. The patients were impaired on the recency discrimination task, but performed normally on content identification. As predicted, performance in temporal order memory was correlated with performance on the WCST, but accuracy in recency judgments was also correlated with performance on the content recognition task. Thus, for MS patients both recognition memory and frontal lobe function (as indexed by the WCST) seemed to influence temporal memory. This is not surprising since Hirst and Volpe (1982) found marked deficits in recency discrimination among amnesic patients whose performance on neuropsychological tests of frontal lobe functioning was entirely normal. Whether or not similar relationships would obtain among PD patients is not known, but it seems premature to attribute their impairments in temporal memory entirely to frontal dysfunction.

More recently Sullivan, Sagar, Gabrieli, Corkin, and Growdon (1989) have suggested that the deficits in temporal memory exhibited by PD patients may be part of a more general disturbance in cognitive sequencing. The basis of this suggestion was the finding that PD patients performed very poorly on the Picture Arrangement subtests of the WAIS-R (Wechsler, 1981), although their scores on the Vocabulary subtest of the same instrument were normal. AD patients, by contrast, showed deficits on both WAIS-R tests. Using a much simpler picture sequencing test, Beatty and Monson (1990b) also found impairment in both nondemented and mildly demented PD patients. Deficits on the picture sequencing test were correlated with impairment on a motor sequencing test and on the WCST, but not with performance of nonsequential motor acts or neurological measures of disability. These findings are consistent with the hypothesis that sequencing difficulties in PD might be consequent to disturbances in critical frontal lobe circuits. However, impairments in picture sequencing were also associated with difficulties on a test of facial perception, suggesting that sequencing is multiply determined.

Summary and Conclusions

Although dementia severity is a major determinant of memory perform-ance, the literature reviewed above suggests four differences in the performance of AD and subcortical patients on explicit memory tests. First, the capacity to encode information semantically seems largely preserved in HD, PD, and MS, but seriously compromised in AD. Second, recognition memory deficits are consistently milder in the subcortical diseases than in AD. Third, forgetting rates within the first several minutes after acquisition are consistently accel-erated in AD, but normal or only slightly higher than normal in the subcortical diseases. Fourth, retrograde amnesia is temporally graded in AD, but equally severe across time in the subcortical diseases.

These observations are consistent with the view that the memory distur-bances of patients with subcortical diseases are largely the result of retrieval difficulties, at least early in the course of their disease. With disease progres-sion and decline in overall mental status, impairments in encoding and storage often emerge, but these deficits seem to be less serious than those of comparably demented AD patients. Thus, one major difference in the explicit memory sys-tems of patients with cortical as opposed to subcortical dementias appears to be the degree to which encoding and storage mechanisms are degraded.

Comparisons of implicit memory in HD and AD patients support the concept that there may be distinct systems subserving motor skill learning and other classes of implicit memory. Studies of PD patients, however, greatly complicate the picture. Until the empirical contradictions regarding the per-formance of PD patients on various tests of implicit memory are resolved, any conclusion about the role of neostriatal mechanisms in implicit memory is premature.

The concept that memory and other cognitive disturbances in subcortical dementia arise because of dysfunction in circuits involving the frontal lobes is attractive on anatomical grounds alone. However, the tasks studied are com-plex and poor performance can arise for a number of reasons. Further, the performance of individual patients varies greatly, both on tests that are sensi-tive to prefrontal lesions such as the WCST as well as on other measures. Similarities in the overall pattern of performance of groups of patients with frontal lesions or subcortical disease may prove to be superficial when patterns of performance on an extensive battery of measures are examined with corre-lational or regression techniques. Dysfunction of frontal lobe circuitry un-doubtedly contributes to memory and other cognitive disturbances in subcortical disease, but it is unlikely to be the only significant factor.

References

Albert, M. L. (1978). Subcortical dementia. In R. Katzman, R. D. Terry & K. L. Bick (Eds.), *Alzheimer's disease, senile dementia and related disorders, Aging, Vol. 7.* New York: Raven Press.

Albert, M. L., Feldman, R. G., & Willis, A. L. (1974). The "subcortical dementia" of progressive supranuclear palsy. *Journal of Neurology, Neurosurgery, and Psychiatry, 37,* 121-130.

Albert, M. S., Butters, N., & Brandt, J. (1981). Development of remote memory loss in patients with Huntington's disease. *Journal of Clinical Neuropsychology, 3,* 1-12.

Albert, M. S., Butters, N., & Levin, J. (1979). Temporal gradients in the retrograde amnesia of patients with alcoholic Korsakoff's disease. *Archives of Neurology, 36,* 211-216.

Alexander, G., DeLong, M. R., & Strick, P. (1986). Parallel organization of functionally segregated circuits linking basal ganglia and cortex. *Annual Review of Neuroscience, 9,* 357-382.

Asso, D. (1969). WAIS scores in a group of Parkinson patients. *British Journal of Psychiatry, 15,* 555-556.

Beatty, P. A., & Gange, J. J. (1977). Neuropsychological aspects of multiple sclerosis. *Journal of Nervous and Mental Disease, 164,* 42-50.

Beatty, W. W. (1989). Remote memory for visuospatial information in patients with Huntington's disease. *Psychobiology, 7,* 431-435.

Beatty, W. W., & Butters, N. (1986). Further analysis of encoding in patients with Huntington's disease. *Brain and Cognition, 5,* 387-398.

Beatty, W. W., Goodkin, D. E., Monson, N., Beatty, P. A., & Hertsgaard, D. (1988). Anterograde and retrograde amnesia in patients with chronic progressive multiple sclerosis. *Archives of Neurology, 45,* 611-619.

Beatty, W. W., Goodkin, D. E., Monson, N., & Beatty, P. A. (in press). Implicit learning in patients with chronic progressive multiple sclerosis. *International Journal of Clinical Neuropsychology.*

Beatty, W. W., Goodkin, D. E., Monson, N., & Beatty, P. A. (1989). Cognitive disturbances in patients with relapsing remitting multiple sclerosis. *Archives of Neurology, 46,* 1113-1119.

Beatty, W. W., & Monson, N. (1989). Geographical knowledge in patients with Parkinson's disease. *Bulletin of the Psychonomic Society, 27,* 473-475.

Beatty, W. W., & Monson, N. (1990a). Semantic priming in multiple sclerosis. *Bulletin of the Psychonomic Society, 28,* 397-400.

Beatty, W. W., & Monson, N. (1990b). Picture and motor sequencing in Parkinson's disease. *Journal of Geriatric Psychiatry and Neurology, 3,* 192-197.

Beatty, W. W., & Monson, N. (1991). Memory for temporal order in multiple sclerosis. *Bulletin of the Psychonomic Society, 29,* 10-12.

Beatty, W. W., & Monson, N. (in press). Lexical priming and pursuit rotor learning in patients with Parkinson's disease. *International Journal of Clinical Neuropsychology.*

Beatty, W. W., Monson, N., & Goodkin, D. E. (1989). Access to semantic memory in Parkinson's disease and multiple sclerosis. *Journal of Geriatric Psychiatry and Neurology, 2,* 153-162.

Beatty, W. W., & Salmon, D. P. (1991). Remote memory for visuospatial information in patients with Alzheimer's disease. *Journal of Geriatric Psychiatry and Neurology, 4,* 14-17.

Beatty, W. W., Salmon, D. P., Butters, N., Heindel, W. C., & Granholm, E. L. (1988). Retrograde amnesia in patients with Alzheimer's disease or Huntington's disease. *Neurobiology of Aging, 9,* 181-186.

Beatty, W. W., Staton, R. D., Weir, W. S., Monson, N., & Whitaker, H. A. (1989). Cognitive disturbances in Parkinson's disease. *Journal of Geriatric Psychiatry and Neurology, 2,* 22-33.

Boll, T. J., Heaton, R. K., & Reitan, R. M. (1974). Neuropsychological and emotional correlates of Huntington's chorea. *Journal of Nervous and Mental Disease, 158,* 61-69.

Boller, F., Mitzutani, T., Roessmann, U., & Gambetti, P. (1980). Parkinson's disease, dementia and Alzheimer's disease: Clinicopathological correlations. *Annals of Neurology, 1,* 329-335.

Bradley, V. A., Welch, J. L., & Dick, D. J. (1989). Visuospatial working memory in Parkinson's disease. *Journal of Neurology, Neurosurgery and Psychiatry, 52,* 1228-1235.

Brandt, J., Folstein, S. E., & Folstein, M. F. (1988). Differential cognitive impairment in Alzheimer's disease and Huntington's disease. *Annals of Neurology, 23,* 555-561.

Brandt, J., Strauss, M. E., Larus, J., Jensen, B., Folstein, S. E., & Folstein, M. F. (1984). Clinical correlates of dementia and disability in Huntington's disease. *Journal of Clinical Neuropsychology, 6,* 401-412.

Brown, R. G., & Marsden, C. D. (1988). Subcortical dementia: The neuropsychological evidence. *Neuroscience, 25,* 363-387.

Butters, N., Albert, M. S., Sax, D. S., Miliotis, P., Nagode, J., & Sterste, A. (1983). The effect of verbal mediators on the pictorial memory of brain-damaged patients. *Neuropsychologia, 21,* 307-323.

Butters, N., Granholm, E. L., Salmon, D. P., Grant, I., & Wolfe, J. (1987). Episodic and semantic memory: A comparison of amnesic and demented patients. *Journal of Clinical and Experimental Neuropsychology, 9,* 479-497.

Butters, N., Sax, D. S., Montgomery, K., & Tarlow, S. (1978). Comparison of the neuropsychological deficits associated with early and advanced Huntington's disease. *Archives of Neurololgy, 35,* 585-589.

Butters, N., Wolfe, J., Martone, M., Granholm, E. L., & Cermak, L. S. (1985). Memory disorders associated with Huntington's disease. *Neuropsychologia, 23,* 729-743.

Caine, E. D., Bamford, K. A., Schiffer, R. B., Shoulson, I., & Levy, S. (1986). A controlled neuropsychological comparison of Huntington's disease and multiple sclerosis. *Archives of Neurology, 43,* 249-254.

Caine, E. D., Ebert, M. H., & Weingartner, H. (1977). An outline for the analysis of dementia: The memory disorder of Huntington's disease. *Neurology, 27,* 1087-1092.

Cummings, J. L. (1986). Subcortical dementia: Neuropsychology, neuropsychiatry, and pathophysiology. *British Journal of Psychiatry, 149,* 682-697.

Cummings, J. L. (1988). Intellectual impairment in Parkinson's disease: Clinical pathologic, and biochemical correlates. *Journal of Geriatric Psychiatry and Neurology, 1,* 24-36.

Cummings, J. L., & Benson, D. F. (1984). Subcortical dementia: Review of an emerging concept. *Archives of Neurology, 41,* 874-879.

Cushman, L. A., Como, P. G., Booth, H., & Caine, E. D. (1988). Cued recall and release from proactive interference in Alzheimer's disease. *Journal of Clinical and Experimental Neuropsychology, 10,* 685-692.

El-Awar, M., Becker, J. T., Hammond, K. M., Nebes, R. D., & Boller, F. (1987). Learning deficits in Parkinson's disease: Comparison with Alzheimer's disease and normal aging. *Archives of Neurology, 44,* 180-184.

Eslinger, P. J., & Damasio, A. R. (1986). Preserved motor learning in Alzheimer's disease: Implications for anatomy and behavior. *Journal of Neuroscience, 6,* 3006-3009.

Fischer, J. S. (1988). Using the Wechsler Memory Scale-Revised to detect and characterize memory deficits in multiple sclerosis. *Clinical Neuropsychologist, 2,* 149-172.

Flowers, K. A., Pearce, I., & Pearce, J. M. S. (1984). Recognition memory in Parkinson's disease. *Journal of Neurology, Neurosurgery, and Psychiatry, 47,* 1174-1181.

Folstein, M. F., Folstein, S. E., & McHugh, P. R. (1975). "Mini-Mental State": A practical method for grading the cognitive state of patients for the clinician. *Journal of Psychiatric Research, 12*, 189-198.

Freedman, M., & Oscar-Berman, M. (1986). Selective delayed response deficits in Parkinson's and Alzheimer's disease. *Archives of Neurology, 43*, 886-890.

Freedman, M., Rivoira, P., Butters, N., Sax, D. S., & Feldman, R. S. (1984). Retrograde amnesia in Parkinson's disease. *Canadian Journal of Neurological Sciences, 11*, 297-301.

Globus, M., Midworf, B., & Melamed, E. (1985). Cerebral blood flow and cognitive impairment in Parkinson's disease. *Neurology, 35*, 1135-1139.

Granholm, E. L., & Butters, N. (1988). Associative encoding and retrieval in Alzheimer's and Huntington's disease. *Brain and Cognition, 7*, 335-347.

Grant, I., McDonald, W. I., Trimble, M. R., Smith, E., & Reed, R. (1984). Deficient learning and memory in early and middle phases of multiple sclerosis. *Journal of Neurology, Neurosurgery, and Psychiatry, 47*, 250-255.

Gurd, J. M., & Ward, C. D. (1989). Retrieval from semantic and letter-initial categories in patients with Parkinson's disease. *Neuropsychologia, 27*, 743-746.

Halgin, R., Riklan, M., & Mishiak, H. (1977). Levodopa Parkinsonism and recent memory. *Journal of Nervous and Mental Disease, 164*, 268-272.

Harrington, D. L., Haaland, K. Y., Yeo, R. A., & Marder, E. (1990). Procedural memory in Parkinson's disease: Impaired motor but not visuoperceptual learning. *Journal of Clinical and Experimental Neuropsychology, 12*, 323-339.

Hart, R. P., Kwentus, J. A., Harkins, S. W., & Taylor, J. R. (1988). Rate of forgetting in mild Alzheimer-type dementia. *Brain and Cognition, 7*, 31-38.

Hart, S. A., Smith, C. M., & Swash, M. (1985). Recognition memory in Alzheimer's disease. *Neurobiology of Aging, 6*, 287-292.

Heaton, R. K., Nelson, L. M., Thompson, D. S., Burks, J. S., & Franklin, G. M. (1985). Neuropsychological findings in relapsing-remitting and chronic-progressive multiple sclerosis. *Journal of Consulting and Clinical Psychology, 53*, 103-110.

Heindel, W. C., Butters, N., & Salmon, D. P. (1988). Impaired learning of a motor skill in patients with Huntington's disease. *Behavioral Neuroscience, 102*, 141-147.

Heindel, W. C., Salmon, D. P., & Butters, N. (1989). Pictorial priming and weight biasing in dementia. *Society for Neuroscience Abstracts, 15*, 343.

Heindel, W. C., Salmon, D. P., & Butters, N. (1990). Pictorial priming and cued recall in Alzheimer's and Huntington's disease. *Brain and Cognition, 13*, 282-295.

Heindel, W. C., Salmon, D. P., Shults, C. W., Walicke, P. A., & Butters, N. (1989). Neuropsychological evidence for multiple implicit memory systems: A comparison of Alzheimer's, Huntington's, and Parkinson's disease patients. *Journal of Neuroscience, 9*, 582-587.

Helkala, E.- L., Laulumaa, V., Soininen, H., & Riekkinen, P. J. (1988). Recall and recognition memory in patients with Alzheimer's and Parkinson's diseases. *Annals of Neurology, 24*, 214-217.

Hirst, W., & Volpe, B. T. (1982). Temporal order judgments with amnesia. *Brain and Cognition, 1*, 294-306.

Huber, S. J., & Paulson, G. W. (1985). The concept of subcortical dementia. *American Journal of Psychiatry, 142*, 1312-1317.

Huber, S. J., & Paulson, G. W. (1987). Memory impairment associated with progression of Huntington's disease. *Cortex, 23*, 275-283.

Huber, S. J., Paulson, G. W., Shuttleworth, E. C., Chakeres, D., Clapp, L. E., Pakalnis, A., Weiss, K., & Rammohan, K. (1987). Magnetic resonance imaging correlates of dementia in multiple sclerosis. *Archives of Neurology, 44*, 732-736.

Huber, S. J., Shuttleworth, E. C., & Freidenberg, D. L. (1989). Neuropsychological differences between the dementias of Alzheimer's and Parkinson's diseases. *Archives of Neurology, 46,* 1287-1291.

Huber, S. J., Shuttleworth, E. C., & Paulson, G. W. (1986). Dementia in Parkinson's disease. *Archives of Neurology, 43,* 987-990.

Huber, S. J., Shuttleworth, E. C., Paulson, G. W., Bellchambers, M. J. G., & Clapp, L. E. (1986). Cortical vs. subcortical dementia: Neuropsychological differences. *Archives of Neurology, 43,* 392-394.

Jambor, K. L. (1969). Cognitive functioning in multiple sclerosis. *British Journal of Psychiatry, 115,* 765-775.

Josiassen, R. C., Curry, L. M., & Mancall, E. L. (1983). Development of neuropsychological deficits in Huntington's disease. *Archives of Neurology, 40,* 791-796.

Kaszniak, A. W., Garron, D. C., & Fox, J. H. (1979). Differential effects of age and cerebral atrophy upon span of immediate recall and paired-associate learning in older patients suspected of dementia. *Cortex, 15,* 285-295.

Kaszniak, A. W., Wilson, R. S., & Fox, J. H. (1981). Effects of imagery and meaningfulness on free recall and recognition memory in presenile and senile dementia. *International Journal of Neuroscience, 12,* 264-270.

Katzman, R. (1986). Alzheimer's disease. *New England Journal of Medicine, 314,* 964-973.

Kopelman, M. D. (1985). Rates of forgetting in Alzheimer-type dementia and Korsakoff's syndrome. *Neuropsychologia, 23,* 623-638.

Kopelman, M. D. (1989). Remote and autobiographical memory, temporal context memory, and frontal atrophy in Korsakoff and Alzheimer patients. *Neuropsychologia, 27,* 437-460.

Lees, A. J., & Smith, E. (1983). Cognitive deficits in the early stages of Parkinson's disease. *Brain, 106,* 257-270.

Litvan, I., Grafman, J., Vendrell, P., Martinez, J. M., Janque, C., Vendrell, J. M., & Barraquer-Bordas, J. L. (1988). Multiple memory deficits in patients with multiple sclerosis: Exploring the working memory system. *Archives of Neurology, 45,* 607-610.

Lyon-Caen, O., Jouvent, R., Hauser, S., Chanu, M. P., Benoit, N., Widlocher, D., & Lhermitte, F. (1986). Cognitive function in recent-onset demyelinating diseases. *Archives of Neurology, 43,* 1138-1141.

Martin, A., & Fedio, P. (1983). Word production and comprehension in Alzheimer's disease: The breakdown of semantic knowledge. *Brain and Language, 19,* 124-141.

Martone, M., Butters, N., Payne, M., Becker, J. T., & Sax, D. S. (1984). Dissociations between skill learning and verbal recogniton in amnesia and dementia. *Archives of Neurology, 41,* 965-970.

Matison, R., Mayeaux, R., Rosen, T. J., & Fahn, S. (1982). Tip-of-the-tongue phenomenon in Parkinson's disease. *Neurology, 32,* 567-570.

Mattis, S. (1976). Mental status examination for organic mental syndrome in the elderly patient. In L. Bellack & T. B. Karasu (Eds.), *Geriatric Psychiatry.* New York: Grune & Stratton.

Meudell, P. R., Butters, N., & Montgomery, K. (1978). The role of rehearsal in the short-term memory performance of patients with Korsakoff's and Huntington's disease. *Neuropsychologia, 16,* 507-510.

Miller, E. (1975). Impaired recall and memory disturbance in presenile dementia. *British Journal of Social and Clinical Psychology, 14,* 73-79.

Milner, B., Petrides, M., & Smith, M. L. (1985). Frontal lobes and the temporal organization of memory. *Human Neurobiology, 4,* 137-142.

Morris, R. G. (1986). Short-term forgetting in senile dementia of the Alzheimer type. *Cognitive Neuropsychology, 3,* 77-97.

Moss, M. B., Albert, M. S., Butters, N., & Payne, M. (1986). Differential patterns of memory loss among patients with Alzheimer's disease, Huntington's disease, and alcoholic Korsakoff's syndrome. *Archives of Neurology, 43,* 239-246.

Ober, B. A., Dronkers, N. F., Koss, E., Delis, D. C., & Friedland, R. P. (1986). Retrieval from semantic memory in Alzheimer-type dementia. *Journal of Clinical and Experimental Neuropsychology, 8,* 75-92.

Ober, B. A., Koss, E., Friedland, R. P., & Delis, D. C. (1985). Processes of verbal memory failure in Alzheimer-type dementia. *Brain and Cognition, 4,* 90-103.

Pillon, B., Dubois, B., Lhermitte, F., & Agid, Y. (1986). Heterogeneity of cognitive impairment in progessive supranuclear palsy, Parkinson's disease, and Alzheimer's disease. *Neurology, 36,* 1179-1185.

Pirozzolo, F. J., Hansch, E. C., Mortimer, J. A., Webster, D. D., & Kusowski, M. A. (1982). Dementia in Parkinson's disease: A neuropsychological study. *Brain and Cognition, 1,* 71-83.

Rao, S. M. (1986). Neuropsychology of multiple sclerosis: A critical review. *Journal of Clinical and Experimental Neuropsychology, 8,* 503-542.

Rao, S. M., Hammeke, T. A., McQuillen, M. P., Khatri, B. O., & Lloyd, D. (1984). Memory disturbance in chronic progressive multiple sclerosis. *Archives of Neurology, 41,* 625-631.

Rao, S. M., Leo, G. J., & St. Aubin-Faubert, P. (1989). On the nature of memory disturbance in multiple sclerosis. *Journal of Clinical and Experimental Neuropsychology, 11,* 699-712.

Raymond, P. M., Stern, R. A., Authelet, A. M., & Penney, D. (1987). A comparison of the California Verbal Learning Test performance among patients with multiple sclerosis, right hemisphere vascular lesions, and normal controls. *Journal of Clinical and Experimental Neuropsychology, 9,* 49.

Riklan, M., Whelinan, W., & Cullinan, T. (1976). Levodopa and psychometric test performance - 5 years later. *Neurology, 26,* 173-179.

Sagar, H. J., Cohen, N. J., Sullivan, E. V., Corkin, S., & Growdon, J. H. (1988). Remote memory function in Alzheimer's disease and Parkinson's disease. *Brain, 111,* 185-206.

Sagar, H. J., Sullivan, E. V., Gabrieli, J. D. E., Corkin, S., & Growdon, J. H. (1988). Temporal ordering and short-term memory deficits in Parkinson's disease. *Brain, 111,* 525-539.

Sahakian, B. J., Morris, R. G., Evenden, J. L., Heald, A., Levy, R., Philpot, M., & Robbins, T. W. (1988). A comparative study of visuospatial memory and learning in Alzheimer-type dementia and Parkinson's disease. *Brain, 111,* 695-718.

Saint-Cyr, J. A., Taylor, A. E., & Lang, A. E. (1988). Procedural learning and neostriatal dysfunction in man. *Brain, 111,* 941-959.

Salmon, D. P., Granholm, E. L., McCullough, D., Butters, N., & Grant, I. (1989). Recognition memory span in mildly and moderately demented patients with Alzheimer's disease. *Journal of Clinical and Experimental Neuropsychology, 11,* 429-443.

Salmon, D. P., Kwo-on Yuen, P. F., Heindel, W. C., Butters, N., & Thal, L. J. (1989). Differentiation of Alzheimer's disease and Huntington's disease with the Dementia Rating Scale. *Archives of Neurology, 46,* 1204-1208.

Salmon, D. P., Shimamura, A. P., Butters, N., & Smith, S. (1988). Lexical and semantic priming deficits in patients with Alzheimer's disease. *Journal of Clinical and Experimental Neuropsychology, 10,* 477-494.

Sandberg, P. R., & Coyle, J. T. (1984). Scientific approaches to Huntington's disease. *CRC Critical Reviews in Neurobiology, 1,* 1-44.

Schacter, D. L. (1987). Implicit memory: History and current status. *Journal of Experimental Psychology: Learning, Memory, and Cognition, 13,* 501-517.

Shimamura, A. P., Salmon, D. P., Squire, L. R., & Butters, N. (1987). Memory dysfunction and word priming in dementia and amnesia. *Behavioral Neuroscience, 101*, 347-351.

Sullivan, E. V., & Sagar, H. J. (1989). Nonverbal recognition and recency discrimination deficits in Parkinson's disease and Alzheimer's disease. *Brain, 112*, 1503-1517.

Sullivan, E. V., Sagar, H. J., Gabrieli, J. D. E., Corkin, S., & Growdon, J. H. (1989). Different cognitive profiles on standard behavioral tests in Parkinson's disease and Alzheimer's disease. *Journal of Clinical and Experimental Neuropsychology, 11*, 799-820.

Taylor, A. E., Saint-Cyr, J. A., & Lang, A. E. (1986). Frontal lobe dysfunction in Parkinson's disease: The cortical focus of neostriatal outflow. *Brain, 109*, 845-883.

Taylor, A. E., Saint-Cyr, J. A., & Lang, A. E. (1987). Parkinson's disease: Cognitive changes in relation to treatment response. *Brain, 110*, 35-51.

Taylor, A. E., Saint-Cyr, J. A., & Lang, A. E. (1990). Memory and learning in early Parkinson's disease: Evidence for a "frontal lobe syndrome." *Brain and Cognition, 13*, 211-232.

Tröster, A. I., Jacobs, D., Butters, N. Cullum, C. M., & Salmon, D. P. (1989). Differentiating Alzheimer's disease from Huntington's disease with the Wechsler Memory Scale-Revised. *Clinics in Geriatric Medicine, 5*, 611-632.

Tweedy, J. R., Langer, K. G., & McDowell, F. H. (1982). The effect of semantic relations on the memory deficit associated with Parkinson's disease. *Journal of Clinical Neuropsychology, 4*, 237-247.

Wechsler D. (1981). *WAIS-R Manual.* New York: Psychological Corporation.

Weingartner, H., Burns, S., Diebel, R., & LeWitt, P. A. (1984). Cognitive impairment in Parkinson's disease: Distinguishing effort-demanding and automatic cognitive processes. *Psychiatry Research, 11*, 223-235.

Weingartner, H., Caine, E. D., & Ebert, M. H. (1979). Imagery, encoding, and retrieval of information from memory: Some specific encoding-retrieval changes in Huntington's disease. *Journal of Abnormal Psychology, 88*, 52-58.

Weingartner, H., Kaye, W., Smallberg, S. A., Ebert, M. H., Gillin, J. C., & Sitaram, N. (1981). Memory failure in progressive idiopathic dementia. *Journal of Abnormal Psychology, 90*, 187-196.

Whitehouse, P. (1986). The concept of subcortical dementia: Another look. *Annals of Neurology, 19*, 1-6.

Wilson, R. S., Bacon, L. D., Fox, J. H., & Kaszniak, A. W. (1983). Primary memory and secondary memory in dementia of the Alzheimer type. *Journal of Clinical Neuropsychology, 5*, 337-344.

Wilson, R. S., Como, P. G., Garron, D. C., Klawans, H. L., Barr, A., & Klawans, D. (1987). Memory failure in Huntington's disease. *Journal of Clinical and Experimental Neuropsychology, 9*, 147-154.

Wilson, R. S., Kaszniak, A. W., & Fox, J. H. (1981). Remote memory in senile dementia. *Cortex, 17*, 41-48.

9

Interaction of Language and Memory in Major Depression and Senile Dementia of Alzheimer's Type

V. Olga Beattie Emery

Dartmouth Medical School

Introduction

Pseudodementia is a phenotype approximated by a wide variety of underlying disorders. Although the frequency distribution of disorders presenting as pseudodementia remains unclear, what is clear is that depressive dementia, synonymously referred to as major depression with depressive dementia or depressive pseudodementia, represents a major subclass of the overarching category of pseudodementia (Emery, 1988a). It has long been observed that in the differential diagnosis between dementia and pseudodementia, depressive pseudodementia appears to be the single most difficult disorder to distinguish from nosologically established "organic" categories of dementia, especially primary degenerative dementia of the Alzheimer type (Kiloh, 1962; Starkstein et al., 1989; Wells, 1982).

Historically, dementia has been defined as an acquired, severe, "irreversible" kind of intellectual deterioration secondary to organic brain disease (Bulbena & Berrios, 1986). The attempt to distinguish between "non-reversible" dementing illness and dementia-like presentations that with treatment or passage of time are "reversed," dates back to at least the 1800's (Mairet, 1883). The term "vesanic dementia" was used to designate dementing syndromes that appeared "reversible," until it was replaced by Wernicke's term "pseudodementia" in the late 1800's (Bulbena & Berrios, 1986; Emery, 1988a). The term "vesania" originates from the Latin word "sanus" meaning "sane, sound, healthy." Implied in the conceptualization of both "vesanic dementia" and "pseudodementia" is a functional etiology. Then, as now, parameters of irreversibility-reversibility and structure-function, or put another way, organic versus non-organic, formed the core around which constructs of dementia and pseudodementia were antiposed. Argument has centered around these crosscutting variables for more than a century without resolution, and with pervasive consequences for treatment perspectives.

Accordingly, to date, the conceptual, empirical, and clinical relationships between primary degenerative dementia and depression-related dementia are still not understood. Both depression-related dementia and primary degenerative dementia are age-correlated (Alexopoulos, 1990; Reifler & Sherrill, 1990). Given the ever increasing numbers and proportion of old people in industrialized Western societies (Reeves, 1989; U.S. Department of Health and Human Services, 1984), the understanding of the nature and causes of age-correlated dementing disorders, such as depressive dementia and primary degenerative dementia, must rank high as a research priority.

Nomological Context

In the long-term follow-up (4 to 18 years after diagnosis) of 44 elderly patients with depression-related dementia (M age = 76.5 years), Kral and Emery (1989) found that 79% of these patients had developed primary degenerative dementia. The modal pattern of these patients was as follows: (1) several episodes of major depression/unipolar; (2) one or more episodes of major depression/unipolar during which cognitive functioning was strongly, adversely affected with subsequent return to "normal;" (3) an episode of apparent depression during which the patient presented with an Alzheimer phenotype, with cognitive symptoms subsequently appearing to "reverse," i.e., depressive dementia; and (4) a presentation with an Alzheimer phenotype without remission of cognitive symptoms and with subsequent progressive deterioration consistent with primary degenerative dementia of the Alzheimer type. Where post mortems were permitted (9 patients), neuropathological examination revealed the typical markers of Alzheimer's disease (AD): Neuronal loss, neurofibrillary tangles, and neuritic plaques. On the basis of these longitudinal data, it would appear that a subset of persons with major depression/unipolar are at risk for depressive dementia and, in turn, the majority of persons with depression-related dementia are at risk for primary degenerative dementia.

The association between depressive dementia and subsequent primary degenerative dementia has been documented in other longitudinal studies (Alexopoulos, 1990). The frequency of documented progression of depressive dementia into primary degenerative dementia appears to be related to length of follow-up (Emery & Oxman, in press). For example, at one year follow-up, Murphy (1983) reported 3% of 124 elderly depressives were demented. Rabins, Merchant, and Nestadt (1984) reported that 12% of older depressed patients were demented at two year follow-up. Increasing to a three year follow-up, Reding, Haycox, and Blass (1985) reported that more than 50% of elderly patients diagnosed with depressive pseudodementia demonstrated primary degenerative dementia. And as described in the foregoing, Kral and Emery (1989) found 79 % of cases of depressive pseudodementia evolved into primary degenerative dementia after four to eighteen years (average 8 years).

The meaning of these data is not clear. Although there has been clinical interest in the differential diagnosis between depression-related dementia and the "organic" dementias for many years (e.g., Kiloh, 1962; Roth, 1986; Wells, 1982), the idea that there might exist some fundamental relation b~~~~~~ nosologically distinct categories is relatively new (Emery, 19 Kral & Emery, 1989). Historically, the affective disorders hav ceptualized as having connection with "organic" brain syndr ciation between major depression without dementia, depressiv primary degenerative dementia represents a research frontier gin to know why major depression sometimes progresses to mentia, and why in turn, a substantial proportion of cases of mentia appear to evolve into primary degenerative dementia, mu investigations comparing these populations will be required.

There is at present a paucity of systematic empirical data l relation between depression-related dementia and primary de mentia (for reviews, see Bulbena & Berrios, 1986; Cummings 1988a; McAllister, 1983). Also, studies addressing similarities ar between major depression without dementia and primary deg mentia are almost nonexistent, with only a few exceptions (e.g., 1990; Cassens, Wolfe, & Zola, 1990; Emery & Breslau, 1989; Ha Hamer, & Taylor, 1987; Speedie, Rabins, Pearlson, & Moberg, 1990). And yet recent longitudinal data suggesting depressive dementia might be a transitional state between major depression without dementia and primary degenerative dementia, necessitate a systemative comparison of these two end points of the spectrum.

The study to be described in this chapter involves comparisons of cognitive processing in populations of major depression without dementia and primary degenerative dementia of the Alzheimer type, with the normal aged serving as normative baseline. Previous research on the interface between major depression and AD by the present author (Emery, 1988a; Kral & Emery, 1989), led to the design of this particular study. Similarities and differences in cognitive processing between major depression without dementia and primary degenerative dementia of the Alzheimer type need to be defined before further understanding of depressive dementia can occur. Because cognitive deficits are at the core of the definition of primary degenerative dementia of the Alzheimer type (APA, 1987, p. 107), investigations of cognitive processing in this population, as well as in any populations representing transitional states to it, are crucial for comprehension of the progressive dementing process. In the study being reported, the focus is on cognitive processes of language and memory. Comparison will be made of language and memory deficits in our research populations, that is, major depression without dementia, late onset primary degenerative dementia of the Alzheimer type, also referred to as senile dementia of Alzheimer's type (SDAT), and normal aging. Further, the interaction of language and memory in these populations will be examined.

Language Deficits in SDAT

Only recently has there evolved a consistent interest in the disordered language of AD (Light & Burke, 1988), despite the fact that Alzheimer himself included descriptions of language decrement in his hallmark case report (Alzheimer, 1907). A disturbance of language appears to be an intrinsic part of both early onset AD and SDAT, and is among the earliest of symptoms, showing steady progression, with severity of language dysfunction correlated with severity of illness (Emery, 1985, 1988b, 1988c; Green, Morris, Sandson, McKeel, & Miller, 1990). Ferm (1974) found that only 5% of over 100 patients of both onset types had normative language capability; language was impaired very early in AD and declined steadily. Similarly, Kirshner, Webb, Kelly, and Wells (1984) found disrupted language to be an initial symptom, presaging the diffuse cortical degeneration of AD.

Research relating to language deterioration in AD of both onset types has been focused mainly on naming impairment, formally referred to as nominal aphasia/dysphasia or anomia (e.g., Bayles & Tomoeda, 1983; Huff, 1988; Rochford, 1971; Selnes, Carson, Rovner, & Gordon, 1988; Shuttleworth & Huber, 1988). Naming tasks typically are generated from the morphological-lexical level of the hierarchical semiotic system, and are among the least complex of linguistic functions. The ranks of the semiotic system, expressed in order of increasing complexity, are: phonology, morphology, syntax, and semantics (deSaussure, 1966; Huck & Ojeda, 1987; Yngve, 1986). Studies of language deterioration in SDAT also have provided data on phonological deficits (Benjamin, 1984; Neils, Brennan, Cole, Boller, & Gerdeman, 1988), syntactic deficits (Emery, 1984, 1985, 1986, 1988b; Illes, 1989), and semantic deficits (Bayles & Kaszniak, 1987; Emery, 1985, 1987, 1988b; Green et al., 1990; Knotek, Bayles, & Kaszniak, 1990; Kontiola, Laaksonen, Sulkava, & Erkinjuntti, 1990). Further, in studies comparing linguistic deficits in SDAT at the differing semiotic ranks, it was found that the most complex forms deteriorated first in SDAT, with less complex linguistic forms preserved longer (Emery, 1982, 1985; Emery & Breslau, 1988). Language deterioration appears to occur in reverse order of language development (Emery, 1985). Thus, although language processing in SDAT has anomic components, the decrement is not best described by the term anomia (Emery & Breslau, 1988). The data suggest that the language deficits of SDAT cannot be characterized accurately by any of the extant categories of aphasia, but rather these deficits can be described validly by the concept and term "progressive aphasia" (Emery, 1982, 1984, 1985). Finally, comparisons of deficits in SDAT with that of AD early onset suggest the two populations are neither identical nor coextensive, but form continuous though differing subgroups (Emery, 1988c; Emery & Breslau, 1987).

Language Deficits in Major Depression

In contrast to the beginnings of a nomology related to language processing in SDAT, to date, investigations of the structure of language deficits in major
depression are virtually nonexistent. And yet a comprehensive understanding
of cognitive processing in depression, by definition, requires that language be
examined, in addition to cognitive processes that are commonly the target of
research, e.g., perception, attention, memory, and thought. In one of the less
than handful of studies that exist, Speedie et al. (1990) investigated confrontation naming in depression without dementia, depressive dementia, and primary dementia. Findings include that depressed patients without dementia
performed significantly better than those with dementia of depression on both
number of items correct and speed of response on the confrontation naming
task. Patients with dementia of depression could not be distinguished from
those with primary dementia on these two variables. In another study with
similar findings, Emery (1988a) found no significant differences between depressive dementia and SDAT on language measures of confrontation naming,
repetition, auditory word comprehension, sequential commands, complex
syntax, and reading commands. In contrast, nondemented depressed patients
performed significantly better than their demented counterparts on tasks of
complex syntax, word generation/fluency, sequential commands, and reading comprehension. Discriminant analyses indicated the two populations were
best distinguished by tasks of complex syntax and reading comprehension.

Memory Deficits in SDAT

Rapid loss of memory is a well established feature of the cognitive decline
in AD (Alzheimer, 1907; APA, 1987). It has been found that memory impairment is among the most apparent of early symptoms in AD of both onset types,
and that this impairment has a progressive deteriorating course (Bayles &
Kaszniak, 1987; Pepin & Eslinger, 1989; Thal, Grundman, & Klauber, 1988).
Phases of memory decline in AD/SDAT have also been tentatively suggested
(Kral, 1962; Schneck, Reisberg, & Ferris, 1982). Additionally, there have been
numerous investigations exploring memory deficits in AD of both onsets in
terms of underlying structures and processes, with the overall trend in data
suggesting that although deficits appear in sensory, primary, secondary, and
tertiary memory (Kaszniak, Poon, & Riege, 1986; Poon, 1985), the greatest
decrement appears to be in secondary memory (e.g., Bayles & Tomoeda, 1990;
Moss, Albert, Butters, & Payne, 1986; Partridge, Knight, & Feehan, 1990;
Weingartner et al., 1981). Using another model to describe the nature of memorial representation in SDAT, several investigators found that memory for

new information is impaired prior to memory for old information in SDAT (e.g., Knopman & Ryberg, 1989; Light & Burke, 1988). Further, it has been found that explicit memory is impaired prior to implicit memory (e.g., Emery, 1985; Heindel, Salmon, Shults, Walicke, & Butters, 1989; Landrum & Radtke, 1990; Light & Burke, 1988). Also, there exist cross-cutting data which emanate from experiments using Tulving's (1972) categories of episodic and semantic memory. These data indicate there is impairment in both episodic and semantic memory (e.g., Albert, Butters, & Brandt, 1981; Bäckman & Herlitz, 1990; Eustache, Cox, Brandt, Lechavalier, & Pons, 1990; Helkala, Laulumaa, Soininen, & Riekkinen, 1989; Knotek et al., 1990; Light & Burke, 1988). However, if episodic memory is conceptualized as a subset of semantic memory, the fundamental deficit becomes a function of semantic memory (Bayles & Kaszniak, 1987).

An analysis of the body of research on memory shows the use of multiple overlapping sets of constructs to describe memorial representation. Problems such as lack of an integrated comprehensive conceptual framework, static rather than developmental perspectives, and the problem of phenomenal identity seriously compromise meaningful interpretation of the data on memory in primary degenerative dementia. Nevertheless, in the foregoing studies, one can begin to see some trends that cross-cut the different models, and that begin to inform the process of memory deterioration in SDAT.

Memory Deficits in Major Depression

A review of the data on memory deficits in major depression, as well as the interpretation of these data, reveals many problems and confounds, e.g., a confound between medicated and nonmedicated subjects, and a confound between depression without dementia and depressive dementia being the most notable. In addition, not only does one find the problems of paradigm that beset memory research in general, but one also finds a problem of objective versus subjective memory impairment that is pronounced for research on depression. While memory complaints or self-perceptions of poor memory are an integral part of the major depressive syndrome (APA, 1987), to what degree does major depression involve real memory decrements and what is the nature and pattern of these decrements.

Many studies have reported that performance of depressed patients on memory tests is significantly poorer than that of normal controls (e.g., Emery, 1988a; Hart et al., 1987; LaRue, 1989; Raskin, 1986; Watts, Dalgleish, Bourke, & Healy, 1990). Also, it has been found that performance of nondemented depressed patients differs only quantitatively from that of normal controls, whereas performance of SDAT patients on memory tests differs both quantitatively and qualitatively from normals (Emery, 1985, 1988a; Poitrenaud, Moy,

Girousse, Wolmark, & Piette, 1989). Although every stage or type of information-processing system and/or structure has been implicated in the memory
deficits of depressed persons, there is a convergence in findings suggesting that
learning-related memory deficits are most prominent in major depression (e.g.,
Weingartner, 1986). Explanations as to why depressed persons find it difficult
to learn and remember have included rehearsal problems, encoding deficits,
retrieval impairments, rapid memory decay, resource allocation, processing
impairment, reduced cognitive channel capacity, impairments of metamemory,
and generalized cognitive impairment (e.g., Breslow, Kocsis, & Belkin, 1981;
Calev, Nigel, & Chasen, 1989; Ellis, 1990; Hertel & Hardin, 1990; Raskin, 1986;
Watts et al., 1990). Another set of studies trying to account for the learning
deficits in the memory processing of depressed persons have been focused on
intervening variables of attention and concentration deficits, problems of
motivations, and lack of sustained effort on tasks requiring effortful processing
(e.g., Hasher & Zacks, 1979; Selnes et al., 1989; Weingartner, 1986).

To date, it remains unclear to what extent the performance deficits of the
depressed on memory tasks represent real, objective changes in the structures
of memory. While there does exist neurobiological evidence that depression may
involve changes in the same brain structures or neurotransmitter substances
that underlie memory functions (e.g., Akiskal & McKinney, 1973; Alexopoulos,
1990; Arora, Emery, & Meltzer, in press; Koyama & Meltzer, 1986), the question
as to how much memory decrement in depression is biologically based is
unresolved. Weingartner (1986) pointed out that relatively little systematic
research has been done to contrast memory changes, and other cognitive
changes, in depressed patients with those of other patient groups. Comparisons
of the patterning of memory deficits in depression with patterning of memory
deficits in organic populations, such as AD, should assist in the characterization
of memory in both populations.

For analytical purposes, research on cognitive processing in depression
can be divided into categories of form/structure and content (Simmel, 1971).
While there is research consensus regarding the content of thought, e.g.,
negative thoughts about self and others, negative perceptions of experiences
and future, and so forth (e.g., Beck, 1967; Goodwin & Jamison, 1986), it is
unclear whether major depression also involve an actual change in the form
or structure of thought, i.e., operational level of thinking (Piaget, 1952). Or as
outlined above, although complaints or self-perceptions of poor memory are
part of major depression, what is the extent of structural deficits in memory?
In addition, although persons with major depression use a significantly greater
number of negatively loaded words than do normal controls (Emery, 1988a),
does major depression involve actual form/structural deficits in language
processing?

The study to be reported addresses questions of (1) similarities and differences in patterning on formal/structural variables of language and memory
in major depression without dementia, SDAT, and normal aging, and (2) interaction between language and memory in major depression without dementia,

SDAT, and normal aging. As pointed out in the foregoing discussion, the question of structural language deficits in major depression has been virtually unaddressed. Further, it appears that hitherto there has not been a systematic study of the interaction of language and memory in these populations.

Methods

Participants

Participants were 23 elderly with SDAT (16 women and 7 men), 20 elderly with major depression and no dementia (15 women and 5 men), and 20 normal elderly (13 women and 7 men). Mean ages of the SDAT, depressed, and normal samples were 75.9, 72.6, and 71.7 years, respectively. Age ranges were comparable also. Educational level was controlled with SDAT, depressed, and normal elderly samples having mean educations of 12.4, 12.2, and 13.0 years, in turn. Additionally, variables of race, occupation, native birth, native language, and reading history were controlled.

Excluded from the SDAT sample were persons with cardiovascular disease, a positive ischemia profile, tumors, endocrine or metabolic disease, substance abuse, or neurological signs not part of AD symptomatology. First diagnosis was at age 65 or later. Screening procedures included a dementia medical workup consisting of testing of vital signs, urinalysis, complete blood count with test for venereal disease, B12 - folic acid, diabetic profile, and thyroid abnormality. Other procedures included neurological examination, ECG, and CT scan. SDAT patients met the criteria of DSM-III-R (American Psychiatric Association, 1987) for primary degenerative dementia of the Alzheimer type. SDAT was differentiated from pseudodementia (Bulbena & Berrios, 1986; Emery, 1988a; Wells, 1982) on the basis of medical workup, medical/psychiatric history, onset history, and scores on the Schedule for Affective Disorders and Schizophrenia (Endicott & Spitzer, 1978), Hamilton Depression Scale, Geriatric Depression Scale, Kahn-Goldfarb Mental Status Questionnaire, and Face-Hand Test (Gallagher, 1986; Kahn, Goldfarb, Pollack, & Peck, 1960). Severity of SDAT was determined by the above procedures, as well as the Reisberg Global Deterioration Scale (Reisberg, Ferris, & DeLeon, & Crook, 1982). Of the 23 SDAT patients, seven were in the "mild" category of severity, eight were in the "moderate" group, and eight met criteria for a "severe" designation.

Major depression was diagnosed on the basis of combined criteria from the Research Diagnostic Criteria and DSM-III-R. The Hamilton Depression Scale was used to assess severity, and Geriatric Depression Scale, a self-report measure, served as reliability check on observer ratings. Mean score on the Hamilton Scale at time of assessment was 29.3, and mean score on the Geriatric Depression Scale was 21.4. No depressed patient was psychotic at time of interview. Subjects were either non-medicated or had been off medication two weeks prior to assessment. For theoretical and methodological reasons, the subset of depressed patients presenting with a dementia phenotype, i.e., depressive pseudodementia, was not included in the depressed sample. A discussion of this subsample can be found elsewhere (Emery, 1988a). Persons in both the depressed and the SDAT samples were outpatients or short-term inpatients at a university hospital medical complex.

Normal elderly persons were recruited from the community-at-large. Requirements for participation included noncompromised major organ systems, lack of chronic illness, and vital signs within the normal range. Psychiatric and neurological measures discussed above were administered. Persons scoring in the positive range of any of these measures were not included in the normal elderly sample.

All subjects gave informed consent. In the case of the SDAT patients, consent was obtained from legal guardians as well.

Language Measures

Language processing was assessed by use of the Western Aphasia Battery (WAB) (Kertesz, 1982) and Test for Syntactic Complexity (TSC) (Emery, 1982, 1985, 1986). The formal or structural variables assessed were repetition, naming, auditory verbal comprehension, syntactic processing, and reading comprehension.

The WAB Repetition Test requires repetition of 14 items (e.g., nose, the telephone is ringing). Points are subtracted for errors in word sequence or phonemic errors.

The four WAB tests for naming assessment are Object Naming, Sentence Completion, Responsive Speech, and Word Fluency. The Object Naming Test involves the confrontation naming of twenty objects, such as comb, knife, spoon. Sentence Completion comprises five familiar sentences to complete, e.g., "roses are red, violets are ___." The Responsive Speech Test consists of five simple questions such as, "How many days are in a week?" The Word Fluency Test requires the individual to name as many animals as possible in one minute. The test was administered in both a timed and untimed trial.

The WAB auditory verbal comprehension assessment consists of three tests: Yes/No Questions ("Is the door closed?"), Sequential Commands ("With the book, point to the comb"), and Auditory Word Recognition, which requires recognition of real objects, drawn objects, forms, letters, numbers, colors, body parts, and left-right items.

The WAB Reading Comprehension Test has eight items to be answered. The correct answer depends on sentence or paragraph comprehension, for example, "Shovels and saws are common tools; they have parts made of (farmer, forest, metal, cutting)."

The WAB has demonstrated high reliability and construct validity (Shewan & Kertesz, 1980), with an internal consistency coefficient of .91, and test-retest reliabilities all above .90. Factor analysis used to establish construct validity result in Pearson correlations ranging from .82 to .97 on criterial convergent validation between the WAB and other major aphasia batteries.

The Test for Syntactic Complexity (Emery, 1982, 1985, 1986) is a 36-item instrument designed to assess processing of various complex syntactic relations that were late to develop in the sequence of language learning (Chomsky, 1979). The TSC was devised in such a way that correct linguistic processing, i.e., the correct analysis of meaning, depends directly on correct processing of syntactic complexities. One finds that in spontaneous speech and other unstructured linguistic exchange, meaning is very often apprehended or communicated through use of contextual cues or redundancy (Emery, 1985, 1988b). The TSC was designed to eliminate any cues external to syntactic structure.

The TSC assesses processing of the following forms: (1) prepositions of time sequence ("Do you put on your stockings after your shoes?"); (2) passive subject-object discrimination ("The boy is called by the girl; who is called and who did the calling?"); (3) possessive relations of a reversible construction ("What is the relationship of your brother's father to you?"); and (4) communication of narrative action events which are concrete ("John and Mary run to the hospital really fast") versus communication of abstract and/or logical relations of the same number of words ("John runs faster than George but slower than Humphrey").

The split-half reliability of the TSC is .93, demonstrating internal consistency. The other reliabilities and validity of the test are being determined.

Memory Measures

Nine measures of memory were administered to the 63 participants: Information, Orientation, Mental Control, Digit Span Forward, Digit Span Backward, Verbal Paired Associates, Story Recall, Delayed Story Recall, and Katzman Test for Delayed Recall. The first seven of these measures are from the Wechsler Memory Scale (WMS) (Wechsler, 1973). The test of Information consists of six items of personal and current information, e.g., "How old are you?" and "Who is the President of the United States?" Orientation involves five items of time and place, e.g., "What month is this?" For the measure of Mental Control, the subject is asked to count backward from 20 to one, say the alphabet, and count by three's to number 40. Digit Span Forward goes to a span of eight digits, and Digit Span Backward has a span of seven digits. Verbal Paired Associates consists of 10 pairs of words to be associated across three trials. Six pairs involve commonplace associations such as "North-South," and four pairs of words consist of non-common associations, e.g., "obey-inch." The measure of Story Recall (Logical Memory) consists of a sixty-seven word paragraph, broken up into twenty-four scoring units, telling the story of a scrub woman who was robbed and her subsequent plight, e.g., "rent was due."

The measure of Delayed Story Recall is based on Russell's revision of the WMS (Russell, 1975), and uses the story summed above, requiring the participant to recount as much of the story as possible one-half hour after initial recall. The Katzman Test for Delayed Recall (Katzman, 1983) consists of a single sentence ("John Brown lives at 42 Market Street in Chicago, Illinois."), and assesses recall two hours after original administration.

Because the global memory quotient of the WMS has been criticized for a number of theoretical and psychometric reasons (Russell, 1975), the memory quotient is not used in the present study. In contrast to the problems of construct validity associated with a global memory quotient, the subtests of the WMS/WMS-R, when scored independently of an overall memory quotient, serve as straightforward operationally defined tasks for memory assessment.

Statistical Measures

Four statistical approaches were used. First, to determine significance of difference in means, one-way ANOVAs were used to compare the three samples. The ANOVAs were followed by Scheffé tests. Further, a difference-of-means test using the t-distribution was utilized to obtain more specific information, such as exact t- and alpha levels. Two-tailed tests were used in interpretation of significance. Finally, in cases where sample distributions violated assumptions underlying parametric measures, the non-parametric Kruskal-Wallis one-way ANOVA was used to check validity of results. Second, within-sample comparisons were made of performance in order to focus on the issue of decrement within each sample, relative only to itself. For each sample, percentages of correct answers per test were calculated across the entire sample. The percentage calculated is in essence a group mean percentage, and is derived by dividing the raw score mean per test by the maximum points per test for any one respondent (Emery, 1988a). This procedure was used also to compare a mild subgroup of SDAT with the overall SDAT group percentages, as well as with group percentages of the other research samples. Third, the ω^2 statistic was calculated to determine effect size of tests with the goal of discriminant function and predictive power. Fourth, Pearson correlations were calculated between all measures of language and memory in order to begin to determine extent and nature of interaction between these two cognitive functions. Further, correlations were calculated between measures of organicity and both language and memory.

Results

Results of the study are organized and presented along four lines that correspond to the statistical approaches outlined above.

Differences of Means

Results from the ANOVAs indicate that on all measures of language and memory, there are significant differences between the three research populations at the .0001 level (Tables 9.1 and 9.2). The data suggest a general pattern in which the normal elderly have the highest means, with depressed elderly consistently lower than the normals, although not always significantly so. SDAT means, without exception, are markedly lowest. However, means of the mild subset of SDAT ($n = 7$) are reliably higher than means of the SDAT sample as a whole, and fall consistently between means of the depressed sample and those of the overall SDAT sample. Means of the mild subset of SDAT on language tests are as follows: Word Fluency/Untimed (7.0), Test for Syntactic Complexity (20.5), Sequential Commands (66), Reading Comprehension (34), Yes/No Questions (56.3), Sentence Completion (9.5), Auditory Word Recognition (57.5), Confrontation Object Naming (57.8), Responsive Speech (10), Repetition (80). Means of mild SDAT on memory are: Story Recall Delayed (2.8), Story Recall (6.3), Katzman Delayed (10), Paired Associates (14), Information (2.8), Orientation (3), Digits Backward (4.8), Digits Forward (6), Mental Control (7.5). These means of the mild subset of SDAT can be compared with the means of the other groups as given in Tables 9.1 and 9.2.

Turning to results from t-tests, all comparisons between the SDAT sample as a whole and normals on all measures of language and memory are statistically significant (Tables 9.3 and 9.4). Further, all comparisons between SDAT and major depression without dementia are statistically significant (Tables 3 and 4). Finally, comparisons between the depressed and normals indicate there are significant differences between the two groups on all measures of memory, except Mental Control (Table 9.4). On language assessments, there are significant differences between the depressed and normals on Test for Syntactic Complexity, Reading Comprehension, and Word Fluency/Untimed, but not on the other language measures (Table 9.3).

Comparisons Within Samples

Turning first to the SDAT sample, rank order of difficulty on language, going from most decrement to least decrement, is as follows: Test for Syntactic Complexity (26%), Word Fluency/Untimed (27%), Reading Comprehension (41%), Sequential Commands (53%), Responsive Speech (68%), Sentence

Table 9.1
Comparison of Means by Sample on Measures of Language

Measure of Language (maximum score)	Normal Elderly (*n* = 20)	Major Depression (*n* = 20)	SDAT (*n* = 23)	*F*
Test for Syntactic Complexity (36)	31.5 ± 1.4	25.5 ± 1.6	9.4 ± 1.8	52.76 ***
WAB Reading Comprehension (40)	39.6 ± .4	35.6 ± 1.5	16.4 ± 3.0	36.88 ***
WAB Word Fluency/ Untimed (20)	14.7 ± .8	11.7 ± 1.2	5.3 ± .8	26.13 ***
WAB Sequential Commands (80)	79.2 ± .8	77.9 ± 2.1	42.1 ± 6.4	25.84 ***
WAB Sentence Completion (10)	10.0 ± 0.0	10.0 ± 0.0	6.9 ± .8	14.19 ***
WAB Yes/ No Questions (60)	60.0 ± 0.0	59.9 ± .2	50.2 ± 2.4	14.12 ***
WAB Responsive Speech (10)	9.9 ± .1	10.0 ± 0.0	6.8 ± .8	13.67 ***
WAB Auditory Word Recognition (60)	59.9 ± .1	59.7 ± .2	44.4 ± 3.9	13.24 ***
WAB Confrontation Object Naming (60)	60.0 ± 0.0	60.0 ± 0.0	46.2 ± 3.9	11.06 ***
WAB Repetition (80)	79.6 ± .4	79.5 ± .5	58.0 ± 6.0	11.00 ***

Note. Values reported are the mean plus or minus the standard error of the mean.
*** $p \leq .0001$

Table 9.2
Comparison of Means by Sample on Measures of Memory

Measure of Memory (maximum score)	Normal Elderly (*n* = 20)	Major Depression (*n* = 20)	SDAT (*n* = 23)	*F*
Orientation (5)	5.0 ± 0.00	4.8 ± .12	1.3 ± .29	115.27 ***
Information (6)	5.8 ± .12	5.2 ± .23	1.3 ± .34	96.34 ***
Paired Associates (30)	23.2 ± 1.10	16.6 ± 1.40	6.1 ± 1.40	45.93 ***
Story Recall (24)	11.6 ± .82	7.8 ± .57	2.4 ± .68	45.83 ***
Katzman Delayed Recall (30)	24.5 ± 1.90	13.5 ± 2.60	1.7 ± 1.20	36.03 ***
Mental Control (9)	8.5 ± .22	8.0 ± .43	3.7 ± .71	26.43 ***
Digit Span Backward (7)	4.9 ± .27	3.7 ± .45	1.6 ± .38	20.64 ***
Digit Span Forward (8)	7.1 ± .26	6.0 ± .40	4.0 ± .54	13.77 ***
Delayed Story Recall (24)	5.6 ± .95	2.8 ± .58	.8 ± .35	13.47 ***

Note. Values reported are the mean plus or minus the standard error of the mean.
*** $p \leq .0001$

Completion (69%), Repetition (73%), Auditory Word Recognition (74%), Confrontation Object Naming (77%), and Yes/No Questions (84%). On measures of memory, the SDAT sample had the following percentages of correct answers: Delayed Story Recall (3%), Katzman Delayed Recall (6%), Story Recall (10%), Paired Associates (20%), Information (21%), Digits Backward (22%), Orientation (26%), Mental Control (42%), and Digits Forward (49%). Rank order of percentages correct answers for the mild subset of SDAT, although not identical to that of overall SDAT, is similar. Mild SDAT order of decrement on language, going from most decrement to least, is as follows: Word Fluency/Untimed (35%), Test for Syntactic Complexity (57%), Sequential Commands (83%), Reading Comprehension (85%), Yes/No Questions (94%), Sentence Completion (95%), Auditory Word Recognition (96%), Confrontation Object Naming (96%), Responsive Speech (100%), and Repetition (100%). The corresponding order for mild SDAT on memory is as follows: Delayed Story Recall (12%), Story Recall (26%), Katzman Delayed Recall (33%), Paired Associates (47%), Information (47%), Orientation (60%), Digits Backward (67%), Digits Forward (75%), and Mental Control (83%).

Persons with major depression showed the following rank order of performance deficits on language: Word Fluency/Untimed (59%), Test for Syntactic Complexity (71%), Reading Comprehension (89%), Sequential Commands (97%), Auditory Word Recognition (99%), Yes/No Questions (99%), Repetition (99%), Responsive Speech (100%), Sentence Completion (100%), and Confrontation Object Naming (100%). Memory performance for the depressed sample took the following order of correct answers: Delayed Story Recall (12%), Story Recall (33%), Katzman Delayed Recall (45%), Digits Backward (53%), Paired Associates (55%), Digits Forward (77%), Information (87%), Mental Control (89%), and Orientation (95%).

Normal elderly had the most difficulty with language measures of Word Fluency/Untimed (74%) and Test for Syntactic Complexity (88%). On other language measures, the normal sample had perfect or near-perfect scores. In the memory tasks, rank order of performance deficits for normal elderly is: Delayed Story Recall (23%), Story Recall (48%), Digits Backward (70%), Paired Associates (77%), Katzman Delayed (82%), Digits Forward (88%), Mental Control (94%), Information (97%), and Orientation (100%).

All three research samples showed greater percentage decrement on measures of memory than on measures of language. Mean percentage of correct answers across all measures of memory for the SDAT sample is 22.1%, whereas the summative mean across measures of language is 59.2%. For the depressed sample, summative mean percentage of correct answers for memory is 60.7%, and summative mean percentage for language is 91.3%. For normal elderly, the summative mean for memory assessments is 75.4%, whereas normals got a total of 95.7% of all language questions correct.

Estimates of Effect Size

As shown in Table 9.3, the language tests that best distinguish SDAT from normals are Test for Syntactic Complexity (.68), Word Fluency/Untimed (.61), Reading Comprehension (.57), and Sequential Commands (.43). Also, these same language tests, with somewhat lower ω^2 values, best discriminate SDAT from major depression. Table 9.4 reveals that SDAT and normals are best discriminated by memory tests of Orientation (.79), Information (.79), Katzman Delayed (.72), Paired Associates (.69), and Story Recall (.64). SDAT and depressed samples are best discriminated by three of these same memory tests: Orientation (.76), Information (.70), and Story Recall (.45).

Table 9.3
Estimates of Effect Size for Measures of Language

Measure	Major Depression and SDAT			Major Depression and Normals			SDAT and Normals		
	t	*p*	ω^2	*t*	*p*	ω^2	*t*	*p*	ω^2
Test for Syntactic Complexity	6.8	.0001	.51	2.9	.01	.15	9.6	.0001	.68
WAB Reading Comprehension	5.7	.0001	.43	2.6	.02	.13	7.6	.0001	.57
WAB Sequential Commands	5.3	.0001	.39	.6	ns	-	5.8	.0001	.43
WAB Word Fluency/ Untimed	4.5	.0001	.31	2.1	.05	.07	8.3	.0001	.61
WAB Responsive Speech	4.2	.001	.27	-	ns	-	3.9	.001	.25
WAB Sentence Completion	4.1	.001	.26	-	ns	-	4.1	.001	.26
WAB Yes/ No Questions	4.0	.001	.26	1.0	ns	-	4.2	.001	.27
WAB Auditory Word Recognition	3.9	.001	.25	1.1	ns	-	3.9	.001	.25
WAB Confrontation Object Naming	3.6	.01	.22	-	ns	-	3.6	.01	.22
WAB Repetition	3.5	.01	.21	-	ns	-	3.6	.01	.22

Note. For Major Depression/ SDAT, Major Depression/ Normals, and SDAT/ Normals, degrees of Freedom are 41, 38, and 41, respectively, except where variances are unequal (Hays, 1981).

Normals and major depression involve much lower ω^2 values. Memory tasks distinguishing depressed from normals include the same secondary memory tasks that distinguish SDAT from other samples, i.e., Paired Associates (.25), Story Recall (.25), Katzman Delayed (.21), but only minimally the tertiary memory tasks (Kaszniak et al., 1986) that separate SDAT from the other research samples, i.e., Information (.10) and Orientation (.08). Depressed are also discriminated from normals by language tests of Test for Syntactic Complexity (.15) and Reading Comprehension (.13).

Table 9.4
Estimates of Effect Size for Measures of Memory

Measure	Major Depression and SDAT			Major Depression and Normals			SDAT and Normals		
	t	p	ω^2	t	p	ω^2	t	p	ω^2
Orientation	10.9	.0001	.76	2.1	.05	.08	12.7	.0001	.79
Information	9.7	.0001	.70	2.4	.05	.10	12.6	.0001	.79
Story Recall	6.1	.0001	.45	3.8	.001	.25	8.8	.0001	.64
Paired Associates	5.3	.0001	.39	3.8	.001	.25	9.8	.0001	.69
Mental Control	5.2	.0001	.37	1.1	ns	-	6.5	.0001	.49
Katzman Delayed Recall	4.1	.001	.27	3.4	.01	.21	10.6	.0001	.72
Digit Span Backward	3.6	.001	.22	2.3	.05	.09	6.9	.0001	.52
Digit Span Forward	3.0	.01	.15	2.2	.05	.09	5.2	.0001	.37
Delayed Story Recall	2.8	.01	.14	2.5	.05	.12	4.7	.001	.33

Note. For Major Depression/ SDAT, Major Depression/ Normals, and SDAT/ Normals, degrees of freedom are 41, 38, and 41, respectively, except where variances are unequal (Hays, 1981).

Although the number of mild SDAT patients in our study is too small (n = 7) to reliably utilize the ω^2 statistic for determination of effect size, one can get some idea of tasks that best discriminate mild SDAT from normal elderly through the method of percentage distance. On measures of language, percentage differences between mild SDAT and normals are as follows: Word Fluency/Untimed (39%), Test for Syntactic Complexity (31%), Sequential Commands (16%), Reading Comprehension (14%), Yes/No Questions (6%), Sentence Completion (5%), Auditory Word Recognition (4%), Confrontation Object Naming (4%), Responsive Speech (0%), and Repetition (0%). Thus, the largest difference between mild SDAT and normal elderly language processing is on Word Fluency/Untimed and Test for Syntactic Complexity. On measures of memory, the percentage differences between mild SDAT and normals are: Information (50%), Katzman Delayed (49%), Orientation (40%), Paired Associates (30%), Story Recall (22%), Digits Forward (13%), Delayed Story Recall (11%), Mental Control (11%), and Digits Backward (1%). Thus, the percentage differences between mild SDAT and normals result in a discriminant profile very similar to that of the ω^2 profile distinguishing the SDAT sample in its entirety from normal elderly persons.

The description and understanding of SDAT as a disease process requires a summative approach encompassing core characteristics that cut across all stages of the disease process, and cannot be limited to any single stage of SDAT. However, the differential diagnosis between normals and SDAT is well served by a clear idea of defining characteristics of the mild stage of the disease process.

Table 9.5
Significant Pearson Correlation Coefficients between Language and Memory Tasks for Each Sample

	Info	Orient	Mental C	Digits F	Digits B	Story R	Story RD	Paired A	Katz D
Normal Elderly									
TSC	-	-	.70***	.66***	-	.53*	-	.58**	-
ReadComp	-	-	-	-	-	-	-	-	-
WordFluenc/Un	-	-	-	-	-	-	-	-	-
ResponsiveSP	-	-	-	-	-	-	-	-	-
SentCompletion	-	-	-	-	-	-	-	-	-
ConObNaming	-	-	-	-	-	-	-	-	-
Yes/NoQuest	-	-	-	-	-	-	-	-	-
AudWordRec	-	-	-	-	-	-	-	-	-
SeqCommands	-	-	-	-	-	-	-	-	-
Repetition	-	-	-	-	-	-	-	-	-
Major Depression									
TSC	-	.47*	.60**	-	-	-	-	.56**	-
ReadComp	.58**	-	-	-	-	-	-	-	-
WordFluenc/Un	.48*	-	-	-	-	-	-	-	-
ResponsiveSp	-	-	-	-	-	-	-	-	-
SentCompletion	-	-	-	-	-	-	-	-	-
ConObNaming	-	-	-	-	-	-	-	-	-
Yes/NoQuest	-	-	-	-	-	-	-	-	-
AudWordRec	-	-	.44*	.57**	-	-	-	-	-
SeqCommands	-	-	-	-	-	-	-	-	-
Repetition	-	-	-	-	-	-	-	-	-
SDAT									
TSC	.62**	.66***	.78***	.51*	.56**	.64***	.53**	.72***	-
ReadComp	.70***	.66***	.81***	.57**	.76***	.47*	-	.68***	-
WordFluenc/Un	-	.55**	.47*	-	.53**	.48*	.44*	.52*	-
ResponsiveSp	.63**	.66***	.71**	.50*	.51*	.53**	-	.57**	-
SentCompletion	.55**	.61**	.61**	-	.43*	-	-	.57**	-
ConObNaming	.49*	.52*	.58**	.43*	.57**	-	-	.54**	-
Yes/NoQuest	.46*	-	.61**	.52*	.46*	-	-	.48*	-
AudWordRec	.52*	-	.65***	.45*	-	-	-	-	-
SeqCommands	.63**	.46*	.82***	.58**	.59**	-	-	.58**	-
Repetition	-	.46*	.57**	.62**	.54**	-	-	.71***	-

Note. $*p \leq .05$ $**p \leq .01$ $***p \leq .001$

Pearson Correlation Coefficients between Language and Memory

The significant Pearson correlation coefficients between all measures of language and memory for the three samples can be inspected in Table 9.5. For the normal elderly, the statistical relation between language and memory is generally not significant. There are only four significant correlations, i.e., Test for Syntactic Complexity and Mental Control (.70), Digits Forward (.66), Paired Associates (.58), and Story Recall (.53). Turning to the data for the depressed sample, one finds seven significant correlations between language and memory. And finally, for the SDAT sample, there are 58 significant correlations out of the 90 coefficients between language and memory.

Discussion

Language Processing

Major depression and normal aging. As pointed out by way of introduction, the question of whether or not nondemented patients with major depression have structural language deficits has been virtually unaddressed, and constitutes a basic question of the present study. Answers to this question are important in the consideration of organicity underlying the continuum of depression without dementia, depressive dementia, and primary degenerative dementia.

Results of this study suggest that in comparisons between normal elderly and depressed elderly, the normal elderly have the edge. Data analyses converge to show that on three language measures of ten, there are significant differences between the two samples. Whereas an interpretation of these findings, at this phase of research, cannot be clear-cut, the following suggestions may be useful for the beginnings of explanation.

We can start by examining how the three language measures on which depressed and normal elderly differ are formally distinct from those on which they do not differ. A parameter that appears to distinguish between significant and nonsignificant language measures is complexity. The data suggest that depressed and normal elderly differ significantly on the most complex measures, but not on measures of lesser complexity. More specifically, we can use the semiotic hierarchy (deSaussure, 1966; Emery, 1982, 1985; Yngve, 1986) to address this issue. The four categories relevant to the present discussion are phonology, morphology, syntax, and semantics, representing a hierarchy that approximates a progression from least complex to most complex linguistic demand (Chomsky, 1979; Emery, 1985; Huck & Ojeda, 1987; Yngve, 1986). Placing research findings in the semiotic context, one finds the three measures distinguishing depressed and normals are concentrated in the semiotic ranks of greater complexity. Further, the complexity point is demonstrated not only across the semiotic hierarchy, but also within the ranks. Looking first at the Reading Comprehension of Sentences/Paragraphs Test, this test represents complex semantic processing of explicit rather than implicit interpretation (Light & Burke, 1988). The data show that the depressed made errors exclusively on the last two items of the test, the most complex items. Looking next at the Test for Syntactic Complexity, an exemplar of the syntactic rank, the greatest number of errors occurred on items having the most complex syntactic processing demand. Finally, analyzing requirements necessitated by the Word Fluency Test, one finds what we have termed a metamorphological processing requirement. We have analyzed the word fluency task in great detail elsewhere (Emery & Breslau, 1988), with the conclusion that generative naming tasks are incorrectly regarded as naming tasks per se. The Word Fluency Test is more appropriately regarded as a meta-naming task because of the organizational and categorical demands that are part of the structure of generative naming tasks, and that differentiate generative naming from other naming tasks. In sum, measures on which depressed elderly did significantly worse than normals are complex metamorphological, syntactic, and semantic measures. These are the same measures with highest ω^2 values. Discriminant function analyses indicate that linguistic tasks of greater complexity best discriminate nondemented persons with major depression from the normal aged. Further, these same tasks have the highest correlations with measures of organicity, i.e., Kahn-Goldfarb Mental Status Questionnaire, Face-Hand Test, and Reisberg Global Deterioration Scale (Arora et al., in press; Emery, 1985; 1988b; Emery & Breslau, 1988).

As we zero in on complexity as a mediating variable in depressed elderly linguistic processing, it strikes us that the concept of "complexity" may overlap a concept often invoked in memory research, namely that of "effortful processing." Certain memory operations can be done "automatically," i.e., with minimal energy, attention, and intentionality, whereas other memory operations are "effortful" and require concentrated energy, attention, and intention (Hasher & Zacks, 1979). Let us for the moment integrate the two concepts of "complexity" and "effortful processing." I would propose that the most complex cognitive tasks require the most effortful processing, whereas cognitive tasks of lesser complexity can be done in a more automatic way. Also, in previous research it was found that the most complex cognitive tasks required the greatest synthesis or integration (Emery, 1982, 1985). Thus, the paradigm becomes, the most complex tasks require the greatest integration and most effortful processing. Accordingly, it could be concluded that measures that best differentiate depressed from normal elderly are complex measures that concomitantly require greater integration and effortful processing.

Although this extension of the concept of complexity may have heuristic value, it leave unaddressed the question of why depressed elderly linguistic processing is significantly worse than that of normal elderly on the most complex tasks. While adherents of the effortful processing model often invoke lack of motivation as a causal variable to explain the depressed person's deficit in effortful processing, there is also increasing evidence that effort-demanding and automatic cognitive processing may be determined by different psychobiological mechanisms (Akiskal & McKinney, 1973; Weingartner, 1986). Significant differences in cognitive processing between normal and depressed elderly constitutes a necessary, but not sufficient condition for an organic explanation of depressed elderly cognitive decrement.

Major depression and SDAT. We will shift our attention now to a consideration of major depression in relation to SDAT. Results of this study indicate that the depressed elderly performed reliably better on structural language variables of repetition, naming, auditory verbal comprehension, syntax, and reading comprehension compared to the SDAT sample. Thus, major depression with no dementia impacts less upon formal language processing than does SDAT.

The greatest differences of means between depressed patients and patients with SDAT occur on the most complex measures of language, whereas the smallest mean differences occur on measures of least complexity. This pattern of mean differences is reflected in effect size patterns. Major depression with no dementia is best discriminated from SDAT by semantic, syntactic, and metamorphological measures, i.e., Reading Comprehension, Test for Syntactic Complexity, Sequential Commands, and Word Fluency/Untimed.

Although discriminant function values for depression/SDAT are much greater than those for depression/normals, there is a similarity in pattern. Both sets of ω^2 values indicate that the greatest discrimination occurs with the most complex linguistic measures. Less effective or no discriminant function, at any rate not a quantitatively based discriminant function, is attained with least complex measures. We would posit that the similarity in pattern is due to the fact that complex linguistic tasks are sensitive to organic decrement in our research populations. Previous research has shown there exists a positive correlation between organicity and decrement on complex linguistic tasks for populations of SDAT, depression, and normal elderly (Arora et al., in press; Emery, 1985, 1988b; Emery & Breslau, 1988). The present study replicates this finding. For example, in the SDAT sample one finds the largest Pearson correlations between decrement on the Kahn-Goldfarb Mental Status Questionnaire and decrement on Reading Comprehension (.78), Test for Syntactic Complexity (.77), Sequential Commands (.67), and Word Fluency/Untimed (.64). It would appear that similarity of effect size patterns between depression/SDAT and depression/normals has as its basis a sensitivity to organicity in those measures with greatest discriminant power. Put another way, the data suggest a common factor of organic decline is being picked up by those complex language measures that have the greatest effect size. Accordingly, it is suggested herein that normal elderly, depressed elderly, and elderly with SDAT constitute a continuum of organicity.

An important difference between nondemented patients with major depression and patients with SDAT is that the former make significant numbers of errors only on the most complex language measures. In contrast, the greater organic decrement of SDAT patients results in significant numbers of errors on all language measures, although greatest number of errors occurs on the most complex measures. Qualitatively speaking, of our subject groups, only SDAT patients miss the simplest questions, e.g., "How many days are there in a week?".

Before concluding this section, we will compare the depressed elderly sample with the mild subset of SDAT patients. An understanding of SDAT as a disease process must be an integrated summative understanding that cuts across all stages of the disorder. The description of SDAT cannot be equated with any one of its stages, but must incorporate information from all stages. However, such an overall description cannot be accomplished without study of each of the stages that are part of the disease process. Especially critical for differential diagnostic applications is the description of mild SDAT.

In examining differences of means between depressed elderly with no dementia and mild SDAT, one finds there are no significant differences on language tests of Repetition (80 vs. 79.5), Confrontation Object Naming (57.8 vs. 60), Sentence Completion (9.5 vs. 10), Responsive Speech 10 vs. 10), Auditory Word Recognition (57.5 vs. 59.7), Yes/No Questions (56.3 vs. 59.9), or Reading Comprehension (34 vs. 35.6). In contrast, reliable differences exist between the depressed and mild SDAT on Sequential Commands (66 vs. 77.9), Word Fluency/Untimed (7 vs. 11.7), and Test for Syntactic Complexity (20.5 vs. 25.5).

Memory Processing

Major depression and normal aging. In comparisons of memory processing of nondemented elderly diagnosed with major depression and normal elderly, t-tests indicate differences of means reach significance on all measures except one (Mental Control). Normal elderly do reliably better on memory tasks than do elderly with major depression. Discriminant function values indicate the two groups are best discriminated by Story Recall (.25) and Paired Associates (.25). The samples are least well distinguished by Mental Control (.02) and Orientation (.08).

Translating these findings into information-processing categories, it would appear that tasks of secondary memory, e.g., new learning that requires long-term memory (Kaszniak et al., 1986), best distinguish the depressed from normals. In contrast, major depression and normal aging are least differentiated by tasks of tertiary memory, i.e., tasks involving highly overlearned material and/or personal information, usually from the remote past (e.g., Mental Control).

The measures that best distinguish depressed and normals also can be subsumed under cross-cutting categories of episodic memory and new information (Light & Burke, 1988). Tasks of tertiary memory are not representations of episodic memory or new information, although all overlearned materials and/or personal data were at one time newly learned. The secondary memory tasks distinguishing our depressed and normal samples (e.g., learning a list of verbal paired associates) are more complex and effort-demanding than are tasks involving tertiary memory (e.g., saying the alphabet).

In sum, both the memory tasks and language tasks that best discriminate nondemented depressed elderly from normals are relatively more complex and effort-demanding than are the tasks that discriminate least.

Major depression and SDAT. With respect to the depressed and SDAT samples, data show highly significant differences on all measures of memory. In terms of percentages of correct answers, the SDAT sample shows greatest memory preservation on a measure of primary memory (Digit Span Forward). This finding has its analogue in the domain of linguistic processing; repetition is among the best preserved of language functions in SDAT.

The greatest discriminant power for SDAT and the depressed occurs with Orientation (.76) and Information (.70). Similarly, the greatest effect size for SDAT and normals is also with Orientation (.79) and Information (.79). Overall, these measures involve overlearned material. For this reason the measures are often subsumed under the information-processing category of tertiary memory (Kaszniak et al., 1986). I would suggest that highly overlearned material can be non-personal (e.g., alphabet) or personal (e.g., birthdate). Further, overlearned material can be non-personal from the remote past (e.g., alphabet), personal from the remote past (e.g., birthdate), non-personal from recent times (e.g., President), or personal from recent times (e.g., present age). It is the loss of overlearned personal information from both the past and present that characterizes SDAT, and that especially distinguishes it, quantitatively and qualitatively, from major depression and normal aging. Also, SDAT is distinguished by decrement in current overlearned non-personal information (e.g., President). Although SDAT also involves deterioration of non-personal information from the remote past (e.g., alphabet), this subset of overlearned material appears to be retained longer than current non-personal material.

In earlier work, I have proposed that organic decrement is a continuous variable (Emery, 1988a). Thus, one can view the normal elderly, depressed elderly, and elderly with SDAT as forming a continuum or spectrum of organic decrement. It would appear that overlearned material is relatively unaffected on the less deteriorated side of this organic continuum. The greater organic deterioration of SDAT in relation to our other samples, impacts tertiary memory to an extent not found in the lesser organicity of nondemented depressed elderly. This same pattern holds true for the simplest language functions. The greater organicity of SDAT impacts on naming tests such as Responsive Speech, e.g., "How many days are there in a week?," whereas nondemented depressed elderly and normal elderly do not make errors on these simple questions, in general.

In sum, normal and depressed elderly both have greatest preservation on tertiary memory, followed by primary memory, with secondary memory most deteriorated. The greater organicity of SDAT results in a configuration with primary memory best preserved, followed by tertiary memory, with secondary memory again most deteriorated.

Before moving to the next section, let us take a look at the subsample of mild SDAT in relation to the depressed elderly. The greatest decrement for mild SDAT occurs on the four measures of secondary memory, as it also does for normal elderly, depressed elderly, and the SDAT sample as a whole. Percentages of correct answers for mild SDAT patients versus the depressed are as follows: Delayed Story Recall (12% vs. 12%), Story Recall (26% vs. 33%), Katzman Delayed Recall (33% vs. 45%), Paired Associates (47% vs. 55%), Mild SDAT patients did as well as the depressed on a measure of primary memory, i.e., Digit Span Forward (75% vs. 77%). Interestingly, mild SDAT patients did significantly better than the depressed on Digit Span Backward (69% vs. 53%). In terms of overlearned material, mild SDAT patients had least decrement on overlearned non-personal material from the remote past such as alphabet and numbers, i.e., Mental Control (83% vs. 89%). The greatest percentage distance between mild SDAT and depressed elderly occurs with Information (47% vs. 87%) and Orientation (60% vs 95%). Mild SDAT is best discriminated from both normal aging and major depression by Information and Orientation, just as is the SDAT sample as a whole.

The Relation Between Language and Memory

The positive relation between language and memory increases with an increase in sample organicity. In other words, the less the organic decrement of the sample, the fewer the positive correlations between language and memory. Further, the less the organic decrement of the sample, the greater the number of negative correlations between language and memory, albeit none significant, i.e., 28 for the normal aged, nine for the depressed, and none for the demented. Thus, it would appear that organic decrement is an intervening variable in the positive relation between language and memory.

For the normal aged, there were only four significant correlations between language and memory. All four significant coefficients were positive and involved the Test for Syntactic Complexity. For the depressed, one finds seven significant (positive) correlations between language and memory. Three involved the TSC. Five of the seven significant values involved measures of memory consisting predominantly of overlearned and/or personal material, i.e., Information, Orientation, Mental Control. For the SDAT sample, 58 of 90 coefficients were significant (positive). All measures of language were affected in the interaction between language and memory in SDAT, but not all measures of memory were affected. The Katzman Test for Delayed Recall is not significantly correlated with any measure of language in SDAT. Delayed Story Recall is the second least correlated measure of memory for SDAT. Thus, the data suggest that measures of delayed recall are least correlated with measures of language in SDAT. Further, for both the depressed and normal samples, measures of delayed recall were not correlated with measures of language.

In more theoretical terms, how can one begin to conceptualize the relation between language and memory? The attempt at explanation that follows is heuristic in nature. I would posit that to begin to understand the meaning of the correlation matrix described above, one must ferret out the theoretical connection between "semantic memory" and the "semantic" rank of the semiotic hierarchy. This connection does not appear to have been addressed in the literature.

We can start by looking at the linguistic properties of "semantics." As pointed out earlier, the semiotic system is hierarchical, going from simple to more complex units of language, with categorical ranks of phonology, morphology, syntax, and semantics (Chomsky, 1979; deSaussure, 1966; Huck & Ojeda, 1987; Yngve, 1986). Phonology refers to sound without reference to

meaning, whereas morphology involves the smallest units of meaningful sig-
nalling (parts of words and words). Syntax refers to structure of phrases and
sentences, and includes variables of voice, sentence type, substitution,
pronomial, and prepositional usage. Semantics, the category on which we are
focused at this point, refers to the analysis, organization, and interpretation
of meaning. Whereas phonology, morphology, and syntax form a true hierarchy, semantics cross-cuts both morphology and syntax (Emery, 1982, 1985,
1988b). Semantics, as a linguistic dimension, requires the person render
meaningful a string of parts of words/words, phrases, sentences, paragraphs,
including the concepts inhering in these linguistic units, through processes
of comprehension, analysis, organization, and interpretation. Semantic
processing at the level of the part of word/word is less complex than at the
level of larger aggregates of words (Emery, 1982, 1985).

I would suggest that semantics, as a dimension of language, presupposes
normative memorial function, and that once normative language skills have
been attained developmentally, linguistic processing has as a basic assumption that the linguistic forms being processed will first of all be "remembered."
A person cannot render meaningful parts of words/words if the normative
denotation and connotation of these basic units is not "remembered" or otherwise accessed. Similarly, semantic processing cannot take place at the level
of aggregates of words if rules of normative phrase and sentence structure are
not "remembered."

On the other side of it, does memory depend on normative linguistic
processing? There do appear to be forms of memory that are not linguistically
based. For example, animals appear to have some forms of "memory" that are
not linguistically based. Also, it appears the pre-verbal infant has sensory
memory functions (e.g., visual, auditory, olfactory) that are not linguistic in
nature. However, categories of memory that are essentially defined or characterized as based on words, ideas, concepts, information are, by definition, linguistically based and depend on semantic processing. Therefore, I would propose that "semantic memory" and linguistic processing at the "semantic" level
are "systemically interconnected." The systemic interconnection of these cognitive activities only becomes apparent in the context of pathology. As long as
normative levels of processing exist for both these higher cortical activities, each
activity represents what appears to be an "independent" and specialized function. A prototype might be found in the more tangible body organs, e.g., heart,
lungs. As long as these organs function within a normative range, each organ
has its specialized activities. However, severe dysfunction of any one organ
impacts on the function of others. Thus, semantic memory may presuppose
normative semantic-linguistic processing and semantic-linguistic processing
may presuppose normative semantic memory.

Thus, it follows that the Pearson correlations between language and
memory were negligible for the normal aged of this study. A normal adult, by
definition, has both normative language and memorial processing, thus ful-
filling the underlying requirement for both these higher cortical activities. In

contrast, organic deterioration of either of these cognitive activities impacts on the synergistic, co-dependent function. Thus, the correlation matrix of the present study reflects this interaction with the increasing number of positive correlations between language and memory as sample organicity increases.

Conclusion

To conclude, I have investigated the degree and kind of deficits found in language and memory processing in populations of SDAT, major depression without dementia, and normal aging. In comparisons between the normal and depressed elderly, normal elderly did reliably better. In contrast, impact of the disease process of SDAT was significantly greater than that of major depression. The patterning of deficits in language and memory is consistent with the conclusion that organic decrement is best viewed as continuous. The dichotomous approach to organicity is less productive for understanding the research results. A spectrum approach to depression and dementia is proposed. The utility of such a spectrum approach is underscored by recent findings from structural neuroimaging studies and neurochemical studies. Alexopoulos (1990) found the sizes of lateral ventricles and cortical sulci of patients with old age depression were comparable to those of patients with primary degenerative dementia. In the same vein, Jacoby and Levy (1980) found that elderly depressives had larger ventricles than normal elderly. Further, reduced brain concentrations of norepinephrine and serotonin have been reported for elderly patients with major depression, depressive dementia, and primary degenerative dementia (Alexopoulos, 1990; Arora et al., in press). Although a spectrum approach to depression and dementia is suggested and developed in the present chapter, a full understanding of the natural course of these spectrum disorders can only be attained by repeated assessments of the same individuals over time. Future research includes the systematic longitudinal study of these spectrum disorders. The long-term follow-up approach is required in order to answer basic questions that the present investigation has brought into focus.

References

Akiskal, H., & McKinney, W. (1973). Depressive disorders: Toward a unified hypothesis. *Science, 182*, 20-29.

Albert, M. S., Butters, N., & Brandt, J. (1981). Patterns of remote memory in amnestic and demented patients. *Archives of Neurology, 38*, 495-500.

Alexopoulos, G. (1990). Clinical and biological findings in late-onset depression. In A. Tasman, S. M. Goldfinger, & C. A. Kaufman (Eds.), *Review of psychiatry.* Washington, DC: American Psychiatric Press.

Alzheimer, A. (1907). Über eine eigenartige Erkrankung der Hirnrinde. *Allgemeines Zeitschrift für Psychiatrie, 64*, 146-148.

American Psychiatric Association (1987). *Diagnostic and statistical manual of mental disorders* (3rd ed. rev.). Washington, DC: Author.

Arora, R., Emery, V. O. B., & Meltzer, H. Y. (in press). Platelet serotonin uptake and imipramine binding in the blood platelets of Alzheimer disease patients. *Neurology*.

Bäckman, L., & Herlitz, A. (1990). The relationship between prior knowledge and face recognition memory in normal aging and Alzheimer's disease. *Journal of Gerontology: Psychological Sciences, 45*, 94-100.

Bayles, K. A., & Kaszniak, A. W. (1987). *Communication and cognition in normal aging and dementia*. Boston: Little, Brown.

Bayles, K. A., & Tomoeda, C. K. (1990). Delayed recall deficits in aphasic stroke patients: Evidence of Alzheimer's dementia? *Journal of Speech and Hearing Disorders, 55*, 310-314.

Bayles, K. A., & Tomoeda, C. K. (1983). Confrontation naming impairment in dementia. *Brain and Language, 19*, 98-114.

Beck, A. (1967). *Depression: Clinical, experimental, and theoretical aspects*. New York: Harper and Row.

Benjamin, B. (1984). Phonological performance in gerontological speech. *Journal of Psycholinguistic Research, 11*, 159-167.

Breslow, R., Kocsis, J., & Belkin, B. (1981). Contribution of the depressive perspective to memory function in depression. *American Journal of Psychiatry, 138*, 227-230.

Bulbena, A., & Berrios, G. (1986). Pseudodementia: Facts and figures. *British Journal of Psychiatry, 148*, 87-94.

Calev, A., Nigel, D., & Chazen, S. (1989). Retrieval from semantic memory using meaningful and meaningless constructs by depressed, stable bipolar, and manic patients. *British Journal of Clinical Psychology, 28*, 67-73.

Cassens, G., Wolfe, L., & Zola, M. (1990). The neuropsychology of depressions. *Journal of Neuropsychiatry, 2*, 202-213.

Chomsky, C. (1979). *The acquisition of syntax in children from 5 to 10*. Cambridge, MA: MIT Press.

Cummings, J. L. (1989). Dementia and depression: An evolving enigma. *Journal of Neuropsychiatry, 3*, 236-242.

deSaussure, F. (1966). *Course in general linguistics*. New York: McGraw-Hill.

Ellis, H. C. (1990). Depressive deficits in memory: Processing initiative and resource allocation. *Journal of Experimental Psychology: General, 119*, 60-62.

Emery, V. O. B. (1982). *Linguistic patterning in the second half of the life cycle*. Unpublished doctoral dissertation, The University of Chicago, Chicago.

Emery, V. O. B. (1984). The progressive aphasia of senile dementia Alzheimer's type. In *New advances in Alzheimer's and treatable dementias*. (Audio-Transcript P 28-100-848). Washington, DC: American Psychiatric Association.

Emery, V. O. B. (1985). Language and aging. *Experimental Aging Research Monographs, 11*.

Emery, V. O. B. (1986). Linguistic decrement in normal aging. *Language and Communication, 6*, 47-64.

Emery, V. O. B. (1987). Linguistic cues in the differential diagnosis of Alzheimer's disease. *Clinical Gerontologist, 6*, 59-62.

Emery, V. O. B. (1988a). *Pseudodementia: A theoretical and empirical discussion*. Western Reserve Geriatric Education Center Interdisciplinary Monograph Series. Cleveland: Case Western Reserve University School of Medicine.

Emery, V. O. B. (1988b). Language and memory processing in senile dementia Alzheimer's type. In L. Light & D. Burke (Eds.), *Language, memory, and aging*. New York: Cambridge University Press.

Emery, V. O. B. (1988c). The deficit of thought in senile dementia Alzheimer's type. *Psychiatric Journal of the University of Ottawa, 13*, 2-8.

Emery, V. O. B., & Breslau, L. D. (1987). The acceleration process in Alzheimer's disease: Thought dissolution in Alzheimer's disease early onset and SDAT. *The American Journal of Alzheimer's Care, 2*, 24-32.

Emery, V. O. B., & Breslau, L. D. (1988). The problem of naming in SDAT: A relative deficit. *Experimental Aging Research, 14*, 181-193.

Emery, V. O. B., & Breslau, L. D. (1989). Language deficits in depression: Comparisons with SDAT and normal aging. *Journal of Gerontology: Medical Sciences, 44*, 85-92.

Emery, V. O. B., & Oxman, T. E. (in press). Update on the dementia spectrum of depression. *American Journal of Psychiatry.*

Endicott, J., & Spitzer, R. (1978). A diagnostic interview: The Schedule for Affective Disorders and Schizophrenia. *Archives of General Psychiatry, 35*, 837-844.

Eustache, F., Cox, C., Brandt, J., Lechavalier, B., & Pons, L. (1990). Word association responses and severity of dementia in Alzheimer's disease. *Psychological Reports, 66*, 1315-1322.

Ferm, L. (1974). Behavioral activities in demented geriatric patients. *Gerontology Clinics, 16*, 185-194.

Gallagher, D. (1986). Assessment of depression by interview methods and psychiatric rating scales. In L. W. Poon (Ed.), *Handbook for clinical memory assessment of older adults.* Washington, DC: American Psychological Association.

Goodwin, F., & Jamison, K. (1986). *Manic-depressive illness.* New York: Oxford University Press.

Green, J., Morris, J. C., Sandson, J., McKeel, D. W., & Miller, J. W. (1990). Progressive aphasia: A precursor of global dementia? *Neurology, 40*, 423-429.

Hart, R. P., Kwentus, J. A., Hamer, R., & Taylor, J. R. (1987). Selective reminding procedure in depression and dementia. *Psychology and Aging, 2*, 111-115.

Hasher, L., & Zacks, R. (1979). Automatic and effortful processes in memory. *Journal of Experimental Psychology: General, 108*, 356-388.

Hays, W. (1981). *Statistics.* New York: Holt, Rinehart, & Winston.

Heindel, W. C., Salmon, D. P., Shults, C. W., Walicke, P. A., & Butters, N. (1989). Neuropsychological evidence for multiple implicit memory systems: A comparison of Alzheimer's, Huntington's, and Parkinson's disease patients. *Journal of Neuroscience, 9*, 582-587.

Helkala, E. L., Laulumaa, V., Soininen, H., & Riekkinen, P. J. (1989). Different error pattern of episodic and semantic memory in Alzheimer's disease and Parkinson's disease with dementia. *Neuropsychologia, 27*, 1241-1248.

Hertel, P. T., & Hardin, T. S. (1990). Remembering with and without awareness in a depressed mood: Evidence of deficits in initiative. *Journal of Experimental Psychology: General, 119*, 45-59.

Huck, G., & Ojeda, A. (1987). *Syntax and semantics.* New York: Academic Press.

Huff, F. J. (1988). The disorder of naming in Alzheimer's disease. In L. L. Light & D. Burke (Eds.), *Language, memory, and aging* . New York: Cambridge University Press.

Illes, J. (1989). Neurolinguistic features of spontaneous language production dissociate three forms of neurodegenerative disease. *Brain and Language, 37*, 628-642.

Jacoby, R., & Levy, R. (1980). Computed tomography in the elderly: Affective disorder. *British Journal of Psychiatry, 136*, 270-275.

Kahn, R., Goldfarb, A., Pollack, M., & Peck, A. (1960). Brief objective measures for the determination of mental status in the aged. *American Journal of Psychiatry, 117*, 326-328.

Kaszniak, A. W., Poon, L. W., & Riege, W. (1986). Assessing memory deficits: An informationprocessing approach. In L. W. Poon (Ed.), *Handbook for clinical memory assessment of older adults.* Washington, DC: American Psychological Association.

202   *V. O. B. Emery*

Katzman, R. (1983). *Biological aspects of Alzheimer's disease*. Cold Spring Harbor, NY: Cold
    Spring Harbor Laboratory.
Kertesz, A. (1982). *Aphasia and associated disorders: Taxonomy, localization, and
    recovery*. New York: Grune & Stratton.
Kiloh, L. (1962). Pseudo-dementia. *Acta Psychiatrica Scandinavia, 37*, 336-351.
Kirshner, H., Webb, W., Kelly, M., & Wells, C. (1984). Language disturbance: An initial
    symptom of cortical degeneration and dementia. *Archives of Neurology, 41*, 491-496.
Knopman, D. S., & Ryberg, S. (1989). A verbal memory test with high predictive accuracy
    for dementia of the Alzheimer type. *Archives of Neurology, 46*, 141-145.
Knotek, P. C., Bayles, K. A., & Kaszniak, A. W. (1990). Response consistency on a semantic
    memory task in persons with dementia of the Alzheimer type. *Brain and Language, 38*,
    465-475.
Kontiola, P., Laaksonen, R., Sulkava, R., & Erkinjuntti, T. (1990). Pattern of language
    impairment is different in Alzheimer's disease and multi-infarct dementia. *Brain and
    Language, 38*, 364-383.
Koyama, R., & Meltzer, H. Y. (1986). A biochemical and neuroendocrine study of the
    serotonergic system in depression. In. H. Hippius (Ed.), *New results in depression
    research*. Berlin: Springer-Verlag.
Kral, V. A. (1962). Senescent forgetfulness: Benign and malignant. *Journal of the Candian
    Medical Association, 86*, 257-260.
Kral, V. A. (1983). The relationship between senile dementia (Alzheimer type) and
    depression. *Canadian Journal of Psychiatry, 28*, 304-306.
Kral, V. A., & Emery, V. O. B. (1989). Long-term follow-up of depressive pseudodementia.
    Canadian Journal of Psychiatry, 34, 445-447.
Landrum, R., & Radtke, R. (1990). Degree of cognitive impairment and the dissociation of
    implicit and explicit memory. *Journal of General Psychology, 117*, 187-196.
LaRue, A. (1989). Patterns of performance on the Fuld Object Memory Evaluation
    in elderly inpatients with depression or dementia. *Journal of Clinical and
    Experimental Neuropsychology, 11*, 409-422.
Light, L. L., & Burke, D. (1988). Language and memory in old age. In L. L. Light & D. Burke
    (Eds.), *Language, memory, and aging*. New York: Cambridge University Press.
Mairet, A. (1883). *De la demence mélancholique: Contribution à l'étude de la périencephalite
    chronique localisée et à l'étude des localisations cérébrales d'ordre psychique*. Paris: G.
    Masson.
McAllister, T. (1983). Overview: Pseudodementia. *American Journal of Psychiatry, 140*,
    528-533.
Moss, M. B., Albert, M. S., Butters, N., & Payne, M. (1986). Differential patterns of memory
    loss among patients with Alzheimer's disease, Huntington's disease, and alcoholic
    Korsakoff's syndrome. *Archives of Neurology, 43*, 239-246.
Murphy, E. (1983). The prognosis of depression in old age. *British Journal of Psychiatry, 142*,
    111-119.
Neils, J., Brennan, M., Cole, M., Boller, F., & Gerdeman, B. (1988). The use of phonemic
    cueing in Alzheimer's disease patients. *Neuropsychologia, 26*, 351-354.
Partridge, F. M., Knight, R. G., & Feehan, M. (1990). Direct and indirect memory
    performance in patients with senile dementia. *Psychological Medicine, 20*, 111-118.
Pepin, E. P., & Eslinger, P. J. (1989). Verbal memory decline in Alzheimer's disease:
    A multiple processes deficit. *Neurology, 39*, 1477-1482.
Piaget, J. (1952). *The origins of intelligence in children*. New York: International Universities
    Press.
Poitrenaud, J., Moy, F., Girousse, A., Wolmark, Y., & Piette, F. (1989). Psychometric
    procedures for analysis of memory losses in the elderly. *Archives of Gerontology and
    Geriatrics* (Suppl.), *1*, 173-183.

Poon, L. W. (1985). Differences in human memory with aging: Nature, causes, and clinical implications. In J. Birren & K. W. Schaie (Eds.), *Handbook of the psychology of aging* (2nd ed.). New York: Van Nostrand Reinhold.

Rabins, R., Merchant, A., & Nestadt, G. (1984). Criteria for diagnosing reversible dementia caused by depression: Validation by 2-year follow-up. *British Journal of Psychiatry, 144*, 488-492.

Raskin, A. (1986). Partialing out the effects of depression and age on cognitive functions: Experimental data and methodological issues. In L. W. Poon (Ed.), *Handbook for clinical memory assessment of older adults*. Washington, DC: American Psychological Association.

Reding, M., Haycox, J., & Blass, J. (1985). Depression in patients referred to a dementia clinic. *Archives of Neurology, 42*, 894-896.

Reeves, A. G. (1989). Aging brains: Some observations. *Seminars in Neurology, 9*, 1-4.

Reifler, B., & Sherrill, K. (1990). Dementias: Reversible and irreversible. In A. Tasman, S. Goldfinger, & C. Kaufman (Eds.), *Review of psychiatry* (Vol. 9). Washington, DC: American Psychiatric Press.

Reisberg, B., Ferris, S. H., DeLeon, M., & Crook, T. (1982). The Global Deterioration Scale (GDS): An instrument for assessment of primary degernative dementia. *American Journal of Psychiatry, 139*, 1136-1139.

Rochford, G. (1971). A study of naming errors in dysphasic and demented patients. *Neuropsychologia, 9*, 437-443.

Roth, M. (1986). Differential diagnosis of psychiatric disorders in old age. *Hospital Practice, 67*, 111-125.

Russell, E. (1975). A multiple scoring method for the assessment of complex memory functions. *Journal of Consulting and Clinical Psychology, 43*, 800-809.

Schneck, M., Reisberg, B., & Ferris, S. (1982). An overview of current concepts of Alzheimer's disease. *American Journal of Psychiatry, 139*, 165-173.

Selnes, O., Carson, K., Rovner, B., & Gordon, B. (1988). Language dysfunction in early and late onset possible Alzheimer's disease. *Neurology, 38*, 1053-1056.

Shewan, C., & Kertesz, A. (1980). Reliability and validity characteristics of the Western Aphasia Battery. *Journal of Speech and Hearing Disorders, 45*, 308-324.

Shuttleworth, E. C., & Huber, S. J. (1988). The naming disorder of dementia of Alzheimer type. *Brain and Language, 34*, 222-234.

Simmel, G. (1971). *On individuality and social forms*. Chicago: The University of Chicago Press.

Speedie, L., Rabins, P., Pearlson, G., & Moberg, P. (1990). Confrontation naming deficit in dementia of depression. *Journal of Neuropsychiatry, 2*, 59-63.

Starkstein, S., Rabins, P., Berthier, M., Cohen, B., Folstein, M. F., & Robinson, R. (1989). Dementia of depression among patients with neurological disorders and functional depression. *Journal of Neuropsychiatry, 1*, 263-268.

Thal, L. J., Grundman, M., & Klauber, M. R. (1988). Dementia: Characteristics of a referral population and factors associated with progression. *Neurology, 38*, 1083-1090.

Tulving, E. (1972). Episodic and semantic memory. In E. Tulving & W. Donaldson (Eds.), *Organization of memory*. New York: Academic Press.

U.S. Department of Health and Human Servcies. (1984). *Report of the Secretary's task force on Alzheimer's disease*. Washington, DC: U.S. Government Printing Office.

Watts, F., Dalgleish, T., Bourke, P., & Healy, D. (1990). Memory deficit in clinical depression: Processing resources and the structure of materials. *Psychological Medicine, 20*, 345-349.

Wechsler, D. (1973). *Wechsler Memory Scale: A standardized memory scale for clinical use*. New York: The Journal Press.

Weingartner, H. (1986). Automatic and effort-demanding cognitive processes in depression. In L. W. Poon (Ed.), *Handbook for clinical memory assessment of older adults*. Washington, DC: American Psychological Association.

Weingartner, H., Kaye, W., Smallberg, S. A., Ebert, M. H., Gillin, J. C., & Sitaram, N. (1981). Memory failures in progressive idiopathic dementia. *Journal of Abnormal Psychology, 90,* 196-197.

Wells, C. (1982). Refinements in the diagnosis of dementia. *American Journal of Psychiatry, 139,* 621-622.

Yngve, V. (1986). *Linguistics as a science.* Bloomington, IN: Indiana University Press.

Section IV

PROGRESSION

Memory Functioning in Dementia – L. Bäckman (Editor)

10 Progression of Senile Dementia of the Alzheimer Type on a Battery of Psychometric Tests

Martha Storandt, John C. Morris, Eugene H. Rubin, Lawrence A. Coben, and Leonard Berg

Washington University in St. Louis

Introduction

In 1979 a multidisciplinary longitudinal study of the natural history of Alzheimer's disease compared with healthy aging was begun at Washington University in St. Louis. Over a period of a year and a half, 23 women and 20 men with mild senile dementia of the Alzheimer type (SDAT) were enrolled for study. An equal number of healthy older adults matched for age, sex, and socioeconomic status were enrolled at the same time. This chapter reports the results of the repeated assessment with a battery of psychometric tests of these individuals through July, 1990.

Alzheimer's disease is a progressive, deteriorative disease. As will be described in this chapter, it typically first attacks the individual's ability to learn and remember new information, but as the disease progresses a wide range of higher cortical functions are affected. The rate of progression, however, varies from individual to individual. A number of investigators have sought to find correlates of these rates. Such information would be useful for health care planners and families of affected individuals. It also might provide hints to the mechanisms involved in the disease.

The search for correlates of rate of deterioration in SDAT takes two general forms. The first focuses on risk factors. One commonly examined is age at onset of the disease. It has been suggested that more rapid deterioration occurs in younger individuals (e.g., Diesfeldt, van Houte, & Moerkens, 1986). Other risk factors include concomitant features of the disease in its early stages that may be associated with more rapid decline. For example, Kaszniak et al. (1978, p. 246) found that "expressive language deficit...may indicate a particularly poor prognosis for survival." Earlier reports from our research group also implicated language function and concluded that aphasia in the mild stage of dementia was associated with more rapid progression of SDAT (Berg et al., 1984; Faber-Langendoen et al., 1988).

The other research strategy examines the concomitant rates of change in different types of measures. For example, Luxenberg, Haxby, Creasey, Sundaram, and Rapoport (1987) found that the rate of ventricular enlargement as measured by CT scan was correlated with the rate of decline on a neuropsychological test battery in 10 male patients. A previous report from our research group found that the development of parkinsonism after diagnosis of SDAT in the mild stage was associated with more rapid progression on a global clinical measure of dementia (Morris, Drazner, Fulling, Grant, & Goldring, 1989).

This chapter includes a description of attempts to identify correlates of progression (deterioration) on the battery of psychometric tests included in the longitudinal study. It differs in several important ways from the earlier reports from this same sample that focused on progression (Berg et al., 1984, 1988; Berg & Storandt, 1988; Botwinick, Storandt, & Berg, 1986; Botwinick, Storandt, Berg, & Boland, 1988; Faber-Langendoen et al., 1988; Morris et al., 1989; Rubin, Morris, Storandt, & Berg, 1987; Storandt, 1990; Storandt, Botwinick, & Danziger, 1986).

First, it reports data from a longer follow-up period (over 10 years). Second, the dependent variables were individual rates of progression on a number of specific neuropsychological tests rather than a global clinical index of dementia severity or brief clinical measures. This makes it possible to ask if, for example, specific early features of the disease are associated with more rapid deterioration in certain types of psychological abilities but not others. Third, a larger number of potential correlates of progression were examined. These included demographic variables (age, sex, education, socioeconomic status); behavioral symptoms, depression, language dysfunction, and EEG abnormalities present in the mild stage of the disease; and concomitant indices of progression (rate of cerebral atrophy, development of parkinsonism or psychoticism, occurrence of falls).

Method

Sample

Participants were recruited through referrals from local physicians and announcements in the news media. All participants lived in the community at time of entry into the study and were white, although not by study design. Table 10.1 describes the age at entry, years of education, and the socioeconomic status (Hollingshead, 1957) of the demented and control groups. Exclusion criteria included other neurological and psychiatric disorders, reversible dementias, and other medical disorders (including overmedication) that might

impair cognitive function. A more detailed description of the recruitment procedures is provided elsewhere (Berg et al., 1982).

Table 10.1
Demographic Characteristics of Mild SDAT and Control Groups

Characteristic	*M*	*SD*	Range
Age at entry (yrs)			
SDAT	71.4	5.0	63-81
Control	71.6	5.2	64-81
Education (yrs)			
SDAT	12.5	4.1	8-21
Control	12.5	3.2	8-20
Social position			
SDAT	3.0	1.2	1-5
Control	3.0	1.2	1-4

Note. Social position measured according to Hollingshead
(1957). Each group contains 20 men and 23 women.

Earlier reports of group means on the test battery from this longitudinal
study include only 42 demented individuals (e.g., Storandt, Botwinick,
Danziger, Berg, & Hughes, 1984). One person was not administered the
neuropsychological test battery at entry. He could be included here, however,
because he did receive the test battery at subsequent assessments.

Diagnostic and Staging Criteria

The diagnostic criteria for dementia were threefold: (a) impaired memory
plus impaired cognitive ability in at least two of five other areas (orientation,
judgment and problem solving, community affairs, home and hobbies, personal
care), (b) gradual onset and progression of the disorder, and duration of 6
months or longer (Berg, 1988). These criteria have been validated by postmortem neuropathological examination (Morris, McKeel, Fulling, Torack, &
Berg, 1988). Stage of dementia was determined by the Washington University Clinical Dementia Rating (CDR; Berg, 1984, 1988; Hughes, Berg, Danziger,
Coben, & Martin, 1982). It is a global clinical judgment based on degree of
impairment in each of the six areas included in diagnostic criterion A; CDR =
0 indicates no dementia, and CDR 0.5, 1, 2, and 3 indicate questionable, mild,
moderate, and severe dementia, respectively. The 43 individuals included in
the mild SDAT group all received a rating of 1 (mild dementia).

The diagnosis and clinical rating were based on a 90-min semistructured
clinical interview and neurological examination conducted by board-certified
physicians (three neurologists, one psychiatrist). Part of the interview was with

the research participant, part with a collateral source (usually a spouse or adult child). The interviews were taped and reviewed by another physician on the research team. A subsequent study of this procedure at our Center revealed that the reliability of the ratings is quite good; weighted kappas ranged from .75 to .94 (Burke et al., 1988). For the purpose of this sample, however, cases were included only if both the interviewing and reviewing physicians agreed. Of the 21 demented cases from this sample that have come to autopsy, a diagnosis of Alzheimer's disease has been confirmed in all but two. One was diagnosed as having only Parkinson's disease (despite its absence on clinical examination at entry) and the other as having mesolimbocortical dementia (Torack & Morris, 1986).

Psychometric Test Battery

Based on a review of the literature at the time the study was initiated, tests of a wide range of cognitive abilities were included (Storandt et al., 1984). The 1.5 to 2-hour battery included measures of memory (both verbal and nonverbal, primary and secondary), intelligence, visuospatial and psychomotor abilities, and language (see Table 10.2). Unless specified otherwise, all tests were administered and scored according to standard manual instructions.

Four subtests of the Wechsler Memory Scale (WMS; Wechsler & Stone, 1973) were used: *Mental Control, Logical Memory, Digit Span,* and *Associate Learning.* A self-paced recognition trial for the Associative Learning subtest was added immediately following the third recall trial. The first word of each pair was printed in the middle upper portion of a large index card with four choices, including the correct response word, printed horizontally below. Scores on the digit spans forward and backwards and the easy and hard pairs of the Associate Learning test are reported separately rather than combined as in the standard scoring of the Wechsler Memory Scale.

The Benton (1963) *Visual Retention Test* was used to measure nonverbal memory. Form C was administered with a 10- s presentation rate and a self-paced reproduction interval. Form D was administered as a copy test (i.e., the stimulus was present while it was being reproduced). The score on both forms was number of errors.

Raw scores from four subtests of the Wechsler Adult Intelligence Scale (WAIS; Wechsler, 1955) were included; two were from the verbal section (*Information* and *Comprehension*) and two were from the performance section (*Digit Symbol* and *Block Design*). The Comprehension subtest was dropped from the battery after the eighth time of testing because of its high correlation with the Information subtest and is not included in the analyses reported in this chapter.

In addition to the two performance subtests from the WAIS, three other psychomotor and visuospatial tests were used: *Trailmaking A* (Armitage, 1946), *Crossing-off* (Botwinick & Storandt, 1973) and the *Bender Visual Motor Ge-*

stalt Test (Bender, 1963). The score on Trailmaking A was the number of seconds to complete the task. A maximum of 180 sec each was allowed for Trailmaking and for Crossing-off. The Crossing-off task requires the individual to make a vertical slash through each of 96 horizontal lines arranged in 12 rows of eight on a 8.5 x 11 inch sheet of paper, working from left to right on each line. The score was the number of items completed per sec times 100. The Bender Gestalt was scored according to a modified Hutt-Briskin system (Lacks, 1984); scores range from 0 (no errors) to 12. All protocols were scored by the same clinical psychologist.

The *Boston Naming Test* (Goodglass & Kaplan, 1983a, 1983b) was used to assess confrontation naming. When the revised version of this test was published the records from the longer, original version were rescored to conform to the 60-item revision. *Word Fluency* was measured for the letters S and P (Thurstone & Thurstone, 1949). One min was allowed for production of S words and 1 min for P words. The score was the total number of words produced.

Two additional tests were included in the original version of the battery (Storandt et al., 1984) but were dropped subsequently and are not reported here. A test of very old memory, the Entertainment Questionnaire (Storandt, Grant, & Gordon, 1978) was too difficult even at entry for the mildly demented individuals. The Zung Depression Scale (Zung, 1967) was included to determine the course of depression as the disease progressed. There were no differences between the SDAT and control groups initially because depressed individuals were excluded. This self-report questionnaire, however, was too difficult for the SDAT group as they became more demented.

Procedure

All participants were tested individually with the neuropsychological test battery by trained psychometricians. Because this study was conducted in the context of a program project and later an Alzheimer's Disease Research Center, these same psychometricians were also testing healthy individuals, people in other stages of dementia, and those with other diseases (e.g., Parkinson's disease, depression, multi-infarct dementia, progressive aphasia). They were not told the diagnosis or stage of dementia, although this often became apparent with progression of the disease in the demented individuals reported here.

Generally, participants were tested at the medical center within a week or two of the clinical interview conducted by the physicians. A deliberate decision was made to use a battery of tests that would be portable so that home visits could be made. These were done as needed, including nursing home visits. Attempts to administer the test battery were terminated after a person with a clinical dementia rating of severe dementia (CDR = 3) provided no scorable test responses at an assessment. Other reasons for attrition included death, relocation outside the St. Louis area, other health problems, and refusal. Contact with the participants and their families, however, was maintained by the project staff, and sometimes the person became available for testing at a later assessment point.

Ten times of testing have been completed. Although the original plan of the longitudinal study specified annual assessments, the "annual" periods were sometimes longer than 12 months for reasons unrelated to psychometric testing.

Attrition

Figure 10.1 shows the attrition due to death in the control and demented groups. Only 30% (*n* = 12) of the 43 individuals who were mildly demented at entry into the study were still living as of January 1, 1991, compared with 74% of the healthy controls. Almost all of the demented individuals were lost to study with the psychometric measures some years prior to death because the cognitive deterioration associated with the dementia made it impossible to continue to test them. Floor effects were observed at different times for the different psychometric measures because of variability in test difficulty. Also, some demented individuals reached floor on some tests more rapidly than did others. Only 1 of 43 demented persons was still testable on some measures in 1990. To illustrate this, Table 10.2 shows the numbers of demented individuals with scorable responses on the psychometric tests at entry and every other time of testing thereafter.

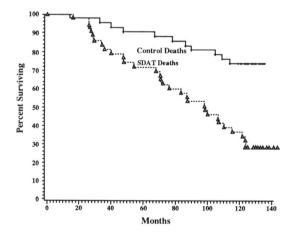

Figure 10.1. Percentage of surviving individuals in demented and control groups from entry into the study in 1979-81 until January 1, 1991.

Table 10.2
*Demented Individuals with Scorable Responses on Psychometric Tests
at Every Other Testing Time (in months)*

Test	Entry	34	66	90	114
a					
WMS Mental Control	38	11	4	1	0
WMS Logical Memory	37	12	3	1	0
WMS Digit Span Forward	42	21	5	3	1
WMS Digit Span Backward	40	13	4	1	0
WMS Associate Learning (recall)					
Easy pairs	41	17	3	1	0
Hard pairs	8	1	0	0	0
WMS Associate Learning (recognition)					
Easy pairs	42	17	4	1	0
Hard pairs	34	13	2	1	0
Benton Visual Retention					
Form C (10-s delay)	42	14	4	2	0
Form D (copy)	42	16	4	3	1
b					
WAIS Information	41	17	4	2	1
WAIS Block Design	32	9	3	2	0
WAIS Digit Symbol	41	13	3	1	0
Trailmaking A	42	13	3	2	0
Crossing-off	42	17	4	2	1
Bender Gestalt	42	15	4	3	0
Boston Naming	41	17	5	3	1
Word Fluency	42	14	4	2	0

Note. Scorable responses are those attempted and not at floor.
[a] Wechsler Memory Scale.
[b] Wechsler Adult Intelligence Scale.

Index of Rate of Progression

The variable attrition described in the previous paragraph made it impossible to use statistical procedures such as repeated measures analysis of variance to examine the course of the disease. Therefore, it was necessary to devise an index of rate of progression. When at least two scorable responses over time were available for an individual, the scores were correlated with time of assessment. This was done for each test in the battery for each individual. The raw regression coefficients of the lines of best fit were computed. These slopes were then used as an index of rate of progression for the individual on each test (Kraemer & Thiemann, 1989). Figure 10.2 shows an example of the rate of progression on the Benton Visual Retention Test, 10-s delay, for a demented individual.

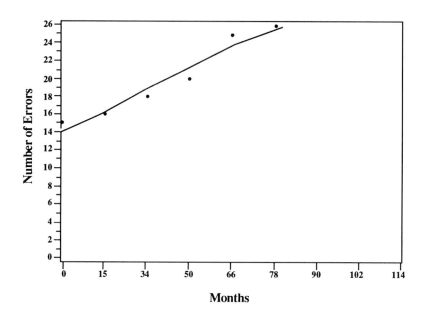

Figure 10.2. Example of rate of progression on the Benton Visual Retention Test (10-s delay) for a demented individual.

It was possible to calculate slopes for only 6 demented individuals on the hard pairs from the recall version of the WMS Associate Learning subtest. This task was too difficult for almost all of these mildly demented individuals even at entry (see Table 10.2). Therefore, this variable was omitted from further analyses. Examination of the distributions of the slopes for each measure indicated extreme skewness for the Logical Memory subtest from the Wechsler Memory Scale. Most of the demented group had very poor performances (near floor) at entry. Therefore, this variable was also omitted from further analysis. For the other tests in the battery the numbers of demented individuals for whom slopes could be calculated are shown in Table 10.3 and ranged from 23 (Trailmaking A) to 34 (Digit Span Forward).

All but 1 of the 43 members of the control group had more than one time of testing. Two variables (WMS Associate Learning Recognition, easy and hard pairs) were too easy for them (i.e., most healthy individuals subjects remained at ceiling). Therefore, slopes were not computed for the control group and comparisons of the demented and control groups do not include these two variables.

Comparison of Demented and Control Groups

Average slope indices for the psychometric tests are shown for the demented and control groups in Table 10.3.

Table 10.3
Comparison of Slope Indices of Progression for Demented and Control Groups

Measure	Demented	Control	z [a]
WMS [b] Mental Control	-1.01 (32)	-.06 (42)	5.24***
WMS Digit Span Forward	-.55 (34)	.04 (42)	5.28***
WMS Digit Span Backward	-.47 (32)	-.01 (42)	4.15***
WMS Associate Learning			
Recall (easy pairs)	-1.31 (32)	-.09 (42)	4.09***
Recognition			
Easy pairs	-.63 (33)	-- [c]	
Hard pairs	-.29 (31)	-- [c]	
Benton Visual Retention			
Form C (10-sec delay)	1.28 (27)	.29 (42)	4.62***
Form D (copy)	2.33 (29)	-.06 (42)	4.58***
WAIS [d] Information	-1.36 (32)	-.07 (42)	4.91***
WAIS Block Design	-3.20 (27)	-.37 (42)	5.27***
WAIS Digit Symbol	-3.26 (28)	-.89 (42)	3.95***
Trailmaking A	17.72 (23)	2.54 (42)	4.40***
Crossing-off	-8.65 (33)	-4.26 (42)	2.23*
Bender Gestalt	.55 (29)	.12 (42)	3.17**
Boston Naming	-4.10 (33)	-.23 (42)	6.20***
Word Fluency	-2.22 (33)	-.03 (42)	5.41***

Note. Entries are mean slopes followed by the sample size in parentheses. Negative slopes indicate rate of deterioration per year on all variables except the two forms of the Benton Visual Retention Test and the Bender-Gestalt (where errors were scored) and the Trailmaking A (number of sec).
[a] Van der Waerden nonparametric two-sample test.
[b] Wechsler Memory Scale.
[c] Slopes were not computed because most control subjects scored at ceiling.
[d] Wechsler Adult Intelligence Scale.
* $p < .05$. ** $p < .01$. *** $p < .0001$.

Negative signs indicate deterioration on all variables except the two forms of the Benton Visual Retention Test and the Bender Gestalt (where the scores are number of errors) and the Trailmaking A (score = sec). Because the variances of the two groups were unequal in most cases, the nonparametric Van der Waerden test was used to compare the demented and control groups. Significant differences in the slope indices for the two groups were obtained for all psychometric measures.

One-tailed, one-sample t-tests indicated that the mean slopes for the demented group were significantly (all ps < .0028) different from 0 for all the psychometric tests. The mean slopes indicated deterioration on all psychometric measures over time. The mean slope values shown in Table 10.3 indicate the average rate of decline per year. These rates vary, of course, from test to test because of the varying scales of measurement. For example, the mean slope index for the Boston Naming Test indicates an average decline of about 4 items per year on this 60-item test. The mean decrease in speed of performance of the Trailmaking A was approximately 18 s per year. The rate of deterioration on the WAIS Block Design and Digit Symbol subtests was over 3 raw score points per year; the decline in Digit Span Forward was approximately one-half digit per year. These values are based on modest sample sizes and should be interpreted cautiously.

Tests of curvilinear regression were also applied to all psychometric measures for all demented individuals for whom at least four times of measurement were available. Only 9 of the 144 such significance tests conducted were significant at the .05 alpha level. These were spread across 7 individuals. It is clear, therefore, that the course of deterioration in SDAT is linear from the mild stage of the disease until the floor (or ceiling) of the psychometric measure is reached.

Two-tailed, one-sample t-tests for the control group were conducted and indicated significant (ps < .02) deterioration on the following psychometric measures: WAIS Block Design and Digit Symbol, Benton Visual Retention Test (10-sec delay), Trailmaking A, Crossing-off, and Bender Gestalt. As previously indicated, this deterioration was significantly less than observed in the demented group. Slight improvement by the control group over time was observed on the copying form of the Benton Visual Retention Test (p < .025).

If one uses the Van der Waerden z statistic as an indication of the greatest difference between the slopes of the demented and healthy aged groups, it would appear that the greatest rate of decline in the demented group was on two measures of language function: confrontation naming (Boston Naming Test) and Word Fluency. A similar conclusion was reached by Rebok, Brandt, and Folstein (1990), who followed participants over a 2-year period. It should be pointed out, however, that the z statistic for several other measures are almost equally as large. One is a measure of primary memory (Digit Span Forward) and another is a visuospatial test (WAIS Block Design). Thus, substantial decline can be seen on several types of psychological functions.

Attempts to compare rates of decline among psychometric measures may be confounded, however, by the varying difficulty levels of the tests and by initial levels. For example, substantial decline could be detected on the Digit Span Forward subtest because primary memory is not severely affected in mild SDAT. The mean number of digits recalled by the demented group at entry was 5.95, less than one digit below that of the healthy group (6.67) (means are from Table 10.1, Storandt et al., 1984). In contrast, the demented group recognized fewer than two of the hard pairs of the WMS Associate Learning subtest at entry and therefore were much closer to the floor of this test at the beginning of the longitudinal study. Simple comparison of the magnitude of the average slope indices for these two measures would lead one to conclude, wrongly, that primary memory declined more rapidly than secondary memory. A more accurate conclusion is that secondary memory is affected earlier in the course of the disease than is primary memory.

These results are consistent with a vast literature on changes in psychological abilities in normal aging. Verbal skills, for example, are well-maintained, although psychomotor and visuospatial abilities may decline somewhat, as they did here over 10 years in the control group. On the other hand, Alzheimer's disease produces global deterioration—not only in psychomotor and visuospatial abilities, but also in memory (both episodic and semantic, primary and secondary, verbal and nonverbal) and measures of language function, which are probably highly dependent on semantic memory.

Principal Components Analysis

Because the tests included in the psychometric battery were chosen to represent several domains of psychological function thought to be affected by the disease, there was substantial multicolinearity among the various measures. Therefore, a principal components analysis was performed on the slope indices for the demented group ($n = 29$). Individuals with missing slope indices on more than five measures were omitted. Mean values were substituted as necessary for the remainder.

Five components with eigenvalues greater than 1 were extracted, accounting for 72% of the variance. Examination of the rotated (Varimax) factor loadings indicated difficulty in achieving simple structure (i.e., some measures were correlated with more than one component). Further, it was difficult to interpret the factors. Measures from different conceptual domains loaded on the same component, and measures from the same conceptual domain loaded on different components. Rotated factor solutions of 2, 3, and 4 components produced similar results. Part of the problem may be due to the fact that rates of deterioration indexed by the computed slope measures used in this principal components analysis are influenced by the range of difficulty and initial levels on the various psychometric measures as discussed in the previous section. This, in combination with the missing data, small sample size, and large number of variables, makes the results of the principal components analysis highly suspect.

Correlates of Progression

As indicated in the introduction to this chapter, an attempt was made to identify variables that might be related to the rate of progression of Alzheimer's disease. Three broad groups of variables were considered: Demographic, concomitant features present in the mild stage of the disease, and other changes occurring during the course of the disease. Using only the data from the demented group, Kendall tau *b* correlations were computed between each of the slope indices of rate of progression on the psychometric tests and the potential correlate. This nonparametric statistic was used, rather than Pearson *r*s, because the distributions of a number of the potential correlates were skewed. Because interpretations of the signs of these correlations depends on the nature of the scoring of the psychometric tests (errors vs. number correct) as well as the nature of the dummy variable coding used for dichotomous variables, it will be specified in the remainder of the text if the association involves more or less rapid deterioration.

Demographic Variables

The demographic variables that were examined were age at entry into the study, sex (coded 1 = male, 2 = female), years of education, and social position based on the Hollingshead (1957) two-factor index. Duration of the disease (i.e., time between onset of disease as reported by the collateral source and entry into the study) is also included in this section, although the accuracy of such estimates is questionable. Reported duration ranged from 0.9 to 9.0 years.

Only three correlations greater than .30 were obtained in these analyses. Younger individuals progressed more quickly on the copying form of the Benton Visual Retention test (-.36). Women declined more rapidly on the recognition trial for the easy pairs from the WMS Associate Learning subtest (-.35) and the Crossing-off (-.37). The lack of correlation observed in these analyses indicates that progression as measured by the psychometric tests was unrelated to age and the other demographic variables, or to estimated duration of the disease at entry into the study (cf. Burns, Jacoby, & Levy, 1991). It should be pointed out that all of the individuals in the present study were at least in their mid 60s when diagnosed. Studies that have suggested a correlation between age of onset and rate of progression have often included younger individuals (e.g., Heston, Mastrie, Anderson, & White, 1981). Ortof and Crystal (1989) reached a conclusion similar to ours, however, using a sample with a much wider age range.

Early Features

Several features present in the mild stage of the disease were examined as potential correlates of rate of progression on the psychometric tests. Three of these were based on measures obtained from the physicians' interview (Berg et al., 1982) at time of entry. These were of language function, behavioral symptoms, and depression. The two remaining early features were from resting EEGs obtained also at entry into the study (percentage delta and theta wave activity; Coben, Danziger, & Storandt, 1985).

Language dysfunction. Previous reports (e.g., Kaszniak et al., 1978) have suggested that the presence of language difficulties early in the course of the disease is associated with a more rapid course. Therefore scores from the Aphasia Battery (Faber-Langendoen et al., 1988) administered by the physicians as part of the diagnostic interview were correlated with the slope indices of the psychometric measures. The Aphasia Battery was devised specifically for this longitudinal study; it was based on tasks from the Boston Diagnostic Aphasia Evaluation (Goodglass & Kaplan, 1983b). The total score on the Aphasia Battery ranged from 0 (no errors) to 35. Correlations with the slope indices were also computed for five of the Aphasia Battery subscales (expressive language, oral naming, reading comprehension, written naming, and auditory comprehension). Only two of the demented individuals made errors on the other two subscales (word discrimination, body part identification) at entry into the study. These two subscales were omitted from the correlational analyses shown in Table 10.4.

The relation between language difficulties early in the disease as measured by the Aphasia Battery and the rate of deterioration on the psychometric measures is modest to moderate. The strongest correlation with the Aphasia Battery total score was with the easy pairs from the recognition trial of the WMS Associate Learning subtest (-.49). This relationship appears to be due to poor performance on the naming and reading subtests of the Aphasia Battery (Kendall tau *b*s = -.50 and -.59, respectively). These analyses provide little support for the hypothesis that language dysfunction in the mild stage of SDAT is associated with a more rapid course on specific types of psychological abilities.

The modest positive correlation (.34) between the Aphasia Battery scores at entry and decline on the Boston Naming Tests shown in Table 10.4 deserves comment. Some individuals with larger numbers of Aphasia Battery errors at entry were also closer to floor on the Boston Naming Test at entry; the two tests are tapping elements of the same domain. Therefore, these individuals could not have large negative slope indices of rate of deterioration on the Boston Naming Test. This produces a situation wherein individuals with more errors on the Aphasia Battery (and fewer correct responses on the Boston Naming Test) at entry have flatter rates of decline on the Boston Naming Test.

Table 10.4

Correlations (greater than .30) of Aphasia Battery Scores (errors) with Psychometric Slope Indices of Progression in the Demented Group

Measure	Total	Speech	Naming	Reading	Writing	Reception
WMS [a] Mental Control						
WMS Digit Span Forward						
WMS Digit Span Backward				-.37		-.32
WMS Associate Learning						
Recall (easy pairs)	-.33	-.33		-.42		-.34
Recognition						
Easy pairs	-.49		-.50	-.59	-.32	-.41
Hard pairs						-.38
Benton Visual Retention						
Form C (10-sec delay)						
Form D (copy)						-.32
WAIS [b] Information						
WAIS Block Design			-.31			
WAIS Digit Symbol						
Trailmaking A						-.43
Crossing-off						
Bender Gestalt						
Boston Naming	.34		.43		.41	
Word Fluency						

Note. The signs of the correlations have been adjusted so that negative correlations indicate that more rapid decline on the psychometric measures is associated with a larger number of errors on the Aphasia Battery at entry into the study.

[a] Wechsler Memory Scale.

[b] Wechsler Adult Intelligence Scale.

Behavioral symptoms. An earlier report from this project (Rubin et al., 1987) indicated that the behavioral changes in the year prior to entry into the study as reported by collateral sources could be divided into three kinds: Increased passivity, increased agitation, and increased self-centeredness. The presence or absence of these three types of early behavioral changes were correlated with the slope indices of the rate of progression on the psychometric measures.

No correlations greater than .30 were obtained between any of the slope indices for the psychometric tests and either passivity or self-centeredness. There were three correlations greater than .30 between the slope indices and increased agitation: Trailmaking A (-.43), the WAIS Information subtest (.34), and Word Fluency (.31). The direction of these correlations indicated that agitated individuals declined *less* rapidly. Given the modest size of these correlations and the large number of analyses conducted, these results may represent capitalization on chance.

The Hamilton Depression Scale (Hamilton, 1960) was completed by the physicians for all participants to assist with the exclusion of individuals with major depression from the study. Note, therefore, that scores are skewed on this quantitative variable because of the exclusion from the sample of all individuals with scores greater than 16. No correlations greater than .30 were found between the depression scores at entry into the study and the rate of deterioration on the psychometric measures.

EEG. The final two early features examined were percentage delta and percentage theta from the resting EEG (occipital-vertex derivation) obtained at entry into the study (Coben et al., 1985). These two types of slow activity are suggestive of cortical electrophysiological dysfunction. No correlations greater than .30 were obtained with percentage delta. Three correlations greater than .30 were observed for percentage theta. These were with the slope indices for the WAIS Block Design (.34) and Digit Symbol (.43) subtests and Crossing-off (.43). Although these correlations are moderate and may represent capitalization on chance, at least they all involve psychomotor/visuospatial measures. The direction of the association, however, is somewhat surprising in that greater percentage theta at entry into the study is associated with less rapid deterioration on the three psychometric tests.

Concomitant Rates of Progression

Luxenberg et al. (1987) found that the rate of ventricular enlargement as measured by CT scan was correlated with the rate of decline on a neuropsychology test battery in 10 male patients. Nineteen of the demented individuals in our longitudinal study received CT scans suitable for quantitative volumetric assessment at 15 and 34 months after entry (Wippold, Gado, Morris, Duchek, & Grant, 1991). Therefore, analyses were conducted to determine whether the rate of deterioration on the psychometric measures was correlated with a volumetric measure of progression in brain atrophy as measured by CT. This was done with hierarchical multiple regression analyses for each psychometric measure. The psychometric slope index served as the dependent variable. The combined percentage of ventricular and sulcal volume at 15 months after entry was entered as the first independent variable followed by the volume percentage at 34 months. If rate of deterioration on the psychometric test was correlated with rate of atrophy measured by CT scan, then the second CT measure should make a significant contribution to the regression equation. Because of the small sample size, a liberal alpha level of .065 was used.

The results of these analyses indicate that the increase in ventrical and sulcal volume at 34 months over and above that measured at 15 months was associated with the rate of deterioration on three psychometric measures: the 10-sec delay version of the Benton Visual Retention Test (.22), Trailmaking A (.27), and Crossing-off (.26). The values in parentheses are the increments in the R squared when the 34- month CT measure was added to the 15-month CT measure in the regression equation. These values can be interpreted as the percentage of variance in the rate of decline on the psychometric measures that is associated with the rate of brain atrophy measured by CT. All of these measures are visuospatial in nature. One (the Benton) involves memory; the other two do not; they are "speeded" tasks. It is not clear why deterioration on other speeded visuospatial/psychomotor tests included in the battery (e.g., WAIS Block Design or Digit Symbol) were not also correlated with rate of brain atrophy. Given the small sample size available for analysis, it is possible we did not have sufficient statistical power to detect other relations. Alternatively, the three observed relations may be spurious.

The other three variables representing concomitant changes were the occurrence of discrete events. One was the development of one or more signs of parkinsonism (bradykinesia, cogwheel rigidity, resting tremor) in the first 66 months of the study (Morris et al., 1989). A second was whether the person experienced a serious fall within the first 50 months of the study (Morris, Rubin, Morris, & Mandel, 1987). The third was the development of symptoms of psychoticism between the first and second times of assessment. An earlier report from our Center suggested that individuals with symptoms of psychosis (delusions, misidentification syndromes, hallucinations) in the early stage of the disease deteriorated more rapidly (Drevets & Rubin, 1989).

Those individuals who developed signs of parkinsonism were classified as either drug-induced or idiopathic (Morris et al., 1989). The slope indices for the psychometric tests were compared for these two subgroups; no significant differences were obtained. Therefore the two subgroups were combined ($n = 27$) for comparison with those demented individuals who did not develop signs of parkinsonism ($n = 16$). Five correlations greater than .30 were obtained. As might be expected, the development of signs of parkinsonism was modestly associated with more rapid decline on two of the visuospatial tests that required motor responses: The copying form of the Benton Visual Retention test (.34) and Trailmaking A (.36). Development of signs of parkinsonism was also correlated with three tests of memory: Digit Span Forward (-.35) and Backward (-.41) as well as recognition memory of the easy pairs from the WMS Associate Learning subtest (-.43). These correlations provide some support for the idea that the development of parkinsonism is indicative of a more rapidly progressive form of Alzheimer's disease (Morris et al., 1989) that involves accelerated decline not only in psychomotor function but also in memory.

The occurrence of a fall in the first 5 years of study was associated with the slope index for the Bender Gestalt Test (.38), a general test of brain dysfunction. The development of psychotic symptoms during the first 15 months following entry into the study was correlated .44 with the slope index for Trailmaking A. Given the large number of correlations computed, these correlations should be interpreted cautiously.

Summary

It is not surprising that the quantitative indices of rates of deterioration in psychometric test performance indicate a downward course of Alzheimer's disease. Deterioration resulting in death is a hallmark of this progressive disease. The analyses reported here, however, do suggest that the course is essentially linear, although the rate varies from person to person.

In general, secondary memory is affected very early in the course of Alzheimer's disease and is one of the most sensitive measures for differentiating mild SDAT from healthy aging (Storandt et al., 1984). Primary memory, however, also deteriorates as the disease progresses, as do language and psychomotor/visuospatial abilities, as well as memory for information learned long ago (e.g., WAIS Information subtest).

Comparisons of the rates of psychometric test decline with increases in brain atrophy suggest that the two may be related, particularly with regard to some behavioral measures of psychomotor/visuospatial abilities. These comparisons are limited, however, in that only two CT assessments were available, and these assessments were begun after some demented individuals had progressed beyond the mild stage of the disease. At the same time, it is reasonable that more rapid brain atrophy as measured by CT is associated with more rapid behavioral changes in psychomotor and visuospatial abilities that follow the early deficits in memory that are the hallmark of Alzheimer's disease. As more brain areas are affected, atrophy would become more apparent.

The development of signs of parkinsonism was associated with more rapid deterioration on psychometric tests not only of psychomotor performance but also of memory. None of these individuals had parkinsonism at entry into the study. As described previously (Morris et al., 1989), the pathoanatomical correlates of parkinsonism were heterogenous in the brains of those demented individuals available for postmortem examination. The series available for histological study is still too small to determine if the more rapid decline in memory reported here is related to the coexistence of Parkinson's disease, nonspecific degeneration in the substantia nigra, or extranigral changes. Further, the associations reported here are modest in size and were with only some of the measures of memory.

With the possible exceptions of increased rates of brain atrophy and the development of signs of parkinsonism, we found little evidence of predictors of the course of the disease as measured by changes in specific psychometric test performances. Only sporadic and modest correlations with a variety of demographic and other early or concomitant features were obtained. There is little to suggest a meaningful pattern in these obtained correlations, and it is likely they represent chance results based on sampling variability. These results are in agreement with those of Drachman, O'Donnell, Lew, and Swearer (1990) who also failed to find a number of similar potential prognostic features predictive of the course of the disease over a 5-year period.

Acknowledgments

This research was supported, in part, by grant MH 31054 from the National Institute of Mental Health and grants AG 03991 and AG 05681 from the National Institute on Aging.

Thanks are due to Emily LaBarge, who supervised the psychometric testing; Patricia Lacks, who scored the Bender Gestalt tests; and Deborah Smith, Valerie Rice, and Elizabeth A. Grant, who assisted in data analysis.

References

Armitage, S. G. (1946). An analysis of certain psychological tests used for the evaluation of brain injury. *Pychological Monographs, 60,* No. 1 (Whole No. 277), 1-48.

Bender, L. (1963). *Bender Visual Motor Gestalt Test.* New York: American Orthopsychiatric Corporation.

Benton, A. L. (1963). *The Revised Visual Retention Test: Clinical and experimental applications.* New York: Psychological Corporation.

Berg, L. (1984). Clinical dementia rating. *British Journal of Psychiatry, 145,* 339.

Berg, L. (1988). Clinical dementia rating (CDR). *Psychopharmacology Bulletin, 24,* 637-639.

Berg, L., Danziger, W. L., Storandt, M., Coben, L. A., Gado, M., Hughes, C. P., Knesevich, J., & Botwinick, J. (1984). Predictive features in mild senile dementia of the Alzheimer type. *Neurology, 34,* 563-569.

Berg, L., Hughes, C. P., Coben, L. A., Danziger, W. L., Martin, R. L., & Knesevich, J. (1982). Mild senile dementia of Alzheimer type: Research diagnostic criteria, recruitment, and description of a study population. *Journal of Neurology, Neurosurgery, and Psychiatry, 45,* 962-968.

Berg, L., Miller, J. P., Storandt, M., Duchek, J. M., Morris, J. S., Rubin, E. H., Burke, W. J., & Coben, L. A. (1988). Mild senile dementia of the Alzheimer type: II. Longitudinal assessment. *Annals of Neurology, 23,* 477-484.

Berg, L., & Storandt, M. (1988). The longitudinal course of mild senile dementia of the Alzheimer type. In M. Bergener, M. Ermini, & H. B. Stahelin (Eds.), *Crossroads in aging.* London: Academic Press.

Botwinick, J., & Storandt, M. (1973). Speed functions, vocabulary ability, and age. *Perceptual and Motor Skills, 36,* 1123-1128.

Botwinick, J., Storandt, M., & Berg, L. (1986). A longitudinal behavioral study of senile dementia of the Alzheimer type. *Archives of Neurology, 43,* 1124-1127.

Botwinick, J., Storandt, M., Berg, L., & Boland, S. (1988). Senile dementia of the Alzheimer type: Subject attrition and testability in research. *Archives of Neurology, 45,* 493-496.

Burke, W. J., Miller, J. P., Rubin, E. H., Morris, J. C., Coben, L. A., Duchek, J. M., Wittels, I. G., & Berg, L. (1988). Reliability of the Washington University Clinical Dementia Rating. *Archives of Neurology, 45,* 31-32.

Burns, A., Jacoby, R., & Levy, R. (1991). Progression of cognitive impairment in Alzheimer's disease. *Journal of the American Geriatrics Society, 39,* 39-45.

Coben, L. A., Danziger, W. L., & Storandt, M. (1985). A longitudinal EEG study of mild senile dementia of Alzheimer type: Changes at 1 year and at 2.5 years. *Electroencephalography and Clinical Neurophysiology, 61,* 101-112.

Diesfeldt, H. F. A., van Houte, L. R., & Moerkens, R. M. (1986). Duration of survival in senile dementia. *Acta Psychiatrica Scandinavica, 73*, 366-371.

Drachman, D. A., O'Donnell, B. F., Lew, R. A., & Swearer, J. M. (1990). The prognosis in Alzheimer's disease: "How far" rather than "how fast" best predicts the course. *Archives of Neurology, 47*, 851-856.

Drevets, W. C., & Rubin, E. H. (1989). Psychotic symptoms and the longitudinal course of senile dementia of the Alzheimer type. *Biological Psychiatry, 25*, 39-48.

Faber-Langendoen, K., Morris, J. C., Knesevich, J., LaBarge, E., Miller, J. P., & Berg, L. (1988). Aphasia in senile dementia of the Alzheimer type. *Annals of Neurology, 23*, 365-370.

Goodglass, H., & Kaplan, E. (1983a). *Boston Naming Test scoring booklet.* Philadelphia: Lea & Febiger.

Goodglass, H., & Kaplan, E. (1983b). *The assessment of aphasia and related disorders* (Appendix 1-28). Philadelphia: Lea & Febiger.

Hamilton, M. (1960). A rating scale for depression. *Journal of Neurology, Neurosurgery, and Psychiatry, 23*, 56-62.

Heston, L. L., Mastrie, A. R., Anderson, E., & White, J. (1981). Dementia of the Alzheimer type: Clinical genetics, natural history, and associated conditions. *Archives of General Psychiatry, 38*, 1085-1090.

Hollingshead, A. B. (1957). *Two-factor index of social position.* New Haven, CN: Author.

Hughes, C. P., Berg, L., Danziger, W. L., Coben, L. A., & Martin, R. L. (1982). A new clinical scale for the staging of dementia. *British Journal of Psychiatry, 140*, 566-572.

Kaszniak, A. W., Fox, J. H., Gandell, D. L., Garron, D. C., Huckman, M. S., & Ramsey, R. G. (1978). Predictors of mortality in presenile and senile dementia. *Annals of Neurology, 3*, 246-252.

Kraemer, H. C., & Thiemann, S. (1989). A strategy to use soft data effectively in randomized controlled clinical trials. *Journal of Consulting and Clinical Psychology, 57*, 148-154.

Lacks, P. (1984). *Bender Gestalt screening for brain dysfunction.* New York: Wiley.

Luxenberg, J. G., Haxby, J. V., Creasey, H., Sundaram, M., & Rapoport, S. I. (1987). Rate of ventricular enlargement in dementia of the Alzheimer type correlates with rate of neuropsychological deterioration. *Neurology, 37*, 1135-1140.

Morris, J. C., Drazner, M., Fulling, K., Grant, E. A., & Goldring, J. (1989). Clinical and pathological aspects of parkinsonism in Alzheimer's disease. *Archives of Neurology, 46*, 651-657.

Morris, J. C., McKeel, D. W., Jr., Fulling, K., Torack, R. M., & Berg, L. (1988). Validation of clinical diagnostic criteria for Alzheimer's disease. *Annals of Neurology, 24*, 17-22.

Morris, J. C., Rubin, E. H., Morris, E. J., & Mandel, S. A. (1987). Senile dementia of the Alzheimer's type: An important risk factor for serious falls. *Journal of Gerontology, 42*, 412-417.

Ortof, E., & Crystal, H. A. (1989). Rate of progression of Alzheimer's disease. *Journal of the American Geriatrics Society, 37*, 511-514.

Rebok, G., Brandt, J., & Folstein, M. F. (1990). Longitudinal cognitive decline in patients with Alzheimer's disease. *Journal of Geriatric Psychiatry and Neurology, 3*, 91-97.

Rubin, E. H., Morris, J. C., Storandt, M., & Berg, L. (1987). Behavioral changes in patients with mild senile dementia of the Alzheimer's type. *Psychiatry Research, 21*, 55-62.

Storandt, M. (1990). Longitudinal studies of aging and age-associated dementias. In F. Boller & J. Grafman (Eds.), *Handbook of neruropsychology: Vol. 4. Section 8: Aging and dementia (Part 1).* Amsterdam: Elsevier.

Storandt, M., Botwinick, J., & Danziger, W. L. (1986). Longitudinal changes: Patients with mild SDAT and matched healthy controls. In L. W. Poon (Ed.), *Handbook for the clinical memory assessment of older adults.* Washington, DC: American Psychological Association.

Storandt, M., Botwinick, J., Danziger, W. L., Berg, L., & Hughes, C. P. (1984). Psychometric differentiation of mild senile dementia of the Alzheimer type. *Archives of Neurology, 41,* 497-499.

Storandt, M., Grant, E. A., & Gordon, G. C. (1978). Remote memory as a function of age and sex. *Experimental Aging Research, 4,* 365-375.

Torack, R. M., & Morris, J. C. (1986). Mesolimbocortical dementia. *Archives of Neurology, 43,* 1074-1078.

Thurstone, L. L., & Thurstone, T. G. (1949). *Examiner manual for the SRA Primary Mental Abilities Test.* Chicago, IL: Science Research Associates.

Wechsler, D. (1955). *Manual: Wechsler Adult Intelligence Scale.* New York: Psychological Corporation.

Wechsler, D., & Stone, C. P. (1973). *Manual: Wechsler Memory Scale.* New York: Psychological Corporation.

Wippold, F. J., II, Gado, M., Morris, J. C., Duchek, J. M., & Grant, E. A. (1991). Senile dementia and healthy aging: A longitudinal CT study. *Radiology, 179,* 215-219.

Zung, W. W. K. (1967). Depression in the normal aged. *Psychosomatics, 8,* 287-292.

11   Impaired and Preserved Semantic Memory Functions in Dementia

Han F. A. Diesfeldt

Stichting Verpleeghuizen Nederland

Introduction

Memory impairment is commonly regarded as the hallmark of the dementia syndrome. This has not always been so. For example, the 1980 Edition of the Diagnostic and Statistical Manual of Mental Disorders (DSM-III) states that the essential feature of dementia is a loss of *intellectual* abilities (American Psychiatric Association, 1980, p. 107). The most recent edition (DSM-III-R) mentions "demonstrable evidence of impairment in short- and long-term memory" as the first diagnostic criterion for dementia (American Psychiatric Association, 1987, p. 103). The difference is interesting, because it implies a priority of impaired *episodic* over impaired *semantic* memory as the hallmark of dementia.

Is dementia mainly an impairment of episodic, or of semantic memory? The question thus stated requires some explanation. The concepts of short- and long-term memory are here linked to episodic memory, and intellectual abilities to semantic memory. Indeed, semantic memory is defined as the system for storing and retrieving knowledge of the world, and can therefore be regarded as the basis of human intelligence. Episodic memory is a system whereby we store and retrieve personally experienced events tagged for time and location (*where* and *when* and a given event did happen). In fact, the forgetfulness for recent events and the inability of dementia patients to learn and recall arbitrary lists of items (a common test of episodic memory) reflect disturbances of episodic short- and long-term memory. However, there is growing evidence that the dementia syndrome implies impairments of both episodic and semantic memory (Herlitz, 1991). The presence of these impairments is universally accepted as a necessary condition for the diagnosis of dementia.

In this chapter, I will concentrate on the variable pattern of selective impairments in semantic memory in two dementia patients. An in-depth functional analysis of their cognitive capacities showed that their impairments of semantic memory were not unitary, but fell apart into several distinct syndromes. The disruption of semantic memory may manifest itself in different ways in different patients. According to the definition of semantic memory as a person's mental thesaurus, containing organized knowledge of the world, the diversity of deficits may be very large if semantic memory is impaired. Semantic memory includes knowledge of the meaning of words, arithmetic knowledge, geographical knowledge, knowledge of social customs, knowledge of people, the color of things and their smells and textures (Baddeley, 1990). So what does it mean to say that semantic memory is impaired or preserved in patients suffering from a dementing disease? It is most important then that investigators be specific about the type of tasks they used and the kind of semantic memory they discuss. It is quite possible that individual patients with a dementing disease have intact semantic capacities in one functional area (e.g., visual knowledge), but are impaired in other areas (e.g., linguistic knowledge; Martin, 1987; Martin et al., 1986). Primary degenerative dementias are selective in the locus and type of brain damage. Even within one domain of, for example, linguistic knowledge, clear differences can be revealed between lexical knowledge and syntactic competence. Group studies may conceal the differential impairments in several domains of semantic memory.

The false impression of homogeneous impairment of all semantic memory processes would also result from studies of dementia patients who are in the advanced stage of their illness. The multiple cognitive impairments associated with a severe dementia significantly limit the assessment of specific functions. Patients who are studied in an earlier stage are more likely to reveal differential impairment. After the discovery of the very interesting dissociation between episodic and semantic impairments in several forms of dementia and amnesia, investigators of dementia have taken growing interest in studies of the differential impairments within the domain of semantic memory. This task may be approached by the method of single-case studies. Studies of individual patients can reveal striking dissociations between cognitive functions and thereby show how higher functions are fractionated into impaired and preserved categories of performance.

The single-case approach is also attractive from a clinical point of view. Clinical practice is predominantly concerned with individual patients and their unique pattern of impairments and preserved abilities. Revealing this pattern by utilizing both psychometric test batteries and theoretically based tests, borrowed from experimental and cognitive psychology, the investigator lays a sound basis for any advice and treatment offered to individual patients.

In the following, two case studies will be presented of patients suffering from dementia of the Alzheimer type. These case studies are intended as demonstrations of an experimental, process-oriented approach to the detailed functional analysis of deficits within the domain of semantic memory.

Case Presentation I

BHJ was admitted to a psychogeriatric day-care department in October 1983. He was then 73 years old, right-handed, and had worked as a receptionist in a hotel. He was a native Dutch speaker with 7 years of formal education. In 1980 he had sought neurological consultation since he experienced increasing difficulty in remembering words, names, addresses and telephone numbers. A full medical work-up did not disclose any illness that could explain his complaints. He had no history of hypertension, heart disease, diabetes, head injury, or alcohol abuse. Since ten years he used a hearing-aid in his left ear. There was no family history of dementia or other neurologic or psychiatric disease. The EEG did not disclose any abnormalities.

As the complaints persisted, a repeat EEG and a CT scan were made in 1982. The EEG was again normal. The CT-scan showed mild atrophy but no definite ventricular or sylvian fissure asymmetry. His symptoms worsened and he was referred to the day care center for a full neuropsychological evaluation and treatment. As he told me, his primary problem was "his head," saying that "he had lost and forgotten everything." The patient complained about memory problems and was clearly frustrated about his word-finding difficulties. Apart from that, he was cheerful and alert, and denied any feelings of depression. His orientation to place and time was normal. His physical appearance and social conduct were generally appropriate. He correctly gave his age, date of birth, former occupation, and address. He could also tell the name of the day care center and the days he was expected there.

His speech was well articulated and had normal melodic quality. It was fluent and within the normal range of 100 to 150 words per minute, but his expressive language was evidently abnormal. It contained many circumlocutions, frequent pauses, and few substantive words. He did not use any neologisms. His spoken sentences had a normal grammatical structure. He was able to repeat auditorily presented sentences up to 15 syllables. Auditory digit span was 5 forward and 5 backward. There was no echolalia. He knew and liked to sing the words and melodies of a fixed repertoire of overlearned, popular songs.

Comprehension of spoken language was tested by the Dutch Aphasia Test Battery (DATB) for auditory word comprehension (Berg & Deelman, 1988; Deelman, Koning-Haanstra, Liebrand, & Van den Burg, 1981). The three distractors for each item in this comprehension task are semantically related, phonologically related, or unrelated to the target picture. His auditory word-to-picture matching was slightly deficient (17 out of 18 items correct). His only error was a semantic mismatch. However on a 14-item Same-Category Spoken Word-to-Picture Matching Test his score of 9/14 correct was clearly below normal. In this test the patient has to select (by pointing) a named picture from a set of four objects all belonging to the same semantic category (e.g., kitchen utensils, animals). His performance on a companion Mixed-Category Spoken

Word-to-Picture Matching Test (with distractors from different semantic categories than the target picture) was 11/14 correct (which is also below normal, Butterworth, Howard, & McLoughlin, 1984; Diesfeldt, 1989).

In contrast, his syntactic comprehension was remarkably good. The 45-item task for syntactic comprehension in the DATB asks for pointing to one of two pictures that best represents the meaning of a spoken sentence. His performance of 44 out of 45 was well in the range of normal control subjects. This means that the patient possessed adequate knowledge of syntactic structures, such as prepositions, adverbs, pronouns, possessives, negatives, comparatives, plurals, pronouns, and active and passive verb tenses.

His severe word-finding problems became fully evident on several picture naming tasks. On the picture naming task of the DATB he named only 1 ("orange") out of 18 objects. Most paraphasias (7) missed any meaningful relation to the picture or the target word (e.g., a saw was named "an apparatus to write with," a chair was named "auto," a horse "auto." Some paraphasias (4) described the use of the object and one was a superordinate name. The remaining 5 errors were omissions. Neither tactile presentation of objects nor a verbal description of their function facilitated naming. No improvement occurred when phonemic cues were supplied. Naming of body parts and pointing to named body parts was very deficient too (5/13 and 6/12, respectively). Only body parts with highly frequent names ($\geq$ 100 per million) could be named or pointed to. Color naming was intact for highly frequent names such as "red," "yellow," "green" and "blue," but not for "orange," "pink," "violet," and "beige." In a verbal fluency test, he produced only 2 animal names, 5 articles of clothing, and 3 fruits, each in one minute. He could not reliably identify the article of clothing or the fruit among four written words in a 10-item test decribed by Diesfeldt (1985). He showed a severe deficit on a 31-item proverb-completion test in which he never gave the last correct word of well known cliches such as "more haste, less ... (speed)," "union is ... (strength)," "barking dogs seldom ... (bite)."

The patient was able to name single letters and to read aloud a short text without difficulty. On a test of recognition of words spelled aloud by the examiner, his performance was 100% correct for 21 words being 3 to 9 letters long. His writing was normal in the mechanical sense (orthography), but showed the same disorders of semantic content as his spontaneous speech. He kept a notebook diary in which he recorded significant experiences during the day. He was very fond of crosswords. Though he could not solve these because of his severe dysphasia, he looked for the correct words at the back of the puzzle-book and wrote these in the appropriate spaces vertically and horizontally.

His episodic memory abilities were tested by a four-alternative, forced-choice recognition task (Diesfeldt, 1987). By pointing he showed 100% correct recognition of five pictures after a delay of 10 minutes. He could also easily remember where the examiner had hidden three objects after a delay of 1 1/4 hour. Other evidence of his relatively intact episodic memory was his remarkable ability to date occasional visits to his doctor, the hairdresser, or his family. If a staff member of the day care center was on leave, the patient knew it and remembered when she was expected to return. He correctly anticipated some weeks in advance when he could not attend day care, e.g., because of a birthday-party or holidays. His ability to judge the passage of time and keeping track of ongoing events was quite remarkable and stood in sharp contrast to his severe language impairment. His constructional abilities were also good. This was demonstrated by his normal performance on several constructional tasks, such as copying of designs and the WAIS block-design subtest (See Table 11.1). He could draw a fairly accurate floor-plan of his house.

When the patient was asked to imitate the examiner and carry out the desired movements, he showed parapraxic movements while gesturing how to use a spoon, a hammer, or a key. When asked to demonstrate the use of 12 manipulated objects, he used 9 of those appropriately (such as fork, scissors, or spoon). However, he did not understand how to use a bottle-opener, mistook a comb for a cleaver, and a toothbrush for a nailbrush. On admission to day care there were some signs that the patient did not always understand the meaning of common objects. This contrasted to his sharpness of acuity and attention to visual detail. At home, he was observed to pick up tiny specks of dust from the floor, but he did not recognize pictures of his children. According to his wife he had only recently stopped to be an amateur carpenter after he had tried to glue two pieces of wood with methylated spirit.

From his normal results on Raven's Colored Progressive Matrices it was clear that his occasional misidentification of household objects was not due to failure in visual processing. His score of 28/36 was well in the range for his age group (Diesfeldt & Vink, 1989). He was able to do complex jigsaw puzzles and would spend much of his day playing patience, dominoes, and checkers. He made no errors on a written form of the serial subtraction test (subtract 7s serially beginning with 100, 93, 86, and so forth to 2). The items of the WAIS Arithmetic subtest were transformed so that only the essential numerical elements were (auditorily) presented. The patient's score of 10 out of 16 correct solutions attested his ability to understand and execute the basic operations of addition, subtraction, multiplication, and division. He quickly read the correct time on all 18 items of a clock-reading task, requiring quite complicated expressions such as "twenty-five minutes past eight," "twenty-five minutes to nine," and "a quarter to twelve."

His good numerical skills and intact writing excluded the presence of Gerstmann's syndrome, which is caused by lesions in the dominant inferior parietal lobe. Other symptoms of this syndrome are right-left disorientation and finger agnosia. The patient knew the meaning of left and right, since he was 100% successful on 8 commands involving right-left orientation responses, some of them requiring a mental spatial rotation. On a finger agnosia test (both hands) he could not name fingers or raise named fingers but, with his hand held out of sight, he always (12 trials) correctly discriminated the number of fingers between the two that the examiner touched. On admittance to day care his social function was very adequate. He was independent as to the activities of daily living, though his wife had taken over the household accounts. According to his wife he could dress himself, wash and shave alone, and helped with the housework and gardening. He rode his bicycle without getting lost.

Longitudinal Course

The patient kept visiting our day care department twice weekly during 3 years and 8 months. During this period he participated in repeated psychometric testing, every six months. Changes in social function and dependency were monitored by a standardized behavior rating scale (Van der Kam, Mol, & Wimmers, 1971). The longitudinal course is given in Tables 11.1 and 11.2. He was admitted to a nursing home in 1987, where he died, December 1990, in a state of very severe dementia.

Table 11.1 summarizes the main results of the psychometric tests. His spontaneous speech continued to be fluent during the four years of repeated testing, and was still fluent in 1989 (not included in Table 11.1). His comprehension of written and spoken words was deficient from the outset, and deteriorated further to a complete inability to understand the meaning of nouns and object-pictures. Comprehension of sentences deteriorated much later than word comprehension.

Table 11.1 further shows that BHJ's initial immediate memory performance (digit span) was normal and deteriorated only from the sixth round of testing. As a formal test of sentence repetition the Dutch version of the Repetition Subtest of the Aachen Aphasia Test (AAT) was used (Huber, Poeck, Weniger, & Willmes, 1983). At round 5, the patient's performance was in grade III on a scale ranging from severe (I), moderate (II), mild (III) to no impairment (IV). His repetition performance deteriorated to grade II at rounds 7 and 8.

His visuo-constructive abilities continued to be good as was attested by his relatively high scores on WAIS Block Designs. His performance on Raven's CPM showed that his visual perceptual abilities remained good as long as he could participate in repeated testing. From an analysis of item content it is known that Raven's CPM consists of three main types of problems: two of a predominantly visuospatial type (12 items of simple continuous pattern-completion (S-items in Table 11.1) and 15 concrete dynamic items showing progressive changes in one or two directions (CD-items in Table 11.1). The other 9 items (AD-items) are of an abstract dynamic-reasoning type (Diesfeldt & Vink, 1989). BHJ's performance on the purely perceptual S-items did not deteriorate, his scores on the concrete dynamic items of Raven's CPM were normal and stable until the second half of 1985. Two years later, after admission to a nursing home, he was still able to copy quite complex designs and to play checkers. However, his symptoms of visual agnosia had grown worse. He had to be kept from eating fish-bones, egg-shells, peels of melons or bananas, and from eating paint or drinking from bottles of perfume. In contrast with this very severe agnosia, his sense for time and temporal events remained remarkably

Table 11.1
Longitudinal Course of BHJ's Illness: Psychometric Performance

Year	83	84	84	85	85	86	86	87
1/2 yr period	2	1	2	1	2	1	2	2
Fluency (words/4 minutes)	463	586	519	608	602	581	618[a]	521
Word Comprehension (18)	17	16	12	11	6	3	4	0
Sentence Comprehension (45)	44	45	41	40	40	34	31	23
Category Naming	2	2	3	0	0	0	0	0
Picture Naming (18)	1	2	1	0	0	0	0	0
Demonstrating the use of objects (12)	-	9	10	9	6	6	-	-
Digit Span Forward	5	6	7	7	5	5	5	3
Digit Span Backward	5	5	5	5	4	2	0	-
Repetition AAT Total[b] (150)	-	-	-	-	129	127	113	82
Phonemes (30)	-	-	-	-	30	27	28	18
Monosyllables (30)	-	-	-	-	29	27	28	24
Foreign Words (30)	-	-	-	-	24	28	25	20
Polysyllables (30)	-	-	-	-	24	27	20	16
Sentences (30)	-	-	-	-	22	18	12	4
WAIS Block Design								
Complete patterns (13)	7	7	7	6	8	9	8	6
Within time limit (13)	5	5	5	6	7	6	6	5
Raven's CPM (36)	28	29	28	28	16	27	26	19
Raven's CPM-s (12)	12	12	11	12	11	11	12	11
Raven's CPM-CD (15)	15	15	15	14	5	14	12	7
Raven's CPM-AD (9)	1	2	2	2	0	2	2	1
WAIS Arithmetic (16)	-	10	9	10	9	-	5	-
Serial Subtraction (14)	14	13	13	11	11	-	-	0
Clock Reading (18)	-	18	18	18	15	-	18	12
Delayed Recognition (10)	-	10	9	6	6	6	-	-

Note. Maximum scores are given in parantheses.
[a] Extrapolation based on two-minutes speech sample.
[b] The AAT (Dutch language version) was not available before 1985.

Table 11.2
Longitudinal Course of BHJ's Illness: Behavioral Ratings

Year	83	84	84	85	85	86	86	87	88	89	90
1/2 yr period	2	1	2	1	2	1	2	2	2	2	2
BOP Dependency (46)	3	4	4	4	7	7	7	11	22	27	35
BOP Aggressiveness (10)	0	0	0	0	1	0	1	4	4	1	2
BOP Physical Dis. (6)	0	1	1	0	0	1	0	1	1	2	2
BOP Depression (6)	2	5	2	0	2	1	1	2	2	1	0
BOP Communication Dis (8)	2	2	2	3	2	3	3	5	7	6	8
BOP Inactivity (14)	3	2	3	1	12	3	5	4	7	3	12

Note. Maximum scores are given in parantheses.

intact. In the second half of 1987, two weeks after his admission to a nursing home, he could tell exactly how long he had been there.

There was no progression of any computational deficits until 1986. Even in the second half of 1986 the patient could still read clocks. Only in the second half of 1988 (not in Table 11.1) he had apparently lost the ability of clock-reading. Episodic memory was tested by using a delayed, four-alternative, forced choice picture recognition test. The delay between presentation of 10 target pictures and the recognition test was 35 minutes. Episodic memory appeared to decline from the last half of 1984, which is clearly later than the very significant decline of his semantic memory functions (see Table 11.1).

Table 11.2 shows the course of the patient's illness in terms of behavioral ratings. The higher scores represent more severe levels of dependency, agressiveness, and so forth. It is clear from Table 11.2 that the patient became more and more dependent from 1986 onwards. Periods with aggressive behavior occurred in 1987 and 1988. The first episodes of urinary incontinence were noted in the first half of 1988. His physical abilities did not suffer much. He remained ambulatory. Only occasionally were there signs of depression. Until one year before his death the patient engaged in social interaction and activities, which is shown by his rather low ratings on the Inactivity-scale. Of course, his high ratings on Communication Disorders indicate his increasing dysphasic problems.

According to the NINCDS-ADRDA criteria the clinical diagnosis of probable Alzheimer's disease would be allowed in this case based upon the clearly insidious and progressive decline in mental functioning in the absence of other neurologic, psychiatric, or systemic disorders (McKhann et al., 1984).

Clinical Diagnosis

Since necropsy was not undertaken the neuropathological diagnosis of BHJ's illness remains unknown. The patient did not show the signs of frontal lobe dysfunction that are suggestive of Pick's disease. A CT scan was made in June 1985 (see Figure 11.1).

It was quite evident from BHJ's history that his initial symptoms were word-finding difficulties. However, the neuropsychological examination and the clinical course revealed that his deficits were by no means confined to the purely verbal domain. His loss of semantic knowledge clearly involved both the meaning of words and objects. Snowden, Goulding, and Neary (1989) termed

this syndrome of slowly progressive loss of semantic knowledge in the context of initially preserved episodic memory "semantic dementia."In a similar vein, De Renzi, Liotti, and Nichelli (1987) described a syndrome of semantic amnesia in a 44-year old woman who, after an episode of encephalitis, lost the knowledge of the meaning and attributes of words, but retained the command of syntax and had normal memory for autobiographical events.

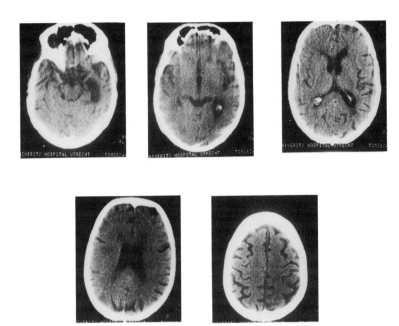

Figure 11.1. CT-scan of BHJ, showing moderate generalized atrophy, with enlarged ventricles and sulci, particularly in the left perisylvian area. The anterior horn of the lateral left ventricle is clearly much larger than normal. The brain's left side is represented on the right side of the CT-scans.

Summary of Clinical Findings: Case Presentation I

In summary, BHJ is a right-handed man, who initially, 70 years old, developed a slowly progressive aphasia and visual agnosia. He died after a course of 10 years in a severely demented state. The pattern of impairments and preserved abilities revealed several remarkable dissociations. During the initial phases of his illness semantic memory suffered more than episodic memory for recent events. Within the domain of semantic memory, language was far more impaired than visual perception, reasoning, arithmetic skills, clock reading, and visuo-constructive abilities. Within the domain of language, lexical comprehension was significantly more impaired than syntactic comprehension. His oral reading was remarkably good relative to his extremely limited comprehension. This means that, at least within the domain of oral reading, phonological knowledge was far better preserved than lexical knowledge. In the domain of visual knowledge his basic perceptual abilities were unimpaired, but there was an inability to recognize the specific meaning of objects, taking the form of an associative agnosia. These dissociations were further analyzed in specific investigations on the nature of the impairments of BHJ's semantic memory.

Experimental Investigations of Semantic Memory

Superordinate Category Knowledge

A series of experimental investigations of semantic memory started in 1984 with a sorting task, involving the assignment of written words to four different category headings. The stimuli for this study were taken from Diesfeldt's (1983) category norms. Within each of six categories half the exemplars were strong, and the other half were weak. Strong exemplars included items that had been named by at least 10% of 100 subjects, whereas weak exemplars had been named by less than 10%. In one session BHJ was asked to sort 74 printed nouns (30 animal names, 20 vegetables and 24 body parts) to one of four categories: "animals," "vegetables," "body parts," or "other." The items were randomized as to category and strength of exemplar. The patient was asked to read each printed item aloud. In another session, two days later, he was asked to sort the names of 30 articles of clothing, 20 musical instruments, and 22 fruits. His knowledge of the relevant category names was tested by presenting him with groups of two or three pictures of objects from three categories. The only categories he could name were "animals" and "articles of clothing." BHJ was then asked to point to the pictures belonging to a category that was named by the examiner. He made no errors on this task. He was also able to match the correct name of five written category names to a given set of object-pictures belonging to a specific category. This indicates that his understanding of the category names used in the semantic judgment task was sufficient for testing his superordinate category knowledge of single nouns.

BHJ used 14 minutes in each session to sort the 74 and 72 words. The results are shown in Table 11.3. BHJ's sorting was significantly better than chance for two categories only: animals (strong exemplars) and body parts.

The individual words, belonging to each of the six categories, were matched for category dominance, but not for frequency of occurrence in Dutch. In general, weak exemplars tended also to be less frequent in Dutch; the Pearson correlation between category dominance and frequency of occurrence was .35 for 146 words. The median frequency was highest for "body parts" and "animals," and lowest for "vegetables" and "musical instruments." That BHJ's performance was associated with the frequency of the items, was demonstrated by an analysis of covariance, with sorting performance as the dependent vari-

Table 11.3
Percentage Correct Semantic Categorization of Written Words
Across Category and Dominance Level

	Period					
	84/1		84/2		86/1	
Categories	HD	LD	HD	LD	HD	LD
Animals	80	13	27	20	47	7
Vegetables	50	10	20	20	30	50
Body-parts	83	67	58	33	25	42
Clothing	40	33	27	40	40	33
Musical instruments	40	20	40	10	40	30
Fruits	36	55	45	36	18	55

Note. HD = high-dominant exemplars; LD = low-dominant exemplars.

able, category as the independent variable and word-frequency as the covariate. The effect of category on BHJ's performance disappeared after controlling for word-frequency (F 5,139 = 1,29). High-frequency words (42/72) were better sorted, regardless of category, than low-frequency words (23/74) (Median test: chi-square = 9.9; p = .002). Thus, the retention of a concept's general category (for example, that a cat is an animal) was better for high frequency than for low frequency items. This word frequency effect is taken as evidence for central damage to the representation of meaning, instead of disordered access to semantic knowledge (Chertkow & Bub, 1990).

The superordinate matching test was repeated twice, first after 8 months and then 2 years later. In this period BHJ's performance deteriorated significantly (McNemar-test for the difference between period 84/1 and 84/2: chi-square = 5,5; p = .02). There was no further deterioration at retesting in period 86/1, except for strong exemplars of the category "body parts." He did not use more time for sorting than at the initial test: 14 to 15 minutes to sort 72 or 74 words. Effects of word frequency could no longer be determined. These results show that initially BHJ's knowledge of some highly frequent object nouns enabled him to match these to their superordinate category label. Over the course of his illness he clearly lost this very general superordinate category information.

Size Judgments for Named and Pictured Animals

In assessing BHJ's knowledge of specific properties of named animals, 17 sets of 3 written animal names, derived from a set of 8 highly frequent names, were presented (e.g., cat, cow, mouse). The patient was asked to underline the "largest" animal. After completion of all 17 items, the test was repeated, asking him to underline the "smallest" animal. His knowledge of the concepts of

"large" and "small" was tested beforehand by asking him to point to the largest, or the smallest item in a row of three letters or geometric designs (trian-
gles, circles) of different size. His 100% correct performance on eight trials
proved that he understood these concepts well.

As Table 11.4 shows, he could not reliably derive attribute knowledge from
written animals names. For example, presented with the names mouse-cat-
horse, he selected "cat" as the largest animal. However, his superordinate
category knowledge (discrimination between the 8 animal names and 8
distractors) significantly exceeded chance.

Table 11.4
*Superordinate Category and Attribute Knowledge for 8 Written
Animal Names*

	Animal	Largest	Smallest
Correct responses (%)	88	29	47
Chance performance (%)	50	33	33

Note. Data from period 84/1.

Table 11.5
*Percentage Correct Category Knowledge (22 Trials) and Attribute
Knowledge (15 trials) for Pictures of Animals Over a Period of 2 Years*

Animal						Largest				
84/1	84/2	Period 85/1	85/2	86/1		84/1	84/2	Period 85/1	85/2	86/1
100	100	100	100	100		67	73	73	60	53

Note. Chance Score = 50%.

On a pictorial version of this test the patient was required to assign 22
colored pictures (derived from Ravensburg Nature Memory) to one of two categories "animal" or "anything else." The 11 pictures belonging to the "anything
else" category depicted flowers and fruits. In order to test his knowledge of the
size of 9 pictured animals, he was asked to point to the largest animal from a
set of 3. On these pictures all animals had about the same size, though in reality
they differed greatly in size (e.g., horse, dog, and hamster). Table 11.5 shows
that the patient perfectly discriminated between animal and non-animal pictures. However, his performance on size judgments, though significantly above
chance, was clearly deficient. It is interesting to note that his superordinate
category knowledge for these animal pictures did not change over a period of

at least two years, whereas his attribute knowledge slowly deteriorated across time.

Category Knowledge: A Comparison Between Words and Pictures

Comparing Tables 4 and 5, it seems that, at least in 1984, the patient derived more conceptual information from pictures than from their written names. Further evidence on this point was found on a test for semantic categorization of pictures and words using 42 black-and-white drawings and their corresponding names (16 animals, 14 articles of clothing, and 12 fruits). All names referred to very common objects. Median word frequency was 10 per million (Uit den Boogaart, 1975). Most names (95%) were judged to belong to the passive vocabulary of a six-year-old child (Kohnstamm, Schaerlaekens, de Vries, Akkerhuis, & Froonincksx, 1981). In the picture-to-category matching task, the patient was given a picture and a card with two category names. He was asked to point to the category to which the pictured object belonged. In the word-to-category matching task the written name had to be matched to the correct category name. Results showed that his category choices were significantly better for pictured objects than for words (chi-square = 7.6; p = .01). Word frequency or age of acquisition had no demonstrable influence on these results.

In a picture-to-name matching task with these 42 pictures, where he had to select the correct name for the picture from two written words which comprised the correct name and a distractor (e.g., a picture of a pear had to be matched to the words "apple" or "pear"), his performance did not exceed chance. These results suggest an underspecification of the codes addressing the semantic system (Bub, Black, Hampson, & Kertesz, 1988). BHJ was able to use the structural cues of pictures to draw inferences about the general category membership of the pictured objects. Knowledge of their specific names, however, was not available. His very impoverished word knowledge did not even allow reliable inferences about the superordinate categories to which the words referred.

Comprehension of Function Words

Though the patient's conceptual knowledge of content words, such as nouns and verbs, appeared to be very poor, he was still able to understand the meaning of syntactic function words, such as prepositions, negatives, and comparatives. This was demonstrated by his good performance on the Sentence Comprehension subtest of the DATB (see Table 11.1). Whereas his Word Comprehension performance started to decline significantly in 1983, his ability to select the correct picture given a spoken sentence was relatively spared until 1986. Although the Sentence Comprehension test involves very common nouns and verbs (e.g., house, tree, boy, girl, to be, to have, walking), BHJ's impaired word comprehension hindered the specific assessment of his knowledge of grammatical function words. In order to overcome the confounding effects of his deficient knowledge of content words, I devised two series of test items that required a minimum of lexical knowledge. In both series, short written sentences served as stimuli and two schematic drawings formed the choice array. The test required the patient to match a written sentence to one of two pictures in which the target and distractor could be easily confused. The only significant elements in the choice arrays were the letters A, B, and C (in the first series of 37 items), and the letter A and the drawing of a square in the second series of 64 items. The first series tested for comprehension of locative prepositions (beside, between, below, above, on, under), comparatives (smaller, larger), and negative-affirmative contrasts. The second series, which became available later, tested for the comprehension of the locative prepositions inside-outside, in-out, beside, and above-below.

Table 11.6 shows that the patient's knowledge of the tested function words was good, at least through 1986, when his Word Comprehension and Sentence Comprehension performance had already deteriorated to a very low level.

Table 11.6
Longitudinal Course of Comprehension (Percentage Correct)
for Locative Prepositions, Comparatives, and Affirmative-
Negative Contrasts

	Period			
	85/2	86/1	86/2	87/2
Test 1	97	100	100	57
Test 2	-	-	100	61

Note. Chance performance = 50%.

Here is thus another example of an interesting dissociation in the domain of semantic memory: The patient's semantic knowledge was normal to good for locative prepositions and other grammatical morphemes, whereas his knowledge of object names was very poor indeed.

Visual Object Perception and Comprehension

Language was apparently not the only function that was impaired in this patient. From clinical observation (impaired recognition of familiar faces, putting inedible things into his mouth, inappropriate use of common household objects), it could be suspected that he also suffered from visual agnosia. The next series of tests to be described here, were intended to analyze his visual functions. Visual object recognition requires the intact functioning of at least three distinct processing stages. First, objects are analyzed for their sensory properties, such as contrast, color, shape, and line orientation. Second, a perceptual classification stage is needed in which a given view of an object is matched to a representation of that object in long-term semantic memory. After this stage of object identification, further associative and functional knowledge about the identified object is derived from long-term semantic memory (Farah, 1990; Humphreys & Bruce, 1989; see also Martin, this volume). Problems in recognizing objects can arise through deficits within or between any of these stages. Therefore, a series of tests was given to BHJ in order to assess the integrity of his basic visual processing, perceptual identification, and semantic classification.

Elementary visual functions. Formal tests of visual acuity and shape discrimination (such as the Snellen eye chart) revealed normal acuity. BHJ could easily read small print. He was also perfectly able to detect the presence or absence of a shape (X or O) against a background of a random black-and-white pattern (Warrington & Taylor, 1978).

On a size discrimination test he reliably detected the difference between asterisks varying in size from 2 mm to 3 mm. He could reliably judge whether two small (2x2 cm) photographs of faces were identical, or portrayed two different people. He even correctly matched photographs to real faces of 6 staff members of the day care center. He correctly read 16 numbers from the first 17 Ishihara plates (Ishihara, 1983) for color-blindness (he mistook 73 for 23) and always selected the correct color out of a choice array of 4 when given one of 11 sample stimuli of different hues. He quickly identified the 3 single items from overlapping line drawings, by pointing to these items in a choice array of 6. The results on these tests, which were given during the first half of 1986, are in complete agreement with his normal performance on Raven's CPM (see Table 11.1). The integrity of his basic visual abilities was further attested by his ability to copy detailed drawings, line by line, of objects that he could barely recognize (see Figure 11.2 and Figure 11.3) and by his normal performance on WAIS Block Designs (see Table 11.1).

Taken together, these results indicate that the patient's object recognition difficulties did not result from impairment in the development of an adequately structured percept (McCarthy & Warrington, 1986b). Therefore, we take a further look into the patient's visual world in search of the stage where his object recognition problems arise.

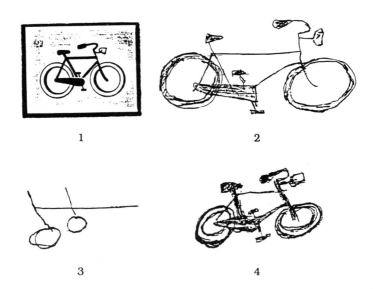

1   2

3   4

Figure 11.2. BHJ's copying of a picture of a bicycle. The first and second pictures portray model and copy (August 1984). The third picture is drawn from immediate memory following a self-paced inspection period (August 1984), and the fourth is drawn in May 1986. When asked to draw from memory, it is quite evident that the patient had difficulty imagining what the named object (e.g., a bicycle) would look like.

   Visual identification: Recognition of visually presented objects. The minimal evidence for intact perceptual identification is success in matching nonidentical presentations of a given object. In order to formally assess this ability several nonverbal tests of picture-to-object matching were given. These visual-visual matching tasks paired real objects with pictures of similar, but not identical objects. The tests used pictures and real objects of 15 fruits, 22 household objects, and pictures and plastic toy models of 11 animals. Table 11.7 shows the results for these matching tasks.

Table 11.7
*Matching-To-Sample Results for 15 Fruits,
22 Household Objects, and 11 Animals*

Stimulus	Choices	% Correct
Fruit pictures	Real objects	93
Real fruits	Pictures	80
Object pictures	Real objects	82
Animal models	Pictures	73

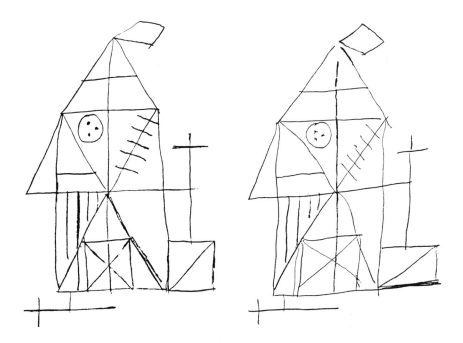

Figure 11.3. Copies of the Rey-Osterrieth Complex Figure in December 1986 (left) and August 1987 (right). BHJ took 5 min and 45 sec, and 4 min and 50 sec, respectively, to complete these drawings. Copying did not reveal any deterioration during this period.

Table 11.8 shows how his performance on a picture to object matching test for 22 household objects deteriorated over the course of two years.

Table 11.8
Percentage Correct Picture-to-Object
Matching of 22 Household
Objects over a Period of 2 Years

		Period		
84/1	84/2	85/1	85/2	86/1
82	95	95	73	59

Typical mistakes on these tests were errors based on structural similarities. Some matchings were based on color, so that the picture of a glass of red wine was matched to the picture of a corkscrew because of its red grip. Particularly informative in this regard was his verbal comments. Comparing pictures and toy models of animals he often overemphasized the external features. The toy model of a "wild sow" was matched to the rhinoceros-picture because both animals bore sharp projections. Only with great hesitation he matched a model of an elephant with its picture, since the model had its trunk up, in contrast to the pictured animal who had its trunk down. Thus, the patient's errors reflected the greater influence of visual properties than the conceptual nature of the stimulus.

His knowledge of color as an object feature was tested with verbal and nonverbal tasks. When provided with their spoken and written names, he was virtually unable to name the colors of objects or substances which have a very specific color. For example, when asked about the colour of snow, he answered "yellow." When asked to name or select the appropriate color of black-and-white line drawings of common objects which have a very specific color, such as banana, ace of hearts, or traffic lights, his performance was very poor (4 correct answers in 18 trials) in the verbal (naming) task and not above chance in the nonverbal (matching) task.

Although his visual sensory functioning appeared to be intact, it is clear that BHJ was not always successful in matching nonidentical presentations of a given object and that he was unable to assign the correct color to line drawings of objects with highly predictable colors. This suggests an impairment in the presemantic perceptual classification stage of visual object recognition (Schwartz & Chawluk, 1990).

Visual semantic processing. The feature-by-feature matching strategy in visual object recognition, already demonstrated on picture-to-object matching tasks, became apparent also on a specially devised test of the patient's knowledge of an object's function and its relation to other objects: The Function Matching Test. This test requires the subject to point to one of four pictures that is functionally related to a target stimulus presented below a horizontal choice array. Only one object in the choice array was related to the target by category or function. A second object was visually, but not functionally similar to the target. The two other distractors were unrelated to the target stimulus. For example, if the target was a comb, the choice array displayed drawings of a pear (unrelated), a head with hair (functional relationship), a rake (visual similarity), and a wheel-chair (unrelated).

The nature of this task was explained by two demonstration trials. BHJ's choices on a 20-item version of this test and the performance of an age-matched group of 26 normal adult control subjects (aged 65 to 93) are given in Table 11.9.

Table 11.9
*BHJ's and a Normal Control Group's Performance on the
Function Matching Test*

Type of match	BHJ Raw score	Control group (N=26)		
		M	*SD*	Range
Functional association	5	18.0	1.5	14-20
Physical similarity	15	1.5	1.4	0-6
Unrelated	0	0.5	0.8	0-2

BHJ's score of 5 functionally and 15 visually related choices was clearly out-side the normal range. This means that he based his matchings on size and shape rather than on concepts of common function. The patient's failure to match by function, given his preserved perceptual classification, reflects a failure of object recognition at the level of visual semantic categorization.

The patient was also given a picture arrangement task comprising 11 sets of three cards demonstrating simple sequentially related actions (Winslow Press, 1980). The cards in a sequence were placed before him in a random order. He was then requested to put the cards in correct order of a logical sequence of actions. His performance of 6 out of 11 correct sequences was clearly less than in a group of 21 normal adults between 70 and 86 years of age (*M* = 9.5; *SD* = 1.3; range 7-11). This disability in understanding the logic of conceptual rela-tions between the pictured actions stood in contrast to his preserved ability to understand the logic of directional movement in the spatial sequences of Raven's CPM (see Table 11.1). Raven's matrices task, which involves geometrical patterns, does not require any knowledge of objects, in contrast to the picture arrangement task that can only be successfully completed if the meaning of the pictured objects or actions is understood.

Summarizing the results of these visual perception and comprehension tests, I conclude that BHJ's elementary visual abilities of acuity, shape dis-crimination, and color perception were unimpaired. However, a severe loss of associative and functional knowledge became evident from his impaired com-prehension of objects and pictures. It is conceivable that this dissolution of semantic memory also negatively affected the presemantic identification of visual objects in the object-to-picture matching tasks. Given the central dam-age to BHJ's memory representations and his normal perceptual abilities, his inability to recognize objects in several modalities (visual, verbal, and tactile) corresponds to *semantic agnosia* in the taxonomy of agnosias given by Humphreys and Riddoch (1987).

Although the damage to the central meaning system could be demon-strated in several sensory modalities, there were indications that the patient's comprehension problems were *material-specific*. Recall the dissociations ob-served between impaired comprehension of content words and preserved comprehension of function words, and between impaired comprehension of pictured action sequences and preserved understanding of the logic of directional movement in Ravens matrices. Next, another material-specific impairment of semantic memory with consequences for episodic recognition memory is described.

Material-Specific Impairment of Nonverbal Episodic Memory: Face Versus Place Recognition

In our regular meetings with this patient, we were struck by his difficulty in face recognition in contrast to his very good ability in recognizing rooms and finding his way in the day care center. For example, the patient was unable to recognize the examiner, except when he was seen in the familiar context of the testing office. Other staff members had comparable experiences; the patient did not recognize their faces, but showed clear evidence of recognition of the spatial environment, and then understood what was expected from him. I tried to investigate this dissociation in a more formal way by designing a test of delayed retention of pictures of faces and landscapes. This test, presented to the patient in the second half of 1986, used the first 12 face pictures from Warrington's Recognition Memory Test (Warrington, 1984) and 12 black-and-white photographs of village scenes or landscapes. For each plate, there was a distractor. The assignment of a landscape as target stimulus or distractor was determined at random. The patient was presented with 12 faces and 12 landscape pictures consecutively in random order, and was allowed to inspect each figure for 5 seconds. Following the presentation of a stimulus, the patient was asked to perform simple calculations (multiply a series of random digits by 2) during 30 seconds. Then two pictures were shown, the target and a distractor, and the patient was asked to point to the picture he had seen before.

The results showed clear discrepancies between landscape recognition and face recognition. Face recognition did not exceed chance performance (7/12) in contrast to landscape recognition, which was perfect (12/12). The difference was significant (Fisher's exact probability test; $p = .04$). Apparently, the patient's episodic memory for faces was more deficient than his episodic memory for pictures of village scenes. This material-specific memory disorder might reflect his associative agnosia for faces, in contrast to his preserved ability to perceive and store images of places and built environments. His better episodic memory for places than for faces could thus be due to material-specific differences in conceptual encoding at the semantic level.

At the Interface of Visual Perception and Language: Oral Reading and Writing

At the interface of visual perception and linguistic competence is the ability to read. This section describes the patient's ability in reading and writing. These abilities typically require both intact processing of visually complex stimulus patterns (words and sentences) and linguistic capacities to derive meaning from print. The study of oral reading at the level of single words can be very instructive because it can show what components (visual, phonological, and/or semantic) in the complex process of translating print into sound are intact or deficient.

Neuropsychological approaches to the study of reading have revealed a number of different patterns of acquired dyslexia, that is, reading impairment resulting from brain damage in a previously competent reader (Marshall & Newcombe, 1973; Patterson, 1981). If an impairment of visual processing is the primary cause of a reading disability, the resulting dyslexia is called peripheral or word-form dyslexia. The second main group are the central dyslexias that affect the ability to derive sound or meaning from print (McCarthy & Warrington, 1990). Since BHJ's visual perceptual abilities were not impaired, a peripheral dyslexia was not expected in his case. Therefore, we directed our attention to the possible existence of a central dyslexia in this patient.

The central dyslexias fall apart in at least two syndromes, "reading without meaning" and "reading via meaning" (Ellis & Young, 1988). Dyslexic patients who read without meaning easily read nonwords, abstract words, and inflected verbs, but have severe difficulty reading words with irregular spelling-to-sound relationships. Their aphasia syndrome is one of fluent speech, poor comprehension, and poor naming. Other dyslexic patients appear to read via meaning. Reading via meaning occurs in patients suffering from deep dyslexia, or phonological dyslexia. Their reading pattern is one of intact irregular word reading, but impaired reading of nonwords, abstract words, function words, and inflected verbs. These two types of central dyslexia can be distinguished by the influence of four major word dimensions on oral reading performance: meaningfulness, regularity of spelling, syntactic class, and imageability or concreteness (Ellis & Young, 1988; Friedman, 1988; Howard & Hatfield, 1987; Marshall, 1987; Patterson, 1981). By presenting a patient with words that systematically vary along these stimulus dimensions, the different types of breakdown within the subcomponents of the complex skill of reading can be determined. BHJ was therefore asked to read several lists of words and nonwords and make decisions on their status (lexical decision).

Visual lexical decision. In lexical decision, the subject must decide whether a printed letter string is a legitimate word in his or her language. This task tests the integrity of the visual input lexicon. The visual input lexicon recognizes familiar words and responds to unfamiliar words (e.g., nonwords) by declaring them "unknown." Recognition of familar words as familiar and nonwords as unfamiliar does not mean that the familar words are also well understood. Lexical decision only tells us something about the early phases in the reading process. Of course, intact lexical decision requires at least an elementary understanding and knowledge of the given words. Words that are deprived of any meaning will not be recognized by the visual input lexicon, so that difficulties in visual lexical decision in the context of normal visual processing of letter strings would indicate a severe disturbance of word comprehension.

BHJ was given a yes-no decision task for 300 written letter strings, half of them being nonwords. Words and three classes of nonwords (pseudowords, orthographically legal nonwords, and illegal nonwords) were selected from the material described by Hudson and Bergman (1985). *Pseudowords* were made by altering one letter of each corresponding Dutch word, vowel to vowel, consonant to consonant. *Legal nonwords* were made of orthographically legal and pronounceable combinations which bore no obvious relationship to any known word in Dutch. *Orthographically illegal nonwords* were scrambled pseudowords which had vowels and consonants, but which broke many of the orthographic rules and were essentially unpronounceable.

Words and nonwords were presented in random order, on two days. The patient took 20 to 21 minutes each day to make his decisions on 150 stimuli. As Table 11.10 shows, he made no errors when deciding on the status of the orthographically illegal nonwords. However, he could less reliably discriminate between words and matched pseudowords, or between words and legal nonwords. The d' values in Table 11.10 show that his sensitivity in discriminating between words and several types of nonwords was greater as the nonwords deviated more from the orthography of his language.

Table 11.10
BHJ's Lexical Decision Performance in the First Half of 1986

Stimuli	% Correct	Hits	False alarms	d'
Words versus matched pseudowords	64	82	54	.81
Words versus legal nonwords	79	93	36	1.84
Words versus illegal nonwords	97	93	0	4.57

It is clear from Table 11.10 that the patient's comprehension disturbance had affected the visual input lexicon for written words. Only if the letter strings violated the rules of the orthography in his language, he could reliably recognize them as nonwords.

Oral reading. BHJ was also asked to read aloud words that varied in meaningfulness, frequency, imageability, syntactic category, and regularity of spelling. The precise nature of the oral reading tasks, with the exception of the Segmentation Task, has been described elsewhere (Diesfeldt, 1991). The Segmentation Task is a test of orthographic knowledge that is derived from McCarthy and Warrington (1986a). Twenty-eight stimulus cards were prepared, each with three words typed with spaces, and 28 cards containing the same words typed without the conventional gap between them. The subject is tested for his or her ability to segment such letter strings into their constituent words.

Length of single words varied between 1 and 4 syllables. Words were combined at random on each stimulus card. Half the words were high-imagery, concrete words, half were low-imagery, abstract words (Van Loon-Vervoorn, 1985). The stimulus cards with and without spaces (A and B, respectively) were tested in an ABAB design. The patient was told that each card contained 3 words, but no information was given as to word length. He was then asked to read the cards aloud. On reading the 84 non-segmented words, which took him almost 5 min (which is somewhat more than the 2 to 3 min he needed to read the 84 normally segmented words), BHJ made only one error.

This performance demonstrates his well preserved orthographic knowledge, which is impressive given his absence of any comprehension of the printed words. His oral reading was also good and within the range of a normal control group for the following stimuli (number of items between parentheses): Single letters (26), numbers (41) (from 1- to 3-digits), high-frequency and low-frequency nouns (64), concrete and abstract words (64), adjectives (17), verbs (41), functon (121), and nonwords (25). Thus, the dimensions of frequency, concreteness, syntactic category, meaningfulness (nonwords), and perceptual distortion (absence of spaces between single words) did not exert any negative influence on the patient's oral reading. However, he made 11 and 10 errors on two different occasions when reading 25 so-called "exception" words that, though very common in Dutch, have comparatively uncommon spelling-to-sound correspondences. He tried to read many of these words using a direct translation from print to phonology. Having lost semantic knowledge about many of the words, it further appeared from his reading of irregular words that BHJ also lost the normal means of transcribing between the stored orthographic unit for the whole-word and its corresponding phonological unit. Patients like BHJ, who apparently have intact whole-word orthographic knowledge but cannot access lexical whole-word phonology, must therefore rely on a strategy of phonologically based grapheme-to-phoneme conversions. The same strategy can be used to read pronounceable nonwords, a task that was not difficult at all for this patient. The patient's dyslexia is known in the literature as "surface dyslexia": A syndrome of non-lexical or phonological reading (Coslett, Roeltgen, Rothi, & Heilman, 1987; Mehler, 1988; Schwartz, Marin, & Saffran, 1979; Schwartz, Saffran, & Marin, 1980; Shallice & Warrington, 1980; Shallice, Warrington, & McCarthy, 1983; Warrington, 1975). This syndrome often occurs in the context of severe semantic and lexical loss. Patients with surface dyslexia have significant difficulty naming objects, and perform poorly on tests of verbal comprehension. In addition, in a test of writing 20 regular and irregular words to dictation, the patient only made errors to words with an irregular spelling-to-sound correspondence. This means that he had an impairment that specifically affects retrieval of the full spelling pattern of once-familiar words from the graphemic output lexicon. Piecemeal phoneme-grapheme conversion was intact, since he could spell regular words correctly.

Summary of the Experimental Investigations of Case I

Summarizing the results of the neuropsychological investigations, I conclude that BHJ developed a severe disorder of comprehension for spoken and written words. His comprehension was also impaired for visual and tactile objects, although this agnosia could not be explained by sensory deficits. The semantic deficits were unrelated to modality of input or output, and could not be influenced by cuing of whatever type. This clearly suggests that his deficits were due to an actual *loss* of semantic information, and not to an impairment in the patient's *access* to an otherwise intact semantic store (Nebes, 1989).

However, an intriguing constellation of spared and impaired abilities was found that appeared to depend on the *stimulus material* the patient was required to respond to. Thus, his understanding of content words was significantly worse than his understanding of grammatical function words, he had an agnosia for faces but not for places, and his knowledge of the orthography of his language was excellent, although he did not have the slightest understanding of the words he could read so perfectly. His performance on many different linguistic tasks provides converging evidence for a dissociation between three main processing components within the language system: The phonological, the syntactic, and the semantic (Berndt, Basili, & Caramazza, 1987). Phonological processes (procedural knowledge of sounds and their structure) appeared to be intact. His speech was fluent without phonemic paraphasias, he could repeat spoken words and sentences, and could read aloud words and nonsense words, provided that they corresponded to a regular orthography. This indicates that the input as well as the output phonological processes were operating efficiently. The syntactic components in language comprehension and production were also preserved. This was demonstrated by his spontaneous speech that contained grammatically well-formed sentences, although it was devoid of content words and often contained semantic errors. His good comprehension of grammatical function words made him understand complex sentences far better than single content words. Clearly his knowledge of the meaning of words and sentences was most impaired. Spontaneous speech, sentence comprehension, repetition, writing and oral reading all showed a pattern of relatively intact phonological and syntactic processes, but impaired semantic processing. In fact, BHJ's impairment is an example of language isolation in which basic visual, phonological, syntactic, and speech output processes can be intact despite the patient's inability to assign meaning to them.

The selective impairment of BHJ's semantic system, causing loss of information about names, attributes, and functions of objects, including a visual associative agnosia, demonstrates that the central representation of meaning can be specifically affected by degenerative brain disease, whereas rule-governed processes of phonology and syntax are spared. The opposite dissociation was found in a second dementia patient, who demonstrated severely impaired phonology, and comprehension and production deficits typical of Broca's aphasia, but whose semantic processing, assessed through picture naming and categorization tasks, was shown to be relatively spared.

Case Presentation II

History and Examination

RKC was a 56 year-old housewive and a native Dutch speaker with 10 years of formal education when she was admitted to our department. She had a five-year history of slowly progressive mental deterioration and apathy. A more extensive report of this patient was published elsewhere (Diesfeldt, 1991).

The history of her neurological illness began in 1980 with significant mood and personality changes (sadness, irritability and self-depreciation). She made errors in shopping and showed serious memory lapses. As the picture suggested the possibility of presenile dementia, a complete physical, psychiatric, and neurological examination with CT scan was performed. No abnormalities could be found by then. However, her intellectual abilities further deteriorated. Previously an avid reader of detective novels, in 1984 she could no longer read. She also lost the ability for writing and needlework, and needed assistance with cooking, simple household chores, and dressing. She began to experience serious difficulty in finding her way in familiar surroundings and had to be looked after around the clock. By then, a repeat CT-scan revealed diffuse widening of the cerebral sulci and enlargement of the ventricular system indicating mild generalized cerebral atrophy. No focal abnormalities were seen in the brain (see Figure 11.4).

No other members of her family had suffered psychiatric illness or progressive dementia. Her parents had died past the age of 75 without symptoms of dementia. The patient was left-handed but had been taught to write with her right hand. At least three family members (sister, aunt, and niece) were known to be left-handed too. There was no history of childhood dyslexia.

The clinical features of multi-infarct dementia such as abrupt onset, fluctuating course, a history of hypertension or a history of strokes, were absent. The clinical history, and the results of the physical, psychiatric, and neurological examinations strongly suggested the diagnosis of Alzheimer's disease (McKhann et al., 1984). In 1986 she was admitted to a psychogeriatric day care department on a schedule of three days a week. In 1987 she became incontinent of urine at night and needed more and more help with several activities of daily life, such as eating, dressing, and toileting. Because of this she was admitted to a psychogeriatric nursing home where her state progressed to a very severe dementia with occasional grand mal fits.

Neuropsychological Data

On admission there were no motor and sensory deficits, nor any visual or hearing problems. Her general lack of initiative and voluntary action was remarkable, but she was fully alert and not excessively distractable. She scored far below the normal score on the Cognitive Screening Test, a standardized

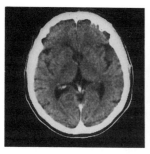
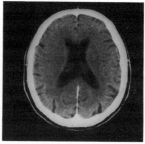
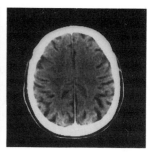

Figure 11.4. A CT-scan of RKC showing diffuse widening of the cerebral sulci and enlargement of the ventricular system. The brain's left side is represented on the right side of the CT-scan pictures. From "Impaired phonological reading in primary degenerative dementia" by H.F.A. Diesfeldt, 1991, *Brain, 114*, p. 1634. Copyright 1991 by Oxford University Press. Adapted by permission.

checklist for orientation to place and time (Deelman, Otten, & Rozema, 1984). On three trials of free recall of five object names presented as pictures, she could name all objects but never recalled more than one object name. On a forced-choice delayed recognition test she did not recognize any of the five objects. This contrasted with her occasional ability to remember recent events, her ability to recognize the staff of the day care center, and her mentioning of their names.

She had normal vision. There were no symptoms of unilateral neglect. She correctly named all colors in an 11-item test of color naming. She could read the single-digit numbers from the Ishihara plates. Calculation ability was severely disturbed. She made two errors (on "5" and "6") on reading a random sequence of the written numbers 1 to 10 aloud, and could not read any multidigit numbers (number alexia). She showed no appreciation of number values if asked to state which of two spoken or written numbers was greater. She could count out aloud from 1 to 20, but not from 20 to 1. She was unable to perform (by oral response) simple tests of the fundamental arithmetical operations of addition, subtraction, multiplication, and division, limited to single-digit numbers. On a standardized clock-reading test she correctly read one out of five clock-faces.

She was apraxic as was disclosed by her severe difficulties with sequencing the acts necessary to reach a given goal (ideational apraxia). She performed normally on tests of buccofacial gestures (e.g., stick out tongue, blow up cheeks), but made clear parapraxic errors when required to execute limb movements (e.g., comb one's hair, drink liquor) on verbal command or by imitation (ideomotor apraxia). She could easily grasp small objects between index finger and thumb of either the left or the right hand. Severe constructional apraxia was disclosed by her complete failure on copying simple drawings.

Her conversational speech was characterized by an abnormally decreased output (less than 30 words per min) associated with a general lack of initiative. Her responses to questions sometimes had an echolalic quality. Many of her sentences lacked a normal grammatical structure. Although she mostly spoke in a soft voice, her speech was not characterized by increased effort, dysarthria, or dysprosody. Striking examples of agrammatism were revealed on the Sentence Production subtest of the DATB (Deelman et al., 1981), where the words she produced to describe action pictures were mostly nouns; action verbs were extremely rare. When prompted to produce a list of words from a given category she could not retrieve a single exemplar of each of the three categories "animals," "articles of clothing," and "fruits."

She had severe difficulties in comprehending of spoken sentences, which were revealed by the Sentence Comprehension subtest of the DATB. Also her performance on the Word Comprehension subtest of the DATB fell far below that of a normal age-matched control group, both in visual and auditory presentation conditions. Her results on these multiple-choice comprehension tasks were difficult to interpret, since mere confrontation with the necessity of making a choice appeared to perplex her. Her far more adequate associative oral responses to the 15 items of a Depression Inventory, however, indicated good comprehension of personally meaningful and emotionally related concepts such as "friends," "sad," and "appetite." Her ability to repeat was tested with the Aachen Aphasia Test. She made no errors on repetition of phonemes and monosyllabic words. She could, however, not reliably repeat words of more than three syllables. Her total score of 103/150 indicates that her problems of repetition were of moderate degree of severity. On the Digit Span subtest of the WAIS, she could only repeat sequences of two digits forward and none backward. When requested to read aloud a very simple short text, she experienced severe difficulties in reading whole sentences, though she could read aloud some isolated words. She failed completely to recognize three-letter words spelled aloud by the examiner, although she was able to repeat the letter-string letter by letter. Writing was severely disturbed. She was unable to sign her name, could not copy single, written words and refused further writing tests.

In striking contrast to her impaired conversational abilities, very poor category fluency, and poor auditory comprehension and repetition, was her good performance on several picture naming tasks. She correctly and quickly named all 10 pictures (with difficult items such as "mushroom" and "pincers") and all six line-drawings of the Object Naming subtest of the CDTB (Diesfeldt, 1987). She also named correctly 17 of the 18 pictures of the Object Naming subtest of the DATB, which was well within the range of an age-matched healthy control group. Thus RKC had a profile of impairments and preserved abilities that was quite different from BHJ's profile: non-fluent spontaneous speech, poor repetition, severe oral reading and writing impairments, but relatively good naming.

Experimental Investigations of Semantic Abilities With Emphasis on
Dissociations Between Two Alzheimer Patients

Naming and Comprehension

Table 11.11 shows the results on several naming and comprehension tests
that were given to both BHJ and RKC. It is clear that RKC performed significantly better on these tasks of semantic memory, except for sentence comprehension.

Table 11.11
*Percentage Correct Naming and Comprehension in Two
Alzheimer patients*

	BHJ	RKC	Chi-square	*p*
Naming				
Pictures (DATB)	0	94	15.06	< .01
Object pictures	0	85	21.04	< .01
Action pictures	15	70	13.07	< .01
Colors	36	100	5.14	< .05
Proverb completion	0	55	15.06	< .01
Comprehension				
Words	17	78	7.69	< .01
Sentences	76	0	32.03	< .01

Note. BHJ's test results are from the first half of 1986.
RKC was tested in the second half of 1986.

The double dissociation between word and sentence comprehension in
these patients is explained by RKC's very impaired immediate memory (repetition), which impeded the comparison of a spoken sentence to a choice-ar-
ray of two simple action-pictures. Figure 11.5 contains examples of the patients'
descriptions of action pictures.

BHJ's descriptions are from the first half of 1986. Note the clear differences between the patients in fluency, paraphasias, agrammatism, use of
prepositions, and use of verbs.

BHJ: "En dat is 'n heertje met en apparaat waar die mee kan slaan" (And that is a young gentleman with an apparatus with which he can strike)

RKC: "Een jongen met een zaag" (A boy with a saw)

BHJ: "En dat zijn twee dames. O nee, dat is een heer, een dame met een heer, en die heer is in een bus en die wordt gebracht door die dame" (And those are two ladies. Oh no, that one is a gentleman, a lady and a gentleman, and that gentleman is in a bus, and that one is brought by that lady)

RKC: "In bad" (In bath)

BHJ: "En dat is een vrouwtje die gaat uit een apparaatje naar de bus" (And that is a little woman who goes from a little apparatus to the bus)

RKC: "De poes, ... weet't niet" (The cat, ... don't know)

Figure 11.5. Description of three action pictures by two Alzheimer patients.

Semantic Categorization

Semantic categorization of written words was tested by presenting both patients with 82 concrete nouns. These were divided into three sets. In the first set the patients were required to sort 40 nouns into "animal" and "non-animal" categories. The two other sets of 20 and 22 nouns, respectively, required the discrimination between "vegetables" and "articles of clothing," and words that did not belong to any of these categories. Table 11.12 shows the differences in performance between the two patients, BHJ having far more difficulty with this semantic classification than RKC. A normal control group of 12 elderly people recognized all category members (100% hits) with a false alarm rate of less than 1%.

Table 11.12
Categorization Performance in Two Alzheimer Patients

	BHJ			RKC		
Category	Hits	FA	d'	Hits	FA	d'
Animals	53	10	1.36	79	0	3.90
Vegetables	50	8	1.41	88	17	2.13
Clothing	33	20	0.40	100	40	3.34
Total	46	12	1.07	87	14	2.21[a]

Note. BHJ was tested in the second half of 1984, RKC in the second half of 1986.
[a] Chi-square = 6.76 ($p < .01$) for McNemar's test of differences between the two patients.

Oral reading

Table 11.13 compares the performance of the two patients on a series of oral reading tests. It is quite clear that RKC's oral reading was deficient for letters, digits, clocks, abstract words, verbs, function words and nonwords, but not for irregular words. There is a double dissociation between the two patients for nonword reading and irregular word reading. RKC had a pronounced difficulty reading nonwords, but not irregular words, while the reverse was true for BHJ. Furthermore it is interesting to note that RKC's, but not BHJ's reading was influenced by the abstract-concrete dimension. Concrete, or high-imagery words are defined as those which have a direct sensory referent. RKC read these words better than abstract, low-imagery words. There was a significant part-of-speech effect in that RKC read nouns better than adjectives, and adjectives better than verbs. In reading, she also made phonological, visual and derivational errors, but no semantic errors.

Table 11.13
Oral Reading Performance (Percent Correct) in two Alzheimer Patients

Test	BHJ	RKC
Letters)	100	63[a]
Numbers		
1 Digit	100	78
2 Digits	100	56
3 Digits	100	-
Clock reading	100	20
High-frequency words	97	88
Low-frequency words	97	78
High-imagery words	97	94
Low-imagery words	97	72[a]
Nouns	96	88
Adjectives	94	82
Verbs	100	63[a]
Functors	97	88[a]
Nonwords	96	32[a]
Irregular words	58	96[a]

Note. Both patients were tested in the second half of 1986.
[a] The difference between patients is significant with McNemar's test; $p < .05$.

RKC's pattern of impaired and preserved reading abilities can best be classified as a phonological dyslexia (Coltheart, 1980; Diesfeldt, 1991; Shallice & Warrington, 1980). Phonological dyslexia is the converse impairment of BHJ's surface dyslexia, which is a syndrome involving non-lexical or phonological reading. RKC's reading performance, in particular her great difficulties in reading nonwords, strongly suggests that the non-lexical reading route was deficient. Instead, she relied on the use of a lexical-semantic route by a procedure of addressed phonology for the pronunciation of familiar printed words. Also the fact that RKC's oral word reading varied with the concreteness of the word indicates that her reading depended on the use of a lexical-semantic route.

These findings are in agreement with the view that the semantic system is partitioned, according to the nature of the information, in a visual-semantic system containing codes for picture names and imageable concrete words, and a verbal-semantic system containing conceptual knowledge of a less sensory, more abstract type (Hillis, Rapp, Romani, & Caramazza, 1990). The visual semantic system would be implied in object recognition, and would via the verbal semantic system mediate access to object names in the phonological output lexicon. Remember that RKC's object naming ability was remarkably good. The visual-semantic system would by the sensory nature of the cognitive codes, mediating the access to names of imageable, concrete words (Coslett & Saffran, 1989; Funnell, 1987; Riddoch & Humphreys, 1987). A verbal-semantic system would contain word meanings that are independent of sensory properties and would be necessary to allow the correct pronunciation of abstract, low-imagery words. According to this model, RKC's access to phonological codes could be mediated by a supportive, visual-semantic system that could understand concrete sensory information and partly compensate for the deficient verbal-semantic system.

RKC's relatively intact object naming and preserved irregular word reading contrasted with the severe dysnomia of BHJ, who showed better reading of nonwords than exception words. BHJ's reading therefore reflected a breakdown in lexical routines and a strong reliance on sublexical routines for retrieving the spoken forms corresponding to written words (Howard & Franklin, 1988). In contrast, for RKC the sublexical route for reading was less reliable, but apparently she could still use a lexical-semantic routine.

By this account, there appears to be a double dissociation between naming impairment and certain types of reading disability in that intact nonword reading and impaired irregular word reading (surface dyslexia) is associatied with severe dysnomia, whereas the reverse pattern of relatively intact object naming and word reading, coupled with disturbed nonword reading is true for phonological dyslexia (Caramazza, Miceli, Silveri, & Laudanna, 1985; Denes, Cipolotti, & Semenza, 1987; Murphy, Pollatsek, & Well, 1988; Patterson, 1982; Patterson & Marcel, 1977; Shallice & Warrington, 1975, 1980).

General Discussion

It is generally held that language deterioration in AD predominantly affects lexical-semantic abilitities, whereas phonological and syntactic operations are largely spared. This was described in Case study I. The study of the second patient, however, shows that phonological abilities may become compromised first, with lexical-semantic processes remaining relatively intact.

The notion that dementia may differentially affect semantic memory abilities is clearly supported by these case studies. In the first patient, the central representation of meaning was severely compromised, whereas the second patient actually used the intact components of a visual-semantic meaning system to compensate for the loss of sublexical phonological abilities.

Other varieties of linguistic impairment in semantic memory in AD have been noted. Diesfeldt (1986) described the mixed trancortical aphasia with isolation of the speech area, caused by primary degenerative brain disease, in a 73-year old woman. Despite her complete lack of spontaneous speech (mutism) and extremely poor comprehension, the patient had a remarkably preserved ability to repeat long sentences and even corrected, in repeating, violations against the rules of grammar. Her preserved repetition ability was taken as evidence for the modular organization of the articulatory loop system in working memory (Baddeley, 1986). Funnell and Hodges (1991) studied a patient whose naming disorder appeared not to be the result of an impairment in the central visual or semantic process (cf. BHJ), but rather caused by a disorder of access from correct semantic descriptions to their name entries in the phonological lexicon.

Different Types of Memory: The Distinction Between Episodic, Semantic, and Procedural Memory Applied to Single-Cases

Tulving's distinction between different types of memory appeared to be useful as a general framework for the analysis of several cognitive skills and abilities in these two patients. Evident strengths of Tulving's (1985) tripartite conceptualization of memory are its simplicity and coherence. It became clear from these case studies that aspects of semantic and procedural memory can indeed dissociate in a systematic way. Thus, preserved phonological and syntactic skills (procedural knowledge) could be demonstrated in a patient whose semantic knowledge was severely impaired. Furthermore, it is known from studies in other aphasic patients and AD patients that they may show semantic priming effects for words they do not understand, indicating intact non-declarative or procedural knowledge in the absence of semantic knowledge (Albert & Milberg, 1989; Chertkow, Bub, & Seidenberg, 1989). In contrast, the second patient suffered from impairments to such elementary procedures as speaking, reading, and writing, but showed relatively preserved object naming and oral reading of high-imagery words. Apparently, she retained sufficient semantic knowledge to partly compensate for her phonological disabilities. Both patients showed relatively good retention of day-to-day events and episodes, a capacity that appeared out of proportion to their impairments in other domains of memory.

According to Tulving's (1985) proposal, episodic memory depends on both procedural and semantic memory. Impairments of semantic processing would therefore predict specific episodic memory impairments for information that is not well understood. This was clearly demonstrated by the first patient whose impairment in episodic recognition of human faces was not the consequence of a general deficit (for his episodic retention of village-scenes was perfect), but was a material-specific learning-deficit, resulting from his agnosia for faces.

A weakness of such gross concepts as episodic, semantic, or procedural memory is that each of these large domains of experience and knowledge may have multiple components. Actually, this was demonstrated in the extensive study of our first patient, where an orderly pattern of preserved and impaired function within the domain of semantic memory appeared to exist. Thus, the impression of homogeneous impairment of semantic memory in group studies of dementia patients may be misleading. Clearly, there are patients who are more impaired in one domain of semantic memory than in others. Single-case studies are very apt to elucidate these differences.

The Longitudinal Approach to the Study of Semantic Impairment in Dementia

Another advantage of intensive individual case-studies is that they may be designed and carried out as longitudinal studies. By following the course of his illness over almost 7 years, we were able to show that BHJ's disorder of lexical and visual comprehension progressed along the lines of a cognitive neuropsychological model that predicts the possibility of selective impairment of lexico-semantic knowledge while rule-governed processes, such as syntax and phonology, are spared. The time lag between semantic impairment and clear signs of loss of grammatical knowledge was almost 4 years in this case. Initially, the patient presented with symptoms of slowly progressive aphasia, but only by following the course of his illness it could be established that a global dementia syndrome eventually developed. It is still an unsettled issue whether a slowly progressive aphasia or agnosia generally ends as a limited impairment to semantic memory, or whether each patient runs the risk of global dementia in the course of the degenerative brain disease that underlies the initial cognitive symptoms. Longitudinal studies using comprehensive neuropsychological assessment are needed to resolve this issue, which is also relevant to the issue of whether patients and their caregivers must be told that progressive aphasia may be a likely precursor for global dementia.

At present, investigators of dementia should know that dementia is not always preluded by a general forgetfulness of recent episodes. We should be aware of the importance of disorders of semantic or procedural memory that might be the initial symptoms of degenerative brain disease. The value of comprehensive and repeated neuropsychological assessments cannot be underestimated. In the domain of semantic and procedural memory many functions can be found to remain intact in dementia. It is very important that we learn how patients use their intact capabilities to compensate for loss in other areas of cognitive function.

References

Albert, M. S., & Milberg, W. (1989). Semantic processing in patients with Alzheimer's disease. *Brain and Language, 37,* 163-171.

American Psychiatric Association. (1980). *Diagnostic and Statistical Manual of Mental Disorders* (3rd ed.). Washington DC: American Psychiatric Association.

American Psychiatric Association. (1987). *Diagnostic and Statistical Manual of Mental Disorders* (3rd ed. revised). Washington DC: American Psychiatric Association.

Baddeley, A. D. (1986). *Working memory.* Oxford: Oxford University Press.

Baddeley, A. D. (1990). *Human memory: Theory and practice.* Hillsdale, NJ: Erlbaum Associates.

Berg, I. J., & Deelman, B. G. (1988). Een waarschuwing voor leeftijdseffecten bij de SAN-afasietest. *Nederlands Tijdschrift voor de Psychologie, 43,* 388-391.

Berndt, R. S., Basili, A., & Caramazza, A. (1987). Dissociation of functions in a case of transcortical sensory aphasia. *Cognitive Neuropsychology, 4*, 79-107.

Bub, D. N., Black, S., Hampson, E., & Kertesz, A. (1988). Semantic encoding of pictures and words: Some neuropsychological observations. *Cognitive Neuropsychology, 5*, 27-66.

Butterworth, B., Howard, D., & McLoughlin, P. (1984). The semantic deficit in aphasia: The relationship between semantic errors in auditory comprehension and picture naming. *Neuropsychologia, 22*, 409-426.

Caramazza, A., Miceli, G., Silveri, M. C., & Laudanna, A. (1985). Reading mechanisms and the organization of the lexicon: Evidence from acquired dyslexia. *Cognitive Neuropsychology, 2*, 81-114.

Chertkow, H., & Bub, D. N. (1990). Semantic memory loss in Alzheimer-type dementia. In M. F. Schwartz (Ed.), *Modular deficits in Alzheimer-type dementia*. Cambridge, MA: MIT Press.

Chertkow, H., Bub, D. N., & Seidenberg, M. (1989). Priming and semantic memory loss in Alzheimer's disease. *Brain and Language, 36*, 420-446.

Coltheart, M. (1980). Deep dyslexia: A review of the syndrome. In M. Coltheart, K. Patterson, & J. C. Marshall (Eds.), *Deep dyslexia*. London: Routledge and Kegan Paul.

Coslett, H. B., Roeltgen, D. P., Rothi, L. G., & Heilman, K. M. (1987). Transcortical sensory aphasia: Evidence for subtypes. *Brain and Language, 32*, 362-378.

Coslett, H. B., & Saffran, E. M. (1989). Preserved object recognition and reading comprehension in optic aphasia. *Brain, 112*, 1091-1110.

De Renzi, E., Liotti, M., & Nichelli, P. (1987). Semantic amnesia with preservation of autobiographic memory: A case report. *Cortex, 23*, 575-597.

Deelman, B. G., Koning-Haanstra, M., Liebrand, W. B. G., & Van den Burg, W. (1981). *S.A.N. Test: Een afasietest voor auditief taalbegrip en mondeling taalgebruik*. Lisse: Swets and Zeitlinger.

Deelman, B. G., Otten, V., & Rozema, J. (1984). Een Nederlandse dementieschaal: Een bewerking van Pfeiffers SPMSQ. *De Psycholoog, 19*, 644.

Denes, G., Cipolotti, L., & Semenza, C. (1987). How does a phonological dyslexic read words she has never seen? *Cognitive Neuropsychology, 4*, 11-31.

Diesfeldt, H. F. A. (1983). *De draad kwijt: Over organisatie van het geheugen bij dementie* [Organization of memory in dementia]. Deventer: Van Loghum Slaterus.

Diesfeldt, H. F. A. (1985). Verbal fluency in senile dementia: An analysis of search and knowledge. *Archives of Gerontology and Geriatrics, 4*, 231-239.

Diesfeldt, H. F. A. (1986). Een psycholinguästisch onderzoek bij een patiënt met echolalie [Psycholinguistic analysis of echolalia and isolation syndrome in a patient with primary degenerative dementia]. *Tijdschrift voor Gerontologie en Geriatrie, 17*, 191-200.

Diesfeldt, H. F. A. (1987). *Psychologisch onderzoek van psychogeriatrische patiënten volgens de methode van Cahn en Diesfeldt*. Laren: Stichting Verpleeghuizen Nederland.

Diesfeldt, H. F. A. (1989). Semantic impairment in senile dementia of the Alzheimer type. *Aphasiology, 3*, 41-54.

Diesfeldt, H. F. A. (1991). Impaired phonological reading in primary degenerative dementia. *Brain, 114*, 1631-1646.

Diesfeldt, H. F. A., & Vink, M. T. (1989). Visuele patroonanalyse en redeneren: Ravens Colored Progressive Matrices bij volwassenen van hoge tot zeer hoge leeftijd [Raven's Colored Progressive Matrices, a test of visuo-perceptual skills and reasoning by analogy in the old-old]. *Tijdschrift voor Gerontologie en Geriatrie, 20*, 241-247.

Ellis, A. W., & Young, A. W. (1988). *Human cognitive neuropsychology*. Hove: Erlbaum.

Farah, M. J. (1990). *Visual agnosia: Disorders of object recognition and what they tell us about normal vision*. Cambridge, MA: MIT Press.

262   *H. F. A. Diesfeldt*

Friedman, R. B. (1988). Acquired alexia. In F. Boller & J. Grafman (Eds.), *Handbook of Neuropsychology* (Vol. 1). Amsterdam: Elsevier Science.

Funnell, E. (1987). Object concepts and object names: some deductions from acquired disorders of word processing. In G. W. Humphreys, & M. J. Riddoch (Eds.), *Visual object processing: A cognitive neuropsychological approach.* Hove: Erlbaum.

Funnell, E., & Hodges, J. R. (1991). Progressive loss of access to spoken word forms in a case of Alzheimer's disease. *Proceedings of the Royal Society of London B, 243,* 173-179.

Herlitz, A. (1991). *Remembering in Alzheimer's disease: Utilization of cognitive support.* Doctoral dissertation, University of Umeå, Umeå, Sweden.

Hillis, A. E., Rapp, B., Romani, C., & Caramazza, A. (1990). Selective impairment of semantics in lexical processing. *Cognitive Neuropsychology, 7,* 191-243.

Howard, D., & Franklin, S. (1988). *Missing the meaning? A cognitive neuropsychological case study of the processing of words by an aphasic patient.* Cambridge, MA: MIT Press.

Howard, D., & Hatfield, F. M. (1987). *Aphasia therapy: Historical and contemporary issues.* Hove: Erlbaum.

Huber, W., Poeck, K., Weniger, D., & Willmes, K. (1983). Der *Aachener Aphasie Test (AAT).* Göttingen: Hogrefe.

Hudson, P. T. W., & Bergman, M. W. (1985). Lexical knowledge in word recognition: Word length and word frequency in naming and lexical decision tasks. *Journal of Memory and Language, 24,* 46-58.

Humphreys, G. W., & Bruce, V. (1989). *Visual cognition: Computational, experimental and neuropsychological perspectives.* Hove: Erlbaum.

Humphreys, G. W., & Riddoch, M. J. (1987). *To see but not to see: A case study of visual agnosia.* Hillsdale, NJ: Erlbaum.

Ishihara, S. (1983). *The series of plates designed as a test for color-blindness.* Tokyo: Kanehara.

Kohnstamm, G. A., Schaerlaekens, A. M., de Vries, A. K., Akkerhuis, G. W., & Froonincksx, M. (1981). *Nieuwe streeflijst woordenschat.* Lisse: Swets & Zeitlinger.

Marshall, J. C. (1987). Routes and representations in the processing of written language. In E. Keller, & M. Gopnik (Eds.), *Motor and sensory processing of language.* Hillsdale, NJ: Erlbaum.

Marshall, J. C., & Newcombe, F. (1973). Patterns of paralexia: A psycholinguistic approach. *Journal of Psycholinguistic Research, 2,* 175-199.

Martin, A. (1987). Representation of semantic and spatial knowledge in Alzheimer's patients: Implications for models of preserved learning in amnesia. *Journal of Clinical and Experimental Neuropsychology, 9,* 191-224.

Martin, A., Brouwers, P., Lalonde, F., Cox, C., Teleska, P., Fedio, P., & Foster, N. L. (1986). Towards a behavioral typology of Alzheimer's patients. *Journal of Clinical and Experimental Neuropsychology, 8,* 594-610.

McCarthy, R. A., & Warrington, E. K. (1986a). Phonological reading: Phenomena and paradoxes. *Cortex, 22,* 359-380.

McCarthy, R. A., & Warrington, E. K. (1986b). Visual associative agnosia: A clinico-anatomical study of a single case. *Journal of Neurology, Neurosurgery, and Psychiatry, 49,* 1233-1240.

McCarthy, R. A., & Warrington, E. K. (1990). *Cognitive neuropsychology: A clinical introduction.* San Diego, CA: Academic Press.

McKhann, G., Drachman, D. A., Folstein, M. F., Katzman, R., Price, D. L., & Stadlan, E. (1984). Clinical diagnosis of Alzheimer's disease: Report of the NINCDS-ADRDA Work Group under the auspices of Department of Health and Human Services Task Force on Alzheimer's disease. *Neurology, 34,* 939-944.

Mehler, M. F. (1988). Mixed transcortical aphasia in nonfamilial dysphasic dementia. *Cortex, 24,* 545-554.

Murphy, L. A., Pollatsek, A., & Well, A. D. (1988). Developmental dyslexia and word retrieval deficits. *Brain and Language, 35,* 1-23.

Nebes, R. D. (1989). Semantic memory in Alzheimer's disease. *Psychological Bulletin, 106,* 377-394.

Patterson, K. E. (1981). Neuropsychological approaches to the study of reading. *British Journal of Psychology, 72,* 151-174.

Patterson, K. E. (1982). The relation between reading and phonological coding: Further neuropsychological observations. In A. W. Ellis (Ed.), *Normality and pathology in cognitive functions.* London: Academic Press.

Patterson, K. E., & Marcel, A. J. (1977). Aphasia, dyslexia, and the phonological coding of written words. *Quarterly Journal of Experimental Psychology, 29,* 307-318.

Riddoch, M. J., & Humphreys, G. W. (1987). Picture naming. In G. W. Humphreys & M. J. Riddoch (Eds.), *Visual object processing: A cognitive neuropsychological approach.* Hove: Erlbaum.

Schwartz, M. F., & Chawluk, J. B. (1990). Deterioration of language in progressive aphasia: A case study. In M. F. Schwartz (Ed.), *Modular deficits in Alzheimer-type dementia.* Cambridge, MA: MIT Press.

Schwartz, M. F., Marin, O. S. M., & Saffran, E. M. (1979). Dissociations of language function in dementia: A case study. *Brain and Language, 7,* 277-306.

Schwartz, M. F., Saffran, E. M., & Marin, O. S. M. (1980). Fractionating the reading process in dementia: Evidence for word-specific print-to-sound associations. In M. Coltheart, K. Patterson, & J. C. Marshall (Eds.), *Deep dyslexia.* London: Routledge and Kegan Paul.

Shallice, T., & Warrington, E. K. (1975). Word recognition in a phonemic dyslexic patient. *Quarterly Journal of Experimental Psychology, 27,* 187-199.

Shallice, T., & Warrington, E. K. (1980). Single and multiple component central dyslexic syndromes. In M. Coltheart, K. Patterson, & J. C. Marshall (Eds.), *Deep dyslexia.* London: Routledge and Kegan Paul.

Shallice, T., Warrington, E. K., & McCarthy, R. A. (1983). Reading without semantics. *Quarterly Journal of Experimental Psychology, 35A,* 111-138.

Snowden, J. S., Goulding, P. J., & Neary, D. (1989). Semantic dementia: A form of circumscribed cerebral atrophy. *Behavioral Neurology, 2,* 167-182.

Tulving, E. (1985). How many memory systems are there? *American Psychologist, 40,* 385-398.

Uit den Boogaart, P. C. (1975). *Woordfrequenties in geschreven en gesproken Nederlands.* Utrecht: Oosthoek, Scheltema, & Holkema.

Van der Kam, P., Mol, F., & Wimmers, M. F. H. (1971). *Beoordelingsschaal voor ouder patiënten.* Deventer: Van Loghum Slaterus.

Van Loon-Vervoorn, W. A. (1985). *Voorstelbaarheidswaarden van Nederlandse woorden.* Lisse: Swets & Zeitlinger.

Warrington, E. K. (1975). The selective impairment of semantic memory. *Quarterly Journal of Experimental Psychology, 27,* 635-657.

Warrington, E. K. (1984). *Recognition Memory Test.* Windsor: Nelson.

Warrington, E. K., & Taylor, A. M. (1978). Two categorical stages of object recognition. *Perception, 7,* 695-705.

Winslow Press. (1980). *Photographic Teaching Materials: Basic Sequences.* Winslow: Winslow Press.

Section V

SUBJECTIVE ASSESSMENT

Memory Functioning in Dementia – L. Bäckman (Editor)

12 Use of Informants' Reports to Study Memory Changes in Dementia

Anthony F. Jorm

The Australian National University

Introduction

Over recent years there has been a concern that laboratory and clinical tests of memory do not relate to everyday life. In an effort to overcome this concern, some researchers have developed questionnaires which ask people about their memory performance in everyday situations. As questionnaires have proved useful in other areas of psychology, the extension of this approach to memory would seem promising. However, while memory questionnaires have proved highly reliable, the evidence on their validity has been disappointing. At best, they show only modest correlations with objectively-tested memory performance. This discrepancy between questionnaires and objective tests has been referred to as the *memory introspection paradox* and attributed to the inability of individuals with a poor memory to remember their own memory performance (Herrmann, 1982). Self-assessment of memory is also distorted by non-memory factors. It has been found that assessing one's own memory as poor is related to depression (O'Connor, Pollitt, Roth, Brook, & Reiss, 1990; Williams, Little, Scales, & Blockman, 1987) and to the personality trait of neuroticism (Poitrenaud, Malbezin, & Guez, 1989). In dementia, the limitations of self-assessment are compounded even further by difficulties in even comprehending a questionnaire.

An alternative which overcomes these disadvantages is to have a questionnaire completed by an informant rather than the subject. Informant's reports retain the advantage of covering everyday functioning, but at the same time avoid the limitations imposed by the subject's own memory and affective state. While informants do not have access to covert aspects of the subject's performance, this may not necessarily be a disadvantage. Even for the subject assessing his or her own memory, covert performance is difficult to judge because subjects have no knowledge of anyone else's covert processes to use as a basis for making comparisons. In being restricted to observable performance, informants may be avoiding a source of potentially distorting information.

The present chapter describes informant instruments which have been developed to assess cognitive performance, including memory performance. It reviews findings on the reliability and validity of these instruments and specifically considers their usefulness for screening and assessment of dementing patients. Finally, the chapter describes some research on the use of an informant questionnaire to study more theoretically-oriented aspects of memory deficits in dementia.

Review of Informant Instruments

A number of informant instruments have been developed in recent years to tap cognitive performance. Many of these cover a broad range of cognitive tasks, rather than just memory, and some assess non-cognitive functions as well. While most informant instruments have been developed for use with elderly subjects, including those with dementia, some have been developed with other groups in mind (e.g., the head injured). All informant instruments are reviewed here, but the focus is primarily on their use with dementing subjects. Sample items from the various instruments discussed below are shown in Table 12.1.

Geriatric Evaluation by Relatives Rating Instrument (GERRI)

The GERRI was developed by Schwartz (1983) to assess the functioning of dementing patients in their home environment. There are 49 items grouped into three clusters: cognitive functioning, social functioning, and mood. Only the cognitive cluster is of interest here. This cluster consists of 21 items, most of which deal with memory functioning. Items are rated by informants on a five-point scale ranging from "almost all of the time" to "almost never."

In the initial study with the GERRI, Schwartz (1983) had informants assess 45 patients with primary degenerative dementia. Each patient was independently rated by two informants. The agreement between the raters was found to be high, with an intraclass correlation of .96 for cognitive functioning. Internal consistency was also very high for the cognitive items (alpha = .95). Validity of this instrument was assessed by comparing demented patients in three stages of severity. The cognitive functioning cluster was found to discriminate these three groups of patients. Although the three clusters were designed to be independent, Schwartz (1983) reported that they were intercorrelated, which could imply that a common factor underlies the three clusters.

Table 12.1
Sample Items From Informant Instruments

Geriatric Evaluation by Relatives Rating Instrument (GERRI)

Remembers name of spouse/children living with him/her.
Does not recognize familiar people.
Remembers where clothes are placed.
Remembers to lock door when leaving the house.

Cognitive Behavior Rating Scale (CBRS)

Has difficulty remembering the names of friends.
Hides objects.
Has difficulty following instructions.
Seems disoriented and confused.

Present Functioning Questionnaire (PFQ)

Problems remembering previous actions on the same day.
Problems maintaining a train of thought.
Problems recognizing the date or day of week.
Problems understanding others.

Cambridge Mental Disorders of the Elderly Examination (CAMDEX)

Does he/she have more difficulty remembering short lists of items, e.g. shopping?
Does he/she have difficulty remembering recent events, e.g. when he/she last saw you, or what happened the day before?
Does he/she have difficulty finding the way about home (or ward), e.g. finding the toilet?
Does he/she have difficulty finding the way around the neighbourhood, e.g. to the shops or Post Office near home?

Relatives' Questionnaire

Forgetting when something happened; for example whether it was yesterday or last week.
Forgetting where he has put something. Losing things around the house.
Unable to pick up a new skill such as a game or working some new gadget after he has practised it once or twice.
Finding that a word is "on the tip of his tongue".

Inpatient Memory Impairment Scale (IMIS)

Has difficulty remembering the names of other patients and staff.
Has difficulty recalling recent family or personal history.
Has difficulty recalling events or activities of the previous day.
Learns new jobs, skills, or recreational activities slowly.

Informant Questionnaire on Cognitive Decline in the Elderly (IQCODE)

Remembering the names of family and friends.
Remembering what day and month it is.
Understanding magazine or newspaper articles.
Knowing about important historical events of the past.

A later study by Rosenbilds, Goldney, Gilchrist, Martin, and Connelly (1986) used the GERRI with 51 patients admitted to a psychogeriatric unit. These patients were also tested with the Mini-Mental State Examination, a brief cognitive screening test for dementia, and nurses rated them with the London Psychogeriatric Rating Scale, which contains a subscale for measuring Mental Disorganization. The informants' ratings on the Cognitive Functioning subscale of the GERRI correlated with both the Mini-Mental State ($r = .59$) and the Mental Disorganization ratings from nurses ($r = .54$). These results support the validity of the relatives' ratings.

Cognitive Behavior Rating Scale (CBRS)

The CBRS was designed by Williams (1987) to cover a broad range of everyday manifestations of cognitive impairment, but also covers some non-cognitive behavioral changes. The 116 items are organized into nine subscales: Language Deficit, Apraxia, Disorientation, Agitation, Need for Routine, Depression, Higher Cognitive Deficits, Memory Disorder, and Dementia. Items were assigned to the various subscales on the basis of groupings by a panel of neuropsychologists. Most items are rated on a five-point scale ranging from "Not at all like this person" to "Extremely like this person," although some items use a scale ranging from "Superior" to "Very Poor."

Only one study has been reported with the CBRS (Williams, Klein, Little, & Haban, 1986). In this study validity was assessed by comparing 30 dementia cases with 30 matched controls. Each of the cognitive subscales was found to discriminate between the two groups. Reliability was assessed in a normal sample in terms of both internal consistency and test-retest. Alphas ranged from .78 to .92 and retest correlations from .61 to .94, indicating acceptable-to-good reliability. The correlations between the subscales were not reported, so it is not known to what extent they are measuring separate constructs.

Present Functioning Questionnaire (PFQ)

The PFQ, developed by Crockett, Tuokko, Koch, and Parks (1989), is a checklist of problems of everyday functioning commonly found in the elderly. The checklist is filled out by a clinician on the basis of an interview with an informant. The items of the PFQ are grouped to cover five areas: memory functioning, everyday skills, language skills, self care, and personality. Although only one section of the PFQ deals with memory, the sections on everyday skills and language skills cover other closely related cognitive activities.

The only data on the PFQ come from a study of 348 referrals to an Alzheimer's Disease and Related Disorders Clinic and 70 normal elderly volunteers. Each of three cognitive subscales was found to discriminate clearly between the memory-disordered and normal groups, providing evidence of their concurrent validity. Internal consistency of these three subscales was found to be high (.80 - .88), but other types of reliability have not been reported. The three cognitive subscales were highly intercorrelated (.57 - .75) indicating they were measuring largely the same construct.

Cambridge Mental Disorders of the Elderly Examination (CAMDEX)

The CAMDEX is a structured psychiatric interview incorporating a mental status examination and cognitive testing of the subject and an interview with an informant (Roth et al., 1986). The informant interview covers a range of areas with items being rated on a three-point scale ranging from "no difficulty" to "great difficulty." The only items relevant here are those covering memory. The interview contains two items about loss of memory for recent events and three items about orientation to person and place. Using data from a community survey of dementia, O'Connor, Pollitt, Brook, and Reiss (1989) calculated informant subscores for memory and orientation and correlated these with objective memory and orientation scores derived from the cognitive testing in the CAMDEX. They found that informant-reported memory was correlated with memory test performance (r = .67), as was informant-reported orientation with orientation test performance (r = .61). These results support the validity of the informants' reports. Unfortunately, the correlation between the memory and orientation subscales was not reported, so it is unknown whether they are tapping independent constructs.

Relatives' Questionnaire

The Relatives' Questionnaire grew out of research by Sunderland, Harris, and Baddeley (1983) on the assessment of everyday memory in head-injured patients. For this study, they developed a set of 35 items dealing with everyday memory functioning which were administered to both the patients and their relatives who acted as informants. The Relatives' Questionnaire was found to discriminate the head-injured group from normals and to correlate with a number of episodic memory tests. By contrast, the Patients' Questionnaire did rather poorly. Multidimensional scaling and cluster analysis were carried out on the items of both questionnaires in an effort to distinguish types of everyday memory failure, but no clear clusters emerged. The Relatives' Questionnaire appeared to be measuring global memory impairment.

In later work by Sunderland, Harris, and Gleave (1984), the Relatives' Questionnaire was revised by retaining the best items of the original questionnaire and adding new ones to give a 28-item version. Items were rated on an eight-point scale of frequency ranging from "not at all in the past 3 months" to "more than once a day." This questionnaire was designed to be administered through the post and was sent to patients and relatives of mild and severe head injury groups. As in the earlier study, there was evidence for the validity of the Relatives' Questionnaire. This discriminated between the two head-injured groups, unlike the Patients' Questionnaire. As before, the Relatives' Questionnaire appeared to be measuring a global factor of memory performance. High intercorrelations were found between the items, with principal components analysis revealing a large first factor.

Subsequently, Sunderland, Watts, Baddeley, and Harris (1986) administered the Relatives' Questionnaire to informants of a group of 60 normal elderly subjects. The questionnaire was administered on two occasions over a period of 3-12 months and the test-retest correlation was found to be poor (r = .51). The subjects were also administered a series of episodic memory tests like those used in the earlier work with head-injured patients. In this study, however, the correlations between the Relatives' Questionnaire and objective tests were found to be poor. The highest correlation was only .26. Sunderland et al.'s (1986) explanation for the poor performance of the Relatives' Questionnaire in this study was that most of the informants were themselves elderly and they may not have accurately recalled instances of memory failure in the subjects.

The most recent study with the Relatives' Questionnaire involved 78 patients who were assessed seven months after a stroke (Lincoln & Tinson, 1989). The patients were also given the Rivermead Behavioural Memory Test, a clinical test battery which uses everyday memory tasks. Supporting the validity of the Relatives' Questionnaire, it was found to correlate moderately well with the Rivermead (rho = .46)

Inpatient Memory Impairment Scale (IMIS)

The IMIS is a 10-item questionnaire which is filled out by nurses (Knight & Godfrey, 1984). Items refer to memory problems likely to be encountered in a hospital setting and are rated from 0 (always) to 5 (not at all). This scale was developed using 20 chronic alcoholic patients, most of whom had been diagnosed with either amnesic syndrome or dementia. Each patient was rated by two nurses and the scores averaged to give greater reliability. Inter-rater reliability was found to be .75 when one rater was used, and rose to .86 when two raters were averaged. Internal consistency of the scale was found to be high (.94). When the IMIS was correlated with a range of memory tests, it was found to correlate .77 with the mean score on practical and experimental memory tasks, .86 with the mean score on questionnaires evaluating orientation and memory for recent events, and .68 with the Wechsler Memory Scale.

In a later study, Godfrey and Knight (1988) used the IMIS with 18 amnesics, 20 chronic alcoholics, and 20 psychiatric patients. Inter-rater reliability was .69 when one rater was used, rising to .81 when two raters were averaged. When the scale was correlated with memory tests, the correlations ranged from .64 to .81. The IMIS was also found to discriminate between the amnesic group and the other two groups. Overall, the validity of the IMIS appears to be excellent, but it is limited in usefulness by being applicable only to hospital residents.

Informant Questionnaire on Cognitive Decline in the Elderly (IQCODE)

An advantage of informant reports over direct cognitive testing is that the informant often has knowledge of the subject's past performance as well as their present performance. Thus, the informant can report on whether the subject's present performance represents a change from that seen previously. Jorm and Korten (1988) developed a 39-item interview to assess cognitive decline in this way. In this interview each item was rated on a five-point scale ranging from "1. Has become much better in the last 10 years" to " 5. Has become much worse in the last 10 years." The interview was made up of items to assess various aspects of memory and intelligence. A preliminary psycho-metric analysis led to 13 items being eliminated, mainly because informants too often felt unable to rate them. The resulting 26-item interview was found to have excellent internal consistency (alpha = .96) and component scores (e.g., memory and intelligence) were found to intercorrelate highly. This finding suggested that the interview was largely measuring a single dimension of cog-nitive decline. The total score for the interview was found to correlate highly with Folstein, Folstein, and McHugh's (1975) Mini-Mental State Examination (r = .74), yet to be relatively independent of indicators of pre-morbid ability, such as level of education and word reading skill.

In later research, a self-administered questionnaire version of the inter-view was developed and dubbed the IQCODE. This questionnaire has now been administered to several different samples of informants: (a) 362 inform-ants who were members of the Alzheimer's Disease and Related Disorders Society and had a dementing relative or friend (Jorm, Scott, & Jacomb, 1989), (b) 613 informants of people aged 70+ who were recruited from the general population (Jorm & Jacomb, 1989), (c) informants of 90 elderly patients at-tending general practitioners (Bowers, Jorm, Henderson, & Harris, 1990), and (d) informants of 69 geriatric patients (Jorm, Scott, Cullen, & Mackinnon, 1991).

The reliability of the IQCODE has been examined in several of these samples. Internal consistency has been found to be high with both dementing subjects (alpha = .93) (Jorm et al., 1989) and subjects from the general popu-lation (alpha = .95) (Jorm & Jacomb, 1989). Test-retest reliability is also high, with a retest correlation of .96 over a few days (Jorm et al., 1991) through to .75 over a year (Jorm & Jacomb, 1989).

Principal components analysis of the IQCODE has shown a large gene-ral factor, despite the diversity of cognitive tasks covered by the 26 items. Jorm et al. (1989) found the first principal component to account for 42% of the variance, with the next three components accounting for only 10%, 7%, and 4% of the variance, respectively. Similarly, Jorm and Jacomb (1989) found the first principal component to account for 48% of the variance, with later components accounting only for 8%, 5%, and 4%. Rotation of these components failed to produce theoretically interpretable factors.

The validity of the IQCODE has been assessed by correlating it with the Mini-Mental State Examination. Bowers et al. (1990) reported a correlation of .75 in a general practice sample, while Jorm et al. (1991) found a correlation of .54 in a geriatric patient sample. These correlations emerged despite the IQCODE purporting to be a measure of decline while the Mini-Mental is a measure of current performance. If the IQCODE reflects decline, it should be uncorrelated with indicators of pre-morbid ability. Indeed, it is virtually uncorrelated both with education (Jorm & Jacomb, 1989) and with word reading skill (Jorm et al., 1991), while traditional tests of cognitive impairment like the Mini-Mental are contaminated by pre-morbid ability (Jorm et al., 1991).

Another method of evaluating validity is via agreement with clinical judgment of dementia. Jorm and Jacomb (1989) reported that the dementing sample and the general practice sample were clearly discriminated by each of the 26 IQCODE items as well as by the total score. Bowers et al. (1990) asked general practitioners to rate patients for dementia on a scale of "not at all," "mild," "moderate," or "severe." They reported a correlation of .65 between the IQCODE and the general practitioners' ratings. Finally, Jorm et al. (1991) compared the IQCODE and Mini-Mental as screening tests for dementia using as the criterion diagnosis by a clinician and by a standardized diagnostic interview. Using receiver operating characteristics to evaluate performance, the IQCODE was found to perform at least as well as the Mini-Mental.

Other Studies of Informants' Reports

There are other studies which have not specifically developed instruments for informants, but nevertheless provide data relevant to the validity of informants' assessments. Probably the earliest informant-based instrument for use with demented patients is the Blessed Dementia Scale (Blessed, Tomlinson, & Roth, 1968). This scale consists of items covering cognitive function, activities of daily living, and personality change. The items are scored by a clinician on the basis of an interview with an informant. Despite the diverse coverage of the items, they are summed to give an overall dementia score. It is therefore impossible to examine the cognitive items alone in most published data. An exception is a study by Erkinjuntti, Hokkanen, Sulkava, and Palo (1988) which reported single-item data on 105 demented patients compared to 123 community residents. They reported that each of the five items dealing with memory clearly discriminated the demented patients from the community residents. In a study of the validity of the Rivermead Behavioural Memory Test, Wilson, Cockburn, Baddeley, and Hiorns (1989) asked relatives of 176 brain-damaged patients to give a rating of everyday memory problems. They found that the relatives' ratings correlated .57 with the Rivermead score, .57 with paired associate learning, .40 with recognition memory for words, and .23 with recognition memory for faces. Finally, Zelinski, Gilewski, and Anthony-Bergstone (1990) reported data on the Memory Functioning Questionnaire, a self-report questionnaire on everyday memory. In one study they gave an informant version of this questionnaire to 31 spouses of their middle-aged and elderly subjects. The informant version was found to correlate highly with a range of memory tests, with multiple correlations ranging from .66 to .77. These correlations were higher than these found with the usual self-report version of the questionnaire.

Conclusions on Informant Instruments

The array of informant instruments available is quite diverse in terms of item coverage (memory vs. general cognitive functioning), the type of informant used (relatives vs. nurses), mode of administration (self completion vs. interview by clinician), and the subject population studied (normal aged, brain damaged, demented, amnesic). Although this diversity might be expected to make generalizations difficult, the findings from informant instruments have, in fact, been remarkably consistent. From the preceding review, the following generalizations can be drawn. First, the reliability of informant instruments is high, whether evaluated in terms of internal consistency, test-retest or interrater reliability. Second, informant instruments seem to be largely measuring a general factor of cognitive functioning. This general factor is revealed by high intercorrelations among subscales, and by large first factors in principal components analyses. Third, informant instruments have moderate to high correlations with dementia screening tests and with tests of episodic memory. Finally, informant instruments discriminate various clinical groups from normals, including cases of dementia, head injury and amnesia. They also discriminate between different levels of dementia severity.

Assessing Theoretically-Interesting Memory Processes

It is clear that informants can make valid assessments of cognitive performance and that their assessments could be useful in clinical practice. A separate issue is whether they can make assessments which would be of use to researchers with a more theoretical interest in everyday memory processes. In other words, do informants observe differences between everyday behaviors which correspond to the theoretical distinctions which cognitive psychologists have made based on laboratory research? The evidence from factor analysis of informant questionnaires shows that they are largely assessing a single global dimension of cognitive performance. Separate factors reflecting theoretically meaningful processes have not emerged in any study. Nevertheless, the issue merits further investigation in order to establish the limits of informant questionnaires as a means of studying memory processes.

To investigate this issue further, items from the IQCODE were classified into subscales on theoretical grounds. First of all, the author and a colleague grouped the items as reflecting either episodic, semantic, or procedural memory. We reached consensus that four of the items reflected episodic memory, seven reflected semantic memory, and one procedural memory. Fourteen items did not clearly fit any of these categories. Because there was only one procedural memory item, this type of memory was not considered further. Table 12.2 shows the items making up the episodic and semantic memory subscales. The distinction between episodic and semantic memory is relevant because of the claim that episodic memory is impaired in both normal aging and Alzheimer's disease (although much more so in the latter), whereas semantic memory is impaired in Alzheimer's disease but relatively unaffected in normal aging (Nebes, 1989).

Another possible distinction is between recent learning and use of previously acquired information. The items were classified by consensus according to this distinction as shown in Table 12.3. There were five items reflecting recent learning and 10 reflecting use of previously acquired information, with the other 11 not being readily classifiable. Conventional clinical wisdom embodied in diagnostic criteria for dementia (World Health Organization, 1990) is that the capacity for recent learning is more impaired than the use of previously acquired information.

Table 12.2
IQCODE Items Tapping Episodic and Semantic Memory

Episodic Memory

Remembering things that have happened recently.
Recalling conversations a few days later.
Remembering where to find things which have been put in a different place from usual.
Remembering things that happened to her/him when s/he was young.

Semantic Memory

Recognizing the faces of family and friends.
Remembering the names of family and friends.
Remembering things about family and friends, e.g. occupations, birthdays, addresses.
Remembering her/his address and telephone number.
Remembering where things are usually kept.
Understanding the meaning of unusual words.
Knowing about important historical events of the past.

These four subscales were examined using data from the study by Jorm & Jacomb (1989). This study involved administering the IQCODE by mail to a general population sample of informants and to a sample of members of the Alzheimer's Disease and Related Disorders Society. The subscales were scored by averaging ratings over each of the items. Thus, each subscale score ranged from 1 to 5, with 1 representing considerable improvement in cognitive function, 5 representing a considerable deterioration, and 3 representing no change.

Table 12.3
IQCODE Items Tapping Recent Learning and Use of Previously Acquired Information

Recent Learning

Remembering things that have happened recently.
Recalling conversations a few days later.
Remembering where to find things which have been put in a different place from usual.
Learning to use a new gadget or machine around the house.
Learning new things in general

Previously Acquired Information

Recognizing the faces of family and friends.
Remembering the names of family and friends.
Remembering things about family and friends, e.g. occupations, birthdays, addresses.
Remembering her/his address and telephone number.
Remembering where things are usually kept.
Knowing how to work familar machines around the house.
Remembering things that happened to her/him when s/he was young.
Remembering things s/he learned when s/he was young.
Understanding the meaning of unusual words.
Knowing about important historical events of the past.

Table 12.4 shows the results. The general population and demented samples were clearly distinguished on each of the four subscales. While greater impairment was rated for episodic memory than for semantic memory, and for recent learning than for use of previously acquired information, this applied to both the samples. Contrary to expectation, the subscales were equally effective at distinguishing the two samples. Furthermore, the pattern of correlations between the subscales suggested that they were measuring largely the same construct. In the general population sample, episodic memory correlated .77 with semantic memory, and recent learning correlated .68 with previously acquired information. Within the demented sample, the correlations were similar, .77 and .58, respectively.

In order to find out whether the episodic and semantic memory subscales of the IQCODE correlate with objective tests of episodic and semantic memory, data were analyzed from a study by Jorm et al. (1991). In this study the IQCODE was administered on two occasions to a sample of geriatric patients,

Table 12.4
Mean Ratings on IQCODE Subscales for General Population and Demented Samples

IQCODE Subscale	General Population Sample (n = 576)		Demented Sample (n = 372)	
	M	SD	M	SD
Episodic Memory	3.37	.51	4.62	.44
Semantic Memory	3.23	.40	4.55	.52
Recent Learning	3.58	.59	4.87	.32
Previously Acquired Information	3.17	.37	4.45	.57

Table 12.5
Memory Tests Used to Construct Objective Scales of Episodic and Semantic Memory Performance

Episodic Memory

Test	Description
Three-word recall	Three words had to be recalled after a filled delay.
Name and address recall	A name and address had to be recalled after a filled delay.
Face recognition	Photographs of faces had to be recognized from distractors after a filled delay.
Figure reproduction	A geometric figure was shown for 10 sec and had to be drawn from memory.

Semantic Memory

Test	Description
Famous people	Subject had to say who certain famous people were.
Word meanings	Definitions had to be given for words.
Sentence verification	Subject had to answer questions like "Is a table a piece of furniture?" and "Is a rug a musical instrument?"
Verbal fluency	As many animals as possible had to be given in a 60 sec period.

along with a standardized interview for the diagnosis of dementia and depression (the Canberra Interview for the Elderly). This interview included a series of brief cognitive tests, some of which tapped aspects of episodic and semantic memory. From these brief tests, separate scales were constructed for the two types of memory. The tests making up the scales are shown in Table 12.5. The reliability of the resulting objective scales was similar, with a retest correlation of .83 for episodic memory performance and .82 for semantic memory performance. The correlation between the scales was .46.

The correlation of the IQCODE subscales with the objective scales of episodic and semantic memory performance is shown in Table 12.6. The results are quite clear-cut. Each of the IQCODE subscales, as well as the total score, had a strong relationship to objectively tested episodic memory. Relationships with semantic memory were only small. Even the semantic memory subscale of the IQCODE was more highly related to objectively-tested episodic memory than to semantic memory.

To find out whether any of the IQCODE items related to semantic memory, each item of the questionnaire was correlated with the objective episodic and semantic memory scale. For every item, a higher correlation was found with episodic memory performance than with semantic memory performance. The highest correlations with semantic memory performance were for the items "Knowing about important historical events of the past" ($r = .42$, $p = .001$) and "Remembering her/his address and telephone number" ($r = .34$, $p = .01$). Although both these items reflect semantic memory, the even higher correlations with episodic memory indicate a lack of specificity in what they are tapping.

Table 12.6
Correlations of IQCODE Subscales with Objective Episodic and Semantic Memory Performance (N = 52)

	Objective Test Performance	
IQCODE Subscale	Episodic Memory	Semantic Memory
Episodic Memory	.51***	.12
Semantic Memory	.64***	.31*
Recent Learning	.62***	.19
Previously Acquired Information	.61***	.27*
Total Scale	.65***	.25*

*** $p < .001$ * $p < .05$

The only conclusion that can be drawn is that informants are largely rating episodic memory, whatever the apparent content of the items. Given that factor analyses of informant questionnaires like the IQCODE have shown a single large general factor, it is possible that this factor reflects episodic memory functioning. If so, then items which have high loadings on the general factor should also correlate highly with episodic memory performance. However, these

items would not necessarily correlate highly with semantic memory performance. To check this possibility, factor loadings from Jorm and Jacomb (1989)
were related to the correlations with objective performance. It was found that
items with high factor loadings also tended to relate strongly to episodic memory
performance ($r = .79$, $p < .001$), but the relationship was weaker for semantic
memory performance ($r = .39$, $p < .05$). This high correspondence between an
item's factor loading and its correlation with episodic memory performance
emerged despite the fact that data from two separate studies were being related. It can be concluded that the general factor found with the IQCODE
reflects episodic memory performance. This conclusion merits replication with
other informant questionnaires.

Conclusion

From these data it appears that informant instruments can provide a good
general measure of cognitive impairment in the elderly and may be useful in
screening for dementia, but they are less useful to researchers wishing to make
theoretically-oriented investigations into the everyday memory performance of
dementia sufferers.

Acknowledgments

Thanks to Helen Christensen for helping with classification of the IQCODE
items, and to Scott Henderson and Helen Christensen for comments on an
earlier draft. Penny Evans typed the manuscript.

References

Blessed, G., Tomlinson, B. E., & Roth, M. (1968). The association between quantitative
    measures of dementia and of senile change in the cerebral grey matter of elderly
    subjects. *British Journal of Psychiatry, 114*, 797-811.
Bowers, J., Jorm, A. F., Henderson, S., & Harris, P. (1990). General practitioners' detection
    of depression and dementia in elderly patients. *Medical Journal of Australia, 153*,
    192-196.
Crockett, D., Tuokko, H., Koch, W., & Parks, R. (1989). The assessment of everyday
    functioning using the Present Functioning Questionnaire and the Functional Rating
    Scale in elderly samples. *Clinical Gerontologist, 8*, 3-25.

Erkinjuntti, T., Hokkanen, L., Sulkava, R., & Palo, J. (1988). The Blessed Dementia Scale as a screening test for dementia. *International Journal of Geriatric Psychiatry, 3,* 267-273.

Godfrey, H. P. D., & Knight, R. G. (1988). Inpatient Memory Impairment Scale: A cross-validation and extension study. *Journal of Clinical Psychology, 44,* 783-786.

Herrmann, D. J. (1982). Know thy memory: The use of questionnaires to assess and study memory. *Psychological Bulletin, 92,* 434-452.

Jorm, A. F., & Jacomb, P.A. (1989). The Informant Questionnaire on Cognitive Decline in the Elderly (IQCODE): Socio-demographic correlates, reliability, validity, and some norms. *Psychological Medicine, 19,* 1015-1022.

Jorm, A. F., & Korten, A. E. (1988). Assessment of cognitive decline in the elderly by informant interview. *British Journal of Psychiatry, 152,* 209-213.

Jorm, A. F., Scott, R., Cullen, J. S., & Mackinnon, A. J. (1991). Performance of the Informant Questionnaire on Cognitive Decline in the Elderly (IQCODE) as a screening test for dementia. *Psychological Medicine, 21,* 785-790.

Jorm, A. F., Scott, R., & Jacomb, P. A. (1989). Assessment of cognitive decline in dementia by informant questionnaire. *International Journal of Geriatric Psychiatry, 4,* 35-39.

Knight, R. G., & Godfrey, H. P. D. (1984). Reliability and validity of a scale for rating memory impairment in hospitalized amnesics. *Journal of Consulting and Clinical Psychology, 52,* 769-773.

Lincoln, N. B., & Tinson, D. J. (1989). The relation between subjective and objective memory impairment after stroke. *British Journal of Clinical Psychology, 28,* 61-65.

Nebes, R. D. (1989). Semantic memory in Alzheimer's disease. *Psychological Bulletin, 106,* 377-394.

O'Connor, D. W., Pollitt, P. A., Brook, C. P. B., & Reiss, B. B. (1989). The validity of informant histories in a community study of dementia. *International Journal of Geriatric Psychiatry, 4,* 203-208.

O'Connor, D. W., Pollitt, P. A., Roth, M., Brook, C. P. B., & Reiss, B. B. (1990). Memory complaints and impairment in normal, depressed, and demented elderly persons identified in a community survey. *Archives of General Psychiatry, 47,* 224-227.

Poitrenaud, J., Malbezin, M., & Guez, D. (1989). Self-rating and psychometric assessment of age-related changes in memory among young-elderly managers. *Developmental Neuropsychology, 5,* 285-294.

Rosenbilds, U., Goldney, R.D., Gilchrist, P.N., Martin, E., & Connelly, H. (1986). Assessment by relatives of elderly patients with psychiatric illness. *Psychological Reports, 58,* 795-801.

Roth, M., Tym, E., Mountjoy, C. Q., Huppert, F. A., Hendrie, H., Verma, S., & Goddard, R. (1986). CAMDEX: A standardized instrument for the diagnosis of mental disorder in the elderly with special reference to the early detection of dementia. *British Journal of Psychiatry, 149,* 698-709.

Schwartz, G. E. (1983). Development and validation of the Geriatric Evaluation by Relatives Rating Instrument (GERRI). *Psychological Reports, 53,* 479-488.

Sunderland, A., Harris, J. E., & Baddeley, A. D. (1983). Do laboratory tests predict everyday memory? A neuropsychological study. *Journal of Verbal Learning and Verbal Behavior, 22,* 341-357.

Sunderland, A., Harris, J. E., & Gleave, J. (1984). Memory failures in everyday life following severe head injury. *Journal of Clinical Neuropsychology, 6,* 127-142.

Sunderland, A., Watts, K., Baddeley, A. D., & Harris, J. E. (1986). Subjective memory assessment and test performance in elderly adults. *Journal of Gerontology, 41,* 376-384.

Williams, J. M. (1987). *Cognitive behavior rating scales.* Odessa, FL: Psychological Assessment Resources.

Williams, J. M., Klein, K., Little, M. M., & Haban, G. (1986). Family observations of every day cognitive impairment in dementia. *Archives of Clinical Neuropsychology, 1,* 103-109.

Williams, J. M., Little, M. M., Scales, S., & Blockman, N. (1987). Memory complaints and abilities among depressed older adults. *Journal of Consulting and Clinical Psychology, 55,* 595-598.

Wilson, B. A., Cockburn, J., Baddeley, A. D., & Hiorns, R. W. (1989). The development and validation of a test battery for detecting and monitoring everyday memory problems. *Journal of Clinical and Experimental Neuropsychology, 11,* 855-870.

World Health Organization (1990). *ICD-10 draft of chapter V: Categories F00-F99, mental and behavioural disorders (including disorders of psychological development). Diagnostic criteria for research.* (WHO/MNH/MEP/87.1, Rev 4). Geneva: World Health Organization, Division of Mental Health.

Zelinski, E. M., Gilewski, M. J., & Anthony-Bergstone, C. R. (1990). Memory Functioning Questionnaire: Concurrent validity with memory performance and self-reported memory failures. *Psychology and Aging, 5,* 388-399.

Subject Index

Mini-Mental State Examination (*see* Psychometric tests)

Mnemonics (*see* Memory training)

Multiple sclerosis, 153-167 (*see also* Subcortical dementia)

N

Naming, 102-108, 114, 119-125, 129-131, 136, 165, 178-179, 183, 192-193, 196, 211, 216, 219, 230, 247-250, 254, 258-259

Neuritic plaques, 19, 31, 124, 136, 176

Neurofibrillary tangles, 19, 124, 136, 176

Noradrenergic system, 110

O

Object naming (*see* Naming)

Omission errors, 11, 17, 46, 48, 230

Organic amnesia, 45-49, 54, 56, 63, 67, 119

Orienting tasks, 75, 77, 109

P

Paired-associate learning, 34, 52, 56, 87, 106, 145, 157, 162, 184,195, 210, 219, 222, 274

Parietal cortex, 18-19, 99,106, 110, 114, 120, 131, 136

Parkinsonism, 208, 222-223

Parkinson's disease, 58, 61, 113-114, 153-167 (*see also* Subcortical dementia)

Perservative errors, 31

PET scan, 136

Phonological storage (*see* Short-term memory)

Picture superiority effect, 74, 136

Preselection effect, 139-140, 143, 146

Preserved functions, 9-10, 18, 20-21, 30, 32, 36, 51, 53-54, 57, 66-67, 75, 83, 88-90, 100-104, 110-114, 131, 140, 143-145, 147, 167, 178, 195-196, 228, 234-235, 245-246, 249-250, 253, 258-259

Primary memory (*see* Short-term memory)

Priming (*see* Implicit memory)

Prior knowledge (*see* Cognitive support)

Procedural learning (*see* Implicit memory)

Pseudodementia, 175-176, 182

Psychometric tests

Benton Visual Retention Test, 210, 213, 216, 222

Boston Naming Test, 102, 130, 211, 216, 219

Dutch Aphasia Test Battery, 229-230, 239, 253

Mini-Mental State Examination, 78, 87, 154, 270, 273-274

Test for Syntactic Complexity, 183-184

Wechsler Adult Intelligence Scale, 107, 166, 210, 231, 253

Wechsler Memory Scale, 56, 160, 184, 210, 214, 272

Western Aphasia Battery, 183-184

Wisconsin Card Sorting Test, 165-167

Psychomotor functions, 210, 217, 221-223, 253

Public information (*see* Retrograde amnesia)

Pursuit rotor task, 111-114, 135-138, 145-146, 161

Q

Qualitative versus quantitative differences, 30, 90-91, 127, 131, 153-154, 160, 180, 196

R

Rate of forgetting
long-term, 20, 51-55
measurement, 51
retention interval, 46-57, 140, 146, 157, 160
savings scores, 56-57, 160
short-term, 15-17, 37, 47-51, 140-141

Rate of presentation, 54, 76-77

Reality orientation (*see* Memory training)

Recency (*see* Short-term memory)

Recognition memory
faces, 31, 84-85, 240, 246, 275
pictures, 32, 36, 52, 76, 158, 161, 230, 234
verbal, 31, 75-78, 105, 139, 159, 210, 218-219, 230, 247, 275
visual forms, 31, 54, 160, 162, 241, 244

Rehabilitation, 143-145 (*see also* Memory training)

Release from proactive interference, 80, 138-142, 158-159

Remote memory, 196 (*see also* Retrograde amnesia)

Retrograde amnesia
general, 57-58
public information, 58-60, 163
temporal gradient, 57-63, 67, 83, 163, 167

Author Index